CLASS, RELIGION AND LOCAL POLITICS
IN WILHELMINE GERMANY

Class, Religion and Local Politics in Wilhelmine Germany

The Centre Party in Württemberg before 1914

David Blackbourn

YALE UNIVERSITY PRESS
NEW HAVEN AND LONDON
1980

An edition of this book, which is only for sale within the Federal Republic of Germany and the German Democratic Republic, is published by Franz Steiner Verlag GmbH, Wiesbaden, on behalf of the Institute für europaische Geschichte, Mainz.

Designed by Caroline Williamson and set in VIP Bembo.

Printed in Great Britain by Ebenezer Baylis and Son Ltd,
The Trinity Press, Worcester and London.

Published in Great Britain, Europe, Africa and Asia (except Japan) by Yale University Press Ltd, London. Distributed in Australia and New Zealand by Book and Film Services, Artarmon, N.S.W., Australia; and in Japan by Harper and Row, Publishers, Tokyo Office.

Library of Congress Cataloging in Publication Data

Blackbourn, David, 1949–
    Class, religion, and local politics in Wilhelmine
Germany.

    Bibliography: p.
    Includes index.
    1. Deutsche Zentrumspartei—History. 2. Württem-
berg—Politics and government. I. Title.
JN3946.Z5B58   324.24302'0943'47   80-11878
ISBN 0-300-02464-9

To my parents

Preface

I discuss the scope of the present book in the Introduction, and try to indicate where I stand in relation to current scholarly debate on Wilhelmine Germany. This Preface has a different and twofold purpose: to give a brief account of how the book came to be written in its present form, and to acknowledge those individuals and institutions without whom it would not have been written.

I began to work on the Centre Party as a research student at Cambridge in 1970. My initial starting-point was a fairly standard one: how to explain the discrepancy between the economic and the political development of imperial Germany. The classic work of Thorstein Veblen, and the then recent works of Ralf Dahrendorf and Barrington Moore, seemed to offer fruitful interpretations of Germany's peculiar 'passage to modernity' (as I would then have put it). So did the studies coming out of West Germany by authors like Hans-Jürgen Puhle, Dirk Stegmann and Hans-Ulrich Wehler. What puzzled me from the beginning, and continued to do so as I came under the spell of the Centre, was how this party fitted in to the general picture. Forty years earlier, Arthur Rosenberg had made some acute but tantalisingly cryptic observations on the way in which the interests and values of the various social groups within the Centre governed the party's generally anti-democratic political stance. Yet there had subsequently been surprisingly little research in these areas. Instead the Centre seemed to crop up quite arbitrarily at different points in the history of imperial Germany, each time under a different kind of historical spotlight. In the 1870s the principal context was naturally the *Kulturkampf*; writers dealing with the 1890s had focused on the internal divisions of the party, or on its key part in the passage of the first navy bill; and the role of the Centre in the election of 1907 appeared to raise a further set of problems. I felt that there were two possible explanations for the apparent difficulty historians had with this awkward party. Either the Centre had in fact been politically inconsistent and uneven in its politics, perhaps because of its sectarian Catholic priorities; or there was an alternative history of the Centre which remained to be written, one which would reveal a fuller and less capricious process whereby the politics of the party were forged out of a complex amalgam of class, regional and sectional interests. It did not occur to me then that these two views were not incompatible. I felt quite strongly that there was a submerged history of the Centre which would repay attention. I first considered trying to write a study of Centre politics in the 1890s, using the succession struggle over the leadership following Windthorst's death as a means of exploring the different levels of political life and reality which made up the Centre. I then decided to concentrate on a local study, settling eventually — for reasons which are discussed below — on Württemberg, rather than on my original choice of Baden. If I still had a model at that stage, it was a work of British rather than German history: John Vincent's *The Formation of the Liberal Party, 1857–68*.

I spent the academic year 1971–2 in Stuttgart, working on the archival sources at the Hauptstaatsarchiv Stuttgart and the rich holding of printed sources in the neighbouring Landesbibliothek. In the Hauptstaatsarchiv I used the range of government papers listed in the Bibliography to this book. I also consulted the private papers of Conrad Haussmann and Hans Kiene (a small collection). In the Landesbibliothek I worked through various kinds of printed source material: parliamentary proceedings and petitions, the articles and statistical information contained in the *Württembergische Jahrbücher*, official descriptions of the various administrative districts of Württemberg, government reports on matters such as agriculture, local newspapers and contemporary pamphlet literature of a diverse kind. A list of these is also provided in the bibliography. What I gained from this was a sense both of the content of Centre politics at state level, and of the meaning which politics had at a level lower than this. What I was trying to understand was how the two were conjoined.

By the time I returned from Stuttgart to Cambridge I had written some fairly extensive drafts on the origins of the Centre Party in Württemberg, and on the party's subsequent relations with the progressive VP and the SPD. In the last months of 1972 I worked this material up into a fellowship dissertation, which contained a rather breathless version of the material to be found in chapters two to six of this book. I continued to work on this material, with a growing conviction that further material was required on Centre politics both locally and nationally. I returned to Germany for the academic year 1974–5, basing myself at the *Institut für europäische Geschichte* in Mainz.

I read much more on the national policies of the Centre, and worked on the private papers of Karl Bachem (Stadtarchiv Cologne), Ernst Lieber (Landesbibliothek Speyer) and Franz von Ballestrem (in family possession). I also returned to Stuttgart to look at further material in the Hauptstaatsarchiv and the Landesbibliothek, and used telephone directories to contact possible relatives of former Centre Landtag deputies. Only then did I realise how common the names Egger and Eggmann are in Swabia. On returning to Cambridge in the autumn of 1975 I added, pruned and generally re-cast the old and new material into a doctoral dissertation which was submitted in 1976. That doctorate provided the foundations of the present book.

I have since made one extended research visit to Germany, in the summer of 1977. The material from that visit has served to extend some points and change the emphasis of others in chapters two, three and six. In the course of preparing and discussing articles, conference and seminar papers on the Centre and related subjects I have, of course, changed my views on a number of things. I am now, I hope, less wilfully iconoclastic than I once was about the importance of the Catholic Church in the fabric of daily and political life among Centre supporters — as anyone will see who consults my Ph.D. dissertation (Cambridge University Library) or, even more, my fellowship dissertation. On an equally crucial issue, I think I am less resistant to the idea that matters of importance occurred in Berlin. What now seems to me necessary is to recognise the existence of different levels and modes of politics, and to try and understand their mutual interaction. I remain convinced that the structure of local and parochial actions and sentiments deserves greater attention — in its own right, not simply as a marginal note or corrective to current wisdom. This second point seems to me important for the way in which we perceive the politics of imperial Germany. Wallace Stevens has expressed my feelings about this better than I could hope to:

> They said 'You have a blue guitar
> You do not play things as they are.'
> The man replied, 'Things as they are
> Are changed upon the blue guitar.'

I agree with the man on this.

I have accumulated many debts of gratitude in the last nine years and it is a pleasure to try and repay some of them now. My initial work on the Centre Party was made possible by a three-year research grant from the Department of Education and Science. I am very grateful for this indispensable support. In my first year of research I also received a Bachelor Scholarship, for which I owe thanks to the Master and Fellows of Christ's College, Cambridge. I am deeply grateful to the Master and Fellows of Jesus College, Cambridge, for electing me to a Research Fellowship in 1973 which made it possible for me to continue my work. I should also like to thank Professor Karl Otmar Freiherr von Aretin, Director of the *Institut für europäische Geschichte, Abteilung Universalgeschichte*, in Mainz, from which institution I received a *Stipendium* and accommodation in 1974–5. On later visits I have continued to benefit from the excellent working conditions and hospitality of the Institute. This book is being published jointly in the historical series of the Institute, and for this too I want to express my gratitude and my sense of pleasure. I am grateful also to the *Deutscher Akademischer Austauschdienst*, London, for providing a grant which made it possible for me to visit Germany in the summer of 1977.

The staff of the archives and libraries which I have used have been unfailingly helpful, and I welcome this opportunity to express my appreciation. I would like to thank the archivists, advisors and assistants at the Hauptstaatsarchiv Stuttgart, the Stadtarchiv Cologne and the Landesbibliothek Speyer. I also received much valuable assistance from the staff of the Württembergische Landesbibliothek Stuttgart and the Cambridge University Library. I am deeply grateful to the staff at the library of the Institute in Mainz for their friendly assistance and advice. I should particularly like to thank Herr and Frau Hugo Lacher and Frau Liselotte Ropers. In hunting for references, addresses and various arcane pieces of knowledge, I have been extremely grateful in recent years for the existence of the German Historical Institute in London. I should like to express my thanks to its Director, assistants and librarians for their kindness and help. I should also like to thank June Neilson, history specialist in the library of Queen Mary College, University of London, whose advice was helpful to me on a number of occasions. Her expertise and friendliness typify the qualities of that institution. I am happy to have taught in the History Department there in the years 1976–9.

A number of individuals were kind enough to provide me with unpublished material in private possession. I should like to thank Dr jur. Carl Wolfgang Graf von Ballestrem for allowing me to use the papers of Franz von Ballestrem. I should also like to express my thanks to the Ballestrem family for their hospitality to me in 1975. I also received valuable information, details of family trees, newspaper cuttings and personal recollections from a number of people in Württemberg. My intention was to trace the relatives of former Centre Landtag deputies, and several of those to whom I wrote went to considerable trouble to track down information useful to me. I am most grateful for all their replies to the letter of a supplicant researcher, and would like to take this opportunity to thank the following: Dr Hans Dentler of Ehingen, Herr Franz Faitsch of Wehingen, Fräulein Anna Herbster of Wiesensteig, Herr Bernhard Rapp of Saulgau, Herr Gebhard Rapp of Saulgau, Herr Johannes Schell of Nendingen, Herr Norbert Schlichte of Ravensburg, Dr Karl Setz of Neresheim, Herr Adrian Speth of Wangen and Herr Wilfried Vogler of Neresheim. My thanks go also to Rainer Vinke of Mainz for his advice at the beginning of this undertaking.

This book has benefited from much kind advice and stimulating discussion. My first and greatest debt is to Norman Stone. He awoke my interest in the subject as an undergraduate, then guided me through the subsequent years of research. His advice, criticism and encouragement were enormously valuable. His confidence in my work was a source of great support to me, and at crucial stages of the research he forced me to think out my ideas more clearly than I would otherwise have done. This book owes much to him, as a research supervisor and as a friend. Joseph Lee and Jonathan Steinberg were extremely kind in giving me advice at an early stage of research, and both have continued to provide encouragement in a characteristically helpful and friendly manner. Jonathan, having acted as my internal Ph.D. examiner, gave generously of his time in discussing the scope and shape of the present book. My other examiner, Volker Berghahn, has also offered me much friendly criticism and advice over recent years. He was kind enough to read the introduction to the book and made a number of most constructive suggestions. Dr D. E. D. Beales read much of the material in chapter two, prior to its appearance in a rather different form in the *Historical Journal*, and gave me the benefit of his advice. I am similarly indebted to Dr David W. Hendon of *Central European History* for his helpful editorial comments on parts of the present work which first appeared in that journal. Professor Karl Otmar Freiherr von Aretin, Claus Scharf, Hans-Jürgen Schröder and John Leslie made valuable comments on my work during the period I spent in Mainz. I am especially grateful to Hugo Lacher in Mainz, who read a copy of my doctoral dissertation and made many constructive suggestions drawn from his deep yet lightly-worn knowledge of the subject. I have also gained much from discussions with Francis Carsten, Dick Geary, Richard J. Evans, James Joll and John Röhl. I want finally to thank my friend and fellow historian of Germany, Geoff Eley. He read the Introduction to this book and gave me his characteristically thoughtful comments. Much more than that, I have gained enormously over the last seven years from our frequent discussions about the history of Wilhelmine Germany. I thank all these friends and colleagues for their advice and encouragement, and others who have written to express an interest in my work. I hope they will find something to enjoy in the present book. The flaws and errors which remain in the book are, of course, entirely my own responsibility.

It is a pleasure finally to thank those friends in Germany whose hospitality has made the work of research more pleasant, particularly Kaspar von Greyerz and Deborah Monroe in Mainz. I am also grateful to John Nicoll and Caroline Williamson of Yale University Press for the efficient, friendly and civilised way in which they have dealt with the manuscript. My final and largest debt of gratitude is to my parents. The book is dedicated to them as a small token of that gratitude.

Birkbeck College, London
October 1979

Contents

Abbreviations

BB	*Beilage-Band*
DP	Deutsche Partei
HStaASt	Hauptstaatsarchiv Stuttgart
KW	*Das Königreich Württemberg* (1863 or 1904 edition cited)
LB	Landesbibliothek
LT	*Landtagsverhandlungen*
PB	*Protokoll-Band*
SPD	Sozialdemokratische Partei Deutschlands
StA	Stadtarchiv
VP	Volkspartei
WJbb	*Württembergische Jahrbücher*
ZWLG	*Zeitschrift für württembergische Landesgeschichte*

Introduction

I

The publication in 1961 of Fritz Fischer's *Griff nach der Weltmacht* opened up a debate with implications beyond Germany's responsibility for the outbreak of the First World War.[1] In emphasising German expansionist ambitions prior to 1914, as well as during the war itself, Fischer helped to direct the attention of historians back to the *Kaiserreich*. A greatly intensified study of the period from 1871 to 1918 was thus initiated, illuminated (although the light has sometimes been blinding) by fierce controversy over 'continuity' in the recent German past. Moreover, although Fischer's own methodological approach was largely a traditional one, he was responsible for shifting the terms in which continuity was discussed. When this had been considered before, it was usually in the context of the peculiar problem posed by militarism in the German nation's external relations.[2] The documentation in *Griff nach der Weltmacht* made it difficult, in the first place, to sustain the distinction between the 'bad Germans' in the army High Command and the Pan-German League, and the 'good Germans' like Bethmann Hollweg. This had the effect, eventually, of clearing a good deal of the ground previously staked out by apologist historians. Secondly, Fischer's work suggested to historians the fruitfulness of looking at the domestic economic and social structure

---

1. F. Fischer, *Griff nach der Weltmacht* (Düsseldorf, 1961). Fischer hardened his views in a second book, *Krieg der Illusionen* (Düsseldorf, 1969). On the debate initiated by Fischer, see I. Geiss, 'Die Fischer-Kontroverse', *Studien über Geschichte und Geschichtswissenschaft* (Frankfurt/Main, 1972), pp. 108–98; J. Moses, *The Politics of Illusion* (London, 1975).
2. Perhaps the most impressive work of this kind was written by one of Fischer's principal opponents: G. Ritter, *Staatskunst und Kriegshandwerk*, 4 vols (Munich, 1954 ff). This view can also be found in the widely-read account by Gordon Craig, *The Politics of the Prussian Army, 1640–1945* (Oxford, 1955).

of imperial Germany as a means of explaining German foreign policy in the period up to the gamble of July 1914.[3]

The new school of historians which has emerged in the wake of Fritz Fischer has been responsible, in particular, for deepening our understanding of the domestic roots of German foreign policy. Phenomena like Germany's first bid for colonies in the 1880s, the Tirpitz Plan for the battle fleet and the background to the crisis of July 1914 have been brought within a general framework of interpretation which stresses the 'primacy of domestic politics' (*Primat der Innenpolitik*).[4] At the risk of over-simplifying a set of views which is by no means monolithic,[5] the key points of this framework may be summarised as follows.

From the middle of the last century there was a marked discrepancy between the dynamism of the German economy on the one hand, and the absence of a corresponding 'modernity' in political life and social values on the other.[6] This was, in turn, a result of the peculiar pattern of German economic development, in which state-led industrialisation and close links between industry and the banks made possible rapid rates of growth *without* the need for a direct conflict between the claims of industry and agriculture. Germany enjoyed the economic advantages of the latecomer, but at a cost. Industrial and commercial capital did not, as in Britain or the USA, win a clear victory over agrarian interests; rather, they compromised. This process was first clearly evident during the Great Depression after 1873, when heavy industry and estate-based agriculture in particular — 'iron and rye' —

3. This stimulus was clear in work done during the 1960s; it was explicitly acknowledged by the authors of the second *Festschrift* for Fischer in 1978. D. Stegmann, B.-J. Wendt and P.-C. Witt (eds), *Industrielle Gesellschaft und politisches System: Beiträge zur politischen Sozialgeschichte* (Bonn, 1978), pp. v–vi.
4. See, especially, H.-U. Wehler, *Bismarck und der Imperialismus* (Cologne, 1969); V. R. Berghahn, *Der Tirpitz-Plan. Genesis und Verfall einer innenpolitischen Krisenstrategie unter Wilhelm II* (Düsseldorf, 1971). The phrase *Primat der Innenpolitik* is, of course, Eckart Kehr's inversion of the famous Rankean axiom. See E. Kehr, *Der Primat der Innenpolitik*, ed. H.-U. Wehler (Berlin, 1965).
5. This point has been well made by Wolfgang J. Mommsen, 'Domestic Factors in German Foreign Policy before 1914', *Central European History*, 6 (1973), pp. 3–43. Despite the limitations of space, the summary which follows is an attempt to present the views in question in as full and rounded a manner as possible.
6. A classic consideration of this discrepancy, first published in 1915, is Thorstein Veblen's *Imperial Germany and the Industrial Revolution*. The influential and important book by Ralf Dahrendorf, *Gesellschaft und Demokratie in Deutschland* (Munich, 1969), has also looked at the 'German problem' in this way, and the recent concern of German historians, particularly H.-U. Wehler, with modernisation theory has helped to establish this way of approaching German history.

were the joint beneficiaries of a return to tariff protection in 1879.[7] Despite its periodic breakdown, this defensive partnership continued in the years up to 1914, forming for example the economic basis of the much-cited *Sammlungspolitik* around the turn of the century, when heavy industry benefited from naval construction and agriculture was given the quid pro quo of higher tariffs.[8]

This pattern of economic development is alleged to have had important corollaries at the social level. In the first place, it constituted a serious defeat for the forces of bourgeois liberalism in Germany, whose weakness had already been prefigured in 1848. The vicarious satisfaction taken in Bismarck's 'revolution from above' in 1864–71 was, it has been argued, a further capitulation by the German bourgeoisie, for it signified their assent to the continuing role which the Junker aristocracy would play in the new Prussian-dominated German state. The acceptance by bourgeois liberalism of the return to tariff protection marked a culmination of these attitudes: it was an even clearer example of a fateful willingness to compromise with the old, pre-industrial élite of landowners. Moreover, acquiescence in the anti-consumer orientation of the tariffs, together with support for the anti-socialist law of 1878, suggested that fear of emerging organised labour would be enough to drive bourgeois liberalism into the arms of the old élite. As Marx had written: 'In France the bourgeoisie conquered so that it could humble the people; in Germany the bourgeoisie humbled itself so that the people should not conquer.' In subsequent decades this self-humbling was manifested in what has been called the 'feudalisation' of the middle classes in Germany, an aping of the values of the landowning élite as transmitted through the reserve officer corps, a bureaucracy whose upper ranks continued to be dominated by Junkers, and student corporations. Faced with the spectre of Demos, the German bourgeoisie was allegedly reinforced in its defensive alliance with the traditional élite which still set the social tone of Prussia–Germany.

The distorted economic and social arrangements of the *Kaiserreich* had fateful consequences in the political sphere, it is argued, both domestically and in the foreign policy which was generated as a

7. H. Rosenberg, *Grosse Depression und Bismarckzeit. Wirtschaftsablauf, Gesellschaft und Politik in Mitteleuropa* (Berlin, 1967); H. Böhme, *Deutschlands Weg zur Grossmacht. Studien zum Verhältnis von Wirtschaft und Staat während der Reichsgründungszeit 1848–1881* (Cologne, 1966), pp. 530–86; M. Stürmer, *Regierung und Reichstag im Bismarckstaat 1871–1880* (Düsseldorf, 1974), esp. pp. 278–88.
8. E. Kehr, *Schlachtflottenbau und Parteipolitik, 1894–1901. Versuch eines Querschnitts durch die innenpolitischen, sozialen und ideologischen Voraussetzungen des deutschen Imperialismus* (Berlin, 1930); D. Stegmann, *Die Erben Bismarcks: Parteien und Verbände in der Spätphase des Wilhelminischen Deutschlands; Sammlungspolitik, 1897–1918* (Cologne, 1970), pp. 59–97.

response to political problems at home. The central problem was the survival of a pre-industrial, aristocratic élite which stubbornly resisted the forces threatening to undermine its position. This élite was entrenched in the Prussian army and bureaucracy and, by virtue of the three-class franchise, also preserved a power-base in the lower house of the Prussian Landtag. In addition, this élite retained its position in national politics as a result of the domination of the Reich by Prussia. The *Bundesrat*, which alone could initiate legislation, was effectively dominated by Prussia; the Reich chancellor was always (with the telling exception, briefly, of Caprivi) simultaneously the prime minister of Prussia; and the Kaiser was the king of Prussia. The chancellor was responsible not to the Reichstag but to the Kaiser, who ruled not as a constitutional monarch but 'as an instrument of the lord'.[9]

However, just as agriculture and aristocracy could only, at best, blunt the forces of industry and the middle class by means of a defensive alliance, so politically the old élite was faced with a permanent challenge to its stranglehold. Bismarck by introducing universal suffrage to the Reichstag with the intention of 'dishing the liberals' had in fact given a hostage to fortune. Neither the use of repression against Catholics and the labour movement, nor the whipping up of nationalist hysteria at election time, could arrest the growth of oppositional forces. The defeat of the pro-Bismarck parties in the Reichstag election which preceded and occasioned his fall in 1890 made this clear. His successors were therefore left with the task of attempting, in increasingly difficult circumstances, what Bismarck himself had failed to achieve: to square the circle of the Prussian–German political system.[10]

It has been maintained that this problem was tackled by recourse to a more vigorous application of the techniques Bismarck himself had used.[11] The first of these was repression, or at least the reminder that force remained the *ultima ratio*: the advocates of reform were to be cowed by the 'permanent threat of *Staatsstreich*' (coup d'état). More positively, the rulers of Wilhelmine Germany sought to counteract the forces of actual and potential opposition by integrating them. The churches and the family allegedly played an important part in this, while the army became the 'school of the nation'. The political parties,

9. Wilhelm II in 1910, cited in V. R. Berghahn, *Germany and the Approach of War in 1914* (London, 1973), p. 86.
10. On 'Bismarck's heirs', see Stegmann, *Die Erben Bismarcks*; J. C. G. Röhl, *Germany without Bismarck* (London, 1967); J. A. Nichols, *Germany after Bismarck* (Cambridge, Mass, 1958).
11. On the following, see particularly H.-U. Wehler, *Das Deutsche Kaiserreich 1871–1918*, (Göttingen, 1973), chs. II and III.

too, were encouraged to become the mere vehicles of economic interest groups and to give up their reforming ambitions. At the same time, and in line with this, the system of economic protection and 'compensations', begun in 1879 with the tariffs and followed by Bismarck's social legislation of the following decade, was extended. The peasantry, too, was protected (although much less than the large landowners)[12] and the loyalty of the petty bourgeoisie was to be guaranteed by means of 'reinsuring' their economic position through an active, interventionist *Mittelstandspolitik*. Finally, it is argued, the uncertainties and apprehensions of groups like the peasantry and *Mittelstand* were mobilised behind the status quo by means of a manipulative demagogy which identified certain groups as responsible for all their ills. The Jew, a symbol of aggressive modernity, was the most obvious scapegoat figure in an ideology which was both anti-capitalist and anti-socialist.[13]

This kind of diversionary tactic, designed to draw attention away from outstanding social and political reforms, reached its apogee in the uses to which foreign policy was put. This, too, had a negative and a positive side. In a negative sense, the tactic was partly a matter of encouraging xenophobia in order to rally support during an election campaign, as in 1907; it was partly a matter of sabre-rattling at a time of particular domestic political crisis, as in 1911; while, at the most general level, France the 'arch-enemy' and 'perfidious Albion' provided — like the internal 'enemies of the Reich' — acceptable targets on which the populace could vent its frustrations.[14] In positive terms, it is argued that the deflection of potential criticism of the status quo was achieved by a policy of 'social imperialism', which encouraged an identification among broad sections of the population with imperial Germany's great-power ambitions. The single most important policy directed to this end was the naval programme launched by the first naval bill of 1898: 'Tirpitz's naval policy was nothing less than an ambitious plan to stabilise the Prusso-German political system and to paralyse the pressure for change.'[15]

The deferred costs of failure to modernise the political system of

12. The argument that agricultural protection was largely a Junker device foisted on the peasantry is a general one, but is perhaps most sharply formulated in A. Gerschenkron, *Bread and Democracy in Germany* (Berkeley, 1943). For an alternative view, see below, pp. 110–11; and J. C. Hunt, 'Peasants, Grain Tariffs, and Meat Quotas: Imperial German Protectionism Reexamined', *Central European History*, 7 (1974), pp. 311–31.
13. Wehler, *Kaiserreich*, pp. 110–18.
14. For a succinct statement of this view, see P.-C. Witt, 'Innenpolitik und Imperialismus in der Vorgeschichte des 1. Weltkriegs', K. Holl and G. List (eds), *Liberalismus und imperialistischer Staat* (Göttingen, 1975), pp. 7–34.
15. Berghahn, *Germany and the Approach of War in 1914*, p. 29. For a more detailed account, Berghahn, *Der Tirpitz-Plan*, pp. 90–173.

imperial Germany still had to be met, however. Stabilisation was the objective. Yet the very comprehensiveness of the demagogic practices by which the German ruling élite sought to avoid painful choices made such ploys self-cancelling. After 1909 and even more after 1912, it has been argued, government was characterised by a growing paralysis. Moreover, the projection outwards of domestic conflicts had created an unprecedented instability in international relations, causing further problems for the imperial government. In the first place, the economic policies pursued by the *Kaiserreich* bred antagonism among Germany's European neighbours. Heavy industry had been propped up by means of the battle fleet; but Britain had been alienated as a result. The great estates had been helped by protective tariffs; but this in turn, together with aggressive attempts to open up the Russian market, had antagonised the Tsarist government. More fundamentally, *Sammlungspolitik* committed imperial Germany both to the maintenance of a powerful army (appealing to Junker landowners and representing 'Prussian' values) and a growing navy (appealing to bourgeois industrialists and representing 'national' values). As a result Germany sowed suspicion in the minds of both her neighbours on land, France and Russia, and the predominantly naval power, Britain. The faulted internal developments of the Reich therefore laid the basis of a self-fulfilling encirclement.

At a financial level, the armaments policy of the Reich was a mounting burden, given political limits to the extent of indirect taxation and the landowning Conservatives' intransigence over the imposition of death duties.[16] At the same time, the diversionary tactics of the ruling élite nurtured exaggerated expectations among the German public, which stood in stark contrast to the actual failure of diplomatic bluster — over the second Moroccan crisis, for example. The position after the 1912 Reichstag elections, with stepped-up spending on the agenda for both army and navy in a Reichstag where the SPD was the largest single party and the Conservatives remained intransigent, was critical. It was — so it has been argued — one which could only encourage the leaders of the Reich to seek a way out of the domestic political impasse by means of a further demagogic 'flight forward' into war.[17]

16. This entire subject has been superbly illuminated by P.-C. Witt, *Die Finanzpolitik des deutschen Reiches von 1903–1913* (Lübeck and Hamburg, 1970).
17. Among the important works on this subject, see Fischer, *Griff nach der Weltmacht*; Fischer, *Krieg der Illusionen*; Berghahn, *Germany and the Approach of War in 1914*; Wehler, *Kaiserreich*, ch. III, 8, 'Die Flucht nach vorn'; D. Groh, ' "Je eher, desto besser". Innenpolitische Faktoren für die Präventivkriegsbereitschaft des Deutschen Reiches 1913/1914', *Politische Vierteljahresschrift*, 13 (1972), pp. 501–21. For an overview of this problem, see Mommsen, *Central European History* (1973).

II

This approach to the study of imperial Germany is formidable and comprehensive. It has not only provided a model for the relationship between domestic and foreign policy which would repay consideration by historians of Britain, France and Russia before 1914.[18] The study of pre-1914 German domestic politics has in itself received a powerful fillip, and it is with this that the present introduction is chiefly concerned. The historical school working within this framework has a number of important achievements to its credit. The importance of studying patterns of comparative economic development has been established; the study of 'social history' has acquired persuasive advocates;[19] the work of previously neglected historians like Eckart Kehr and Hans Rosenberg has been fruitfully rediscovered; and monographs on a wide range of subjects, from crime and anti-semitism to financial policy and the role of economic interest groups, have emerged out of the new school.[20]

All new departures bring problems in their train, however, and this is necessarily true of a school whose exponents have in the course of academic controversy been obliged constantly to reiterate their right to put forward such views in the first place. One problem is that positions may harden in the course of such reiteration. There is, moreover, the related danger that works in the field which are readily assimilable neither to the one view nor to a polemically defined opposite view will fall into the interstices of historical debate. The observations which follow are made, therefore, in a prudential rather than a polemical spirit. They are an attempt to indicate and make explicit some of the main points where I differ in my approach from

18. See the interesting comments of James Joll, 'War Guilt 1914: A Continuing Controversy', *Aspekte der deutsch-britischen Beziehungen im Laufe der Jahrhunderte* (Stuttgart, 1978), pp. 60–80.
19. See, for example, H.-U. Wehler, *Geschichte als Sozialwissenschaft* (Frankfurt/Main, 1973); and 'Vorüberlegungen zu einer modernen deutschen Gesellschaftsgeschichte', Stegmann, Wendt and Witt (eds), *Industrielle Gesellschaft und Politisches System*, pp. 3–20; J. Kocka, 'Sozialgeschichte-Strukturgeschichte-Gesellschaftsgeschichte', *Archiv für Sozialgeschichte*, 15 (1975), pp. 1–42; and 'Theorien in der Sozial- und Gesellschaftsgeschichte: Vorschläge zur historischen Schichtungsanalyse', *Geschichte und Gesellschaft*, 1 (1975), pp. 9–42.
20. On the subjects mentioned, see the following: D. Blasius, *Bürgerliche Gesellschaft und Kriminalität. Zur Sozialgeschichte Preussens im Vormärz* (Göttingen, 1976); R. Rürup, *Emanzipation und Antisemitismus. Studien zur 'Judenfrage' der bürgerlichen Gesellschaft* (Göttingen, 1975); Witt, *Finanzpolitik*; S. Mielke, *Der Hansa-Bund für Gewerbe, Handel und Industrie 1909–1914. Der gescheiterte Versuch einer antifeudalen Sammlungspolitik* (Göttingen, 1976); H.-P. Ullmann, *Der Bund der Industriellen. Organisation, Einfluss und Politik klein- und mittelbetrieblicher Industrieller im deutschen Kaiserreich 1895–1914* (Göttingen, 1976).

the school whose framework of interpretation has been outlined above.

The first of these differences concerns the general question of social and political change in imperial Germany. In one sense this has been identified as a central problem in current treatments of the *Kaiserreich*: how did traditional élites preserve their position in the face of new forces thrown up by change? The effect of posing the question in this way, however, has been to create a curiously static picture of imperial German politics and society. This is evident in the widespread use of terms like *Dauerkrise* (permanent crisis) and 'permanent threat of *Staatsstreich*' to describe the functioning of the imperial political system. It can also be seen in the way concepts like *Sammlungspolitik* and social imperialism have been elaborated to assert a long-term continuity in the methods used by the ruling élite to maintain the status quo.[21] Coupled with a view of politics which lays particular stress on the practice of manipulation from above, this approach has produced an interpretation in which an apparent pattern of continuity has come to obscure the underlying process of change in imperial politics. It is with this process of change, itself both contradictory and operating at different levels, that this introduction is principally concerned. It is focused particularly on the shifts in both the scope and the nature of German politics between unification and the end of the nineteenth century.

It marked a fundamental change, in the first place, when a political nation was created out of the German state established on paper in 1871, a process concluded by about the 1890s. Institutionally the Reich was increasingly consolidated in a formal sense into a unified nation–state in the first two decades of its existence. The extension of the communications network, the establishment of the Reichsbank, legislation to create a uniform system of weights and measures, patent laws and so on: these made the Reich a flesh-and-blood reality. At the same time the growing competence of government in economic, fiscal and social matters also marked a pronounced centralising tendency at the institutional level. This had its constitutional counterpart in the shifting centre of gravity away from the Bundesrat towards the Reichstag. This was not necessarily synonymous with a shift in the real distribution of power; but it did mark an important change in the

---

21. On these points, see the pertinent criticisms made by the following: T. Nipperdey, 'Wehlers "Kaiserreich". Eine kritische Auseinandersetzung', *Geschichte und Gesellschaft*, 1 (1975), pp. 539–60; H.-G. Zmarzlik, 'Das Kaiserreich in neuer Sicht?', *Historische Zeitschrift*, 222 (1976), pp. 105–26; R. J. Evans, 'Wilhelm II's Germany and the Historians', R. J. Evans (ed), *Society and Politics in Wilhelmine Germany* (London, 1978), pp. 11–39; G. Eley, 'Die "Kehrites" und das Kaiserreich: Bemerkungen zu einer aktuellen Kontroverse', *Geschichte und Gesellschaft*, 4 (1978), pp. 91–107.

formal framework within which politics were conducted. Even to the extent that the dominant political mode was manipulative, its locus had been altered by the 1890s. Imperial state secretaries were less concerned with the federal states and their plenipotentiaries in the Bundesrat, more concerned with key political leaders in the Reichstag.[22] In this respect the opening of a new Reichstag building in the early 1890s was symbolically appropriate.

This was only part of the story, however. The emergence of a national politics viewed from above was complemented by the emergence of a political nation from below. The latter, no less than the former, constituted a significant change in the framework of politics. 1871 had been wholly satisfactory to no one party. The south German governments, Junker Conservatives, Catholics and middle-class Liberals would all have preferred something different. Only in a limited sense, in fact, was the *Kaiserreich* — compared with the French Third Republic founded at the same time — even the form of German state which divided men least. In the first place, the minorities of Danes, Alsatians and Poles (along with the Hanoverian Guelphs) organised separatist parties, which at the peak of their electoral popularity won an aggregate of around 10 per cent of the vote and over 10 per cent of the seats to the Reichstag. Secondly, the 1870s and 1880s saw successive onslaughts against Catholics and the labour movement in which major parts of the newly-unified population were treated not so much as dissident citizens, but effectively as inhabitants of an occupied state. When this is considered in conjunction with the low turn-out at the first six Reichstag elections prior to 1887,[23] then it is clear that in the first decades of the Reich's existence the conditions for a truly national politics did not exist.

Yet by the 1890s the institutional basis of a political nation had been forged below as well as above. Support for the separatist national parties tailed off and their supporters were largely integrated within national-based parties (principally the Centre). The *Kulturkampf* was wound up, and the anti-socialist law lapsed. This, of course, is to deny neither the importance of the 'ghetto mentality' which persisted among both Catholics and the labour movement, nor the continuing discrimination which they and the national minorities faced. Indeed, an analysis of both the discrimination and its effects plays a major part in

---

22. See, especially, M. Rauh, *Föderalismus und Parlamentarismus im Wilhelminischen Reich* (Düsseldorf, 1973). The present writer does not, however, agree with Rauh's fiercely polemical attacks on what he calls the 'critical school', made in his most recent book, *Die Parlamentarisierung des Deutschen Reiches* (Düsseldorf, 1977), esp. pp. 9–14.
23. Turn-out at the six Reichstag elections between 1871 and 1884 ranged between 50.7% and 63.1%.

this study.[24] But it remains of great importance that from the 1890s the discrimination these groups faced was at the economic, social and political level, rather than the result of overtly repressive administrative powers — that it was located, in other words, in the sphere of civil society. The decline of mere repression, therefore, had the effect of actually increasing the importance of politics in public life. At the same time, steadily increasing turn-out at elections created a numerical enlargement of the political nation.

This change in the formal, external conditions under which politics was conducted was accompanied, moreover, by an inner transformation which can be summed up as the emergence of interest politics. This was partly the product of vicissitudes in economic development, as the working class, artisans and peasantry were affected in different ways by the rapid rate of change. It was also partly a result of the growing interventionist role of government in economic and social life, which greatly extended the field of struggle between groups and classes over the division of resources. At the same time, the growth of communications, the press and education extended the range of issues which were regarded as 'political'. The spread of interests unleashed by these two parallel developments was indicated by one south German government which commented sourly on the agitation of 'the homeopaths, the anti-inoculationists, the pro-cremationists, the agrarians and the publicans'.[25] These changes have been noted, indeed stressed, by those historians whose views were outlined earlier; but they have usually been considered in the context of the raw material they provided for a manipulative élite. The anxieties and aspirations of the peasantry and *Mittelstand*, in particular, were allegedly exploited by the ruling class for the purpose of bolstering up the institutional and political status quo.[26] Demagogic intentions of this kind were undoubtedly widespread; they nevertheless tell only half of the story. In this study stress is placed on the fact that these manifestations of ferment from below themselves contributed to a re-definition of the political nation. To governments, and political leaders in general, these rude interruptions were as much

24. For the labour movement and this problem, see G. A. Ritter, *Die Arbeiterbewegung im Wilhelminischen Reich* (Berlin, 1959); G. Roth, *The Social Democrats in Imperial Germany* (Totowa, N.J., 1963); D. Groh, *Negative Integration und revolutionärer Attentismus* (Frankfurt/Main and Berlin, 1973).
25. Hauptstaatsarchiv Stuttgart, E41, Anhang II, Bü 4, 'Votum des Staatsministeriums' concerning Württemberg constitutional reform in 1897.
26. Wehler, *Bismarck und der Imperialismus*, pp. 473, 480–1; Wehler, *Kaiserreich*, pp. 102, 140; H. A. Winkler, 'Der rückversicherte Mittelstand', W. Rüegg and O. Neuloh (eds), *Zur soziologischen Theorie und Analyse des 19. Jahrhunderts* (Göttingen, 1971), pp. 163–79. On the peasantry in particular, see H.-J. Puhle, *Agrarische Interessenpolitik und preussischer Konservatismus im wilhelminischen Reich, 1893–1914* (Hanover, 1966).

a threat as an opportunity. Their institutionalisation was not passive and automatic; rather, it entailed a change in the very nature of politics.

These changes had a marked effect on the political parties, and a concern with the realignment of political partisanship at the close of the nineteenth century is the second point at which this study has an emphasis different from that of much recent work. The political parties have continued to be somewhat neglected, occupying rather a blank space between the wire-pullers of government and the functionaries of the various pressure groups and *Verbände*. Our ignorance on the subject of individual party developments and the outcome of elections, for example, remains enormous.[27] It was the parties, however, which acted as the essential mediators of change. At the formal level the extension of the political nation eroded the basis of 'notable politics' (*Honoratiorenpolitik*) within the parties. Political control through a handful of notables was no longer appropriate or adequate when the demands of interest groups, the careful selection of candidates and intensive electioneering were the key problems. The changing composition of the Reichstag revealed the withdrawal of those unwilling or unprepared to assume the new burdens — on the hustings, in local party work, and in parliamentary committees — which politics began to demand.[28]

The new issues not only helped to modify the organisational structure of the parties: the content of party politics and party conflict was also altered. In the 1870s constitutional questions, the consolidation of the new nation and the relationship between church and state had absorbed a large amount of political energy. By the 1890s growing economic and social conflicts dominated. As the parties annexed the extra-parliamentary pressure groups, so they altered both their own practice and their own vocabulary. *Zollpolitik*, *Mittelstandspolitik* and *Beamtenpolitik* replaced *Grossdeutschland*, *Kleindeutschland* and the *Kulturkampf* as the currency of everyday political exchange.

The parties faced this challenge with differing degrees of success.

27. There are studies of only two Reichstag elections of the thirteen which took place between 1871 and 1912: G. D. Crothers, *The German Elections of 1907* (New York, 1941); J. Bertram, *Die Wahlen zum Deutschen Reichstag vom Jahre 1912* (Düsseldorf, 1964). See also, however, B. Vogel, D. Nohlen and R.-C. Schultze, *Wahlen in Deutschland. Theorie, Geschichte, Dokumente 1848–1970* (Berlin, 1971); A. Milatz, 'Reichstagswahlen und Mandatsverteilung 1871 bis 1918', G. A. Ritter (ed), *Gesellschaft, Parlament und Regierung. Zur Geschichte des Parlamentarismus in Deutschland* (Düsseldorf, 1974), pp. 207–23.
28. See T. Nipperdey, *Die Organisation der deutschen Parteien vor 1918* (Düsseldorf, 1961); P. Molt, *Der Reichstag vor der improvisierten Revolution* (Cologne and Opladen, 1963).

The SPD was geared from the start to articulating the material demands of its supporters on matters like the cost of living and housing. The bourgeois parties had to create machinery for expressing their supporters' demands, just as they had to confect a new political style in place of *Honoratiorenpolitik*. The Conservatives reacted to the popular discontent unleashed by the agricultural crisis with a demagogic new programme and the formation of the *Bund der Landwirte*. They were thus able to secure, though only by dint of a painful readjustment, the political allegiance of a significant part of the Protestant peasantry.[29] The Centre Party was still more energetic, recognising that its very survival depended on its response. The *Volksverein für das katholische Deutschland* (People's Association of Catholic Germany) and a plethora of interest groups under the aegis of the party were established to immunise Catholics against 'materialism' in general and the blandishments of proletarian, petty-bourgeois and agrarian 'sectional' interests in particular. This institutional and organisational density, in fact, became a hallmark of the Centre Party as much as of the SPD.

Bourgeois liberalism was the chief victim of this changing political climate. Left liberalism to some extent reconstituted itself after 1900: it wooed new social groups like the growing white-collar class, and it adopted certain 'American' techniques of electioneering.[30] The National Liberals, however, went into decline at every level. Politically they were ill-equipped either to counter the anti-capitalist, anti-liberal resurgence institutionalised within the Conservative and Centre parties, or to harness the newer nationalist currents represented in the various *nationale Verbände*. Organisationally the party was slower than any other to cast off the patrician insouciance of *Honoratiorenpolitik*. The combined effect of these weaknesses was serious electoral decline, as the National Liberal electorate was squeezed between Left and Right.[31]

The connection between economic and social change on the one hand and political realignments on the other was, of course, outlined by Hans Rosenberg in his seminal work *Grosse Depression und Bismarckzeit*. Rosenberg made many fruitful suggestions on the way in

---

29. Puhle, *Agrarische Interessenpolitik und preussischer Konservatismus*.
30. See, for example, Friedrich Naumann's Heilbronn election campaign of 1907, master-minded by Ernst Jäckh, described in T. Heuss, *Erinnerungen 1905–1933* (Tübingen, 1963), pp. 58–64. More generally, P. Gilg, *Die Erneuerung des demokratischen Denkens im Wilhelminischen Deutschland* (Wiesbaden, 1965).
31. The lowest point of National Liberal Reichstag electoral fortunes was in 1898, when they received only 12.5% of the total poll. Nevertheless, the average 14% of the vote polled by the party in the subsequent three elections contrasts with the 23.5% average during the elections of the 1870s and 1880s.

which the Great Depression discredited liberal capitalism, prompted protectionist economic demands, stimulated a more rabid form of anti-semitism and generally brought about changes in political partisanship. Rosenberg's work was intended, however, as a stimulus to detailed research, not as a hard-and-fast product of such research, and considerable problems of interpretation remain. It is difficult in the first place to escape the conclusion that in recent years the Great Depression has become, analytically, a blunt instrument.[32] Given the relative paucity of information, already mentioned, about political parties and elections, the complexities of the process of change even over the years 1873–96 remain obscure at many points. The 1880s, in particular, have received too little attention. As a result, perhaps, there has been a tendency to replace the de-mythologised landmark of 1871 with the new, decisive landmark of 1878–9. Taken together, the anti-socialist law, the return to tariffs, the purging of the Prussian bureaucracy under von Puttkamer and Bismarck's turn away from the Liberals are held to have signified an effective 're-founding' of the Reich.[33]

As already indicated, however, the real reconstituting of the political nation in Germany occurred not as the result of deliberate manipulation from above, whether in 1866–71 or 1878–9, but as the outcome of a ferment within society; and in this process the late 1880s and above all the 1890s marked the watershed. In this relatively short period was concentrated an extraordinary explosion of new organisations bent on exerting pressure on the government and the political parties. These included the principal anti-semitic political parties, the earliest *Mittelstand* organisations, the major *nationale Verbände*, the Evangelical League, the German Peace Society and the German Feminist Movement. It was this period, too, which saw the founding of the *Bund der Landwirte* and the *Volksverein für das katholische Deutschland*, as well as a large number of the Centre Party's other auxiliary organisations among diverse social groups. In the first half of the 1890s, moreover, both the SPD and the Conservatives formulated important new programmes, while the Centre Party was under considerable pressure to do so from its agrarian wing. When these developments are considered together with the decline of National Liberalism and the emergence of the Centre as an

---

32. There has been a considerable debate in England over whether or not there actually was a Great Depression. See S. B. Saul, *The Myth of the Great Depression* (London, 1969). As the economic unity of the period 1873–96 has been made the basis in German historiography for wide-reaching assumptions about social and political developments, it appears even more necessary to look again at this question.
33. See the literature cited above in n. 7.

indispensable party of government, it becomes apparent that the 're-founding' of the Reich should more properly be located in the 1890s. It was then that the mould in which imperial politics had been set in the 1860s and 1870s was broken and re-cast.

If one looks at imperial Germany from a regional perspective, the crucial importance of the 1890s is underlined. This consideration of the 'periphery' of Prussia–Germany as well as the 'centre' is the third major respect in which the present study has a focus different from that of influential recent work. Such an approach need no longer be adopted defensively. It has a long pedigree in French and British historiography; and in Germany there is also a well-established tradition of local studies, with the difference that these studies have commonly not been integrated within broader frameworks of interpretation. In recent years, however, works on Baden, Hesse and Württemberg during the 1850s and 1860s,[34] together with a number of important monographs on the Weimar Republic,[35] have illustrated the valuable contribution of regional studies to our understanding of modern German history. There are heartening signs that this may soon apply also to the study of the *Kaiserreich*.[36]

In most of the German states outside Prussia (and sometimes, at the municipal level, within Prussia itself), a consideration of local politics in the 1890s provides a means of bringing into sharper focus those changes which we have already noted taking place at national level. Here, more than at Reich level, politics had remained frozen until then in an archaic pattern established in the 1860s. The suffrage was narrow or indirect, or both; *Honoratiorenpolitik* predominated, with state legislatures containing a correspondingly large number of officials and local government representatives; and party-political alignments continued to be based on *kleindeutsch—grossdeutsch* or 'pro-governmental'–'anti-governmental' differences (the two categories frequently overlapping). All these features helped to maintain for the National

34. L. Gall, *Der Liberalismus als regierende Partei: Das Grossherzogtum Baden zwischen Restauration und Reichsgründung* (Wiesbaden, 1968); N. M. Hope, *The Alternative to German Unification. The anti-Prussian Party. Frankfurt, Nassau and the Two Hessen 1859–1867* (Wiesbaden, 1973); D. Langewiesche, *Liberalismus und Demokratie in Württemberg zwischen Revolution und Reichsgründung* (Düsseldorf, 1974).
35. R. Heberle, *Landbevölkerung und Nationalsozialismus. Eine soziologische Untersuchung der politischen Willensbildung in Schleswig-Holstein 1918 bis 1932* (Stuttgart, 1963); J. Noakes, *The Nazi Party in Lower Saxony 1921–1932* (Oxford, 1971); G. Pridham, *Hitler's Rise to Power: The Nazi Movement in Bavaria 1923–33* (London, 1973).
36. K. Möckl, *Die Prinzregentenzeit. Gesellschaft und Politik während der Ära des Prinzregenten Luitpold in Bayern* (Munich and Vienna, 1972); J. C. Hunt, *The People's Party in Württemberg and Southern Germany, 1890–1914* (Stuttgart, 1975); T. D. White, *The Splintered Party. National Liberalism in Hessen and the Reich 1867–1918* (Cambridge, Mass. and London, 1976).

Liberals in state legislatures outside Prussia, and in the town halls of the Rhineland, a powerful or even dominant position through to the last decade of the century.[37]

The 1890s brought a change in almost all of these states. Material discontent among the working class, peasantry and *Mittelstand*, often articulated by particular sub-groups like state railway workers, publicans or shopkeepers, coupled with a more general social ferment ('the agitation of the homeopaths, the anti-inoculationists, the pro-cremationists', etc.) brought pressure from 'out of doors' which helped to change both the form and the substance of state politics. These pressures affected the normally 'pro-governmental' parliamentary groupings as much as they affected governments themselves. The old political alignments were broken, and cleavages appeared instead increasingly on class or sectional lines. Social Democrats and agrarians entered the state parliaments either for the first time, or in significantly greater numbers, and local Centre parties were effectively reconstituted as bodies which were more tightly organised, more populist and more electorally successful than before. Liberalism, especially National Liberalism, was the victim here even more than at national level, its collapse startlingly telescoped into a period of a mere few years. The electoral fat off which it had lived for three decades was quickly burned up, and the inability of liberalism to survive the breakdown of *Honoratiorenpolitik* was clearly exposed. Electoral reform after 1900 in states like Baden, Bavaria and Württemberg only served to underline this.[38]

The pattern of state politics in imperial Germany tends, therefore, to reinforce the points already mentioned at which present interpretations are in need of broadening or of revision: the manner in which social pressures 'from below' brought political change; the realignment of the political parties as they channelled, absorbed and orchestrated these pressures (or failed to do so); and the central importance of the 1890s as a watershed in both of these processes.

---

37. J. J. Sheehan, 'Liberalism and the City in Nineteenth Century Germany', *Past and Present*, 51 (1971), pp. 116–37, esp. pp. 126–37; and 'Deutscher Liberalismus im postliberalen Zeitalter', *Geschichte und Gesellschaft*, 4 (1978), pp. 29–30.
38. Some examples will illustrate this. In Baden National Liberal Landtag representation declined seriously in 1891, then more sharply still from 1907, following electoral reform. In Bavaria the National Liberals' Landtag strength declined from 58 seats in 1893–9 to 24 in 1907–11. In Hesse the National Liberals held 37 Landtag seats in 1890, only 18 in 1902. In Württemberg the 1890s were also the watershed, although in Prussia this fell in the 1880s. Saxony was the major exception to the general pattern, a state where the suffrage was restricted and the local National Liberals were exceptionally energetic in trying to tap new social forces and political currents. Details in H. Kalkhoff (ed), *Nationalliberale Parlamentarier des Reichstages und der Einzellandtage 1867–1917* (Berlin, 1917), statistical tables, pp. 272, 303, 338, 371, 405.

Some historians who have looked recently at the effects after 1900 of these changing party strengths and realignments have done so from the perspective of 'democratisation' and the obstacles to it in imperial Germany. The *Grossblock* in Baden and the reformist impulse of Conrad Haussmann and Friedrich Payer in the Württemberg *Volkspartei* have, in particular, lent themselves to such speculations.[39] What, it has been asked, was the balance of advantages and disadvantages facing those who sought party coalitions to press for 'parliamentarisation'; and what does this tell us about Reich politics in general? These questions are clearly important. At least since Arthur Rosenberg posed the problem of the 'failure' of a 'Gladstonian coalition' to take shape in imperial German politics, the 'failure' of various reformist coalitions to materialise has occupied the minds of historians.[40] Taking German history to task for its sins of omission can, of course, become a dangerous historical exercise. It is, however, of obvious interest to know what *did* happen to the political parties in a period of great ferment, particularly as a number of recent studies have tended to suggest that many of the divisions in both society and polity were not the result of any conscious manipulation from above, but rather proceeded spontaneously from the nature of the political parties themselves and their constituencies.[41] The present work, which deals at some length with the interests, aspirations and perceptions which divided the parties from one another, tends to support this conclusion.

What follows is presented, however, not only as a study in microcosm of the problems facing would-be reformers and coalition-builders in imperial Germany, but also as a study of local politics as such. It should not be read as an attempt to replace the question 'Who ruled in Berlin?' with the question 'Who ruled in Stuttgart?' Rather, it is an attempt to focus on the popular sentiments which sustained local politics: to try and re-direct some attention, that is, not only from the 'centre' to the 'periphery' but also from politics 'above' to politics 'below'. Any such effort to plot the nature of (let alone changes in) popular consciousness is hazardous, and must necessarily be incomplete. The attempt nevertheless seems necessary. It is clear that neither the machinations of political leaders nor the

39. See, for example, B. Heckart, *From Bassermann to Bebel. The Grand Bloc's Quest for Reform in the Kaiserreich, 1890–1914* (New Haven, 1974); Hunt, *The People's Party in Württemberg*; R. A. H. Franz, *Das Problem der konstitutionellen Parlamentarisierung bei Conrad Haussmann und Friedrich von Payer* (Göppingen, 1977).
40. A. Rosenberg, *Imperial Germany*, transl. I. F. D. Morrow (London, 1931), p. 18. I have also posed this question in a number of articles, and do so as well in the first chapter of the work which follows.
41. This comes out particularly clearly in Hunt, *The People's Party in Württemberg*.

temper of popular sentiment can be studied in isolation. Indeed, it will
be argued below that the degree of interaction between the two was
growing in imperial Germany, just as the two-way contact between
'centre' and 'periphery' was on the increase. In view of the mounting
volume of work being produced on the *Kaiserreich*, it may be hoped
that before too long we will have a clearer idea of the terms on which
this interaction proceeded. For the moment there is certainly a need to
try and recover something of the fabric of local politics. In the absence
of this, important arguments about the effects on the electorate of
'manipulation' and 'diversionary strategies' run the risk of remaining
disembodied, even when the intention to manipulate or divert can be
demonstrated. The approach to politics solely from the top down, in
other words, may be misleading. For examination of 'the affects, the
whisperings, the motions of the people' within the limited compass of
a locality suggests a level of ambiguity and flux in attitudes during the
years before 1914 much greater than often supposed.

A good example of this concerns the assumption made in a good
deal of recent writing on imperial Germany, that there was a
straightforward connection between social change and 'anti-modernist'
reactions, particularly among the peasantry and *Mittelstand*. The
connection was actually a good deal less straightforward. Reactions to
an unevenly changing social fabric were themselves uneven.[42] On the
land and in the small towns, for example, new patterns of dress,
furnishing and diet were evident, although this occurred alongside a
frequently sharp resentment of the agencies which made it possible —
like the mail-order catalogue and the travelling salesman. Similarly,
the anti-urban animus which can be detected in rural communities was
not always indiscriminate: it often directed itself against genuine
objects of grievance, such as interest rates and prices which were fixed
in the distant town. Yet, at the same time, urban liberals who scorned
the 'idiocy of rural life' could point smugly to the persistence of a
belief in witchcraft or sorcery on the land. What does seem clear is
that the extension of communications in this period penetrated the
smallest localities, although its effects were contradictory. The leaven
introduced by an altered sense of time and space often served to
'modernise' the form but not the content of local social consciousness:
customary values were thus re-cast and took on a new appearance.
Pilgrimages were undertaken by railway. The hawker or gipsy was
replaced by the travelling salesman as the *bête noire* of small towns and

42. On the following points, see my article, 'The *Mittelstand* in German Society and
Politics, 1871–1914', *Social History*, 4 (1977), pp. 426–8.

villages, castigated now by letters to the local press rather than by physical violence.

These contradictions and ambiguities informed the changed politics which crystallised in the 1890s. The narrow political nation forged in the 1860s had been conditioned by the construction of major railway links, a city press and the political mobilisation of the *Honoratioren*; the new political nation re-cast in the 1890s was conditioned by the local branch line, the small-town press and the political mobilisation of the masses. Like the broader process of social change, this process of political change was two-way: it operated upwards as well as downwards. On the one hand, an unprecedentedly large part of the population was attached 'from above' to a politics which already enjoyed an existence in parliamentary institutions and clubs; on the other hand, politics itself underwent a change as it acquired the imprint of popular aspirations. Class and sectional interests formed part of this imprint; the articulation of local identity, local grievances and local aspirations — *as such* — formed another, important, part. If there was a growing sense of national politics at the local level, then in an important sense national politics became at the same time parish-pump politics writ large.

The achievements of recent work on imperial Germany are very considerable. Central to these achievements has been the identification of manipulative intentions among the political élite. Yet the way in which this manipulative and demagogic mode of politics actually worked requires further elucidation. If concepts of this kind are to be put to work usefully in the study of imperial Germany, then this will perhaps be best achieved through a sympathetic approach to the forms of political interpenetration described above. That is why the political parties are of such significance, for they occupied the ground on which pressures from 'centre' and 'periphery', from 'above' and 'below', met. In studying them, one is studying the manner in which newly conscious sectional and local sentiment was mediated, modified and often manipulated. That is the central concern of the present study.

III

It may be useful to close this introduction with some comments on the particular ground covered by the study. The large gaps which exist in our knowledge of German political parties in this period have already been alluded to. The Centre Party has been subject to particular neglect. The standard work is still Karl Bachem's nine-volume history, written in the 1920s and published between 1927 and 1932.[43] Bachem's work remains an enormously valuable account both of the Centre and more generally of politics in imperial Germany. It was written, however, by a Centre politician with the assistance of party colleagues to whom it was submitted for comments before publication. It is essentially an official history. Since Bachem research on the Centre has been sketchy. The political caesura of 1933 interrupted scholarly enquiry, and the loss and physical destruction of sources in the period 1933–45 has also hampered research. The most significant contribution since 1945 to the study of the Centre Party is that of Rudolf Morsey, but his major concern has been with the period after 1917.[44] Two books have appeared recently in the United States which deal with the Wilhelmine Centre,[45] and Karl Möckl's study of politics in pre-1914 Bavaria gives an excellent account of the party in that state. Nevertheless, work on many important aspects of the Centre — the regional organisations, the party press, the *Volksverein für das katholische Deutschland*, the economic interest groups under the aegis of the party — is slight. If we are eventually to have a general history of the Centre to replace Bachem's, many gaps in our knowledge must first be filled.

There is, additionally, a major problem of interpretation involved in dealing with the Centre. In general accounts of this period the Centre usually appears as a narrowly sectarian and politically opportunist party. This view was a commonplace among contemporaries and it has persisted for a number of reasons. In the first place, it has been reinforced by the introverted nature of much work by those within the tradition of political Catholicism. The *Zentrumsturm* (Centre tower) which Julius Bachem warned against in 1906[46] continues to revenge itself on the party: both the underdeveloped state of research on the Centre and the conventional view of the party are in part a legacy of the historical isolation and inbred cultural separatism of German Catholicism, dating back at least to the *Kulturkampf*. There is, however, a further reason why the Centre still appears in historical accounts as a clerically-motivated party dedicated to unscrupulous

---

43. K. Bachem, *Vorgeschichte, Geschichte und Politik der Deutschen Zentrumspartei*, 9 vols (Cologne, 1927–32).
44. R. Morsey, *Die Deutsche Zentrumspartei 1917–1923* (Düsseldorf, 1966). Morsey has, however, written a number of articles dealing with the Centre Party prior to 1914. See, in particular, 'Die deutschen Katholiken und der Nationalstaat zwischen Kulturkampf und dem Ersten Weltkrieg', *Historisches Jahrbuch*, 90 (1970), pp. 31–64.
45. J. K. Zeender, *The German Center Party 1890–1906* (Philadelphia, 1976); R. J. Ross, *Beleaguered Tower: The Dilemma of Political Catholicism in Wilhelmine Germany* (Notre Dame, Ind., 1976). See also U. Mittmann, *Fraktion und Partei. Ein Vergleich von Zentrum und Sozialdemokratie im Kaiserreich* (Düsseldorf, 1976).
46. J. Bachem, 'Wir müssen aus dem Turm heraus', *Historisch-politische Blätter*, 137 (1906), pp. 376–86.

politicking. This derives from the difficulty experienced by recent historians in accommodating the Centre within their interpretations on the same terms as other political parties and movements. Two out of many examples of the Centre's 'awkwardness' in this respect may be cited. First, the Catholic bourgeoisie and the Centre Party clearly adopted an affirmative stance towards Germany's expansionist foreign policy. But, equally clearly, they were infected with the social values of neither bureaucracy nor officer corps: Catholics were discriminated against in appointments to both, while the strong Catholic anti-duelling movement testified to their alienation from 'Prussian' values.[47] The position of the Catholic peasantry and *Mittelstand* was similarly ambiguous. As this study will try to show, their material interests and the pressure they exerted on behalf of them were crucial to the politics of the Centre. But these interests had only the most oblique relationship to the problem of 'iron and rye'; and study of both the interests and their articulation has languished.

Despite the fruitful concern of recent historians with the economic and social context of politics, therefore, the Centre still seems to exist as a disembodied political creature. This emerges clearly in Eckart Kehr's classic formulation of the basis of *Sammlungspolitik*, from which so much recent research has proceeded. According to Kehr, the reconciling of National Liberals and Conservatives was a matter of economic interests, a trade-off between industry and agriculture, iron and rye, the fleet and agricultural tariffs. The role of the Centre, by contrast, is approached very differently. Here it is purely political considerations, rather than a combination of economic, social and political ones, which is stressed; and the Centre's support for the first navy bill is explained solely as the result of the offer to the party of the political hegemony in imperial Germany.[48]

Neither the view of the Centre as a sectarian Catholic party, nor the related view of it as a party of unscrupulous tacticians, is entirely without truth. The Centre, after all, *was* the party of German Catholics, gaining over half of the Catholic vote even in the Reichstag election of 1912, when the party lost fourteen seats. The Catholic-ness of the Centre was not contingent but central to the party's nature. This is not to say, however, that the Centre was a clerical party which acted as the political arm of the Catholic church. As this study attempts to show, there was in fact a marked de-clericalisation of the Centre from the 1890s in particular, at the level of both policies and personnel, measures and men. At the same time, while it is true that

47. See Chapter One below.
48. Kehr, *Schlachtflottenbau*, p. 205.

almost all Centre voters were Catholic, it is not true that almost all Catholics voted for the Centre. To have been a Catholic was a necessary not a sufficient condition of supporting the party. Many ceased to do so, despite their religion; and many who continued to support the party did so for reasons which were residually rather than primarily religious.

It was partly a by-product of the fact that the Centre increasingly appealed to the worldly interests of its heterogeneous supporters that the party acquired its reputation for political unscrupulousness. Balancing above the conflicting interests, there was a marked tendency for the party leadership over quite short periods of time to lean first one way, then another. Here too, though, the half-truth has obscured the rest of the story. The Centre was indeed almost universally regarded by contemporaries as untrustworthy and hence incapable of forming alliances (*bündnisunfähig*). Yet, as most of its political opponents recognised, this applied more to the tactics of the party than its strategy. As this study will attempt to demonstrate, in crucial political, economic and social matters the policy of the Centre was by no means the outcome of a disembodied, ultra-tactical mode of politics peculiar to the party.

What follows is therefore an attempt to present a fuller picture of the Centre, in which the particular political position occupied by the party is related to broader forces at work in German Catholic society. The first chapter deals with the party at national level, and offers an explanation as to why both the values of the Centre's leaders in Berlin and the extra-parliamentary pressure on the party from its supporters should have combined to guide the Centre on to a generally pro-governmental and anti–Left course. In the course of this analysis a number of points are brought out which have been raised earlier in this introduction: the importance of pressure 'from below' on political parties, including the Centre; the centrality of the 1890s, when against a background of such pressures the Centre underwent crucial changes in leadership, policy and political style; and the significance of divisions between political parties — in this case, between the Centre and the parties of the Left — which resulted from genuine differences of both interests and values.

The remainder of the study consists of a detailed examination of the Centre Party in Württemberg. The choice of Württemberg was based on a number of considerations. In the first place, Catholics in that state made up about a third of the population, and lived in areas which were clearly separate and largely backward in an economic and social sense. For this reason the politics evolved by the Centre Party locally mirrored the politics of the national party, where the similar overall position of Catholics in the Reich helped to bring about a comparable politics of resentment. Secondly, Württemberg offers a good example of those important changes in the nature of the Centre Party in the 1890s which are dealt with at national level in the first chapter, and have been more generally alluded to in this introduction. More detailed consideration of both these points can be found in the text.

The general advantages of a regional study have already been mentioned. Such a study makes it possible to look in detail at the emergence of the party locally, at the positions it took up towards a body of government legislation, and at its changing relationship to the other political parties. It also makes it possible to consider, within a manageable compass, the relationship between party leadership and supporters. This is dealt with specifically in a chapter on organisation, but occupies an important place throughout. What emerges is the constant tension between the more lofty political ambitions of the leaders in Stuttgart, and the role which the Centre played in the self-understanding of back-benchers, local newspaper readers and ordinary supporters. The forging of Centre policy out of the interaction between the political calculation of party leaders and the aspirations of Centre supporters in the state provides the book with its unifying idea.

CHAPTER 1

The Centre Party in German Politics, 1890–1914

I

Between 1890 and 1914 the Centre Party was, in Friedrich Naumann's words, 'the measure of all things in German politics'.[1] Throughout this period it possessed a quarter of all the seats in the Reichstag, and held the balance of power between Left and Right. Its importance, from the standpoint of Bismarck's successors as chancellor, stemmed from the electoral and parliamentary decline of the National Liberals and Conservatives, the parties making up the *Kartell* through which Bismarck had governed in the Reichstag. After 1890 these no longer commanded a majority and other parties had to be won over by the government.[2] With the SPD permanently hostile, this narrowed the government's choice down to the Progressives and Centre, either of which would give the *Kartell* parties a majority, and both of which were to be used to this effect. The Progressives, however, were used only sparingly, above all during the period of the Bülow Bloc, 1906–9. They were regarded as unreliable because of their historic anti-militarism, and they were also moving to the left at this time as a result of leadership fears that their supporters might otherwise defect to the SPD. The Centre was therefore the only alternative,[3] and for most of the Wilhelmine period successive chancellors depended on it for their parliamentary majorities.

1. F. Naumann, *Die politischen Parteien* (Berlin, 1910), p. 39.
2. Röhl, *Germany without Bismarck*, pp. 45–6; Stegmann, *Die Erben Bismarcks*, pp. 29–31.
3. A Hohenlohe memorandum in 1898, after the Reichstag elections, summed up the dilemma: 'The election statistics provide irrefutable evidence that it will not be possible in the foreseeable future to form a majority from the so-called national parties. One must therefore seek to win over one of the opposition parties. The only party which comes into consideration here is the Centre, the overwhelming part of which is monarchist.' C. zu Hohenlohe, *Denkwürdigkeiten der Reichskanzlerzeit*, ed. K. A. von Müller (Stuttgart, 1931), pp. 451–3. For earlier calculations by Caprivi, leading to the same conclusion, see Röhl, *Germany without Bismarck*, p. 80.

At the same time the Centre showed itself willing to become a 'party of government' (*Regierungspartei*). The party's support for the re-introduction of tariffs in 1879 and for social legislation in the following decade had already marked a retreat from the purely negative, oppositional standpoint of the 1870s.[4] In the 1880s Centre leaders like Windthorst frequently stressed how pleased they would be to adopt a still more positive role, if given some encouragement by the Reich's rulers. The accession of Wilhelm II, initially higher popular with Centre leaders, the fall of Bismarck and the death of Windthorst were the outward signs of a decisive caesura in the early 1890s. For the following two and a half decades, under a new generation of leaders, the Centre became a dependable ally of successive chancellors. Its leading members now, for the first time, occupied important honorary posts in the Reichstag, while men like Ernst Lieber, Peter Spahn and Karl Trimborn built up close relations with state secretaries in the imperial government. The change was most apparent in the party's consistent support for government legislation. Under the leadership of Ernst Lieber, until his death in 1902, the Centre supported Caprivi's 'New Course', most notably the trade treaties with Russia, Romania, Spain and Austria; the financial reforms of 1896 (the 'lex Lieber'); the new German Civil Code (*Bürgerliches Gesetzbuch*); the first and second navy bills (1898 and 1900); the military bill of 1899; and the important new tariffs passed through the Reichstag in 1901–2. It was with some justice that Lieber referred to the Centre as the 'governing party', and hardly surprising that the party's opponents should sourly refer to Lieber himself as the *Reichsregent*.

Following Lieber's death the collective leadership of Spahn, Hertling, Trimborn and Gröber followed his broad policy, making the Centre a continuingly essential part of the government's majority, except for the Bülow Bloc years of 1906–9. Prior to 1906 the Centre supported the financial laws of 1904 and 1906, the commercial courts law of 1904, the 1905 military law and the 1906 navy law. After the interlude of the Bloc the Centre returned to the governmental fold to enable the passage of the finance reforms of 1909, and to support the increasing spending on armaments in the years up to 1914.[5]

Almost all of this legislation was passed in opposition to the growing

4. Note Windthorst's remark in the course of the 1879 Reichstag tariff debate: 'Herr Bamberger has labelled us the picked troops of the chancellor. I wish he had been speaking the truth. For nothing could be more agreeable to us than always to be fighting on the side of the chancellor.' D. Fricke (ed.), *Die bürgerlichen Parteien in Deutschland 1830–1945*, 2 vols (Leipzig, 1968–70), II, p. 886.
5. On the change of the Centre into a party of government, see especially Morsey, *Historisches Jahrbuch* (1970).

SPD parliamentary group, much of it also against the votes of the Progressives. The consistent pro-governmental stance of the Centre was therefore accompanied by a tendency to ally politically with the parties of the Right, especially with the Conservatives. This was not an entirely novel departure. Even during the *Kulturkampf*, many Conservatives had been profoundly disturbed by the implications of liberal attacks on the Catholic Church, and correspondingly sympathetic to the Centre.[6] In the 1880s, as the Centre demonstrated its support for tariffs and anti-laissez-faire legislation, the groundwork for future Centre–Conservative cooperation was laid: the group of Conservatives around Hammerstein and the *Kreuz-Zeitung* was especially anxious to foster this relationship, and Bismarck complained of the 'constant flirtation' of the *Kreuz-Zeitung* with the Centre.[7] From the 1890s Conservative leaders orientated towards the 'social question', like Kardorff and Levetzow, worked closely with their Centre counterparts. From this time the two parties cooperated in supporting a host of conservative economic measures, such as agrarian protection, stock exchange controls and measures to support independent artisans and shopkeepers by swingeing taxes on department stores and 'mobile capital'.[8] The formal expression of this growing Centre–Conservative alliance was the foundation of the *Schwarz-Blau Block* to fight the 1912 Reichstag election.

The Centre, however, always had an alternative to its pro-governmental, pro-Conservative course: to join what Arthur Rosenberg called a 'Gladstonian Coalition' of the centre–left, running from itself, as the party of German Catholics, through the Progressives, to the SPD.[9] The idea of such a coalition was not just the later intellectual construct of a historian engaged politically on the Left. Certainly the rulers of imperial Germany, forced to rely on Centre votes in the Reichstag, expressed periodic concern that the party would throw in its lot with the Left. The tendency of the Centre to avoid committing itself in advance either for or against a government bill heightened the nervousness of those in the Wilhelmstrasse, while reminding them of Bismarck's implacable belief in the unreliability of the party; and the fact that most of the Centre's leaders after the early 1890s were recruited from the more democratic southern and western parts of the Reich served to heighten government apprehensions on this score.

6. E. Hüsgen, *Ludwig Windthorst* (Cologne, 1911), p. 198.
7. N. Rich and M. H. Fisher (eds), *The Holstein Papers*, 4 vols (Cambridge, 1955–63), II, p. 191.
8. M. Spahn, *Das deutsche Zentrum* (Mainz and Munich, 1907), p. 99 ff.
9. See Introduction n. 40.

Centre and SPD did, in fact, have much in common. Drawing their support from the poorest parts of the population, they formed the two great mass parties in Wilhelmine politics, equipped with the most extensive auxiliary organisations rooted among the people. If the SPD had a million members by 1914, the mass organisation of the Centre Party, the *Volksverein für das katholische Deutschland*, had 865,000 (in 1900 it was only 500,000), along with a budget of 700,000 Marks per annum.[10] Significantly, it was in the Centre and SPD that the phenomenon of the professional politician noted by Max Weber was most apparent, and it was in their respective organisations that career politicians like Matthias Erzberger and Friedrich Ebert first rose through the ranks of party functionaries to achieve prominence. Both parties, too, had suffered under exceptional legislation, the *Kulturkampf* May Laws in one case, the anti-socialist law in the other; and both, having gained electoral support and positions of parliamentary importance at liberal expense, turned to announce the bankruptcy of liberalism as an economic, political and cultural force.

At a time when the Progressives were moving closer to the SPD, an alliance of these two parties with the Centre would have commanded a Reichstag majority at all times after 1890. Clearly, an alliance of this sort would not initially have been capable of forcing ministers on the Kaiser; but it would have placed the autocratic constitutional practices of the Reich under severe and permanent pressure. A political alignment of these parties might have precipitated reform: it would certainly have called the hand of those on the Right who threatened a *Staatsstreich*. It was, after all, these three parties which moved decisively against the imperial government by supporting Erzberger's Peace Resolution in 1917; and it was the same three parties, as members of the 'Weimar coalition', which carried Weimar democracy on their shoulders in the early 1920s.[11] By adhering to an alliance of this kind, the Centre itself might have anticipated later events and developed into a constitutional conservative party within a genuinely parliamentary system — which (as the CDU/CSU) it has since become. The Centre chose, however, to support the Progressives and SPD only sporadically before 1917, whether in the Reichstag, in state parliaments or in elections. The remainder of this chapter will attempt to explain why the Centre should have found cooperation with the Left — most especially the SPD — so difficult.

---

10. J. Rost, *Die wirtschaftliche und kulturelle Lage der deutschen Katholiken* (Cologne, 1911), p. 190.
11. See Morsey, *Zentrumspartei*.

II

The attitude of the Left towards the Catholic Church was naturally a major obstacle to better relations with the Centre. The Progressives were anti-clerical by tradition, and while the SPD regarded religion as a 'private matter', the party was in practice consistently hostile to the Church, critical both of its teachings and of its social role. The Centre had laid the foundations of its formidable political position in the 1870s, in defending the Church and its members against Bismarck's *Kulturkampf*. While the SPD and many individual Progressives had not, in fact, supported this assault on the Church, the Centre nevertheless regarded Bebel's 'state of the future' (*Zukunftsstaat*) with as much suspicion as it had regarded the policies of Bismarck and Falk. In the years after 1900 Centre fears for the autonomy of the Church were kept alive particularly by the constant attacks of both Progressives and SPD on the clerical control over education.[12]

Several points have to be made here, however. First, these important differences existed also in the Weimar Republic, when they did not prevent a substantial measure of cooperation between the parties. Second, and more fundamentally, the Centre was never simply a clerical party. The name of the party was deliberately chosen to reflect this fact,[13] and many clerical Catholic politicians spurned the Centre at its inception, while other frustrated clerical diehards continued to do so at regular intervals over the following years. Even in the early years of its existence, moreover, the Centre stood for more than just Catholic resentment against a two-thirds Protestant state. The party identified itself too with south German opposition to a Prussian-based Reich, and with the dissatisfaction of economically backward regions and social groups at incorporation within a large, dynamic new political unit.[14] The support which the Centre received from the Guelphs, backward, traditionalist and anti-Prussian, was symptomatic.

Thirdly, relations between the Centre and the Left deteriorated from the 1890s, precisely when the former was sloughing off those clerical remnants of its character which remained. With the dismantling of

---

12. See, for example, the Centre leader Hertling on the importance of the struggle over education in Prussia: G. von Hertling, *Erinnerungen aus meinem Leben*, 2 vols (Munich, 1919–20), II, pp. 8–9.

13. Hüsgen, *Windthorst*, pp. 94–9; Spahn, *Das deutsche Zentrum*, pp. 33–47.

14. A good example of the contrast between Protestant towns, with their industry, commerce and bureaucracy, and the Catholic countryside, is to be found in Baden during its *Kulturkampf*. See F. Dor, *Jacob Lindau, Ein Badischer Politiker und Volksmann, in seinem Leben und Wirken geschildert* (Freiburg, 1909). This situation has been well treated recently by Lothar Gall, *Zeitschrift für die Geschichte des Oberrheins* (1965).

Kulturkampf legislation and the declining persecution of Catholics, the Centre drew a dwindling return from electoral appeals to confessional loyalty.[15] By the 1890s, to be a Catholic was still largely a necessary but by no means a sufficient condition for voting Centre. The increasing fragility of its hold on Catholics as Catholics was a source of serious concern to party leaders, who began to emphasise the popular, social policies of the Centre, and called for an end to confessional politics. Support for tariffs and legislation like stock exchange controls testified to the growing adherence of Centre leaders to a very worldly *Sozialpolitik*. Evidence of this change can be seen in the founding of a plethora of peasant and artisan associations in these years, but most of all in the founding, shortly before Windthorst's death, of the *Volksverein für das katholische Deutschland*. The *Volksverein* was set up to provide the Centre with an organisational backbone in changed political conditions, and to impose the social and political objectives of the Berlin leadership on the idiosyncratic and often clerically-minded Centre groups in the south.[16] It was faced from the outset with the rival claims of the episcopacy, who wished to use the *Volksverein* as a confessional weapon aimed at the anti-Catholic Evangelical League. These attempts at control by Bishop Korum of Trier, and Jesuit elements, were strongly resisted by Windthorst, for they stood in direct opposition to his own attempts to declericalise the Centre. Later efforts by Korum, Cardinal von Hartmann and Cardinal Kopp were resisted equally firmly by Franz Brandts and Karl Trimborn, the *Volksverein* organisers.[17]

The non-clerical nature of the Centre was best illustrated by its hostility towards attempts by Rome and the German bishops to dictate party policy on Reich military bills. As early as 1880 Rome had suggested that a favourable attitude towards Bismarck's seven-year military bill (*Septennat*) might lead to a reduction of *Kulturkampf* legislation; but the Centre chairman, Franckenstein, made it clear that the party was completely independent of clerical influence in this sphere.[18] In 1887, when the *Septennat* came up for renewal, Bismarck tried to put pressure on the Centre through Rome to support the measure. A note was passed to Centre leaders Franckenstein and

15. Thus Felix Porsch, a Silesian Centre leader, wrote to Cardinal Kopp that the spirit of the *Kulturkampf* years had waned, that Centre men now weighed matters up very carefully where once they had followed blindly. H. Gottwald, *Zentrum und Imperialismus*, dissertation (Jena, 1966), p. 129.
16. Nipperdey, *Organisation*, p. 281; Spahn, *Das deutsche Zentrum*, pp. 82–3.
17. StA Cologne, Karl Bachem Papers, 59: memoranda of Karl Bachem on the founding of the *Volksverein*; H. Cardauns, *Karl Trimborn* (M-Gladbach, 1922), p. 73.
18. StA Cologne, Karl Bachem Papers, 55: copy of a letter from Franckenstein's son to Felix Porsch, 19 October 1914, with Bachem's own comments added.

Windthorst through the papal nuncio in Munich, di Pietro, urging Centre acceptance of the bill in the interests of the Church. The reply was, once again, an unambiguous statement of Centre Party autonomy in all political matters, and a refusal to modify its opposition to the *Septennat*.[19]

In 1893, finally, faced with the need to secure Centre support for his 'big' military bill, Caprivi also failed with the same ploy. Cardinal Kopp, a favoured intermediary in negotiations between Berlin and the Vatican, and von Ballestrem, a conservative Silesian member of the Centre, went to Rome while the bill was being discussed. They returned reporting that the Pope would be pleased to see the bill passed, and that he recommended discussions between Centre leaders and the German bishops. If the bishops were divided, the Pope had continued, the party was to heed the advice of those who were most experienced in such affairs, a clear hint from Rome that the pro-bill position of Kopp would be more favourably received in the Vatican than the anti-bill posture of men like Bishop Krementz of Cologne. The Centre leaders, especially Lieber, were incensed at this attempted interference, and once again the clerical overtures were disregarded.[20] The elections which followed the Centre's firm opposition to Caprivi's 'big' military bill showed how the clerical conservatives in the party — Kopp, Ballestrem, Huene — were, in Karl Bachem's words, 'isolated' in the Centre.[21]

In later years this declericalisation of the Centre became even more emphasised, particularly in the dispute between party and episcopacy over inter-confessional trade unions. When, in 1906, Julius Bachem published his famous article 'We must leave the tower', calling for a final abandonment of the Centre's confessional character, he already had the great majority of the party behind him. Those who continued to demand a narrowly clerical party were as isolated as the Silesian rebels in 1893; many left the party, or simply failed to be adopted as

---

19. StA Cologne, Karl Bachem Papers, 56, 61b: memoranda of Karl Bachem dealing with the reactions of Centre leaders to the crisis and the discussions of the *Reichstagsfraktion*. See also Hüsgen, *Windthorst*, pp. 231–2; Hertling, *Erinnerungen*, II, pp. 64–6.

20. StA Cologne, Karl Bachem Papers, 56, 66c; Pfälzische LB Speyer, Ernst Lieber Papers, S. 195, Schädler to Lieber, 20 June 1893. The near unanimity of Centre politicians over this issue can be gauged not only from the memoranda and letters of the bill's opponents, like Bachem, Lieber and Schädler, but also from the diary accounts of Franz von Ballestrem, a prominent Silesian member of the Centre and one of the few to urge a more pliant line. See especially folder IX of the unpublished papers in family possession.

21. StA Cologne, Karl Bachem Papers, 56: Bachem memorandum on the Centre and the military bills of 1887, 1890 and 1893.

candidates at elections.[22] It is perhaps worth pointing out the sharp contrast with France, where political Catholicism as a broad and popular social movement suffered from the interference of a conservative episcopacy, which first delayed *Ralliement* by its obdurate resistance, then damned the movement by its support.[23] In Germany, Centre leaders never allowed the bishops, or Rome, to dictate the politics of the party. If the Centre was happy to receive concessions to the Church as a reward for its support of government policy — the return of impounded property, and permission for the banned Redemptorist Order to return to the Reich, for example — this was by no means a dominant aspect of party policy.

There were, of course, many issues on which Centre policy followed closely the position of the Church: education, cremation, mixed marriage and the role of the family are examples. It is also the case that party leaders sought wherever possible to avoid conflict with the episcopacy, while at the same time the parish clergy provided an essential organisational prop for the Centre in the constituencies. Circumstances had changed, however, since the *Kulturkampf*. In the years after 1890 issues which involved the position of the Church were dwarfed by Centre involvement in legislation on military and naval programmes, and on economic and social matters. And while the Centre continued to concern itself centrally with discrimination against Catholics, the thrust of its policy was aimed at alleviating the position of the more general Catholic 'ghetto', rather than at specific proscriptions on the Church and Catholic worship. Thus at the end of the 1890s, Lieber and the rest of the party leadership decided that in return for their support of the Mittelland canal they would demand not the relaxation of the anti-Jesuit law but a reform of the Rhineland electoral law which discriminated against Catholic communities.[24]

It was not the supposed clerical policy of the Centre which cut the party off from the Left. This was the result, rather, of policies embarked upon by Centre leaders as a form of assertion that German Catholics were no longer prepared to be treated as a Cinderella community; that they wished to emerge from the economic backwardness, social discrimination and political and public impotence which had previously been their lot. It is to the grievances and

---

22. The intransigent deputies Roeren and Bitter are good examples of those who left the *Fraktion*. Morsey, *Zentrumspartei*, pp. 36–40; L. Bergsträsser, *Geschichte der politischen Parteien in Deutschland* (Munich, 1960), pp. 175–7; J. Bachem, *Erinnerungen eines alten Publizisten und Politikers* (Cologne, 1913), pp. 180–1.
23. T. Zeldin, *France 1848–1945*, vol 1, *Ambition, Love and Politics* (Oxford, 1973), pp. 646–8.
24. Cardauns, *Trimborn*, pp. 83–4.

aspirations nurtured within the Catholic community, and their effects on a new generation of Centre Party leaders, that we shall now turn.

III

The generation of Centre leaders which emerged in the 1890s had perspectives very different from those of the party's leaders in the previous two decades. The earlier generation had formulated their policy at a time when unification by the sword was still a fresh memory and when flesh and blood still had to be given to the bare bones of the Reich constitution. In those decades the *Kulturkampf* and anti-socialist law had treated major parts of the newly-unified population as overt enemies of the state, almost as occupied populations. The earlier preoccupation of the Centre with attacks on a Church whose priests were regularly being imprisoned was a natural result of the position in which German Catholics found themselves in the fluid and uncertain first decades of the Reich. The new men, by contrast, reflected the changed conditions of German politics after the external and internal consolidation of the Reich. Their emphasis was not so much on the position of Catholic worship and the Catholic Church within a recently unified and still loosely federal Reich, but on the economic, social and political equality of Catholic citizens within the consolidated German state.

While the 1880s saw the repeal of the more crass forms of discrimination against Catholic worship, inequality remained apparent in most other spheres. In 1908, Catholics in Prussia still paid less than a sixth of total income tax in the state, although they made up a third of the population: in the extreme case of Aachen the non-Catholic one-twenty-sixth of the population paid a third of the income tax. The picture of relative Catholic poverty which this represented was similar in other states.[25] Such evidence of Catholic 'backwardness', seized upon by the Evangelical League for its anti-Catholic propaganda, was not restricted to income. In Baden, only 36 per cent of students were Catholic in a state where they constituted 60 per cent of the population; in Prussia the figures were 25 per cent and 36 per cent respectively. Among academics the disparity was even more pronounced. In 1896–7, Catholics provided only 11.75 per cent of the lecturers in the non-theological faculties of Prussian universities, only 8.75 per cent of the *Privatdozenten* (unsalaried lecturers), and only 16.5 per cent of the professors. In Bavaria at the same time, only 43 per

25. Rost, *Die wirtschaftliche und kulturelle Lage*, pp. 82–3.

cent of all professorial chairs were held by Catholics in a state where they made up 71 per cent of the population.[26]

This discrimination was felt above all in appointments to official posts, especially in Prussia. Silesia (56 per cent Catholic) and Trier (80 per cent Catholic) had no Catholic *Regierungsrat* in the lifetime of the Reich; Alsace-Lorraine (80 per cent Catholic) had only one Catholic *Statthalter* (the later Chancellor, Hohenlohe). Oppeln, where all but one of the 19 *landräthliche Kreise* were predominantly Catholic, had only three Catholic *Landräthe* in 1911, while in Posen there were only two Catholic *Landräthe* in 1911, while in Posen there were only two Catholic *Landräthe* out of twenty-seven, although twenty-six of the *Kreise* had a Catholic majority. Discrimination also existed, however, in the economically more advanced and urbanised Prussian Rhine Province, and in non-Prussian states. In all, Catholics provided only sixty-five (14 per cent) of the Reich's 487 *Landräthe* in 1911.[27] A similar pattern can be discerned right down to the municipal level: in many places where Catholics made up a majority or a large minority of the population, professional employees in the municipal gas and electricity works, abattoir, hospital and architecture department were commonly non-Catholic.

It was against this background of severe inequality that, from about the 1890s, the Centre began to reflect a growing demand among middle-class Catholics for a fairer and fuller share in various areas of German national life. One index of this was a more affirmative mood among businessmen, aware of the under-representation of Catholics in industry and commerce and anxious that the shortfall be made good.[28] The mood was still more pronounced, however, among the non-business middle class. Catholic civil servants and academics, and would-be members of those professions, began to react more strongly to the discrimination which they encountered; particularly, in the case of academics, to the continuing widespread prejudice that Catholics could never exercise the disinterest required of scholarship.[29] The tone adopted generally by Catholic intellectuals became brisker and less apologetic. This was clear in the emergence from its 'inner exile' of a periodical like *Hochland*, and it was demonstrated also in the successive revised editions of the Görres *Staatslexikon*, as it took up a position

---

26. Ibid, pp. 98–9.
27. Ibid, pp. 163–6; A. Neher, *Die wirtschaftliche und soziale Lage der Katholiken im westlichen Deutschland* (Rottweil, 1927), pp. 48–9.
28. Gottwald, *Zentrum und Imperialismus*, p. 24 ff.
29. The best example of this is the 'Spahn affair' in 1901, the outcry which followed Martin Spahn's appointment to a chair of history at the new University of Strassburg. For accounts of the affair, see *Schulthess' Europäischer Geschichtskalender, 1901* (Munich, 1902), pp. 145–7; Ross, *Beleaguered Tower*, pp. 26–8.

within German intellectual life which was both more confident and more outward-looking.[30] The appearance, finally, of newspaper articles and books written by Catholics and dealing with the problem of 'Catholic backwardness', its causes and possible solutions, was in itself evidence of a mounting awareness that the Catholic community should assert itself.

This movement for greater recognition added a new slogan to contemporary debate: the 'parity question' (*Paritätsfrage*). In its narrowest sense the phrase was applied to the prospects of Catholics seeking entry to, or promotion within, the civil service. More generally, it articulated a demand for the equality of Catholics as citizens within the state. First taken up nationally at the 1891 annual Assembly of German Catholics in Mainz, the issue was seldom absent from the agenda of subsequent assemblies.[31] The desire for a greater degree of acceptance and recognition achieved particularly powerful expression at the political level. It can be seen in the phrase of a Centre agent in Siegen, writing to Lieber about the political circumstances necessary locally for the Centre to 'come into its own'.[32] The growing awareness of anti-Catholic electoral gerrymandering, and moves to end it in Baden and the Rhineland, were signs of a similar sentiment. It was evident, above all, in the attitudes of the new generation of Centre leaders which emerged in the 1890s and guided the party on to its pro-government course.

This new generation was a perfect embodiment of the broader aspiration to parity among middle-class Catholics. For just as the 1890s saw a de-clericalisation of the Centre, so it was marked also by the emergence of a more bourgeois leadership. A number of prominent aristocrats died in these years: Franckenstein, Schorlemer-Alst and Löe-Teporten. Many more lost their seats in the 1893 election on the issue of the 'big' military bill; and in the same year a number of prominent Silesian aristocrats, whose policy over the military bill had been defeated in the Centre, resigned their party posts and declined correspondingly in power.[33] The weakening of aristocratic influence could be seen in the composition of the Centre

30. C. Bauer, *Deutscher Katholizismus. Entwicklungslinien und Profile* (Frankfurt/Main, 1964), p. 54 ff.
31. StA Cologne, Karl Bachem Papers, 92–6: material on the *Paritätsfrage*.
32. Pfälzische LB Speyer, Ernst Lieber Papers, B. 10, G. Brust to Lieber, 26 July 1893. The phrase was an extremely common one among Centre politicians and in the party press.
33. An excellent insight into the feelings of Ballestrem, who resigned as chairman of the Centre *Reichstagsfraktion*, and of his fellow-Silesians Huene, Letocha and Matuschka is contained in folder IX of the Ballestrem papers, especially the diary entries from 27 April to 4 June 1893, and a long memorandum written in 'Herbst 1893'.

group in the Reichstag. Whereas in 1876 aristocrats constituted over a third of the Centre's ninety Reichstag deputies, by the end of the 1890s they numbered only a handful.[34] The declining presence and power of the party's aristocratic wing was general: it was most marked in Bavaria, Westphalia and the Rhineland, but even in Silesia residual aristocratic influence scarcely extended beyond the state itself.[35] The process could, moreover, be observed at all levels of the party. It was evident both in the exclusion of the Rhineland aristocrat Count Oppersdorff from the influential Augustinus Press Association, and in the accession of Ernst Lieber to the Centre leadership over the rival claims of the Silesian von Huene. Attempts to rehabilitate such men in the guise of a 'party directory' advising the parliamentary leaders of the Centre were unsuccessful;[36] and tacit acknowledgement of this changing balance of power came with the stream of high-born Catholic defectors — Schorlemer-Lieser, Prince Hatzfeld, Prince Lichnowsky, the Duke of Ratibor — to the Conservatives.[37]

On the other hand, the new bourgeois leadership had few roots in industry and commerce, a reflection partly of the continuing under-representation of Catholics in these areas of national life. It is noteworthy that a significant group of entrepreneurs among Centre deputies both in the Reichstag and Prussian Landtag consisted of men who owned printing and publishing works. The size of this group, however, like the related strength of journalists in the Centre, was not so much evidence of a capitalist upthrust as a legacy of the *Kulturkampf*, when these branches absorbed talent denied an outlet in

34. Molt, *Der Reichstag*, p. 92, shows that the total number of aristocrats in the Centre *Fraktion* between 1893 and 1914 was only twenty-three. Further details can be obtained from M. Schwarz, *MdR. Biographisches Handbuch der Reichstage* (Hanover, 1965).
35. In Silesia even so eminent a figure as Cardinal Kopp was forced to admit to Hohenlohe in 1898 that he had no influence on Centre election strategy outside Silesia itself. Hohenlohe, *Denkwürdigkeiten*, pp. 450–1. Even within Silesia the influence of Kopp and the aristocratic conservatives was modified by the existence of other political figures who stood close to the major party leaders. StA Cologne, Karl Bachem Papers, 86c: correspondence between Bachem and Felix Porsch in June 1898. On the impotence of Centre aristocrats like Preysing and Löwenstein in Bavaria, see Hertling, *Erinnerungen*, II, p. 291; Möckl, *Die Prinzregentenzeit*, pp. 281, 313–14.
36. Pfälzische LB Speyer, Ernst Lieber Papers, L. 243, Lieber to Gröber, 14 June 1894, where Lieber writes of a conspiracy in which Julius Bachem was prominent to rehabilitate the 'statesmanlike' Huene; but the idea was received in hostile fashion by most of the Centre *Fraktion*. The major attempt to re-establish aristocratic conservative influence came, however, from a Rhenish/Silesian axis of Löe, Hoensbroech and Huene, with ideological backing from Oberdörffer, author of a reactionary unofficial Centre programme. Lieber Papers, G. 24, Gröber to Lieber, 20 June 1894; G. 30, Gröber to Lieber, 8 July 1894. In particular, these aristocratic forces were putting financial pressure on the Centre newspaper *Germania* to try and alter its too 'democratic' line.
37. Stegmann, *Die Erben Bismarcks*, p. 31.

the civil service or the universities.[38] There were, of course, Catholic entrepreneurs who played an important part in local Centre politics: Cahensly in Limburg, Bell in Essen, Urfey in Krefeld. Others were the political confidants of major Centre leaders; this was true of Lieber's relationship with Cahensly, and with the Württemberg industrialist, Braun. And, of the national leaders, Karl Trimborn had a considerable income from business interests,[39] while Richard Müller, the Centre financial expert, was a textile magnate in Fulda. The number of such men was limited, though, and fewer throughout the years 1890–1914 than in the National Liberal or Progressive parties.

The new leaders reflected bourgeois Catholic aspirations faithfully, in that they were largely men of the non-business middle classes, above all lawyers. Ernst Lieber was a lawyer; so were three of the four men who constituted the collective leadership of the Centre after Lieber's death in 1902 — Trimborn, Peter Spahn and Adolf Gröber (the fourth, Hertling, was an academic). In addition, a large number of the party's most prominent Reichstag figures, who made up the 'transmission belts' between Berlin and Centre organisations in the individual states, shared this profession: in the Rhineland and Westphalia, Fritzen, Würmeling, Julius and Karl Bachem; in Silesia, Porsch, Stephan and Nadbyl; in Hesse, Schmitt; in Württemberg, Alfred Rembold; and in Baden, von Buol, Fehrenbach, Marbe and Zehnter.[40] Their specialist skills both in drafting legislative measures in committee and debating them in plenary sessions clearly helped to determine this concentration of lawyers in the upper echelons of the Centre; and the indifferent quality of many members of successive intakes of Centre deputies to the Reichstag led to a further concentration of work-load and political initiative on to this group, endowing its members with a discernible *esprit de corps*. Above all, the more rigorous demands both of electioneering and of parliamentary business in the 1890s and after, compared with the 1870s, made lawyers both more fitted and more willing to conduct the leadership of the party than other groups like businessmen, the clergy or the aristocracy.[41]

38. Hermann Cardauns, for example, influential editor of the *Kölnische Volkszeitung*, had been thwarted in an academic career. H. Cardauns, *Aus dem Leben eines deutschen Redakteurs* (Cologne, 1912), pp. 72–4.
39. Rudolf Martin, *Jahrbuch des Vermögens und des Einkommens der Millionäre in der Rheinprovinz* (Berlin, 1913), p. 83, estimated Trimborn's wealth in 1911 at 1–2 million Marks. Gottwald, *Zentrum und Imperialismus*, pp. 27–31, has valuable details on those Centre politicians who did have major business interests.
40. K. Bachem, *Zentrumspartei*, V, pp. 27–8.
41. Hertling noted in his memoirs how different it was campaigning in the 1890s, compared with earlier decades. By the latter period it was necessary to make speeches in the smallest village. Hertling, *Erinnerungen*, II, p. 176.

Yet these advantages could also be weaknesses. Financially, for example, the new leaders were relatively isolated and exposed, as the episode of the Centre's Berlin newspaper, *Germania*, revealed. In the 1890s powerful aristocratic supporters of the paper threatened to remove their backing on political grounds; but Lieber's confidant Cahensly had some difficulty arranging alternative support among the Catholic business community.[42] At a more fundamental level, the position of the lawyers who led the Centre made them more susceptible to cooptation by the government of the day. As lawyers, their very freedom from the obligation to run an estate or business meant that they lacked an independent basis of social power like that possessed by the Catholic aristocrats formerly active in the Centre or the entrepreneurs active in other German parties.

What the Centre leaders did have was a solid block of a hundred Reichstag seats, and these they showed every willingness to use: partly to build up credit and goodwill with the government which could be drawn on in demanding specific legislative measures; and, more generally, to prove that the Centre, like the Catholics it represented, was not 'hostile to the Reich' (*reichsfeindlich*). It might, in fact, be more accurate to describe those at the head of the Centre Party as political brokers rather than political leaders;[43] and as brokers they were concerned less with power than with influence and respectability. Lieber especially, the 'malcontent Nassauer' of earlier years, shed the angularity and prickliness he had previously shown towards authority and assiduously cultivated his contacts with chancellors and state secretaries.[44] An almost desperate desire to please was manifest in many aspects of Lieber's behaviour in these years: his suggestions to ministers on how best to circumvent opposition to their measures; his

42. Pfälzische LB Speyer, Ernst Lieber Papers, G. 24, Gröber to Lieber, 20 June 1894. See also Gottwald, *Zentrum und Imperialismus*, pp. 136–7; Zeender, *Center Party*, p. 36, n. 4.

43. For some fruitful general observations on the modern political role of lawyers, see M. Weber, 'Politics as a Vocation', H. H. Gerth and C. Wright Mills (eds), *From Max Weber* (London, 1948), esp. pp. 94–5. When Centre leaders are considered in this way, a certain amount of light is cast on two obvious features of the party in the Wilhelmine period: its role as a mediator of interest group demands, and its strikingly (if often exaggerated) 'pure political' character, a trait which particularly antagonised its opponents.

44. The *Beiblatt* of the *Mecklenburgische Blätter*, 18 September 1903, described Lieber in the late 1890s, 'when he had shed the last remnants of his "*Musspreusse* from Aschaffenberg" and "malcontent Nassauer" egg-shell, and had happily transformed himself into a byzantine-governmentalist, pro-Reich, pro-army, pro-navy "hurrah-patriot" through to the skin'. StA Cologne, Karl Bachem Papers, 67b, newspaper cutting. On Lieber's earlier attacks on Windthorst's leadership for being too pro-governmental, see M. Spahn, *Ernst Lieber als Parlamentarier* (Gotha, 1906), pp. 21–2; K. Wolf, *Ernst Lieber 1838–1902* (Wiesbaden, 1950), p. 236.

ingratiating and conspiratorial arrangements to meet for discussions with Reich treasury secretary Posadowsky about a projected tobacco tax without alerting the 'sniffing pack of hounds' in the press;[45] and his advice to Hohenlohe on how to time Reichstag business in 1899 in order to neutralise the intriguing of Prussian finance minister Miquel.[46] This pattern of self-abasement coupled with arrogant expectations of influence was to reach its height in the conduct of Lieber's successors in the years between 1902 and 1906.

Lieber and his fellow Centre leaders were determined to appear 'two hundred per cent German'. It was for this reason that the sense of pique was so great in the Centre on those occasions when the party was faced with the loss of its position. This was the case, for example, at the end of the 1890s, when Miquel attempted to reactivate the Bismarckian *Kartell*, and in 1906 when Bülow succeeded temporarily in forging a government majority out of Conservatives, National Liberals and Progressives. On both occasions the Centre saw itself faced with the loss of what it had seized at the beginning of the 1890s: the intoxicating novelty of influence exercised to confirm its own respectability.

The deft single-mindedness with which the Centre used its Reichstag position, and the seemingly arrogant hauteur which accompanied its parliamentary hegemony, was a source of antagonism to all the other parties. The party's tactical deployment of its voting strength was frequently attacked as 'horse-trading', and such conduct was widely disliked, frequently even reviled. The antagonism was, however, particularly great on the Left. When the Progressives were offered a place as a partner of government — something which seemed a possibility under Caprivi's New Course, and was more substantially held out to them as a member of the Bülow Bloc — they showed themselves eager to grasp the opportunity. But the Progressives were neither so large and stable, nor so politically flexible as the Centre, and their reaction to the position acquired by the Centre was correspondingly embittered by their own failure to achieve one like it.

The SPD, too, was antipathetic to the way the Centre exercised its key role; and this reflected the very different response of the German labour movement and German Catholics to the experience of having previously been the outlaws of German society. While the Centre led German Catholics — middle-class Catholics particularly — in an

45. Pfälzische LB Speyer, Ernst Lieber Papers, L. 39, Lieber to Posadowsky, 10 July 1894. For similarly conspiratorial communications, see ibid, L. 36, L. 37, L. 38, Lieber to Posadowsky, 24 June, 29 June and 3 July 1894.
46. Hohenlohe, *Denkwürdigkeiten*, pp. 397, 523–4, 535, 545.

attempt to transcend the ghetto mentality which had been inherited from the *Kulturkampf*, the SPD stood at the head of a labour movement which still remained self-consciously outside 'respectable' society.[47] It is true, of course, that both the revisionists and the south German SPD reformists were responsible for breaching the ideological purity and self-sufficiency of the labour movement; and the extent to which the majority SPD group under Kautsky was effectively reformist was to be fully revealed in 1914. In day-to-day political matters, however, the SPD group in the Reichstag took its lead from the most intransigent Prussian and Saxon party branches. In accordance with this it was bitterly critical of the Centre's conduct. While the Centre was prepared by means of judicious amendments to try and find a means of passing almost any government bill, even one unpopular with many of its own supporters (like the navy programme), the SPD in the Reichstag took an attitude of principled opposition to all measures which it could not fully support. Instead of finding in the Centre an ally which, in line with its professed anti-militarism, consistently opposed army and navy expenditure, the SPD found rather a party which customarily reserved its position on the first reading of such a measure, argued at the committee stage for a more equitable distribution of the additional tax burden, and voted for the government on the third reading.[48]

The hostility which the Centre's method of parliamentary procedure aroused on the Left was fully reciprocated. The Reichstag leadership élite of the Centre, legal draftsmen and apostles of procedural rectitude, had a scornful, professional impatience with everything they regarded as 'obstructive' and 'negative'. This outlook was apparent even in their relations within the Centre Party. Lieber again furnishes a good example: a man lacking in patience towards those of his colleagues who made little positive contribution to the legislative process, and intemperately hostile to criticism from the Centre press, parts of which he viewed as enemies of his party's attempt to secure its position in Wilhelmine politics.[49] His attitude was shared by others, however. Richard Müller, as a financial expert, attacked the 'idiocy' of the agrarians' extreme demands; Georg Hertling lamented the lack of constructive parliamentary potential among his fellow Bavarians; and Karl Bachem complained along the same lines about the 'nonentities' in the Centre group, who owed their position to special interests

47. See the works cited in n. 24, p. 10.
48. For some shrewdly critical comments on this aspect of the Centre's practice, see F. Naumann, *Demokratie und Kaisertum* (Berlin, 1900), p. 126.
49. See the letters from Lieber to Posadowsky, cited in n. 45 above. The Lieber Papers, L. 243, Lieber to Gröber, 14 June 1894, demonstrates a similar attitude of impatience and contempt towards the party press on Lieber's part.

rather than to their usefulness in contributing to the serious business of legislation.[50]

For such Centre leaders, who elevated parliamentary compromise and cooperation almost to the status of a credo, the attitude of the Left — above all, that of the SPD — was undignified and irresponsible. This can be seen in the reactions of Peter Spahn and Karl Bachem to the filibustering speeches of Arthur Stadthagen, the SPD representative on the Reichstag committee dealing with the Civil Code. The anger that Stadthagen's tactics aroused in a man like Bachem signified the gulf which separated Centre and SPD: the former trying to demonstrate its loyalty to the national cause, the latter reacting to its pariah status with an undifferentiated hostility to the efforts of the bourgeois parties. It is a telling comment on this difference that, while the work of the Centre representatives on the committee was singled out by the Kaiser for special praise, Stadthagen's obstructionist role was at least in part the result of the gaol sentence for lèse majesté which hung over him.[51]

These differences over parliamentary responsibility were a general source of conflict between Centre and Left. They assumed a particular importance, however, in the years between 1898 and 1902. In these years the political anchorage of the Centre was relatively uncertain. Despite its efforts, the party had not at this time established the degree of close collaboration with the government which was to characterise the years 1902–6. The political events of 1897, moreover, were thoroughly alarming to the Centre. A number of state secretaries favourable to the Centre were dropped, while the Prussian finance minister and new vice-president of the Prussian Ministry of State, Miquel, was attempting to construct an alliance of National Liberals and Conservatives in a policy of *Sammlung* which Centre leaders believed to be aimed against them. At the same time, the Centre feared that a victory for the Right in the 1898 Reichstag elections might lead to a *Staatsstreich*.[52] These circumstances might be expected

50. Fricke, *Die bürgerlichen Parteien*, II, p. 896; Pfälzische LB Speyer, Ernst Lieber Papers, H. 142, Hertling to Lieber, 26 March 1891; StA Cologne, Karl Bachem Papers, 21, copy of *Augustinus-Blatt*, containing a speech by Bachem to the Augustinus Press Association annual general meeting, 2 September 1900.
51. See the numerous and comprehensive memoranda of Bachem on the negotiations over and passage of the civil code: StA Cologne, Karl Bachem Papers, 7.
52. On the background to 1897, *Sammlungspolitik* and the fear of *Staatsstreich*, see: Röhl, *Germany without Bismarck*, pp. 246–51; D. Stegmann, 'Wirtschaft und Politik nach Bismarcks Sturz. Zur Genesis der Miquelschen Sammlungspolitik 1890–1897', I. Geiss and B.-J. Wendt (eds), *Deutschland in der Weltpolitik des 19. und 20. Jahrhunderts. Fritz Fischer zum 65. Geburtstag* (Düsseldorf, 1973), pp. 161–84; G. Eley, 'Sammlungspolitik, Social Imperialism and the Navy Law of 1898', *Militärgeschichtliche Mitteilungen*, 15, 1 (1974), pp. 29–64.

to have pushed the Centre towards closer cooperation with the Progressives and SPD; they had certainly led to support from the Centre for Progressive candidates in the elections, and even to demands from Richard Müller that the Centre collaborate electorally with the SPD in certain states.[53]

In the event the Centre turned away from a policy of confrontation with the government, despite the latter's clear move to the right following the re-shuffle of 1897. The reasons for this were complex. Partly, the fear of *Staatsstreich* was itself double-edged: it cowed some Centre leaders into a conciliatory position.[54] Furthermore, despite the personal dislike of Miquel harboured by Centre leaders (especially Lieber), the party could plausibly assume that it would continue to form a necessary part of the government's majority. Tirpitz's approaches over the first navy bill could only confirm such assumptions. There was, though, a further consideration which hardened the Centre in its non-cooperation with the Left: the continuing differences over the question of parliamentary propriety, brought to a head in the period after 1898. Between 1898 and 1903 the Left, particularly the SPD, employed an unprecedented level of obstructionist tactics in the Reichstag. Between December 1898 and April 1903, three SPD deputies alone — Bebel, Singer and Stadthagen — were called to order by the Reichstag President seventy times, and reprimanded on fifty-four occasions.[55] The impact of this was heightened by the fact that most of the parliamentary turmoil was concentrated in the periods covered by discussion of two measures: the Lex Heinze and the 1902 tariffs. On 4 December 1902, Singer was called to order three times and refused to leave the chamber when formally expelled from the sitting. Ten days later, during the nineteen-hour final sitting on the tariff bill, the SPD deputy Antrick spoke for eight hours in an attempt to delay passage of the measure. The outrage felt by the Centre over this behaviour was equal to the outrage felt by the Left over the legislation itself. Bachem referred to the 'revolution in parliament'; 'obstruction', he declared, 'is open war'.

53. On Centre support for the Progressives: StA Cologne, Karl Bachem Papers, 86c: Bachem to von Hagen, 5 June 1898; to Porsch, 30 May 1898 and 4 June 1898; to Wacker, 2 June 1898; to Eugen Richter, 10 June 1898; to Fischbeck, 1 June 1898; to Graf Schulenburg, 7 and 13 May 1898. Richard Müller went so far as to suggest either open or secret Centre support for the SPD in certain constituencies in Hesse, Nassau and Thuringia; but Bachem would only countenance support for Progressives or left-leaning National Liberals. Ibid, 86d: Müller to Bachem, 19 and 22 May 1898; Bachem to Müller, 20 and 27 May, 1898.
54. StA Cologne, Karl Bachem Papers, 88: memorandum, 24 June 1898.
55. Calculated from the lists of reprimands and calls to order in J. Seidenberger, *Der parlamentarische Anstand unter dem Reichstagspräsidium des Grafen von Ballestrem nebst parlamentarischem Lexikon* (Cologne, 1903), pp. 69 ff.

The reactions of Trimborn and Gröber were similar, and it was the latter who drafted a bill designed to limit speeches on procedural motions to five minutes.[56] In subsequent years the Centre remained a staunch supporter of measures to prevent a recurrence of obstructionist tactics like those used in 1902.[57]

Centre and Left were, of course, divided over the substance of economic measures like the tariffs of 1902, and the reasons for this will be discussed in the following section. The procedural aspects of their mutual antagonism should not, however, be underestimated. In their different responses towards parliamentary rectitude, Centre and SPD represented two different reactions to what, in the 1870s and 1880s, had been a common fate as *reichsfeindlich* outsiders. The SPD, even after the turn of the century, was neither willing nor able to grasp respectability and achieve positive integration into German society and politics. The Centre, on the other hand, was desperately concerned to prove that Catholics and their political leaders would be the equal of other Germans in national feeling, if only they were given the chance to show it.

IV

While the Centre's role in the game of politics in Berlin frequently appeared to its opponents as mere politicking or horse-trading, we have seen how its actions should, in fact, be seen in the context of feelings which were widespread within the Catholic community. Centre policy received much of its force from the sense of discrimination among its middle-class supporters. While the Centre became a vehicle for the aspirations of middle-class Catholics, however, it also acted as a vehicle for the grievances of a broader, mass Catholic constituency. This, too, had the effect of dividing the Centre from the Left.

Centre and Left drew their mass support from different social groups. The SPD was squarely based on the working class, particularly in the larger towns. The Progressives competed with the SPD for this part of the electorate, but also — especially after 1900 — looked towards the rapidly growing white-collar and petty professional groups like primary school teachers for support. The

---

56. On the obstruction during the tariff debates, and Centre reactions, see folder IX, Ballestrem papers; Cardauns, *Trimborn*, p. 113; Seidenberger, *Der parlamentarische Anstand*, pp. 9 ff.
57. Like the government attempt in 1906 to reduce the Reichstag quorum. K. Bachem, *Zentrumspartei*, VI, pp. 305–7.

Centre, by contrast, found some support among all parts of the population, from the Rhineland middle class to Westphalian miners, and from Silesian aristocrats to Bavarian peasants. This was the legacy of the party's position as the defender of Catholic interests during the *Kulturkampf*, and the existence of this following among different social groups has been remarked on by all historians who have dealt with the Centre. It was also stressed by party leaders themselves, for whom the fact that the Centre was 'a true people's party which embraces all estates and classes' was important.[58] At a time of growing antagonism between town and country, industry and agriculture, capital and labour, they could maintain that the Centre alone eschewed the politics of sectional interest groups. Buttressing their claim that the Centre was entitled to a key political role, they argued that it alone was free from the blinkered class politics of the other parties, whether the industry lobby of the National Liberals, the agrarian pressure of the Conservatives, or the SPD advocacy of working-class hegemony.[59]

Centre leaders certainly took seriously the need to preserve a balance of interests between the social groups which formed their actual or potential constituency. A telling example of their sensitivity to this problem came in the decisions on where to hold the annual Assembly of German Catholics, effectively the Centre Party conference. Alternate city and small town venues were selected, to ensure that no part of the Centre electorate felt slighted; and when several small towns argued that their facilities were inadequate the Centre industrialist Carl Custodis was asked to look into the feasibility of a mobile assembly hall to solve this problem.[60] The nurturing by the Centre of a range of economic interest groups among all classes testified to the same concern, as did the demand in all Centre election programmes between 1871 and 1914 for a 'balanced justice' (*ausgleichende Gerechtigkeit*) in the passage of legislation which affected various social groups. As Karl Trimborn claimed at a *Volksverein* meeting in 1905: 'The Centre is not purely a workers' party, a peasants' party or a *Mittelstand* party; it is a universal people's party.'[61]

In fact the Centre by no means drew its support evenly from each of these groups. Its potential constituency remained that of German Catholics, who at the beginning of the twentieth century remained

58. From the 1903 Reichstag election programme. L. Bergsträsser, *Der politische Katholizismus; Dokumente seiner Entwicklung*, 2 vols (Munich, 1921–3), II, p. 330.
59. There is a brilliantly succinct summary of Centre arguments like this, from one of the party's opponents, in Naumann, *Die politischen Parteien*, p. 75.
60. StA Cologne, Karl Bachem Papers, 19: material on the constituting of the general committee of the *Generalversammlung der Katholiken Deutschlands*.
61. *Kölnische Volkszeitung*, 17 April 1905, cited in J. Wernicke, *Kapitalismus und Mittelstandspolitik* (Jena, 1922), p. 422.

significantly under-represented both in the great urban areas and in the characteristic occupations of an industrial society. This was recognised and given expression in the spate of books mentioned earlier analysing Catholic 'backwardness'.[62] In 1912 Catholics made up only 25.8 per cent of city-dwellers in the Reich, although they constituted 36.5 per cent of the total population. In Baden, where 48 per cent of Jews and 35 per cent of Protestants lived in towns, the figure for Catholics was a mere 20 per cent.[63] Catholics were also much more heavily represented in the ranks of peasants, artisans and shopkeepers than among the owners of capital or the wage and (particularly) salary-earning classes. In 1907, 37.5 per cent of the German population made a living from agriculture: the figure for Catholics was 44.2 per cent. It has been estimated that one third of a million more Catholics were dependent on primary production for a livelihood than their share of the overall population warranted.[64] It is perhaps significant too that while Catholics were under-represented in most industrial branches and in commerce, they were over-represented in a number of traditional occupations: glassware production, the manufacture of time-pieces, spinning and the preparation of wood. The social and occupational structure of Catholic Germany was reflected in the major areas of Centre support, which formed a backward fringe to the south, east and west of the Reich. The party's strongholds were largely in the rural and small-town areas: Ermland in East Prussia; the rural areas of West Prussia; the Upper Palatinate in Bavaria, along with Swabia, Upper and Lower Bavaria; the southern, least industrialised part of Württemberg; the rural areas of the Rhineland around Trier, Aachen and Cologne; the Breslau and Oppeln areas of Silesia; and the agricultural Münsterland and Sauerland in Westphalia. Of the 113 Reichstag seats won by the Centre and its allies in 1907, seventy-eight were in constituencies where agriculture and small business predominated.[65]

At a time when German political parties were increasingly becoming the vehicles of economic interests, Centre and Left therefore drew their support from potentially antagonistic groups: SPD and Progressives from the dependent working-class and white-collar consumers, the Centre from the traditional *Mittelstand* of small businessmen and retailers, and from independent primary producers.

62. See esp. Rost, *Die wirtschaftliche und kulturelle Lage*, and Neher, *Die wirtschaftliche und soziale Lage*.
63. Rost, *Die wirtschaftliche und kulturelle Lage*, p. 180.
64. Ibid, pp. 19, 79.
65. H. Gabler, *Die Entwicklung der Parteien auf landwirtschaftlicher Grundlage von 1871–1912*, dissertation (Berlin, 1934), p. 16, cited in Gottwald, *Zentrum und Imperialismus*, p. 41.

The Wilhelmine Centre Party was, moreover, particularly susceptible to the demands of these groups, notwithstanding its claims to stand 'above the interests'. Not only was the growth of agrarian, artisan and shopkeeper self-consciousness making these groups more vocal and generally demanding in the claims they made on the established political parties: with the declining impact of appeals to confessional loyalty, the Centre faced particular difficulties of control. In addition, seventy-three of the seats held by the Centre in the Reichstag were safe seats (*Stammsitze*), in Centre hands uninterruptedly from 1874 to 1914.[66] The possession of these seats proved double-edged in its effects. It cut down the cost of fighting elections, but in the absence of serious political opponents it encouraged interest groups to press the party organisation for special policies, or even special candidates. As the leaders were hampered by a decentralised party structure and the unreliability of an eccentrically undisciplined Centre press, rebels of this kind could frequently demand a high price for their loyalty.

The way in which these interests worked on Centre policy and helped to divide the party from the Left can be seen in the case of agrarian agitation. Discontent among the producers of agricultural produce was widespread throughout the Reich in the first half of the 1890s. The immediate cause of this was the collapse in prices, which coincided with the negotiation by Caprivi of a new round of trade treaties lowering the protective tariffs on grains, meat, wine and other produce. The roots of the discontent were deeper, however. The flight from the land, the rising cost of labour, indebtedness and the growing burden of taxation and insurance contributions not only worked against primary producers: all could be blamed directly or indirectly on Germany's transition from an *Agrarstaat* to an *Industriestaat*, a transition which it was feared would consign the agricultural interest to permanent neglect and impotence.[67]

Within the Centre there had been agrarian rumblings even in the 1880s. The leader of the Westphalian Peasant Association, Schorlemer-Alst, resigned both his Reichstag and Prussian Landtag seats in protest against the Centre's acceptance under Windthorst of only limited increases in agricultural tariffs. As long as tariffs continued to rise, if only slightly, discontent could be contained; but

---

66. Molt, *Der Reichstag*, pp. 58–9.
67. On the agrarian background: S. R. Tirrell, *German Agrarian Politics after Bismarck's Fall* (New York, 1951); H. Haushofer, *Die deutsche Landwirtschaft im technischen Zeitalter* (Stuttgart, 1963); Puhle, *Agrarische Interessenpolitik und preussischer Konservatismus*; H. Lebovics, ' "Agrarians" versus "Industrializers". Social Conservative Resistance to Industrialism and Capitalism in late Nineteenth Century Germany', *International Review of Social History*, 15, 1 (1967), pp. 31–65; K. D. Barkin, *The Controversy over German Industrialization 1890–1902* (Chicago, 1970).

when the treaties negotiated by Caprivi with Italy and Austria received official Centre support a storm of protest broke within the party. Schorlemer, having resumed his parliamentary activities, attacked Lieber's policy fiercely; so did the agrarian conservative from Silesia, Huene, and the leader of the Rhineland Peasant Association, Löe-Teporten, while the Bavarian Orterer spoke of the 'great alarm' over the commercial treaties in south Germany.[68] In the event party unity survived the test, partly because residual attachment to Catholic Italy and Austria muted some of the criticism of the treaties. Even so, five Reichstag deputies from Baden eventually voted against both treaties, while twenty-eight Centre men were absent from the vote over the Austrian and thirty-four from the vote on the Italian treaty.[69]

The election of 1893, fought against the background of rising rural agitation symbolised by the formation in the same year of the *Bund der Landwirte* and the *Bayerischer Bauernbund*, showed the strength of agrarian feeling within the Centre. The *Allgemeine Zeitung* claimed that a 'very considerable part' of the party's Reichstag group was in favour of the pro-tariff Free Economic Union, and that some had decided in May, shortly before the dissolution, to declare their adherence to it. Lieber was forced to call a party meeting, where it was decided that membership of the Union was a party, not a personal, matter.[70] In Bavaria the agrarian issue, combined with anti-Prussian particularism and fears of higher taxation supported by the Centre, caused the party to lose three seats to secessionists who joined the *Bayerischer Bauernbund*, and two more to the Conservatives.[71] While the Centre was able to prevent wholesale secessions in Bavaria, difficulties remained. It is significant that the most prominent Bavarian Centre leader, Hertling, was able to exert little influence on these developments, and the Berlin leadership was obliged to turn to the more agrarian-orientated Bavarian leaders, Schädler, Pichler and

68. Möckl, *Die Prinzregentenzeit*, p. 450; Tirrell, *German Agrarian Politics,* pp. 103, 121; K. Müller, 'Zentrumspartei und agrarische Bewegung im Rheinland, 1882–1903', K. Repgen and S. Skalweit (eds), *Spiegel der Geschichte; Festgabe für M. Braubach zum 10. April 1964* (Münster, 1964), p. 833.
69. Nichols, *Germany after Bismarck*, p. 149; Müller, *Spiegel der Geschichte*, p. 833; Tirrell, *German Agrarian Politics*, pp. 120–3; K. Bachem, *Zentrumspartei*, V, pp. 253–4.
70. *Allgemeine Zeitung*, 4 August 1893, cited in Tirrell, *German Agrarian Politics*, p. 188. When, after exhaustive *Fraktion* discussions, the Centre finally decided not to join the Free Economic Union, it was not essentially because of substantive objections to the economic policies of the latter but because of the common *Fraktion* discipline joining would have entailed. StA Cologne, Karl Bachem Papers, 70: draft letter from Hompesch, chairman of the *Fraktion*, to Ploetz, chairman of the Free Economic Union, December 1894.
71. K. Bachem, *Zentrumspartei*, V, pp. 294–5; VIII, pp. 25–7, 36; Tirrell, *German Agrarian Politics*, pp. 190–1.

Orterer, to try and keep the 'wild men' like Georg Heim under control.[72] Already by 1893, therefore, the later Centre accommodation of agrarian pressure was prefigured.

The elections of 1893 also produced tensions in other Centre strongholds. In Westphalia, for instance, Schorlemer demanded that four seats be set aside by the party for agrarian special candidates. The Centre leadership was unwilling to see the careful balance of candidates from different social groups set aside in this way, and at a meeting in Münster the local agents (*Vertrauensmänner*) of the Westphalian branch of the party rejected Schorlemer's demand. The latter then decided to put up his agrarian candidates against the Centre, and to found a new newspaper in Münster, *Der Westfale*. Two other 'wild' candidates also stood against the official Centre men on an agrarian platform, and only after the defeat of these candidates could Schorlemer be reconciled with the Centre leadership.[73] In the Rhineland too, where agrarian opposition within the Centre was to prove more protracted, Löe, having grudgingly accepted the Italian and Austrian treaties, began to attack Lieber again in 1893. Referring to the pending treaty with Russia, he accused the Centre leader of wishing to turn the party into a vehicle for 'industry and the stock exchange'.[74] Löe and his associate in the Rhineland Peasant Association, Hoensbroech, refused to endorse the official 1893 election address of the Centre, and attempts by Fritzen to conciliate the agrarians failed.[75] The Rhineland branch of the party entered the election openly divided, the rebels declaring that they would be bound to unity only on issues concerned with religion and the Church.

In the following year agrarian opposition intensified, as the agricultural crisis deepened and the Rumanian, Serbian, Spanish (1893) and Russian (1894) trade treaties sharpened the agrarian consciousness. Lieber had termed the 1891 treaties the 'great deed of the new era'; but he was now obliged to tread warily, as it had been rumoured that as many as fifty to sixty Centre deputies might vote against the remaining treaties.[76] His tactic was to stress how Centre policy was, in fact, preserving an element of tariff protection against SPD demands for total repeal. But Lieber continued to draw the fire of Centre

72. Nipperdey, *Organisation*, p. 288; Möckl, *Die Prinzregentenzeit*, pp. 454 ff.
73. The other 'wild', or agrarian candidates, apart from Schorlemer, were in the constituencies of Arnsberg and Paderborn. See the article in the *Kölnische Volkszeitung*, 28 May 1912, copy in StA Cologne, Karl Bachem Papers, 66b. See also K. Bachem, *Zentrumspartei*, V, pp. 23–4, 291–2; Nipperdey, *Organisation*, pp. 277–80.
74. Müller, *Spiegel der Geschichte*, p. 835; Tirrell, *German Agrarian Politics*, p. 311.
75. StA Cologne, Karl Bachem Papers, 66b: Hermann Cardauns' memorandum on the Rhineland agrarian movement, the Russian trade treaty and the founding of the *Rheinische Volksstimme*; also Hoensbroech to Bachem, 27 May 1893.
76. Tirrell, *German Agrarian Politics*, p. 294.

dissidents: from wine-growing constituencies which feared especially the effect of the Spanish treaty; from grain producers in general, who feared a glut of imports from eastern Europe; and from Bavarians in particular, who were concerned about the impact of the Rumanian treaty on imported agricultural produce transported along the Danube. When the voting on these treaties took place, all semblance of unity within the Centre was lost. Less than half (forty-four) of the Centre deputies in the Reichstag followed official party policy on the Rumanian treaty; forty-nine voted against, and a further six were absent. Of the Bavarians, two were absent and twenty-eight voted against, with none supporting the party leadership. Voting on the Russian treaty, where cheap grain imports were the crucial issue, confirmed the extent of the agrarian opposition within the Centre. Lieber, tactically adept, had raised the issue of the anti-Jesuit law in the Reichstag, in an attempt to distract attention away from agrarian problems and cement party unity. Despite this, only forty-five deputies voted in favour of the treaty, with thirty-nine against and fifteen absent.[77]

The crisis in the first half of the 1890s had a deep impact on Centre leaders, who recognised the seriousness of the disaffection. As Karl Bachem wrote gloomily to Lieber in September 1895, the peasantry in the Rhineland — his own area — was behind Löe's movement, and while their economic position remained as it was little could be done to detach them from this allegiance.[78] Hermann Cardauns, editor of the *Kölnische Volkszeitung*, came to a similar conclusion in a memorandum of the following year.[79] Lieber himself saw the agrarian discontent as the gravest threat to the unity of the Centre since its founding. In a letter to Schädler in June 1894, he wrote of the formation of economic interest groups in the party, adding that at no time since the *Kulturkampf* had this internal disunion in the Centre been so pronounced.[80] Lieber was strongly affected by the agitation at a personal level. He complained in one letter of May 1894 of a 'war of extermination' against him in the Centre's agrarian press, while six weeks earlier he had written to Heinrich Otto of the Augustinus Press Association actually considering whether or not to retire from public life.[81]

77. Spahn, *Ernst Lieber als Parlamentarier*, p. 37; Tirrell, *German Agrarian Politics*, pp. 243–5, 294.
78. Pfälzische LB Speyer, Ernst Lieber Papers, B. 237, Karl Bachem to Lieber, 28 September 1895; StA Cologne, Karl Bachem Papers, 14: material on the Rhineland agrarian movement in 1894–5.
79. StA Cologne, Karl Bachem Papers, 66b.
80. Pfälzische LB Speyer, Ernst Lieber Papers, L. 32, Lieber to Schädler, 6 June 1894.
81. Gottwald, *Zentrum und Imperialismus*, pp. 150–1.

In the remaining years of the decade, nervousness about the agrarian wing of the party was endemic among Centre leaders. Bachem records how, at the two Catholic Assemblies held in Bavaria (Munich, 1895, and Landshut, 1897), interruptions from agrarian dissidents were anticipated.[82] The memorandum by Cardauns mentioned above had already suggested that there might be trouble in the Rhineland during the 1898 Reichstag elections, a prediction which turned out to be accurate. And over a range of issues Centre leaders in Berlin had to reckon with demonstrations of discontent. The navy programme, for example, was highly unpopular, especially in Bavaria, with Centre voters, who feared both an increase in taxation and a strengthening of industry at the expense of agriculture.[83] The decision of the Prussian government to construct a Mittelland canal linking the Rhine to the Elbe and Weser also divided the Centre, for similar reasons. It was seen by agrarians as a measure which would encourage the flight from the land (and thus higher labour costs) in the short term, and constitute a further tilting of the scales between agriculture and industry in favour of the latter. Karl Trimborn, passing on to Lieber the results of a Rhineland Centre Party committee meeting, suggested that while a vote against the canal would lose no seats in the Rhineland, a vote in favour might well have that effect in agricultural constituencies.[84]

It was hardly surprising in view of all this that, in a party which was always attuned to the need to offer material concessions to its voters, a more pro-agrarian feeling should have made itself felt among the Centre leadership after the crisis of the early 1890s. Adolf Gröber, writing to Lieber in 1897 to stiffen his resolve in dealings with the Rhineland agrarian rebels, complained bitterly that a large part of the Bavarian Centre stood closer to the *Bauernbund* leadership than to the Centre leadership in Berlin.[85] And it certainly was the case that Centre candidates were chosen locally in Bavaria on the basis of not allowing themselves to be outflanked by the agrarians of the *Bauernbund*.[86] Similar complaints that agrarian interests were being too much accommodated could be found in other regions. August Grunau, a Centre agent in the Lower Rhine town of Goch, wrote to Lieber in

82. StA Cologne, Karl Bachem Papers, 15, 17: Bachem memoranda.
83. Kehr, *Schlachtflottenbau*, esp. p. 131.
84. Pfälzische LB Speyer, Ernst Lieber Papers, T. 20, Trimborn to Lieber, 29 July 1899: Trimborn, as chairman of the Rhineland provincial committee of the Centre, reporting a committee meeting attended by all major local leaders two days earlier in Mönchen-Gladbach.
85. Gottwald, *Zentrum und Imperialismus*, pp. 65–6, n. 163.
86. Nipperdey, *Organisation*, p. 277.

1896, arguing that too little was being done to resist agrarian pressure: with the resources of the clergy behind it, he argued, the leadership should be prepared to adhere more firmly to its policy of justice for all social classes and economic groups. In the Rhineland he singled out Karl Bachem especially as a man too ready to compromise with the agrarian *frondeurs*: 'The Centre has conceded too much the partially justified complaints of the peasants and aristocratic disturbers of the peace, that too little has been done in recent years for agriculture, and the impression has been created that certain gentlemen in the Centre, of whom Herr Deputy Bachem is one, believe they can win back the peasantry through unheard-of concessions over the margarine question.'[87]

It is perhaps worth taking the 'margarine question' alluded to by Grunau, and using it to look more generally at the sort of problems agrarian demands could pose for the Centre leadership. Legislation which made the manufacture and sale of margarine more difficult, in the interests of butter producers, was clearly of special interest to Grunau, himself the proprietor of a margarine factory.[88] Nevertheless, his arguments reveal the extent of the Centre dilemma. First, while the Lower Rhine towns of Goch and Cleve might well have drawn a large part of their livelihood from margarine production, as Grunau claimed, in the majority of Centre constituencies primary producers and small businessmen outweighed the importance of large-scale manufacturing. Faced with the risk of losing either working-class consumers to the SPD or agricultural producers to the agrarians, the line of least resistance for the Centre would generally be to trim its policy in favour of agricultural interests. As the Centre paper, the *Rheinisch-Westfälische Zeitung*, pointed out in 1906, at a time when the Bavarian Centre rebel Georg Heim was threatening to form his own purely agrarian party, such a party at national level could cost the Centre fifty seats.[89] Secondly, while the aristocrat-led agrarian movement in the Rhineland might have produced hostility among the lower clergy, this was certainly not the case generally in Centre areas. Rather than being the pliant agents of Berlin policy, as Grunau seemed

---

87. Pfälzische LB Speyer, Ernst Lieber Papers, G. 63, Grunau to Lieber, 6 February 1896.
88. Grunau, in fact, had great difficulties with agrarian attacks on him. The *Rheinische Volksstimme*, 9 May 1897, published an article claiming that a conserving agent Grunau used at the Jürgen Prinzen margarine factory contained arsenic. *Der Rheinische Bauer* repeated this allegation in its issue of 15 May 1897, and Grunau took legal action. Pfälzische LB Speyer, Ernst Lieber Papers, G. 62, Grunau to Lieber, 27 May 1897, enclosing a circular the former had issued on the affair and sent to the newspapers involved.
89. H. Renner, *Georg Heim, der Bauerndoktor* (Munich, 1960), p. 99.

to suggest, parish priests — at least in Trier, Bavaria, Baden and Württemberg — were in fact frequently to be found at the head of the agrarian movement. The Trier Peasant Association, for example, was also calling for stringent anti-margarine legislation, and its leader was a priest, Georg Dasbach.[90]

A deference to agrarian demands on the part of the Centre leadership was discernible in the 1890s; and initiatives on the margarine question were an indication of this spirit of accommodation. As early as 1887 the Centre had supported restrictive legislation, but with the massive rise in margarine production in the last years of the century and the dip in butter prices in the middle of the 1890s the party was prepared to support more radical moves. Centre committee members in the Reichstag supported demands that the substance be dyed an obnoxious colour to differentiate it from butter: a demand which was only spuriously connected with either hygiene or trades' description considerations, as contemporaries recognised. The enemy was margarine as such, and the legislation which was finally passed with Conservative, Centre and Anti-Semite votes was an unambiguous sop to the dairy interest and a blow to the consumer.[91] There were other features of the Centre's policy in these years which demonstrated the party's willingness to accede to agrarian demands. It supported a ban on futures trading on the stock exchange, for example, a measure long called for by agricultural interests which blamed low grain prices on the alleged machinations of Jewish dealers in Berlin.[92] The Centre was also prominent in the progressive establishment of a quota system for the import first of live animals, then of meat. By 1900 meat imports of almost all kinds were excluded from the Reich under this legislation, once again purportedly in the interests of consumers, in fact a clear concession to agrarian clamour.[93]

Above all, the Centre's position on tariffs underwent a striking modification as the date for the re-negotiation of the Caprivi trade treaties approached. As early as the Reichstag elections of 1898 there were rumblings among Centre supporters in rural areas. The volatile temper of peasant opinion was illustrated by a by-election in May 1899 in the Lower Bavarian Reichstag constituency of Straubing,

90. See the resolution of the Trier *Bauernverein*, 17 April 1895, calling not only for legislation against margarine, but a ban on the import of live animals, meat, milk and cheese: StA Cologne, Karl Bachem Papers, 14.
91. U. Teichmann, *Die Politik der Agrarpreisstützung. Marktbeeinflussung als Teil des Agrarinterventionismus in Deutschland* (Cologne, 1955), pp. 463–74.
92. Ibid, pp. 213–16.
93. For the Centre's position on the *Fleischbeschaugesetz* of 1900, see Hohenlohe's journal entry for 7 March 1900: Hohenlohe, *Denkwürdigkeiten*, pp. 567–8; Teichmann, *Die Politik der Agrarpreisstützung*, p. 569 ff; Hunt, *Central European History* (1974), pp. 313–16.

where the official Centre candidate held off his *Bauernbund* challenger by only 6,068 votes to 5,975.[94] Karl Bachem also noted an 'edgy mood' among agricultural producers on the Lower Rhine in the same period.[95] It is instructive to examine the reactions of Bachem, a representative member of the Centre leadership group, to the groundswell of demands for higher tariffs. By the last two years of the 1890s he had come round to a very different position from that which he had held in the early years of the decade. The right-wing call for *Sammlung*, for example, which included a programme for considerably greater agricultural protection, was dismissed by Bachem because of its anti-Centre political implications. But the economic demands of *Sammlungspolitik* — including higher tariffs — he was able to label simply the 'old Centre programme'.[96] By 1900 Bachem was talking more explicitly still of the Centre accepting the need for a higher tariff wall. Speaking in September 1900 to the Augustinus Press Association, he argued that even the pre–Caprivi, pre-trade-treaties level of protection, which at the time he had voted to reduce, was an inadequate safeguard for the interests of agriculture.[97]

By 1901 agrarian feeling was running so high among Centre supporters that wholesale secessions from the party to the *Bund der Landwirte* were feared.[98] Under this pressure the Centre fought throughout the plenary and committee debates on the side of the Conservatives, its pro-agriculture position becoming especially marked when Lieber died after the first reading, and the leadership of the party over the tariff question was entrusted, significantly, to the agrarian-orientated landowner, Karl Herold. As the *Kölnische Volkszeitung* remarked: 'The Centre has become notably agrarian in committee. Herold has taken over the leadership and operated with a tact and mastery which one would not believe of a simple agriculturalist. He was able to hold his party together, so that it could say to Posadowsky: on this basis the tariff will never be passed. So the Centre has bound itself to the agrarian side in a manner which some will find uncomfortable.'[99] The Centre demand for higher tariffs was tailored closely to its constituents' requirements in relation to two

94. *Schulthess' Europäischer Geschichtskalender, 1899* (Munich, 1900), p. 96.
95. StA Cologne, Karl Bachem Papers, 86c: copy of a letter from Bachem to (?), 5 June 1898.
96. Ibid, 86c, Bachem to Stolze, in the Dessau-Zerbst constituency, 13 June 1898: 'In its wording the official *Sammlung* programme is nothing other than the old Centre economic programme.'
97. Ibid, 21: Bachem speech on the political situation to the Augustinus Press Association.
98. Barkin, *The Controversy over German Industrialization*, p. 230.
99. *Kölnische Volkszeitung*, 14 October 1902, cited in F. Jacobs, *Deutsche Bauernführer* (Düsseldorf, 1958), p. 89.

particular crops. The Caprivi tariffs had left barley and oats especially vulnerable, with the level of protection at 2 Marks and 2.80 Marks respectively, compared with 3.50 Marks on rye and wheat. The Bülow proposals in 1901, although raising the general level of grain tariffs, proposed once more to discriminate against oats and barley, crops which were intensively cultivated in south and west German Centre strongholds. The work of Herold and the Bavarian Heim was largely responsible for revising these proposals: the level finally accepted for rye was 5.50 Marks, for wheat and oats 5 Marks, and for barley 4 Marks. Within the overall steep increase in agricultural protection for which the Centre voted, the percentage and absolute increases in the tariffs in which Catholic peasants were chiefly interested were greater than the increases in the tariffs on grains more identified with east Elbian estates.[100]

The tariff legislation of 1902 marked the high point of Centre accommodation of agrarian truculence within its own ranks. With the erection of a high protectionist barrier against the import of all major grains, a comprehensive prohibition on foreign meat imports (tightened still further in 1909) and discrimination against margarine manufacturers, the Centre, together with the Conservatives, played a major part in helping to cushion agricultural producers from the effect of imports at world price levels. The other side of the coin, of course, was the disadvantageous effect of its policy on working-class and other consumers, to whose costs the tariffs added an estimated 600,000,000 Marks, while returning only 78,000,000 Marks in the form of a widows' and orphans' insurance scheme (which proved to be largely window-dressing).[101] The years which followed the passing of the tariffs saw a rapid rise in prices, particularly of the lower-class consumers' staple, bread.[102] This, in turn, produced a flaccid rise in the consumption of more diversified foodstuffs, and hence to a working-class diet which was less balanced than in non-protectionist countries like Britain and the Netherlands.[103]

One effect of the Centre's growing agrarian tendency was the loss of Catholic working-class support. A straw in the wind was the 1901 by-election in Duisburg, held at the height of the tariff controversy, where the Centre lost a significantly large number of working-class votes to the SPD.[104] The passage of the tariffs made clear the damage

100. Barkin, *The Controversy over German Industrialization*, pp. 240–2.
101. Ibid, p. 239.
102. An enquiry in 1909 among the families of 300 metalworkers showed that an average 11% of all expenditure, and 23% of all expenditure on food, was devoted to bread. Teichmann, *Die Politik der Agrarpreisstützung*, pp. 569–71.
103. This case is put most vigorously by Gerschenkron, *Bread and Democracy*.
104. *Schulthess' Europäischer Geschichtskalender, 1901* (Munich, 1902), p. 121.

done to this part of the Centre electorate. In 1903 the Reichstag elections brought great successes to the SPD in Catholic urban constituencies like Duisburg, Essen, Mainz and Munich. The dissatisfaction of working-class Catholics was demonstrated in Bochum, where it was not in the Protestant north of the constituency that the SPD increased its vote most, but in the southern Catholic areas of Wattenscheid, Gelsenkirchen, Herne and Eitel-Wanne.[105] By 1912 the Centre proportion of the total votes cast at Reichstag elections had fallen from 27.9 per cent in 1874 to 16.4 per cent, its share of the Catholic vote from 83 per cent to 54.6 per cent.[106] The seats which the Centre had forfeited to the SPD — including Cologne, Düsseldorf, Mainz, Metz, Mülhausen, Munich, Strassburg and Würzburg — suggested that much of the loss was accounted for by disenchanted Catholic workers.

Centre policy also provoked bitterness on the Left, among SPD and Progressive politicians who drew most of their support from working-class and lower-middle-class consumers. Here 1902 marked a real climacteric, permanently establishing the Centre, in the eyes of the Left, as the *Brotverteuerer*; and the various measures in subsequent years through which the Centre confirmed its pro-agrarian standpoint, such as the finance reforms and the meat law of 1909, only served to harden this antagonism. The conflict between the interests of primary producers and consumers, filtered into politics through the medium of pressure-groups, played a major role in driving a wedge between the Centre and the parties of the Left.

V

The Centre was no less divided from the Left by its articulation of a *Mittelstandspolitik* addressed to artisans, small businessmen and petty retailers. Few Centre leaders came from this milieu themselves, of course, although there was an important exception in Matthias Erzberger, who had also been an active organiser in the artisan movement. These interests were nevertheless a powerful presence in the Centre: of the 230 deputies who represented the party in the Reichstag between 1893 and 1918, 39 (17 per cent) belonged to these groups.[107] Nor did the parliamentary strength of the *Mittelstand* groups

105. On Centre working-class opposition to the tariff policy, Nipperdey, *Organisation*, p. 280, n. 1. On 1903 election losses to the SPD, O. Hue, 'Die Katholischen Arbeiter und das Zentrum', *Neue Zeit*, 21, 2 (1903), pp. 473–6.
106. J. Schauff, *Die deutschen Katholiken und die Zentrumspartei* (Cologne, 1928), p. 75; Morsey, *Historisches Jahrbuch* (1970), pp. 34–5.
107. Molt, *Der Reichstag*, pp. 78, 216–17.

in the Reichstag and state parliaments correspond fully to the weight they had within the Centre. The drift of working-class Catholics away from the Centre was a reflection of — but also helped to reinforce — the willingness of the party to address itself to both agricultural and lower-middle-class interests. It is significant, for example, that the influence of artisans and shopkeepers was considerable not just in the rural and small town areas where the safe Centre seats were located, but also in the more vulnerable urban constituencies. Thus in Cologne it was members of these groups, rather than working-class Catholic trade unionists, who dominated the lower reaches of the party organisation,[108] while in Munich the Christian trade union leader and Centre supporter Karl Schirmer complained of the undue strength of the *Mittelstand* wing within the party.[109] The bloc of lower-middle-class interests in the Centre became both larger and more influential after the turn of the century, as the organised *Mittelstandsbewegung* seemed to offer a potentially dangerous alternative focus of allegiance to Centre voters. Like the agrarian movement in the 1890s, the *Mittelstand* movement presented the Centre with the threat of being outflanked, and helped to mould its economic policies accordingly.

Like primary producers, members of the business *Mittelstand* feared loss of livelihood and independent status as a result of uncontrolled industrialisation. Artisans and small businessmen had been adversely affected by the liberal commercial codes of the 1870s: these laid the basis for an increasing concentration of production in large concerns which monopolised raw materials and, through economies of scale, enjoyed an inbuilt advantage over the smaller producer.[110] Already by the 1890s the majority of coopers, tanners, nailmakers, basket-makers and coppersmiths saw their livelihoods threatened, as concentration coupled with new industrial processes, mass production and changing consumer demand created a situation of secular decline for the small

108. Cardauns, *Erinnerungen*, p. 158; Nipperdey, *Organisation*, p. 270.
109. K. Schirmer, *50 Jahre Arbeiter* (Duisburg, 1924), p. 31. The *Mittelstand* leaders within the Munich Centre Party included the bookbinder, Nagler, leader of the guild-orientated city artisans and a committee member of the *Mittelstandsvereinigung für Handel und Gewerbe*. Stegmann, *Die Erben Bismarcks*, p. 250.
110. As an example of the process of concentration, the number of business concerns in Arnsberg fell by 16.75% between 1875 and 1895, while the total number employed in business rose by 155%. In Münster during the same period the fall in the number of concerns was 30%, the rise in the total number employed 300%. A. Noll, 'Wirtschaftliche und soziale Entwicklung des Handwerks in der zweiten Phase der Industrialisierung', W. Rüegg and O. Neuloh (eds), *Zur soziologischen Theorie und Analyse des 19. Jahrhunderts* (Göttingen, 1971), pp. 199, 201.

man.[111] Master craftsmen in other, major branches frequently found themselves reduced to a peripheral or auxiliary role as concentration proceeded:[112] tailors, masons, shoemakers and carpenters were particularly affected. In the last decades of the nineteenth century the demand became more insistent from these interests for a return to the *status quo ante* 1871; for legislation which would curb the free play of economic forces held responsible for depriving the artisan of capital, labour and outlets.[113] Retailers, too, began to organise in the last decade of the century, first at local, then at regional and national level, in order to put pressure on the political parties. Their main grievances were two-fold. On the one hand they objected to the leviathan department stores, with their auxiliary services of travelling salesmen, advertising, special offers and motorised delivery. On the other hand they also wished for legislative controls over the consumer cooperatives, whose operations were expanding, and which interposed themselves between producer and customer.[114]

The Centre, in its economic policy, followed a line which was largely that of the *Mittelstand* interest groups. As Hertling worriedly wrote to Lieber in 1895, he was disturbed at how completely the party had identified itself with the demands of the 'artisan party'.[115] It was the Centre which stimulated the state authorities in Prussia and elsewhere to change the tender system used to assign government contracts, in favour of a less rigid practice more favourable to small producers. It was the Centre, too, which was foremost in demanding an end to prison manufacturing which competed with local artisans.[116]

---

111. On this, see the paper delivered by Bücher to the annual general meeting of the *Verein für Sozialpolitik*, Cologne 1897: *Schriften des Vereins für Sozialpolitik*, 76 (1898), pp. 16 ff. Between 1882 and 1895 the number of independent weavers also declined by 43%, hat-makers by 42%, millers by 32%, rope-makers by 35%, brewers by 24% and varnishers by 21%.

112. K.-H. Schmidt, 'Die Rolle des Kleingewerbes in regionalen Wachstumsprozessen in der zweiten Hälfte des 19. Jahrhunderts', I. Bog *et al* (eds), *Wirtschaftliche und soziale Strukturen im säkularen Wandel: Festschrift f. Wilhelm Abel z. 70 Geburtstag*, 3 vols (Hanover, 1974), III, *Wirtschaft und Gesellschaft in der Zeit der Industrialisierung*, pp. 726–7.

113. It has been estimated that *Handwerk* accounted for only 8.8% of business capital stock in 1895, only just over half its share twenty years earlier. Noll, *Zur soziologischen Theorie*, p. 205. On the movement among artisans, from the 1873 founding of the *Verein selbständiger Handwerker und Fabrikanten* to the demand for guilds and restrictive legislation, see Winkler, *Zur soziologischen Theorie*, pp. 163–79; and S. Volkov, *The Rise of Popular Antimodernism in Germany. The Urban Master Artisans, 1873–1896* (Princeton, 1978).

114. R. Gellately, *The Politics of Economic Despair: Shopkeepers and German Politics 1890–1914* (London, 1974), pp. 45–50.

115. Pfälzische LB Speyer, Ernst Lieber Papers, H. 168, Hertling to Lieber, 5 November 1896. Hertling refers caustically in his memoirs to the Bavarian Centre as the party of 'grain tariffs and compulsory guilds'. Hertling, *Erinnerungen*, II, p. 54.

116. Wernicke, *Kapitalismus und Mittelstandspolitik*, p. 424.

Most important of all, it was the Centre and Conservatives which agitated for, and supported, the 1897 revision of the *Reichsgewerbeordnung* (RGO), a change of course in economic policy as fundamental as the return to high agricultural protection in 1902. Under the law of 26 July 1897, the powers of the already existing voluntary craftsmens' guilds were strengthened, and provision was made for local authorities to sanction compulsory guilds where particular conditions were met.[117] Together with tighter regulation of the right of an artisan to call himself a master and stricter control of apprentices by masters, the provisions of the law went some way towards restoring an enclave of guild exclusivity within a modern industrial economy. Moreover, provision for the setting up of artisan chambers like those already enjoyed by agriculture constituted a decision effectively to guarantee the existence and importance of a particular interest group, by endowing it with a corporate, public function and organisation. It was this policy, in which the Centre vied with the Conservatives and the various *Mittelstand* political groups for leadership, which has led one historian to write of the 'reinsured *Mittelstand*'.[118]

The Centre also took the lead in demanding measures which protected small retailers. The party rightly claimed responsibility for bringing about the Reich law of 1896 on 'unfair competition', with its strict controls on closing-down sales, special offers, the sphere of competence of travelling representatives and advertising. In subsequent years the Centre produced a constant stream of bills and interpellations in the Reichstag and state parliaments, aimed at further controls on large retail concerns, itinerant traders and consumer cooperatives. The high point of these efforts on behalf of small shopkeepers was reached in the attack on the department store. Two main lines of assault were employed by those concerned to minimise the competition small retailers faced from department stores, and the Centre played a pioneering role in developing both. First, the party had shown in Münster how police regulations over the use of buildings could be used to deprive large retail outlets of the right to sell to the public in many parts of their premises.[119] Secondly, the Bavarian Centre had initiated the weapon of the special turnover tax, a fiscal lever for use against the department store which was imitated in most other German states. With a majority in the Bavarian Landtag, the militantly

117. Ibid, pp. 834 ff.
118. Winkler, *Zur soziologischen Theorie*, has given his article the title 'Der rückversicherte Mittelstand'.
119. Wernicke, *Kapitalismus und Mittelstandspolitik*, p. 420.

anti-department store Centre Party forced a turnover tax from the rather reluctant government in 1899, and called — without complete success — for still stricter taxes six years later. In Prussia, Baden, Württemberg and elsewhere similar measures were also passed with Centre encouragement and support.[120] That these measures were deliberately aimed at the department store, the particular *bête noire* of the shopkeepers, was indicated by their provisions: these were not simply for a progressive tax, in the conventional sense, but for a tax on turnover specifically tied to other variables like the number of branches, size of personnel and range of goods sold.

There were many contradictions involved in the Centre Party's *Mittelstandspolitik*, and these will be considered in detail in subsequent chapters. Many party leaders tacitly accepted the large share of responsibility which small businessmen and shopkeepers themselves bore for their problems. Many, too, were sceptical of what could be achieved by measures like department store taxation. As the Bavarian Centre leader Schädler confided to the department store owner Oskar Tietz: 'Dear Tietz, we must do something to counter the seething state of popular feeling; they want a department store tax; we know that is unjust and economically stupid, but the others are the majority.'[121] To the extent, however, that the Centre contributed to the 'reinsurance' of the *Mittelstand*, it was bound to antagonise the parties of the Left. Any success which such measures had would, like agricultural protection, necessarily add to the price paid for goods by the consumer. This was unacceptable to parties whose appeal was precisely to these groups. Moreover, in measures to protect the artisan or shopkeeper, the Centre did not only run up against Progressive believers in the unfettered development of industry and commerce: like the Progressives the SPD viewed the small man as an outmoded figure, doomed to extinction in the struggle against larger, more competitive rivals, and vainly trying to turn the clock back by appealing to the government through the parties for special privileges. The SPD opposed attempts to create sheltered enclaves where inefficient or marginal producers and retailers could escape the imperatives of the market; and on all issues of this kind the party allied itself unequivocally with the Progressives and the entrepreneurs in the ranks of their leadership.[122]

120. Ibid, pp. 628 ff.
121. G. Tietz, *Hermann Tietz: Geschichte einer Familie und ihrer Warenhäuser* (Stuttgart, 1955), p. 46.
122. Representative of the SPD position is the pamphlet by Adolf Braun, *Die Warenhäuser und die Mittelstandspolitik der Zentrumspartei* (Berlin, 1904), with its fierce attack on the attempts by the Centre to turn back the clock.

VI

The anti-Left alignment of the Centre between 1890 and 1914 was not determined by traditional clerical obscurantism or by the strength of aristocratic influence within the party. The events of the early 1890s, especially the struggle over the 1893 military bill, marked the beginning of a decisive decline in the importance of both these elements. Rather, the alignment of the Centre was largely the outcome of two other factors, both having their origins in the demands of German Catholics for an end to the neglect they had previously encountered.

First, a new generation of political leaders emerged, men who were no longer primarily conditioned by the need to defend the Church from attack, but by the desire to establish equality of treatment for Catholics as citizens. This was the essence of the 'parity question' (*Paritätsfrage*). By following a policy of affirmation, the Centre leaders embodied the national feeling and aspiration towards acceptance of middle-class Catholics, demanding in return concessions over grievances like discrimination in public appointments. This new departure was reinforced by two other developments in the Reich. The dismissal of Bismarck and the parliamentary arithmetic of the Reichstag after his departure created an attitude among successive chancellors which was more accommodating to this Centre desire to play a more positive role. In addition, the growing unity and sphere of competence of the Reich, along with the increasing volume of legislation on economic and social matters in particular, changed the Reichstag itself from a debating chamber to a political market-place. The new Centre leaders were supremely well-equipped to respond to this change. Led in the *Kulturkampf* years by the orators Windthorst and Mallinckrodt, the Centre was from the 1890s in the hands of politicians with highly-developed negotiating skills, like Lieber and Peter Spahn. As the party moved from the outside to the inside of German politics, the corollary of its new course was an impatience with other parties which were not willing to offer customary support to the government of the day. This impatience often expressed itself in attacks on the position of the Conservative Right and the Anti-Semites. Even more, though, it was directed against what were stigmatised as the obstructionist tactics of the Left, above all of the SPD.

The other main cause of the Centre's anti-Left alignment lay in the social structure of its grassroots support. German Catholics, over-represented in backward rural regions and in pre-industrial occupations, had long felt oppressed by what they saw as the alien policies of urban administrative and financial institutions. Their grievances were a Catholic variant of the broader disenchantment of large sections of the peasantry and *Mittelstand* with the economic and social direction Germany had taken since 1871. By the 1890s these social groups among the Catholics were prepared, like other and similar pressure groups in Wilhelmine politics, to demand economic concessions from the government. The policies called for by these interests within the Centre were, however, antipathetic in many important respects to those of the groups forming the constituency of the Left. Centre leaders, keenly aware of where their major electoral strength was based, articulated these agrarian and *Mittelstand* grievances much more vocally than those of the Catholic working class, and on a host of issues, from the tariff to department store taxation, made common cause with the Right against the Left.

These two sets of demands on the Centre — from the Catholic middle class on the one hand, the Catholic peasantry and *Mittelstand* on the other — both had their origins in the grievances and aspirations of the broader Catholic community; and both, as we have seen, had the political effect of dividing the Centre from the Left. But these demands were by no means identical, or even mutually compatible in their aims and content. In embodying middle-class aspirations to a domestic place in the sun, Centre leaders accepted the pattern of economic and social development in the years since 1871, asking only that the proportion of Catholics in the administrative, academic, professional and business community increase. Alongside this, the party supported policies which were an expression of the way German state and society were developing, such as the naval programme; again they added the caveat only that Catholics be given credit for their national feeling. This presented a sharp contrast to the Centre's role as a vehicle for peasant and lower-middle-class grievances emanating from the countryside and small towns. Here the party was faced with supporters who distrusted the very nature of economic and social change, remained suspicious of civil servants, academics and businessmen alike, and were notably hostile to costly measures like naval expansion.

In addressing itself to such divergent sets of values and aspirations, the Centre Party could rely to some extent on a residual confessional loyalty to keep conflict in check. But as the defection of Catholic aristocrats and the Catholic working class showed, this had clear limits. The survival of the Centre depended in the end on the political weapons it could forge; on organisation, and on the formulation of policies and slogans flexible enough to be manipulated by leaders who became particularly adept at the practice. The result was a surface symmetry in the Centre's policy which party leaders claimed as a 'balancing' of interests. In fact, no hidden hand guided the interests of German Catholics into a harmonious balance: they were, rather, orchestrated by a leadership which overcame successive contradictions in its policy by successive injections of demagogy. The spectre of the Left played a vital, if passive, role in this; for in creating a demonology of the Left, the Centre created the conditions of its own unity.

This element in Centre policy requires stress, for it helps to explain an apparently curious feature of the party's policy in Wilhelmine Germany. The emergence from the more democratic west and south German states of a new, largely middle-class leadership generation orientated towards the social problems of Centre voters might, at first sight, have been expected to produce a greater degree of friendliness towards the Left. And indeed, on specific issues like electoral reform, and over short periods, there was cooperation between Centre and SPD in the south German states. As we have seen, however, it was only an apparent paradox that the Centre, despite the more democratic features of the new leadership, more consistently supported the Right. Both this alignment, a critical one for the problem of democratisation in Wilhelmine Germany, and the demagogy which accompanied and conditioned it, can be most effectively examined in detail by looking at the Centre's emergence and politics in one of the south German states where it enjoyed a strong local power-base: Württemberg.

CHAPTER 2

Württemberg in the Nineteenth Century and the Emergence of the Centre Party

I

Württemberg has a number of advantages for a study of the Centre Party. It was representative of those south and west German areas which were chiefly identified with the changes we have already noted in the nature of the Centre in the later nineteenth century: a shift away from a residual clerical bias, away from aristocratic leadership, and towards a greater concern with social issues. In addition, the Württemberg Centre Party possessed in Adolf Gröber[1] a powerful local leader who was also one of the most prominent members of the leadership group in Berlin, and representative of the new departure in the 1890s. His relationship with the Catholic hierarchy in the state mirrored that of his mentor Windthorst with Rome and the German bishops. Moreover, the Catholics in Württemberg, as in the Reich as a whole, constituted a minority of one-third, living in clearly delimited areas in a state where religious boundaries were sharply drawn.[2]

The most important of these areas was Oberschwaben, acquired in stages from the Habsburgs, Bavaria and Baden at the beginning of the nineteenth century, and corresponding to that part of the administrative division of the *Donaukreis* which lay south of the Danube. There were also two smaller pockets of Catholics, in the

---

1. Adolf Gröber, born in Riedlingen, Württemberg, 11 February 1854, was the son of a prosperous goldsmith and engraver. He graduated from the *Gymnasium* in Stuttgart in 1872, studied law at Tübingen, Leipzig and Strassburg, and entered the Württemberg state judiciary in 1877. He had reached the position of state prosecutor in Ravensburg when political activity interrupted his legal career. Entered the Reichstag for the XV Württemberg constituency in 1887, and the lower house of the Landtag in 1889, representing his home town. In Württemberg he was the unchallenged leader of the local Centre Party until his death in 1919. In Berlin he quickly became a confidant of Windthorst, and from the 1890s was regarded as one of the most important south German leaders of the Centre.
2. See maps, pp. 242–3.

Schwarzwaldkreis around Rottweil, Rottenburg and Spaichingen, and in the area of the *Jagstkreis* near the towns of Ellwangen, Aalen, Schwäbisch Gmünd and Neresheim. What they had in common was a peripheral position in the Protestant state, once more a microcosm of that in which German Catholics as a whole found themselves. This was an important conditioning factor, for the outlying, inaccessible Catholic strongholds were divorced not only from the peculiarly militant, pietistic brand of Protestantism espoused in *Alt-Württemberg*.[3] Trade links with Bavaria and Switzerland marked the separation of Catholics, in Oberschwaben especially, from the economic as well as the religious life of the state, which was centred on Stuttgart and the Protestant Neckar valley. Just at St Gallen and Lucerne provided a haven from religious intolerance, so a trade in agricultural produce through the port of Friedrichshafen linked the Catholic peasantry of Tettnang and Waldsee more closely with their Swiss market on the far shore of Lake Constance than with their fellow-citizens north of the Danube.[4]

Isolation and separateness played a relatively small role before the beginning of the century, when communications in the state were uniformly bad and the Protestant areas as under-developed economically as the Catholic ones. When industrialisation did come, however, it was uneven. The Catholic areas lagged behind, and the grievances generated by a sense of neglect and exploitation by bureaucrats and liberal politicians in Stuttgart helped to establish a popular basis for the Centre Party. The lateness of the party's emergence in Württemberg at the state level reflected the comparative importance of economic and social factors over purely confessional ones. The state experienced nothing like the Rhineland or Baden form of the *Kulturkampf*, which might have stimulated the founding of a party giving expression to the religious apprehensions of Catholics. On the contrary, Württemberg at the height of the *Kulturkampf* was an 'oasis of peace'.[5] The Centre came into existence at the local level only in 1894, entering the Landtag for the first time in the following year alongside the legalised SPD and the newly-formed agrarians. Like these parties it responded to — while helping to channel — pressing economic and social concerns on the part of the electorate. Correspondingly, the Centre leadership stressed from the outset what in the national party had come to the forefront only later: the central importance of the social question.

3. H. Haering, 'Württemberg und das Reich in der Geschichte', *ZWLG*, 7 (1943), pp. 315–16.
4. C. Bauer, *Politischer Katholizismus in Württemberg bis zum Jahr 1848* (Freiburg, 1929), p. 19.
5. K. Bachem, *Zentrumspartei*, VIII, ch. 8, pp. 347–56: 'Die Oase des Friedens'.

II

It will be useful, first, to consider the characteristic features of economic and social development in Württemberg before 1848, shared largely by Protestant and Catholic areas. Many of the grievances of local Catholic communities after mid-century can only be understood against the background of the accumulated discontents of the earlier years. Moreover, the tensions which existed in 1848 between the political objectives of the 48ers and the more parochial and material aspirations of the mass of the population also prefigured the difficulty which liberal politicians were to have later in the century in maintaining the allegiance of the Catholic peasantry and *Mittelstand*. In this sense the roots of the Centre Party extend back well beyond the 1870s and 1880s.

Württemberg as a whole remained economically backward until after the middle of the century. A memorandum of Finance Minister von Weckherlin in 1832 revealed that there were only 250 industrial establishments in the state, employing 4,500 people.[6] In Oberschwaben the most industrialised town, Ravensburg, had only 13 factories in 1836; at this time there was a total of nearly 1,500 artisans employing a further 650 assistants. In 1837 Waldsee still had no factories at all.[7] While a few concerns numbered up to 200 employees, the state remained overwhelmingly rural and agricultural, even by contemporary German standards. Industry was diversified, localised and small-scale. Traditional crafts were practised alongside agriculture in the small towns of the Schwarzwald, Alb and Oberschwaben, which were cut off from major trade routes. Often these crafts, like wood-carving, the production of gold and silver ware, watch-making and the small-scale manufacture of leather and cotton goods, represented only the evening or winter occupation of the peasant family.[8]

This backwardness was partly the result of the state's natural and geographical disadvantages. Württemberg lacked mineral deposits, and waterways, with the exception of the Neckar, were unnavigable. The handicap of a position on the fringes of the German trade area was compounded by the difficulty of internal communications, caused in general by high and irregular terrain, in particular by mountains which divided the state from south-east to north-west. Only a small number of roads linked Württemberg with the more richly endowed Baden to

6. P. Gehring, 'Von List bis Steinbeis', *ZWLG*, 7 (1943), p. 422.
7. E. Schwab, P. Weiss and K. Holtermann (eds), *100 Jahre Oberschwäbische Industrie- und Handelskammer Ravensburg 1867–1967* (Ravensburg, 1967), p. 155.
8. Gehring, *ZWLG* (1943), p. 422.

the west, despite a long common border.[9] This closed, backward economy was also adhered to because, like the pattern of agricultural holdings on which it was based, it was considered socially if not economically desirable. Thus, for example, the inheritance laws, and the excessive sub-division of holdings which they produced, were generally recognised as an economic evil. The official *Zentralstelle für die Landwirtschaft* came to this conclusion as early as 1826; and Friedrich List, who made the first classic study of subdivided holdings in the Neckar valley and Schwarzwald, argued that 'the subdivision of land is the misfortune of the state and precisely the reason why no factories develop'.[10] But reform was inhibited by fear of the social consequences of industrialisation. A writer in the *Württembergische Jahrbücher* in 1839 warned of the characteristic evils which would accompany the growth of a factory-based proletariat: 'hopelessness and dependence on the factory owner, the destruction of family life and the spreading of immorality'.[11] When List urged on the government the need to promote factories and thereby stimulate the economic life of the state, von Weckherlin retorted that 'factories are the greatest danger, for they bring men up to be either beggars or agitators'. He argued that Württemberg should remain a self-sufficient economy, in order that the livelihood of thousands was 'not made subject to the good fortune of one single factor owner, so that no one fashion or measure from outside is able to reduce our manufacturers to wretchedness'.[12] Agriculture, in particular, supposedly provided the sturdiest basis for a sound economy and social order; and in a report to the King in 1823 von Weckherlin argued that agricultural production was to be regarded as the keystone of the economy, the production of other goods an interlocked but ancillary element.

This view, a commonplace among governments,[13] found a popular resonance. Peasants and members of the *Mittelstand* viewed their property not as a competitive undertaking but as a patrimony: a small but secure stake in the social order. The rural population had been confirmed in the possession of its land by the edict of 1817 abolishing feudal dues, and emancipation followed a very different pattern from

9. E. Marquardt, *Geschichte Württembergs* (Stuttgart, 1961), p. 336; W. Ehmer, *Südwestdeutschland als Einheit und Wirtschaftsraum* (Stuttgart, 1930), p. 15.
10. H. Hoffmann, *Landwirtschaft und Industrie in Württemberg* (Berlin, 1935), p. 39, n. 1; Marquardt, *Geschichte Württembergs*, p. 335.
11. *WJbb* (1839), p. 71.
12. Gehring, *ZWLG* (1943), p. 414.
13. For expressions of this view in Baden, Bavaria and Bremen, see: W. Fischer, *Wirtschaft und Gesellschaft im Zeitalter der Industrialisierung* (Göttingen, 1972), pp. 98–101; A. Popp, *Die Entstehung der Gewerbefreiheit in Bayern* (Leipzig, 1928), pp. 132–3; U. Branding, *Die Einführung der Gewerbefreiheit in Bremen und ihre Folgen* (Bremen, 1951), pp. 14, 27.

that established in Prussia.[14] The Württemberg peasantry had been favoured by a number of factors in retaining its land. Emancipation coincided with a period of political instability, which helped to secure for the peasantry more indulgent treatment than might otherwise have been the case. Furthermore, government solicitude in maintaining Württemberg as an *Agrarstaat* extended beyond the setting up of a *Zentralstelle des landwirtschaftlichen Vereins* and an agricultural college in 1817: some of the financial burdens of redemption payments were assumed, and credit was made available for the rural population to weather the severe agricultural crisis of the 1820s. Finally, lords like the Hohenlohe accepted rent without trying to buy up peasant holdings: capital was invested instead in land outside the state and even in colonial ventures. The peasantry clung to what it had. Those lords who did attempt to purchase land were resisted, and when an outside money-lender obtained a property through foreclosure, the local community would combine, force the creditor to sell off the land below market price and restore it to the owner. Government theory and peasant practice were united in resisting change,[15] and the peasant economy as a result retained a strong element of self-sufficiency.

The manufacturing and commercial *Mittelstand* was stunted by this self-sufficiency, which ensured that no clear division of labour took place. A typical case was that of the father of Geo Ehni, later liberal politician, who combined the roles of smallholder, glazier and publican.[16] Even in the towns where a division of labour had occurred, demand remained at a rudimentary level, so that for example in Tettnang in the 1830s and 1840s 'manufacture . . . was of negligible importance and restricted principally to those branches supplying the needs of everyday life'.[17] Moreover, the *Mittelstand* entertained fears similar to those of the peasantry about the social effects of economic change. Wilhelm Jung, a factory owner in Göppingen, described in 1845 the entrepreneurial ignorance and timidity of the state's manufacturers, their inability to cast off the mental shackles of the guild system. He noted especially the suspicion with which an

14. See W. von Hippel, *Die Bauernbefreiung im Königreich Württemberg*, 2 vols (Boppard, 1977); E. Schremmer, 'Die Auswirkung der Bauernbefreiung hinsichtlich der bäuerlichen Verschuldung, der Gantfälle und des Besitzwechsels von Grund und Boden', K. E. Born (ed), *Moderne deutsche Wirtschaftsgeschichte* (Cologne and Berlin, 1966), pp. 67–85.
15. As one contemporary said: 'Right up to the present time, the governing idea in Württemberg has been a real antagonism to the whole factory system, while for public opinion Württemberg was an *Agrarstaat* and should remain one', E. C. Dinkel, 'Uber die bäuerlichen Credit-Verhältnisse in Württemberg', *Zeitschrift für die gesamte Staatswissenschaft* (1856), p. 564. Cited by Schremmer, *Moderne deutsche Wirtschaftsgeschichte*, p. 435, n. 31.
16. K. Schmidt-Buhl, *Schwäbische Volksmänner, 17 Lebensbilder* (Stuttgart, 1908), p. 107.
17. *KW* (1907), IV, p. 457.

expanding business was regarded.[18] Artisans and shopkeepers, like the peasantry in the surrounding countryside, were concerned to satisfy largely static needs. In the small-town economy it was not the aggressive spirit of competition which governed mens' thinking, but the economically and socially conservative *Nahrungsprinzip*; that a man could expect a level of business adequate to maintain himself and his family in a manner which was appropriate (*standesgemäss*), but should not attempt to win customers from his fellow-citizens.[19] In their different ways, therefore, peasant and artisan, shopkeeper and publican, saw a common interest in resisting the threat which they saw posed by industrial society, where uncontrolled economic forces outran the sanctions of the community.

Resistance was only partial, however. A combination of rising population and a series of bad harvests put pressure on agriculture both to feed itself and remain solvent. Although the rise in population was lower than in north Germany[20] it was serious enough where holdings were chronically divided and no increased yield could be obtained. Moreover, the state passed through three agricultural crises within forty years, first between 1809 and 1817, then from 1822 to 1827, and finally in the years 1847 to 1854.[21] The pressing need for rural credit had been met by the government up to the 1820s, but was subsequently satisfied largely by private creditors who were subject to no governmental control once their statutes had been approved. With no restrictions on the free sale of property, they could acquire land to re-sell, often further sub-divided, on the basis of long term repayments at high interest rates. Despite the attempts of local communities to prevent the incursions of the money lender, and damp down the inflation of prices, the value of land continued to rise steeply up to 1847. The previously landless rural lower classes were free to go on the market to obtain a small plot, smallholders to supplement their patrimony. Together with the overall rise in population, this unleashed a demand which gave the advantage to the outside seller. Since interest

18. W. Jung, *Der Gewerbsmann und die gewerblichen Verhältnisse Württembergs* (Ulm, 1845), p. 24.
19. On the social and moral implications of the *Nahrungsprinzip*, see M. Walker, *German Home Towns. Community, Estate and General Estate 1648—1871* (Ithaca, N.Y., 1971), esp. p. 101.
20. The population of Württemberg rose between 1817 and 1850 from 1.39 m. to 1.8 m.
21. In 1816–17, when wet and cold ruined the grain crop, bread was reportedly being baked from grass and dried potato peelings. G. Dehlinger, 'Uberblick über die Entwicklung der Landwirtschaft in Württemberg seit der Mitte des 18. Jahrhunderts', *WJbb* (1897), I, p. 59. The same extreme situation recurred in 1847, when the government was forced to buy 300,000 *Zentner* of grain for distribution. W. Reinöhl, *Revolution und Nationalversammlung 1848. Schwäbische Urkunden (Reden, Berichte, Tagebuchblätter, Gedichte)* (Stuttgart, 1919), pp. 20–1.

rates followed land prices, debts were frequently contracted at an artificially over-valued level. The result was chronic indebtedness. The sum of agricultural debt in 1841, expressed as a proportion of property value, was 11 per cent.[22] The number of forced sales rose annually between 1840 and 1847, while the sum accruing to creditors in this way increased from 1.8 million *Gulden* in 1832–3 to 14.3 million in 1847–8.[23]

Artisans suffered a similar fate in these years, as the dismantling of guild authority produced growing competition from former journeymen who could now set up independently, and from factories both in Württemberg and outside.[24] The corporate system was not finally abolished until 1862, but its hold was critically weakened: in 1845 Wilhelm Jung argued that it had effectively 'sunk into nothing' and that those who appealed to the government for help were given no encouragement.[25] Faced with loss of security and rising costs the artisan, like the peasant, fell into debt. Moreover, the collapse of peasant purchasing power itself brought many small businesses down. The result was widespread bankruptcy: between 1840 and 1847 the number of artisans subject to forced sales was 5,772, while the figures for tradesmen and publicans were 592 and 580 respectively.[26] It is not surprising that one historian has claimed that it was 'the characteristic small business class . . . of the small towns [which] felt the growing need most strongly'.[27]

Economic distress in Württemberg was therefore very considerable from the mid-1840s until the middle of the following decade, and the high level of emigration was one index of this.[28] Social unrest was also pronounced, exacting major and rapid concessions from aristocracy and crown in 1848 and providing the groundswell which sent an overwhelming number of radical democrats to the Frankfurt Parliament. The twenty-eight deputies at Frankfurt certainly represented obliquely the resentments of their electors: opposition to the privileged aristocracy and *Geldpatriziat*, to bureaucratic intrusions on communal autonomy, and to Prussia and the *Zollverein*. But there

22. *KW* (1863), p. 437.
23. Schremmer, *Moderne deutsche Wirtschaftsgeschichte*, p. 75.
24. W. Buzengeiger, *Die Zusammenhänge zwischen den wirtschaftlichen Verhältnissen und der politischen Entwicklung in Württemberg um die Mitte des 19. Jahrhunderts*, dissertation (Ulm, 1949), p. 28, gives an account of the impact made by the liberal economic legislation of 1828 and 1836.
25. Jung, *Der Gewerbsmann*, p. 26.
26. *WJbb* (1847), pp. 179 ff.
27. V. Valentin, *Geschichte der deutschen Revolution von 1848–9*, 2 vols (Berlin, 1930–1), I, p. 150.
28. The population fell by 75,000, as a result of emigration, between 1849 and 1855. The 1849 level was not reached again until 1864. *KW* (1863), pp. 314–15.

was a significant tension between the politicians at Frankfurt and grassroots feeling, for the social complexion and deliberative manner of many of the twenty-eight set them apart from attitudes in the countryside and small towns. Most believed strongly in the rule of law and voted, too, for the abolition of corporal and capital punishment; but unrest in Württemberg was marked by extreme violence, and a typical petition from Ravensburg gave 'the assurance that if the princes should be so foolish as to oppose the wishes of the people, the strong arms of the petitioners would persuade them'.[29] Again, with the important exception of Moriz Mohl, they were not anti-semitic, although this was a major strain in the unrest.[30] More generally, the club atmosphere in Frankfurt, the formal political sophistry of the Württemberg academics, officials and poets, caused antagonism at home, from the local chauvinism and suspiciousness noted by Robert Mohl, which saw the small town as the centre of the world. While urbane liberal leaders sought to assuage popular impatience, it was reported from Ulm that there was 'little trust for the learned men of the Paulskirche, who are viewed as too theoretical and moderate'.[31]

Charges of this kind levelled against 'theoretical' men obsessed with constitutional matters were to be regularly re-formulated in later years by political parties like the Centre. So, in a re-worked form, were many of the popular social grievances which came to the surface in 1848. It may therefore be useful to examine these grievances briefly. Most obviously, of course, hostility directed itself against the aristocracy and even more their officials, the visible symbols of the oppression and indebtedness of the peasant. The burning of records of debt and pamphlets calling for the murder of all officials testified amply to popular feelings: indeed, the events of 1848 were in many ways a violent parody of the Peasant War in the sixteenth century.[32] But the removal in 1848–9 of the last outstanding feudal injustices marked the final occasion when peasant *jacquerie*, real or figurative, was directed against the aristocracy and its officials. There were already other objects of antagonism which were to have continuing importance in the future.

29. T. Schnurre, *Die württembergischen Abgeordneten in der konstituierenden National-versammlung zu Frankfurt am Main* (Stuttgart, 1912), p. 12.
30. Valentin, *Geschichte der deutschen Revolution*, I, p. 344; P. Sauer, *Die jüdischen Gemeinden in Württemberg und Hohenzollern* (Stuttgart, 1966), p. 8.
31. Schnurre, *Die württembergischen Abgeordneten*, p. 30.
32. Valentin, *Geschichte der deutschen Revolution*, I, pp. 344–51; T. S. Hamerow, *Restoration, Revolution, Reaction. Economics and Politics in Germany*, (Princeton, 1958), pp. 107–9.

The first of these was the government, whose swollen bureaucracy was a major butt of criticism. Although theoretically committed to the support of agriculture and the *Mittelstand*, the government had proved unreliable both in the provision of rural credit and in preserving the guild system. On the other hand, it had not undertaken a policy such as List advocated of factory development coupled with protectionism, which might have eased the problems of the peasantry and small business.[33] A government in limbo, it appeared to the countryside and small towns as a distant authority packed with non-native officials, whose only practical activities outside Stuttgart were interfering with communal autonomy in matters like citizenship rights and collecting taxes. Hostility towards the financial burden of a parasitic bureaucracy was reflected in widespread calls for an end to official 'scribbling' (*Vielschreiberei*), as well as in demands for the abolition of the standing army and pruning of the civil list. Typical was an address from the citizens of Ebingen to the King, calling for 'the lowering of taxes and duties through simplification of the state budget and limitation of the high pensions and salaries of the top officials'.[34] The popular climate was indicated in the advice given by David Friedrich Strauss to his friend, Ernst Rapp: 'Tell no one you were a Privy Councillor';[35] and many of those elected to the Frankfurt Parliament were able to overcome the disadvantage of an official background only by pointing to their resignation or dismissal.

More direct objects of attack than the government were the money lenders and the liberal economic system in general. This was especially so on the land. As one commentator noted, the peasants 'did not willingly accommodate themselves to the present-day state of the credit market, in that they frequently decry the demand for punctual payment of interest as personal oppression, a normal increase in the interest rate as usury, the recalling of capital because of too low interest as godlessness, and the exaction of an outstanding debt as

33. On the oscillations between a 'forward' and 'backward' course on the part of state governments in Germany from 1820 onwards, see Walker, *German Home Towns*, pp. 283 ff. He provides (p. 357) an excellent summary of the result of this: 'The two alternative attacks on the [social] problem — to liberalise economy and society so as to absorb the outsiders, or to protect and strengthen existing institutions against penetration and dissolution — were contradictory; and as a consequence no effective policies were formed and there was little legislation to guide action.'
34. *Schwäbischer Merkur*, 9 March 1848. On hostility to officials and calls for a return to the imagined pristine virtues of *das gute, alte Recht*, Schnurre, *Die württembergischen Abgeordneten*, p. 4; Haering, *ZWLG* (1943), p. 294. Wilhelm Blos, who experienced the events of 1848 in Konstanz, discussed in his memoirs the animus against 'alien' academics and officials, as indicated in the popular phrase *Mucker- und Schreibertum*. W. Blos, *Denkwürdigkeiten eines Sozialdemokraten*, 2 vols (Munich, 1914–19), II, p. 67.
35. Reinöhl, *Revolution und Nationalversammlung 1848*, p. 24.

hard-heartedness'.[36] The Jews especially became a scapegoat for economic ills. Traditionally barred from working the land or taking up an 'honourable' craft, they had, as in other European states, played an important economic role as money lenders, dealers and middlemen. They made up, for example, almost all the thirty-two cattle dealers recorded at Laupheim in 1856, and the same was true in the 1830s and 1840s in Mergentheim, Saulgau, Oberndorf and Bopfingen.[37] In 1848 they were therefore readily identified as enemies, and the anti-semitic strain in the unrest brought to the surface the undercurrent of inchoate despair felt by the peasantry in the face of manipulation by outsiders to the community. The artisan, too, found a convenient, composite enemy in the liberal economic system, and demands for the reconstruction of the guild system were widespread in Württemberg. The vote in favour of freedom of trade by a number of the state's deputies at Frankfurt was received with hostility, and the artisans of Tuttlingen were typical in their praise of the guild system and their emphatic protest against 'the freedom of trade, which is nonsensical for our conditions, but which so many progressive men profess'.[38]

Hatred of Prussia, finally, focused many resentments under one head. Württemberg was overwhelmingly *grossdeutsch*: all the 103 petitions received from the state at Frankfurt demanded an Austrian rather than a Prussian empire.[39] This was partly the result of traditional emnity, but also had economic grounds. It was assumed that in a Prussian Germany there would be higher taxes to support the army. It was also generally argued that Württemberg would be better off under the Austrian protectionist system, rather than having to face the industry of the north in a free trade system. Schoder, a member of the Frankfurt Assembly, wrote that 'if Austria leaves the German Federal State, then the victory of the free trade men may be decisive; but then, too, good-bye southern Germany'.[40] Those who favoured a Prussian-based Germany gave indirect support to fears of this kind, for Otto Abel was typical of this minority when he praised Prussia in an 1848 pamphlet for 'the liveliest traffic in goods and ideas'.[41] It would be wrong, however, to assume that popular arguments against Prussia were compounded simply of tradition and self-interest. In fact,

36. Dinkel, *Zeitschrift für die gesamte Staatswissenschaft* (1856), p. 574, cited in Schremmer, *Moderne deutsche Wirtschaftsgeschichte*, p. 75.
37. Sauer, *Die jüdischen Gemeinden*, pp. 34, 70–1, 118–19, 142.
38. Schnurre, *Die württembergischen Abgeordneten*, p. 9.
39. On the unanimity of anti-Prussian feeling in the state, see the letters of Moriz Mohl to his brother Julius, between 30 May 1848 and 21 April 1849: K. Demeter, *Grossdeutsche Stimmen 1848/49* (Frankfurt/Main, 1939), pp. 54–60.
40. Schnurre, *Die württembergischen Abgeordneten*, p. 84.
41. A. Rapp, 'Württembergische Politiker von 1848 im Kampf um die deutsche Frage', *Württembergische Vierteljahrshefte für Landesgeschichte*, 25 (1916), p. 577.

Prussia, like the official, the factory owner and the Jew, was a symbol of alien manipulation, potent in inspiring fear beyond actual events. There was an element of *grande peur* when crowds from Tübingen and Reutlingen were told that they were to be made Prussian and a Prussian *Oberpräsident* installed in Stuttgart.[42] The case of Dr Conrad Hassler, Ulm representative at Frankfurt, demonstrates the temper of popular feeling. In December 1848 he was praised by his constituents for following their wishes more than other deputies; but returning after casting his vote to offer the German crown to Prussia he had the window of his room smashed and a torch hurled in.[43]

In 1848 the Catholic third of Württemberg shared many of their grievances with the Protestant majority. They had particular objections to the bureaucracy which, through the Catholic Church Council especially, kept the Church in a position of humiliating dependence on the state. The Council published 377 ordinances between 1802 and 1842, almost twice as many as the episcopal authorities. It decided the length of sermons and established the hours when confessions could be heard. The education and appointment of priests, like the control of seminaries, was subject to state authority.[44] Most objectionable was felt to be the subordination of natural Catholic communities to the administrative convenience of the state capital. Rottenburg had been chosen as the head of the see because of its proximity to Stuttgart: Catholics would have preferred a town in Oberschwaben, or at least the choice of Ellwangen or Rottweil. In Rottenburg, a town without strong Catholic traditions or a cathedral, the bishop was obliged to share his residence with a seminary, in the buildings of an old Carmelite convent.[45] Even after the establishment of Rottenburg as the seat of the bishop, the examination of priests continued to take place in Stuttgart. Characteristic of the bureaucracy's stranglehold was its refusal to allow newspapers representing Catholic interests;[46] and its instinctively repressive nature was revealed in the decision to deny a Wangen bookseller, Gebhard Lingenöhl, the right to open a lending library, a project supported by five local Catholic priests. Lingenöhl, it was argued, 'as a supporter of the Jesuits and the Ultramontanes, could only cause harm with his lending library'.[47]

Catholics also had strong religious grounds for preferring Austria to

42. Schnurre, *Die württembergischen Abgeordneten*, p. 72.
43. Ibid, p. 103.
44. Bauer, *Politischer Katholizismus*, p. 14; K. Bachem, *Zentrumspartei*, I, pp. 230, 234–5.
45. Bauer, *Politischer Katholizismus*, p. 19; K. Bachem, *Zentrumspartei*, I, pp. 233–4.
46. W.-S. Kircher, *Adel, Kirche und Politik in Württemberg 1830–1851. Kirchliche Bewegung, Katholische Standesherren und Demokratie* (Göppingen, 1973), pp. 157–9.
47. R. Schenda, *Volk ohne Buch. Studien zur Sozialgeschichte der populären Lesestoffe 1770–1910* (Frankfurt/Main, 1970), p. 207.

Prussia, and in 1848 they were the most anti-Prussian of all the Württemberg communities. But in preferring Austria to Prussia, Catholics expressed their feelings less as Württemberg particularism than as a sense of even narrower regional identity — as in the toast 'to Oberschwaben and Austria'.[48] One historian has even suggested a comparison between Oberschwaben in 1848 and the Vendée.[49] This was a feature of attitudes among both Catholics and Protestants. Only in the large towns like Stuttgart and Heilbronn did more cosmopolitan and republican ideas win supporters. On the land and in the small towns feelings ran high on parochial issues like the colour of the uniform worn by the local militia;[50] but what interest there was among either confession in wider political problems tended to take on a confused, contradictory form. The Protestant peasantry of Weinsberg, after rising and burning records of indebtedness, gave three cheers to the King; the Ravensburg Catholics, in their petition to Frankfurt, envisaged a German republic composed of individual monarchies.[51]

Still of central importance was a stubborn loyalty to locality and commune (*Gemeinde*), the basic units of social life; and within the commune was a determination to preserve *Mittelstand* respectability, not to sink into pauperism. For, much as small property-owners opposed court and officialdom, their bitterness was directed too against the lower class: in 1847 and 1848 there was mounting fear of the urban mob and of the increase in begging and theft.[52] There was a widespread feeling that even the most dependent and unreliable worker received better treatment from the government than virtuous and solid citizens. One Württemberg petition to Frankfurt complained that 'the humanity shown to the workers exceeds the limits of common sense, only the artisan, the productive *Mittelstand*, has been deserted'.[53] Similar sentiments were expressed by a community of Schwarzwald peasants, in whose petition local loyalties and concern for respectability were linked to a fear of abstract outside theorists. They began by stressing the features peculiar to their area of the Schwarzwald, particularly primogeniture. If the free divisibility and sale of land were to be established in the basic law, they argued, free independent properties might easily become mere marginal holdings,

48. Schnurre, *Die württembergischen Abgeordneten*, pp. 86–7.
49. Kircher, *Adel, Kirche und Politik*, pp. 230–5.
50. O. Elben, *Lebenserinnerungen 1823–1899* (Stuttgart, 1931), p. 118.
51. Valentin, *Geschichte der deutschen Revolution*, I, p. 351.
52. Reinöhl, *Revolution und Nationalversammlung 1848*, p. 21. On this problem see also Walker, *German Home Towns*, pp. 358–9; and W. Conze, 'Vom "Pöbel" zum "Proletariat" ', *Vierteljahrschrift für Sozial- und Wirtschaftsgeschichte* (1954), p. 352.
53. Buzengeiger, *Die Zusammenhänge*, p. 49.

their owners reduced by vicissitudes of harvest or market to the dependence of the 'proletariat'. If any 'levelling' was to be done, it would be better to turn the proletariat into respectable peasants and artisans by encouraging diligence, and through controlled emigration.[54]

This was of a piece with events elsewhere in Germany in 1848: it indicated the precarious hold of both moderate and radical politicians — in Württemberg the Liberals and Democrats — on those whose grievances were articulated more in social than political terms.[55] The active political nation in Württemberg was very small: the number of newspapers and their readers, for example, was a mere handful. This was the result partly of the heavy hand exercised by the absolutist state;[56] it derived also from widespread illiteracy, lack of mobility and resistance to 'outsiders' (from Stuttgart as much as Frankfurt). Discomfited and undermined by this, Liberals and Democrats in their different ways stressed even more the purely political opportunity presented by 1848. This compounded their dilemma. The instinctive radicalism of many among the peasantry and *Mittelstand*, finding itself neglected and lacking any other outlet, frequently expressed itself in violent opposition to those who, from their Olympian detachment, seemed to threaten doctrinaire and unwanted innovation. Thus the impoverished vintners of Cannstatt mounted an attack on the house of Ludwig Pfau, republican and translator of Proudhon, and razed it to the ground.[57]

Many other manifestations of popular feeling indicated the general difficulty which liberal politicians faced. Although they could partly subsume popular dissatisfaction with the political status quo, how were they effectively to harness the oblique currents of peasant and petty-bourgeois rancour behind their own leadership? This remained a major problem into the second half of the century, despite advances in mobility and formal political organisation. When political life in the state became more active in the 1860s, following a decade of reaction and de-politicisation, popular indifference to parliament and elections continued to be widely noted.[58] This persisted through to the last

54. G. Franz, *Quellen zur Geschichte des deutschen Bauernstandes in der Neuzeit* (Darmstadt, 1963), pp. 443–4.
55. This subject has been excellently illustrated by Dieter Langewiesche, in his recent study *Liberalismus und Demokratie*. Some interesting comments on the gap between the leadership of political movements in the middle of the century, and popular feeling, can be found in F. J. Stetter, 'Anfänge einer konservativen Partei in Württemberg', *Besondere Beilage des Staatsanzeigers für Württemberg*, 12, 31 December 1926, pp. 281–9.
56. On pre- and post-publication censorship by the Württemberg government of books and popular pamphlets, see Schenda, *Volk ohne Buch*, pp. 112 ff, 135–7.
57. Blos, *Denkwürdigkeiten*, II, pp. 75, 185.
58. A. Weinmann, *Die Reform der württembergischen Innenpolitik in den Jahren der Reichsgründung 1866–1870* (Göppingen, 1971), pp. 90, 121.

years of the century; and when the popular presence in politics did make itself felt, the heirs of the Liberals and Democrats were not the main long-term beneficiaries. Rather, both the Agrarians and the Centre emerged when the politically-orientated, anti-governmental liberalism of the kind represented by the 48ers began to lose the allegiance of its former rural and small town constituency. It is to this process we must now turn: to the question why the communities of the Catholic minority should have become alienated from a political movement which had previously been able to command their — albeit sometimes unenthusiastic — support.

III

The Centre was not formed at state level in Württemberg until 1894, and it is the lateness of its emergence which makes it difficult to explain the party's origins in terms of the anti-Prussian feeling which was so evident in areas like the Rhineland. As we have already seen, Catholic Württemberg was overwhelmingly *grossdeutsch* in 1848, but so was Protestant sentiment. This was perhaps the strongest common bond in the state, and the Württemberg deputies at the Paulskirche reflected by and large the views of both confessions. Nor did the events of the 1860s and 1870s, although they led to the creation of a strong local National Liberal party, deprive Catholics of a vehicle for expressing *grossdeutsch* feeling. The anti-Prussian strain of liberalism survived more powerfully in Württemberg than elsewhere, producing in the *Volkspartei* (VP) a specifically Swabian form of a liberal Progressive party.[59] Catholics therefore had no need to create a party which was anti-Prussian and particularist; and the potential leaders of such a party were content to remain within the VP fold. The most prominent Catholic politician of the years between 1850 and 1890 was Rudolf Probst, a VP leader who sat with the Centre group in Berlin as a Reichstag deputy, but was adamant in refusing to countenance what he considered the unnecessary formation of a Centre party at the state level.[60]

At the time of the Centre's foundation locally, the VP had not

59. Schmidt-Buhl, *Schwäbische Volksmänner*, pp. 1–18; F. Payer, 'Mein Lebenslauf', typed ms. (Stuttgart, 1932), pp. 12–13; K. Simon, *Die württembergischen Demokraten. Ihre Stellung und Arbeit im Parteien- und Verfassungssystem in Württemberg und im Deutschen Reich 1890–1920* (Stuttgart, 1969), p. 10.
60. On Probst's views, see A. Hagen, *Gestalten aus dem Schwäbischen Katholizismus*, 4 vols (Stuttgart, 1948–63), I, pp. 296 ff; O. Burkart, *Die Zusammensetzung des württembergischen Landtags in der geschichtlichen Entwicklung*, dissertation (Würzburg, 1922), p. 104.

modified its anti-Prussian stance: indeed, it fought the 1895 Landtag elections on an anti-governmental platform strikingly reminiscent of Karl Mayer's earlier anti-Prussian campaigns of the 1860s, with Prime Minister Hermann von Mittnacht cast as Bismarckian villain. If any party relinquished its old particularist notions in the 1890s it was, as we have seen, the Centre, whose leaders in Berlin — among them the founder of the Württemberg Centre, Adolf Gröber — now began to change course and make the Centre a national party of government. If Catholics in Württemberg wished in the 1890s to cast a vote against the power of Prussia and its institutions, the protest would have been registered most effectively by voting for the particularist and still anti-militarist VP. In fact, a generation after Königgrätz, the 'diplomatic phase' of Prussia's relations with the southern states had ended: the Reich had become more integrated as a state, and anti-Prussian feeling no longer played such a central role in Württemberg politics. If it had, the Centre would perhaps have been more embarrassed than its local VP opponents.

Neither can the change in the political allegiance of Catholics in Württemberg be readily understood within the chronology of anti-Catholic feeling in the state. The slights against Catholics which existed in the first half of the century remained, along with the outlawing of teaching orders and discrimination in public appointments, as standing reproaches to Catholic *amour-propre*. But the high point of active anti-Catholic feeling was in fact reached in the 1850s. No struggle in later years was as fierce as that waged by the Lower House of the Landtag against the Concordat of 1857, as anti-clerical and anti-Catholic elements combined successfully to prevent its ratification.[61] No Catholic party emerged from this defeat, or in the following decades. There was no full-blooded *Kulturkampf* in Württemberg: Karl I (1864–91) was personally favourable to the Church, encouraged the setting up of Catholic charitable institutions and even attended the sermons of the Jesuit Petrus Roh.[62] No Centre party therefore came into existence in Württemberg, as in other parts of the Reich, with the initial function of defending the Church against persecution. Catholic members of the Lower House continued to sit with the various Protestant-dominated parliamentary groups, the majority joining Probst in the umbrella grouping of the Left, the remainder sitting with the pro-governmental *Landespartei*. While Catholics in the later 1880s and early 1890s were concerned about the

---

61. K. Bachem, *Zentrumspartei*, IV, p. 251; A. Scheuerle, *Der politische Katholizismus in Württemberg während der Jahre 1857–1871*, dissertation (Tübingen, 1923), pp. 33 ff.
62. K. Bachem, *Zentrumspartei*, VIII, p. 59.

intemperate attacks of the Evangelical League and a sharper anti-clerical tendency within the VP, the level of official discrimination remained constant or even diminished. Prominent Catholics in politics and the press remained accordingly lukewarm on the subject of forming a Centre party in the state.[63]

Nor did the Catholic electorate seem anxious, on religious grounds, to withdraw its support from VP politicians when it had the opportunity. At an election in Waldsee in 1862, only a short time after the Concordat controversy, the VP was still able to win the seat with a Protestant candidate against a conservative Catholic.[64] Even the outburst of Catholic fury which was unleashed by the events of 1866–7 left no permanent demand for confessional representation.[65] Two elections held in Gmünd showed that a VP man standing on a radical anti-governmental platform of the traditional kind could still beat a specifically Catholic candidate. In 1868 the conservative Catholic Karle temporarily won the seat by obtaining the rural Catholic vote; but the VP candidate Streich was able to win it back in a by-election the following year.[66] Throughout the 1870s and beyond, Catholic Württemberg continued to vote for VP men of a radical democratic hue, without regard to confession.

It was not until the very beginning of the 1890s that Adolf Gröber, who had been agitating since the 1880s for the foundation of a Centre party, began to receive a livelier response; and within five years the party was constituted and prepared to fight a successful election campaign in 1895. The sudden emergence of the Centre at local level has been largely passed over by historians dealing with Württemberg politics. Their attention has focused instead on the series of reforming parliaments which, from the 1890s, swept away the remaining unelected members of the Württemberg Lower House, revised the systems of local government and education, and introduced a progressive income tax. In works dealing with the watershed which the 1890s undoubtedly constituted in Württemberg politics, it is the role of the VP which has been most closely examined. When the

---

63. Ibid, pp. 60 ff; H. Cardauns, *Adolf Gröber* (M-Gladbach, 1921), pp. 63–7. The *Deutsches Volksblatt*, the most prominent Catholic newspaper in the state, took the position in 1879, for example, that the founding of a Centre Party in Württemberg would be 'unwise and irresponsible'. J. Lange, *Die Stellung der überregionalen katholischen deutschen Tagespresse zum Kulturkampf in Preussen (1871–1878)* (Frankfurt/Main, 1974), p. 250.
64. Scheuerle, *Der politische Katholizismus*, p. 135.
65. In Laupheim, in Oberschwaben, Catholics sacked a Protestant church. G. C. Windell, *The Catholics and German Unity, 1866–1871* (Minneapolis, 1954), p. 6.
66. Scheuerle, *Der politische Katholizismus*, p. 213. In 1870 Catholic Württemberg was the strongest bulwark of VP support. Langewiesche, *Liberalismus und Demokratie*, p. 355.

Centre party has been considered at all, its arrival on the local political stage has been ascribed simply to confessional factors.[67]

This does not, as we have seen, answer the question of why the Centre appeared in Württemberg when it did; why Catholic voters who had previously been prepared to entrust their representation to the VP should now switch their allegiance. It will be argued here that the sudden upthrust of anti-governmental political sentiment in the early 1890s was accompanied by more deep-seated economic and social grievances which came to a head at the same time. The VP was clearly able to put itself at the head of the movement for political reform; but its relationship to manifestations of economic and social discontent was much more uneasy. There was a clear reason for this divide: the predominance in Württemberg of medium-sized holdings and small business concerns, usually and rightly considered a stimulus to political radicalism, also generated a strong current of social conservatism. We have already noted the ambiguities in 1848 of this combination of political radicalism and social conservatism, the petty-bourgeois characteristic of 'red on the outside, white on the inside'. Under the impact of industrialisation it was not the radical politics of the VP but the conservative social policies of the Centre and Agrarians which eventually gained the support of those middling social groups which were facing the future with apprehension. As the success of the Agrarians showed, there was a Protestant peasantry and *Mittelstand* whose grievances could be mobilised against the VP; but such groups were particularly important in the Catholic parts of the state as a result of the distinctive development of these regions after the mid-century. The growing sense of material neglect and exploitation in Catholic rural and small town communities reinforced feelings of religious separateness and geographical isolation which already existed. It was against this background that VP support in areas like Oberschwaben disappeared and the Centre Party turned its natural constituency into an actual political power-base.

Up to 1850 Württemberg stood still economically while other parts of Germany advanced; after that date the Catholic regions of Württemberg stood still while other parts of the state advanced. Although industrial development proceeded initially more slowly than

---

67. See, for example, G. Egelhaaf, 'Württemberg in den fünfundzwanzig Jahren 1891–1916', *Württembergische Vierteljahrshefte für Landesgeschichte*, 25 (1916), pp. 606 ff; Marquardt, *Geschichte Württembergs*, p. 348; R. Menzinger, *Verfassungsrevision und Demokratisierungsprozess im Königreich Württemberg* (Stuttgart, 1969), p. 143; W. Grube, *Der Stuttgarter Landtag 1457–1957* (Stuttgart, 1957), p. 549; Simon, *Die württembergischen Demokraten*, esp. pp. 58 ff; H. Schlemmer, *Die Rolle der Sozialdemokratie in den Landtagen Badens und Württembergs und ihr Einfluss auf die Entwicklung der Gesamtpartei zwischen 1890 und 1914*, dissertation (Freiburg, 1953), pp. 45–57.

in the Reich as a whole, it was nevertheless on a scale much greater than before 1848. The census of occupations in 1861 showed that while from 1835 to 1852 the population had increased by 160,000, and those in industry by only 30,000, in the decade after 1852 the population fell by 13,000 (as a result of emigration), but those engaged in industry rose by 40,000.[68] The proportion of those dependent on agriculture for a living continued to fall steadily, until by 1882 it was less than half (48.5 per cent) of the population. This change was aptly symbolised in the attitudes of those publicly charged with the fostering of business. Before 1848 the government institution which took care of these interests, the *Gesellschaft zur Förderung des Gewerbes*, still shared a weekly newspaper with the agricultural *Zentralstelle des landwirtschaftlichen Vereins*. Even the commercial patent laws were administered by the *Zentralstelle* and published in this essentially agricultural paper. The chairman of the Society for 15 years, Pistorius, believed that the social value of organic economic development should take precedence over mere industrialisation, and favoured the piecemeal encouragement of decentralised artisan concerns.[69] By contrast, the *Zentralstelle für Gewerbe und Handel* set up in 1848 stood for rapid growth and large-scale manufacturing, a doctrine which was propagated in its own publication, the *Gewerbeblatt*. Its chairman from 1855, Steinbeis, was also a leading advocate of laissez-faire: his pressure was an important factor in the government's final abolition of all guild restrictions in 1862, and in the foundation of the Stuttgart stock exchange in the same decade.[70]

Not only was there a tilting of the scales between agriculture and industry, but a basic change in the scale of industry itself. Before 1850 even the large-scale industry which existed was forced to compromise with the tradition of decentralised village crafts by giving out-work: at the beginning of the 1830s the Heidenheim textile firm of Mebold had 25 workers in its factory and 115 outside.[71] After the mid-century the pattern of out-work declined and the capitalisation of factories increased. In the course of the 1850s alone the number of spindles employed in the textile industry increased from 37,000 to 216,000, and by 1863 a government official was already claiming that Württemberg had made 'a rapid transition to factory production, to large-scale production'.[72] One particularly important indicator of industrial

68. Report on the census of occupations: *WJbb* (1862), pp. 283 ff.
69. Gehring, *ZWLG* (1943), pp. 435–6.
70. Ibid, pp. 441–3; Marquardt, *Geschichte Württembergs*, p. 343; R. Kaulla, 'Bankwesen', V. Bruns (ed), *Württemberg unter der Regierung König Wilhelms II* (Stuttgart, 1916), p. 890.
71. Gehring, *ZWLG* (1943), p. 435.
72. *WJbb* (1863), pp. 40 ff; *KW* (1863), p. 551.

development, the machine and machine tools industry, became a central feature of the Württemberg economy. The lack of an indigenous machine-producing branch had been a serious handicap in the first half of the century, resulting in factories using equipment often twenty or thirty years out of date. The rapid development after the 1850s was the basis of the state's growing reputation for quality finished goods.

Against this background of industrialisation and the prosperity which accompanied it, the Catholic parts of the state remained solid in their traditional occupations. The roots of the separate development of Catholic Württemberg are to be found in economic backwardness; and this in turn was based on different traditions of property inheritance and their effects on the size of peasant holdings. This enabled Catholic communities to weather the agricultural crisis better and maintain themselves intact; but it left them at the same time prey to the long-term crisis of agriculture and small business in the last quarter of the century.

Württemberg was not dominated by 'dwarf holdings' like its neighbours Baden and Hesse. Just over 40 per cent of all holdings were small to medium sized, between ten and fifty *Morgen* (six to thirty-five acres). Of the remainder, the larger holdings of over thirty-five acres outnumbered dwarf holdings by three to two. With the exception of Protestant Hohenlohe and the Protestant parts of the Alb the size of holding corresponded to the confessional division, larger on the Catholic side, smaller on the Protestant.[73] In Catholic areas, above all in Oberschwaben, the tradition was for the patrimony to be handed on undivided to a single heir. The typical agricultural unit in Catholic Württemberg was the family farm of large or medium size. Many of these had been supplemented by gains made during the clearing of common land from the end of the eighteenth century.[74] In the Protestant Neckar valley, on the other hand, the absence of primogeniture produced increasingly parcelled plots. The strong contrast emerges from the statistics of average size of holdings: in the Neckarland only 13.8 per cent were greater than thirty-five acres, but in the Oberland the figure was 56.3 per cent, or 20 per cent above the average for Württemberg. Conversely, half of all holdings in the

---

73. The details for the account that follows are from *KW* (1863). On the similarity of the Alb and Hohenlohe — in types of crop, size of holdings, geographical situation, the importance of cattle breeding, communications — see M. König, *Die bäuerliche Kulturlandschaft der Hohen Schwabenalb* (Tübingen, 1958); and Schremmer, *Moderne deutsche Wirtschaftsgeschichte*, pp. 67–85.
74. Hoffmann, *Landwirtschaft und Industrie in Württemberg*, pp. 139–40.

Neckar valley were smaller than six acres, but less than an eighth of those in Oberschwaben.[75]

These differences were decisive in the years of agricultural crisis during the 1840s and 1850s. The heaviest burden of debt and the highest incidence of bankruptcy fell on those areas where dwarf holdings predominated: there the demand for land was greatest and the tendency for debts to be taken on at inflated rates of interest the most marked. In the years 1840–7 the total number of forced sales affecting peasants and landowners was 679: in the *Neckarkreis* the figure was 209, in the *Schwarzwaldkreis* 213 and in the *Jagstkreis* 153; but in the *Donaukreis* it was only 104, or 15.3 per cent of the total.[76] Furthermore, one particularly hard-hit group, the vintners, was hardly represented in the Catholic parts of the state, where wine was produced only in a very small region around Tettnang.[77] In Oberschwaben the worst-affected group was that of the traditional landless village lower class, the *Söldner* and *Köbler*. In the 1840s and 1850s the Catholic owner of a fair-sized family farm had the fear of sharing this fate, but not as yet the experience of it. The choice facing the peasantry of the densely-populated Protestant areas was stark: further sub-division (frequently a physical impossibility), emigration, or migration to the towns. Rural artisans faced a similar dilemma, ruined by peasant poverty. This coercion stimulated the urbanisation and industrialisation of the 1850s and 1860s. But no such alternative forced Catholics to leave their communities or abandon agriculture and local crafts.

The emigration and internal migration figures for Württemberg measured in the census of 1861 showed clearly how the Catholic communities had weathered the crisis. The most severely depopulated areas were almost exclusively Protestant. This applied to all the areas worst affected, which had lost 15–18 per cent of their population since the end of the 1840s: Marbach, Welzheim, Nürtingen, Backnang, Waiblingen, Balingen and Böblingen.[78] The one *Donaukreis* town in this category, Kirchheim, was in the extreme north of the administrative district, and overwhelmingly Protestant in an otherwise Catholic part of the state. There was no net loss of population from Oberschwaben, and four districts — Ravensburg, Waldsee, Saulgau and Biberach — were the only ones in Württemberg, other than garrison towns and growing urban centres, which registered a net

---

75. *KW* (1863), p. 429.
76. *WJbb* (1847), pp. 179 ff.
77. K. C. Hainlen, *Gemeinfassliche natürliche Beschreibung Württembergs. Mit besonderer Beziehung auf die Landwirtschaft* (Stuttgart, 1867), p. 94.
78. *KW* (1863), p. 311.

influx of population. This was the result, perhaps, of the 'numerous agricultural servants' noted by an official account.[79]

The agricultural crisis of the mid-century and its aftermath thus created two distinct economic units within Württemberg: one industrialising fast and largely Protestant, the other agricultural and mainly Catholic. The three main centres of industrialisation were all Protestant. First was the Greater Stuttgart conurbation, formed as the city gradually drew the surrounding communities of Cannstatt, Feuerbach, Untertürkheim, Wangen, Gaisburg and Degerloch within its industrial and commercial orbit. Stuttgart's population increased from 48,000 in 1834 to 63,000 in 1852, doubled in the next twenty years and reached 172,000 by the turn of the century.[80] Cannstatt itself grew from 7,000 in 1850 to 20,000 in 1890: from the exclusive spa town which Balzac had known it became a solidly working-class suburb of Stuttgart and a major railway junction and repair centre.[81] The second area comprised a group of towns in the Neckar valley — Reutlingen, Esslingen and Heilbronn — which were closely linked to Stuttgart, and like the capital city had grown enormously by soaking up labour from the land. The third group consisted of four towns, three in the far north of the *Donaukreis* (Geislingen, Göppingen, Ulm), and one in the *Jagstkreis* (Heidenheim); but both geographically and economically these towns looked west towards Stuttgart and the Neckar, rather than south or east to the isolated Catholic valleys.[82]

Catholics took almost no part in this movement into the towns and factories: in the 1860s, after the first wave of internal migration, none of the six towns over 10,000 was Catholic, only two of the ten of 5–10,000 and only three of the twenty-four of 3–5,000. Catholics made up scarcely one-tenth of the total urban population, but four-fifths of those living in scattered farms and hamlets.[83] This remained essentially true for the next thirty years. The official description of Ellwangen published in 1886 remarked on the 'predominantly agricultural' character of the district: 60 per cent of the inhabitants gained a livelihood directly from the land. In Biberach in 1895, 55 per cent of the population continued to be dependent on agriculture as a source of income, but only 33 per cent on industry and commerce.[84] By the end

79. Ibid, p. 310.
80. L. Dessauer, *Die Industrialisierung von Gross-Stuttgart*, dissertation (Tübingen, 1916), p. 191.
81. Blos, *Denkwürdigkeiten*, II, p. 74.
82. This is clearly shown in map 13, L. Vischer, *Die industrielle Entwicklung im Königreich Württemberg und das Wirken seiner Centralstelle für Gewerbe und Handel* (Stuttgart, 1875).
83. *KW* (1863), p. 349.
84. *Beschreibung des Oberamts Ellwangen. Herausgegeben von dem Königlichen Statistisch-topographischen Bureau* (Stuttgart, 1886), pp. 202, 267; *KW* (1907), IV, p. 14.

of the century the average number of those living off agriculture in the seventeen Reichstag constituencies of the state was 44.5 per cent: in the four constituencies with a Catholic majority the average was 56.2 per cent.[85] It was therefore a Catholic peasantry still intact in its former communities which faced the economic problems of the later nineteenth century; and with it a flourishing *Mittelstand* in derivative occupations like small-scale brewing and milling, and other crafts like metal-working and leather goods manufacture which lived off peasant custom. Moreover, the two decades after the mid-century climacteric proved to be good ones for agriculture and the small businesses and shops it supported, a golden interim between the old crises of dearth and the beginning of a long-term crisis of a different kind, brought on by collision with the world market and its falling prices. In all agricultural regions more land was brought under the plough, the prices of produce and property rose, and Rümelin writing in the early 1860s could claim that agriculture was largely free of debt.[86] Württemberg continued to export grain until 1874,[87] and the wars of 1866 and 1870–1 disguised the advent of a downward turn in prices. Nowhere was this temporary prosperity and optimism more apparent than in Oberschwaben, where it was reported that among the peasantry even the possession of state bonds had become normal.[88]

This situation was decisively altered by declining agricultural returns. Price levels in Württemberg became increasingly determined by world prices which were themselves falling, as new land in North America and eastern Europe was brought into cultivation. Lower freight rates brought cheap agricultural produce to German ports, and after 1871 a railway network of national dimensions opened up the state to these supplies. At the same time, an increased volume of river traffic carried grain up the Rhine to Mannheim, and then on to Heilbronn and Stuttgart, where it was distributed by dealers on the exchanges at a standard price. Harvest failures in 1873, 1876, 1888 and 1889 brought no repetition of earlier price rises, and the dominant trend of world prices was a downward movement to which all three main grains of Oberschwaben were subject. Spelt, for example, the main winter crop, reached 20.68 Marks per 100 kg in 1854, a price attained again for the last time in 1872: after 1882 the price only twice

85. *WJbb* (1898), I, pp. 206–7. Max Miller, *Eugen Bolz, Staatsmann und Bekenner* (Stuttgart, 1951), p. 26, has a good description of Rottenburg in the last decades of the nineteenth century, a *stilles Landstädtschen* while industrialisation was beginning in the surrounding areas.
86. Cited by Dehlinger, *WJbb* (1897), I, p. 71.
87. M. Bühler, *Die Stellung Württembergs zum Umschwung in der Bismarck'schen Handelspolitik 1878/9*, dissertation (Tübingen, 1935), p. 48.
88. *KW* (1863), pp. 437–8.

exceeded 15 Marks. The movement of oats and barley prices was similar.[89]

The loss of income sustained by primary produces was made more serious by the sharp rise in costs which began to affect them at the same time; in particular, the rising cost of farm labour resulting from the competition of railway construction and factories with their attractions of higher wages, more regular and normally shorter hours and greater independence. Between 1882 and 1895 the number of male and female servants resident on farms fell by 1,716, the number of day labourers by over 5,500. While the total number of wage earners in the state increased by more than 50 per cent, the number on the land actually fell by nearly 5 per cent, and shortage and competition combined to raise the wages of male agricultural servants by over 300 per cent between 1860 and 1889, and those of female servants by over 200 per cent.[90] This problem was critical in Catholic communities, where considerable numbers of servants and day labourers had always been considered essential to supplement the labour of family members on medium and large farms. It seems possible that the rising birth rate which now became evident in these areas was at least in part a response to the chronic shortage of non-family labour.[91]

Increased taxes to finance illness, accident, old age and invalid insurance created an additional burden: in the three decades up to the 1890s the total of taxes and contributions rose fourfold, and to this must be added contributions to hail and fire insurance.[92] Falling land prices were an index of growing pessimism and agricultural distress; and they constituted also a drop in the real value of property. This drop in prices was most extreme in Oberschwaben, just as that part of the state had been best placed to profit from the confidence of the better years.[93] Catholic peasants who had escaped the indebtedness of earlier crises now found themselves thrown on the capital market at a time when credit terms were unprecedentedly bad. In the first half of

89. *WJbb* (1896), II, p. 122.
90. *WJbb* (1897), I, pp. 176–9; *Die Landwirtschaft und die Landwirtschaftspflege in Württemberg. Denkschrift Hrsg. von der K. Zentralstelle für die Landwirtschaft* (Stuttgart, 1908), p. 191.
91. A declining rate of infant mortality played a major part in this, of course, for infant mortality had previously been highest in Catholic areas.
92. *WJbb* (1897), I, p. 74. Insurance premiums were especially severe in agricultural insurance because the returns to the companies were smaller and much less reliable. In life insurance, for example, only 50% of income was returned in claims, in agricultural insurance 80%. K. Lindboom, 'Das Privatversicherungswesen', Bruns (ed), *Württemberg unter der Regierung König Wilhelms II*, pp. 915–17.
93. Over the three periods 1880–4, 1885–9 and 1890–4, the fall in land values was actually levelling off in the state as a whole; but in the *Donaukreis* the loss of saleable value was still increasing, from 9.7% in 1880–4 to 12.3% in 1890–4. *WJbb* (1895), p. 21.

the century capital had flowed mainly into the land, but successive crises had destroyed the confidence of creditors in the peasantry. Interest rates rose[94] and capital turned to safer investments in state railways or to industry and commerce where returns were higher. It was complained that money was no longer loaned against a simple promissory note but only on mortgage: by 1897 three-quarters of the debt owed by agriculture was in the form of mortgages. In the *Donaukreis* the total value of mortgage debts taken on increased by 42 per cent between 1874 and 1894: harsh credit terms were being tied to the security of property which was losing both its profitability and its market value.[95]

The first of two government enquiries into the state of agriculture found that the average number of bankruptcies in the state was 37.25 per 10,000 owners. Strikingly, the western, Protestant areas which had been worst affected earlier in the century now escaped more lightly: the figure for the *Neckarkreis* was 31 per 10,000, for the *Schwarzwaldkreis* 23. The less densely populated part of Württemberg, with its larger holdings, was now the centre of the crisis: the figures for the *Jagstkreis* and *Donaukreis* were 52 and 42 per 10,000. The Catholic areas now paid the price for earlier success in resisting debt, foreclosure and rural exodus. This was especially so in the Catholic heartland of Oberschwaben, where Wangen, with 71 bankruptcies per 10,000, was one of the most badly affected communities, and Saulgau (58), Ehingen and Leutkirch (47) and Riedlingen and Tettnang (46) were all well above the state average.[96]

Distress was strongly felt among the Catholic peasantry, for agriculture was at the very centre of life. Rottenberg's newspaper, for example, called itself the *Hopfenzeitung*, after the crop on which the livelihood of many of its readers depended. This same paper was once obliged to remind its readers that 'a newspaper is, so to speak, more than just the *Börsenblatt* [stock exchange gazette] of the peasant'.[97] Adolf Gröber, beginning his legal career in Catholic Neresheim, noted with some impatience that the local peasantry was 'interested in

---

94. In the 1820s interest rates were usually 4%, after the mid-century 5½%. *WJbb* (1897), I, p. 70. In the second half of the century agricultural cooperative banks, after Raiffeisen's model, were established; but they too had to reckon with the vicissitudes to which agriculture were peculiarly prone, and the consequent unreliability of the peasant as a debtor. Stockmayer, an agrarian deputy in the lower house of the Landtag, spoke in 1895 of one such association with an interest rate of 6% 'to encourage prompt repayment'. *Verhandlungen der Württembergischen Kammer der Abgeordneten auf dem 33 Landtag. Protokoll Band I*, p. 120, 10 Sitzung, 8.3.1895 (Henceforth: *33 LT, PB I*, p. 120, 10 Sitz., 8.3.1895).
95. *WJbb* (1895), II, pp. 9, 14.
96. *WJbb* (1893), I, pp. 133 ff.
97. *Rottenburger Zeitung und Neckarbote*, 16 September 1911.

nothing but agriculture'.[98] In the late 1880s this interest acquired a new form, as a series of factors outside their control — new patterns of world trade, the development of railways and canals, the power of the commodity exchanges to fix prices at the expense of the local *Schrannen*, the labour shortage, the vagaries of the capital market — made primary producers aware of their own impotence. At the same time there was a slackening of that solicitude which governments had formerly shown towards agriculture. By the last two decades of the nineteenth century, industry and commerce provided the backbone of state income and government and officials were more concerned with ameliorating the problems caused by industrialisation than with preaching the moral worth of the *Agrarstaat*. The changing official mind was indicated by the development of insurance schemes aimed chiefly at the factory worker, and by a new concern with industrial training programmes. An equally telling sign was the emergence of a new kind of official, like the pioneering Württemberg statistician Losch, whose interests lay in urban housing schemes and suburban railway services.[99]

When the government did investigate agricultural distress, rural disenchantment was plain. It was reported from Ravensburg and Waldsee that the state tax burden was felt as 'oppressive', while the district of Thaldorf commented that its results were 'not of the kind which would win the rural population for social legislation'.[100] Resentment against the Olympian detachment of a distant government resurfaced and played an important role in the elections of the period. But it was not the traditionally anti-governmental VP which now reaped the political reward; and it failed because unlike its political cousins in France, the Radicals, it lost the support of the peasantry and lower middle class in the small towns and villages. The French Radicals consolidated their hold among these groups by pressing parish-pump demands in Paris. Never losing a basic belief in the peasant state as a guarantee of social stability, they abhorred rapid industrial growth and encouraged the safe investment of capital in government bonds rather than in speculative commercial ventures. The agrarian order was underwritten in a practical sense by protective tariffs. Germany's Progressives, by contrast, were Manchester men in their economic views, and nowhere was this more true than in the

98. Cardauns, *Gröber*, p. 26.
99. Losch's overriding interest in the social problems of industrial society put him on close personal terms with Friedrich Naumann's National Social group, for whom he contested a Württemberg Reichstag seat against an agrarian candidate. M. Miller and R. Uhland (eds), *Lebensbilder aus Schwaben und Franken*, IX (Stuttgart, 1963), pp. 403, 406–7.
100. *WJbb* (1895), II, pp. 20 ff.

Württemberg VP. For them, free movement of labour and free trade were central articles of faith and 'cheap bread' a major objective.

The VP tried to counter the unpopularity of this stance by persuading the peasantry that tariffs were a Junker device. But they were largely unsuccessful, although many of their arguments were undoubtedly correct. They were right to point out, for example, that to see tariffs as a long-term solution to the crisis of falling prices was chimerical. For these could not alter the basic problem: after the 1880s Württemberg was unable to provide its rapidly growing urban population with food, and the bakers anyway preferred foreign grain of superior quality once it became available.[101] The VP was also correct in arguing that large estates were the main beneficiaries of high grain tariffs. In fact, protective duties harmed Württemberg agriculture in three distinct ways. First, Prussian grain growers, having priced themselves out of world markets, dumped in southern Germany and so further deflated prices. Secondly, the repercussions of the protectionist barrier harmed a flourishing export of oats to Switzerland. Finally, the one-sided protection of grain worked against the cattle-rearer's interests: it tended to limit his domestic market by making the proportion of the family budget spent on bread exaggeratedly high; and it made cattle feeds more expensive.[102] This was of considerable importance in Oberschwaben, where cattle breeding was more extensive than in any other part of Germany.

This was the case put forward by VP politicians to persuade the peasantry that protection was against its own interests. Approaching the question from a slightly different angle, a number of recent writers have also suggested that small producers had no interest in tariffs because they were producing largely for subsistence.[103] Neither case can be fully sustained. The practice of producing a small marketable surplus of grain was widespread among the peasantry, and it is probable that price movements were subjectively of greater

---

101. A. Bartens, *Die wirtschaftliche Entwicklung des Königreichs Württemberg mit besonderer Berücksichtigung der Handelsverträge* (Frankfurt/Main, 1901), pp. 35 ff. Milling technology in Germany was initially incapable of dealing with the hard wheat from the great plains of central Europe and North America, but by the 1880s new techniques developed in the U.S.A. by millers using prairie wheat had been introduced into Germany, and from that time the remaining advantage of domestic grain was destroyed. See K. W. Hardach, *Die Bedeutung wirtschaftlicher Faktoren bei der Wiedereinführung der Eisen- und Getreidezölle in Deutschland 1879* (Berlin, 1967), p. 67.

102. Gerschenkron, *Bread and Democracy*; H.-B. Krohn, *Die Futtergetreidewirtschaft der Welt 1900–1954* (Hamburg and Berlin, 1957), esp. p. 37.

103. For the contemporary liberal case, see Bartens, *Die wirtschaftliche Entwicklung des Königreichs Württemberg*, p. 54; for the arguments of more recent writers, Bühler, *Die Stellung Württembergs*, pp. 12, 47–8; Hardach, *Die Bedeutung wirtschaftlicher Faktoren*, pp. 120–1.

importance to those operating on a tight margin. The extent of small-scale production for the market among the Catholic peasantry is clear from official sources. In Gmünd the surplus in 1870 from the 130 households of Iggingen was 1,500 bushels of spelt, 1,400 of oats, 130 of barley and 40 of rye. In Degerfeld, also in Gmünd and consisting of 55 households, it was reported that '200–300 bushels of spelt and 250–350 bushels of oats in excess of domestic consumption can be sold outside annually'.[104] In Göttingen the pattern was similar, and seems to have prevailed beyond the turn of the century.[105] In reply to a government enquiry of 1895 the district of Bergatreute in Waldsee, where all three main grains were cultivated, calculated the annual loss to its producers from the price drop at 32,000 Marks: of its 231 households only 17 needed to purchase all their flour and bread; 22 produced at least a part of their requirements on rented land, and a further 43 on their own land; 48 covered all their own domestic needs; and 101 had a surplus to market. There can be no question that the peasant had an interest in the market price of grain.[106]

It was true, of course, as the VP claimed, that German agricultural production was unbalanced; and that a greater emphasis on cattle or dairy farming, on the Danish or Dutch model, was called for to redress the over-production of grain. This did not, however, dispel the problem that the small producer's budget was often finely balanced to include a small profit from spelt, oats or barley. Nor did VP arguments take sufficient account of the fact that rising costs contributed at least as much as falling prices to rural anger. Thus the suggestion that he switch from grain was met with outright suspicion by the small producer, particularly since it came from the champions of that rapid industrialisation which he held responsible for his plight. This reaction found support among cattle breeders who feared a glut from over-production, or a sudden flood of livestock and meat imports,[107] and among dairy farmers whose apprehensions were reinforced by concern over surrogate foodstuffs. Margarine was the main enemy here. The Ravensburg Chamber of Commerce, sensitive to the moods of local customers, reported in 1894 that dairy men were fighting to check the spread of margarine as a butter substitute. Feelings were sufficiently strong for the Chamber to take up the

---

104. *Beschreibung des Oberamts Gmünd. Herausgegeben von dem Königlichen Statistisch-topographischen Bureau* (Stuttgart, 1870), p. 354.
105. Ibid, p. 325; *Gmünder Tagblatt*, 15 April 1902 (report on agriculture).
106. *WJbb* (1895), II, p. 25.
107. Ibid, pp. 14, 25; *WJbb* (1897), I, p. 74. Horse-raisers also feared a flood of foreign imports. On the rising number of imported horses from the 1860s onwards, and reactions to it, see the report in the *Ipf-Zeitung*, 14 September 1899.

movement and propose — as the Centre Party in the Reichstag had done — that, as a disincentive to the consumer, the offending substance be dyed a distinctive and disagreeable colour (their suggestion was violet).[108] Hop growers, concentrated in the Catholic areas of Rottenburg and Tettnang, were also threatened with a curtailed outlet for their crops when improvements in refrigeration reduced the role of hops as a preservative, and freed breweries from the compulsion to buy immediately after the harvest.[109]

All these considerations made it difficult for the VP to impress with its argument that peasant prosperity lay in diversification. Yet, as working-class complaints about dear food became more insistent, the VP was strengthened in its belief that the great Junker estates must be made to suffer and the peasant to see sense. As the gap between town and country widened, the peasantry looked to other parties for a sympathetic hearing. Their discontent came to a head in the early 1890s. Hop prices, always subject to violent fluctuations, dropped to uniquely low levels.[110] Grain prices dipped disastrously: spelt prices went down in 1894 to only 11 Marks per 100 kg, with barley and oats showing the same trend.[111] At the same time, cattle breeders were struck by a series of natural disasters, when cattle was several times struck by foot-and-mouth disease, in 1891 affecting a tenth of all stock. Then in 1893 a chronic shortage of feed reduced stocks by a fifth, with an estimated loss to the peasantry of 30 to 40 million Marks.[112] The liberal economic system bore the brunt of the resentment. Many cattle owners who had previously resisted were forced to assume debts. Complaints were rife about the alleged extortion of Jewish cattle dealers when animals had to be bought on credit by peasants with insufficient capital to re-stock, and liberal economic legislation was blamed for allowing the itinerant trade in cattle.[113]

Above all, the Caprivi trade treaties of the early 1890s provoked violent opposition. The import duty on oats was reduced from 4

---

108. Schwab, Weiss and Holtermann (eds), *Handelskammer Ravensburg*, pp. 58–9.
109. Teichmann, *Die Politik der Agrarpreisstützung*, p. 638. Stuttgart was a major centre both for the chemical industry and the manufacture of sophisticated brewery equipment which made possible the use of surrogates like rice.
110. Ibid, p. 641.
111. *WJbb* (1896), II, p. 122.
112. Lindboom, Bruns (ed), *Württemberg unter der Regierung König Wilhelms II*, p. 911; *WJbb* (1897), I, p. 73.
113. *WJbb* (1895), II, pp. 14, 25. Note also Friedrich Payer's description of his agrarian opponent at a by-election in Besigheim at the same period: 'His campaign was not delicate, and portrayals of the lawyer [i.e. Payer] having the mortgaged cow taken away from the despairing peasant family at the bidding of the Jew played a major part.' Payer, 'Mein Lebenslauf', pp. 35–6.

Marks to 2.80 Marks; on barley from 2.25 Marks to 2 Marks, and on the barley-derivative malt from 4 Marks to 3.60 Marks; cattle breeders were affected by a lowering of the tariff on oxen, calves and on fresh and prepared meat; and hop growing, already suffering low prices, was hit by similar reductions. The support given by the Württemberg VP to Caprivi's measures convinced the struggling peasantry of the free traders' perfidy. One beneficiary of this crisis was the Württemberg *Bauernbund*, formed in 1893 as the local branch of the agrarian *Bund der Landwirte*: it was beginning to make headway in the Protestant regions of Hohenlohe and the Alb which, in terms of geographical location, type of agriculture and social structure, were very similar to the Catholic areas of the *Jagstkreis* and Oberschwaben. The other beneficiary was the Centre itself, many of whose candidates in 1895 were already leaders in agricultural communities, or active in local peasant associations.[114]

IV

The Centre also inherited former VP support among the Catholic *Mittelstand*. Declining peasant purchasing power brought a spate of bankruptcies to small businesses in the Catholic valleys: the Ravensburg Chamber of Commerce noted in 1895 that the difficulties of the agricultural population were especially severe in their effects on artisans and small shopkeepers.[115] In fact, just over four-fifths of all bankruptcies in the decade up to 1892 were in business and trade, of which 'by far the majority fell on small businesses'.[116] At the same time the *Mittelstand* echoed the peasantry in contrasting their own relative poverty with the wealth of Stuttgart and the Neckar valley, and blamed the prevailing laissez-faire philosophy for spawning the industrial and commercial leviathans which threatened to destroy small independent existences.

Four traditional industries of Oberschwaben were particularly badly affected. Artisan tanneries were hit by cheap imported American leather, and the pruning out of small concerns was already well advanced by the middle of the 1890s when the formation of the American Leather Trust tightened the screw further.[117] In the related branch of shoe manufacturing artisan producers were being eliminated by the factory competition of firms like the Salamander concern in

114. See below, Chapter Three, p. 107.
115. Report in *Waldse'er Wochenblatt*, 7 March 1895.
116. *WJbb* (1893), I, pp. 130 ff.
117. Bartens, *Die wirtschaftliche Entwicklung des Königreichs Württemberg*, p. 110.

Stuttgart: between 1882 and 1895 the number of large shoe factories in the state increased from two to twenty.[118] The milling industry faced similar problems. The Upper Rhine milling industry, finding its north German and foreign outlets taken by better-placed competitors, became in turn heavily concentrated in a few large firms based on Mannheim and Heidelberg. These were bent on securing the entire south German market. Württemberg's millers complained that the advantages of scale and organisation possessed by such concerns were helping to turn the domestic industry increasingly into a mere distributor of cheap imported flour.[119] Family-based breweries frequently found themselves in the same dilemma, and this again was a characteristic industry of underdeveloped Oberschwaben.

In a process parallel to that experienced by agriculture, small businesses found themselves forced out of a central place in the economy and left in a marginal position. Resisting the psychological and social loss of status entailed by dropping into the dependent working class, many members of the *Mittelstand* tried to keep afloat in the service sector, as repairers, shopkeepers and publicans. But it was only in the growing towns and cities, if there, that sufficient custom was available to support this mushroom growth, and in smaller towns these occupations were chronically overcrowded. By the 1880s there were over 20,000 tradesmens' businesses in Württemberg, or one to every twenty-two families; and the situation was deteriorating.[120] In the Catholic areas south of the Danube artisans were encouraged by the presence of a growing number of holiday-makers from the towns to sink their savings in a shop or inn; but the rate of bankruptcy was extremely high in these branches, in the 1880s six times as high among inn-keepers and publicans as in the building industry, for example.[121]

For the shopkeeper and publican, like the peasant and artisan, economic change posed certain common problems, particularly the need for credit on satisfactory terms at a time when mortgage payments, taxation, insurance and overheads had to be met from an insecure turnover. These problems were acute in Catholic communities, for the unhealthy expansion of the retail sector was very evident there, and the bulk of insolvencies occurred in towns of under

---

118. Ibid, p. 13. Eight of these twenty had more than 100 employees; and by the time of the war, Jacob Sigle's Salamander factory in the Kornwestheim suburb of Stuttgart employed 3,400 workers.
119. See the petition of small millers: *34 LT, BB (Beilage Band) III*, Beilage 167, p. 483.
120. *WJbb* (1893), I, p. 143. On this subject more generally, see R. Gellately, *The Politics of Economic Despair: Shopkeepers and German Politics 1890–1914* (London, 1974), pp. 30–4.
121. *WJbb* (1893), I, pp. 140–2.

2,000 inhabitants. But if shopkeepers often proved to be their own worst enemies, they naturally found others to blame for their problems: the department stores, which enticed labour and customers out of the small towns and encroached on local markets; and those identified politically with the liberal commercial code of 1862, which had encouraged numerous practices supposedly harmful to retailers, from price-cutting wars and the spread of automatic vending machines, to the sale of bottled beer so anathematised by publicans.

The VP was as unsympathetic to these arguments as to those of the peasantry. Thirty years before VP politicians had been a mixture of lawyers, literary figures and small businessmen. They had addressed themselves to, and articulated the feelings of, the *Mittelstand*.[122] But the VP candidates for the 1895 election included a bevy of 'Manchester men' representing manufacturing and commercial interests: the banker Schnaidt, the merchants Lang, Betz, Schumacher and Schweickhardt, the factory owners Bürk, Käss, Hähnle, Beurlen, Henning and Kraut, the large-scale miller Schmid and the brewery owner Tag.[123] The party's leaders had also changed. Most were now lawyers with strong business ties. Friedrich Payer sat with Hans Hähnle on several boards, and the two men between them held eight different directorships. The Haussmann brothers, Conrad and Friedrich, with their respective brothers-in-law, made up a closely-knit group with multiple commercial interests in Stuttgart, Esslingen, Geislingen and Reutlingen.[124] The advent of Payer and the Haussmanns to the leadership of the VP in the late 1880s pointed up the party's growing inability to speak for *Mittelstand* discontent, and there began a steady drift of these groups towards the *Bauernbund* and Centre.

The changing nature of the VP also stirred the Catholic political élite out of its complacency. For the forceful young VP leaders were attached to free trade and laissez-faire not only as economic tenets, but as part of a buoyant belief in the public and social benefits of entrepreneurial initiative. Just as laissez-faire had proved its superiority over ancient guild restrictions, so it would act as a leaven on the

---

122. Simon, *Die württembergischen Demokraten*, pp. 12–14. See also the accounts of earlier VP politicians in Schmidt-Buhl, *Schwäbische Volksmänner*.
123. Occupations listed in *WJbb* (1895), III, p. 187.
124. *Deutsches Volksblatt*, 3 December 1906; HStaASt, Conrad Haussmann Papers, Q 1/2, 104: *Bauernbund* pamphlet 'An die Landtagswähler des Oberamtsbezirks Münsingen' (n.d. 1906?). The sources here are hostile ones, but the details themselves were commonly known: the tendentious parts of the *Deutsches Volksblatt* article and the *Bauernbund* pamphlet consisted in the suggestion that involvement in these business concerns made the VP leaders a party to the overmighty power of 'Jewish capital'. The VP did not try to deny their business involvements: in 'Mein Lebenslauf', Payer calculated his annual income from this source, by 1917, as more than 40,000 Marks.

inherited rigidities of *ständisch* society. The political corollary of this faith was a belief that government should recognise the social importance of the industrial, commercial and professional middle classes;[125] and the plans and compromise measures already drawn up by ministers in the early 1890s for changes in the taxation, education and local government systems, as well as the constitution, raised the possibility of reforms in this direction.[126]

Prominent and politically engaged Catholics were by no means hostile on the general question of reform. Men like Gröber not only stressed the need for changes in economic and social policy, but also shared some of the political concerns of VP leaders. These included opposition to government interference in elections and a recognition that some reform of both the constitution and local government was overdue. But potential Catholic political leaders viewed with distaste the prospect that the direction of reform might be guided by such self-consciously Cobdenite radicals: this could only help to accelerate the division of society into the wealthy capitalist few and the rootless property-less many. While Catholic peasants and members of the *Mittelstand* had concrete grievances against liberal capitalism of the sort espoused by the VP, the future leaders of the Centre Party had equally great apprehensions about the philosophy of 'Manchesterism'. Hence, while they stressed the need for a balance of classes in society, they saw the nurturing of the peasantry and *Mittelstand* as one antidote to the threatening 'war of all against all': peasants and moderate property owners would provide a bulwark against the excesses of liberal individualism on the one hand and the growing threat of socialist collectivisation on the other.[127] For the future leaders of the Centre, then, the VP was encouraging a social and intellectual ferment from which only the SPD could ultimately benefit. Two specific events of the early 1890s served to sharpen this feeling. First, after Prussia's

---

125. See the articles on Richard Cobden in *Der Beobachter*, 4 and 5 June 1894, part of the collection of newspaper cuttings and other material in HStaASt, B. 41, Anhang II, Bü 4, dealing with constitutional reform. On the VP and the post-1895 'era of reform', see Chapter Four below.

126. HStaASt, E 41, Anhang II, Bü 4, plans for reform of the constitution; HStaASt, E 130a, Bü 576, Nr. 1–9, Bü 577, drafts for the revision of land, building, business, capital and income taxes. See also Menzinger, *Verfassungsrevision und Demokratisierungsprozess*, esp. p. 141. Education and local government laws in 1891 had merely postponed the fundamental decisions about the direction reform should go; and on the eve of the 1895 election the government's draft bill on tax reform was still awaited.

127. These were constantly reiterated themes in the editorials of the *Deutsches Volksblatt* and the speeches of Centre leaders like Gröber and Kiene. See also the 1895 Centre programme, printed in *Politische Zeitfragen in Württemberg. Zwanglos erscheinende Hefte*, 4 (Stuttgart, 1900), pp. 1–6.

lifting of the prohibition on the Benedictines, the absence of male teaching orders in Württemberg was even more strongly felt as a gap in the ranks of those engaged in maintaining social and family discipline.[128] Secondly, the Reich anti-socialist legislation was not renewed and lapsed in Württemberg in October 1890. The local SPD, which had won its first local council seat at Heilbronn in 1885,[129] re-emerged to organise successfully at state level, and in the Landtag election of 1895 won its first seats there.

The early 1890s therefore marked a watershed also in the attitude of potential Centre leaders to the organisation of a party at state level. The example of Rudolf Probst is an illuminating one. As late as January 1889, Gröber was still recording doubts in his diary as to whether Probst, as Württemberg's senior Catholic politician, would ever be willing to lead a Centre Party in the state.[130] Probst's volte-face dated from the following year when the SPD, freed from Bismarck's discriminatory laws, singled out the Centre at its Halle conference as its particular political enemy. Less than a month later, on 23–24 November 1890, Probst was in the chair at a meeting in Ulm, helping to set up a committee to put pressure on the government over the return of banned teaching orders and the need to safeguard confessional schools.[131] In the following years there were a number of meetings between members of the Ulm committee and ministers, and in 1892 a petition was presented to the government and a sharply-worded reproach against government inactivity issued. The theme of these approaches was a common one: only by restoring freedom to teaching orders could the State help the Church to combat threats to the stability of the social order. When, in 1893, Gröber made a further attempt to secure support for a Württemberg Centre Party, Probst this time telegraphed his approval and in the same year formally resigned from the Left group in the Landtag after a life-long political association.[132] Then, as later, Probst gave his reason as the threat to the social order represented especially by the VP educational policy, in which they were 'going hand in hand with the Social Democrats and Anarchists'.[133]

128. K. Bachem, *Zentrumspartei*, VIII, p. 62.
129. G. Kittler, *Aus dem dritten württemb. Reichstags-Wahlkreis. Erinnerungen und Erlebnisse* (Heilbronn, 1910), p. 91.
130. Cardauns, *Gröber*, p. 65.
131. K. Bachem, *Zentrumspartei*, VIII, p. 67.
132. Ibid, p. 75; Cardauns, *Gröber*, p. 67.
133. See Probst's speech at Ochsenhausen, reported in *Deutsches Volksblatt*, 12 January 1895.

V

It is clearly necessary to consider how far the Centre Party which Gröber, Probst and others now began to build in Württemberg was acting simply as the political arm of the Church. Probst was certainly not on bad terms with Rottenburg, but his independence from the hierarchy was as venerable as his mid-century radicalism. He was, and remained, a disciple of Montalembert.[134] Gröber represented the new school of Centre politicians which emerged in the 1890s. He was, of course, concerned about issues which were of special importance to the Church: he took a keen interest, for example, in the attitudes taken by politicians of other Württemberg parties to the anti-Jesuit law.[135] But like his mentor, Windthorst, Gröber saw both the dangers and weaknesses of a political party dictated to by the bishops. From the 1880s, when his political activity in Rottweil brought a clash with the local seminary head,[136] he refused to be deflected by the clerical displeasure he provoked. His relations with successive incumbents at Rottenburg were especially cool. The latter had traditionally sought to keep on good terms with the government; and — perhaps recalling the backlash which followed the founding of a Catholic party in neighbouring Baden — continued to favour the discreet lobbying of ministers on specific issues.[137] Gröber, however, was unwilling to see the cause of Württemberg Catholics remain the preserve of the hierarchy. Through the ballot box and by means of an active social policy, he intended to consolidate a party aimed ideologically at VP and SPD, one which was conservative in its aims but entirely modern in its methods.

This was the significance of the *Volksverein für das katholische Deutschland*, founded in Württemberg four years before the Centre itself and by 1895 already numbering 20,000 members (17 per cent of male Catholics over the age of twenty-one).[138] It had been founded, as curate Kappler said at Waldsee in January 1895, 'as a defence against Social Democracy, but above all against the pernicious economic

134. Scheuerle, *Der politische Katholizismus*, pp. 2–9.
135. G. Egelhaaf, *Lebenserinnerungen*, ed. A. Rapp (Stuttgart, 1960), p. 80.
136. Cardauns, *Gröber*, p. 28.
137. Bishop Hefele, for example, wrote to Probst on 30 October 1877 expressing his unwillingness to see a Centre group in the lower house. Scheuerle, *Der politische Katholizismus*, appendix III, p. 261. See also Miller, *Eugen Bolz*, p. 36. In the 1880s Hefele and his assistant (later Bishop) Reiser felt the founding of a Centre Party in the state would be 'inopportune'. K. Bachem, *Zentrumspartei*, VIII, pp. 60–1. On Gröber's poor relations with Reiser's successor, Keppler, see ibid, p. 74.
138. Cardauns, *Gröber*, pp. 104–5.

aspirations of modern liberalism'.[139] The function of the *Volksverein* locally was to organise and channel both the grievances of the Catholic population against VP 'Manchesterism' and its apprehensions about socialism. In places where the peasantry and rural *Mittelstand* were suspicious of privilege and outside authority, the organisation was an invaluable auxiliary of the Centre. It served the same purpose as peasant and artisan associations in successfully utilising the energies of the radical lower clergy, who normally shared this social background themselves.

It was therefore appropriately under the aegis of the *Volksverein* that the founding of the Württemberg Centre should have taken place. At a meeting of the organisation in Ellwangen at Whitsuntide 1894, the various grievances of Catholics in the state were aired. Speeches were given on the question of schools and teaching orders and a resolution was also passed which 'rejected the liberal view of unconditional economic freedom, which leaves the individual helpless against the free play of economic forces'. In addition, legislative measures were demanded for the defence of the *Mittelstand* in agriculture and business, and for a relief of the tax burden on small and medium sized property owners. A resolution of Gröber's was then passed by the 4,000 present to form a political party to fight the forthcoming Landtag elections. The real founding of the party followed a meeting of the twenty–one–man executive committee of the *Volksverein* together with ten Catholic Landtag deputies, after which a formal programme and electoral address were published.[140]

It was consistent with the origins of the Centre that the party's first full–scale meeting at state level, at Ravensburg on 17 January 1895, should have placed great emphasis on the economic fears of its constituents. Hans Kiene attacked the VP for its advocacy of 'Manchester liberalism', its willingness to countenance 'exploitation and unfair competition' and its opposition to stock exchange taxation.[141] The Centre's leading newspaper in Württemberg, the *Deutsches Volksblatt*, also consistently put the social issue forward as a central concern, in refuting VP and Evangelical League allegations that the party was merely confessionally based. The paper quoted with approval a pamphlet put out by coachbuilder and furniture manufacturer Louis Bauer, which stated: 'It is ultimately neither the Catholic nor Protestant religion which is in danger (rather true

139. Meeting of 30 January 1895, reported in *Deutsches Volksblatt*, 1 February 1895.
140. K. Bachem, *Zentrumspartei*, VIII, pp. 78–9.
141. Report in *Deutsches Volksblatt*, 18 January 1895.

Christianity, and that is something else) but the *Mittelstand*.'[142] It complained that the VP's opposition to indirect taxes would only lead to further fiscal handicaps for the already overburdened peasantry and small business classes: 'Anyone who believes that this is the time to impose still more taxes on the needy peasantry and *Gewerbestand* understands the interests of the people as little as certain lawyers from Stuttgart understand agriculture and business'; and it demagogically invited the authors of the VP programme to leave the capital city and discover the real temper of popular feeling in Spaichingen or Ehingen.[143]

Naturally, in a state which was two-thirds Protestant and had a long tradition of pietistic anti-Catholic feeling, the Centre leadership had to weigh the advantages of appealing to a narrowly confessional resentment among Catholics against the widespread political hostility such a course would provoke. In large-scale meetings and in a prominent organ of opinion like the *Deutsches Volksblatt* the party would clearly have been anxious to avoid incurring the confessional label. Yet, if anything, meetings in small towns and villages, usually presided over by the local clergy, showed an even greater preoccupation with the social and economic parts of the Centre programme. Here, pressing material problems often relegated the lofty concerns of the Centre leadership to an entirely subsidiary role. Thus, at a meeting in the Rottweil constituency, the schoolteacher Deitz 'spoke principally about agriculture and economic questions in the light of the Centre programme, and at the close touched briefly on the schools and orders question'.[144] This ordering of priorities could be read in countless reports of local Centre papers like the *Waldse'er Wochenblatt* or *Ipf-Zeitung*. In both meetings and press reports a sense of confessional rancour was never entirely absent; but 'defence of the Church' slogans played a surprisingly muted part in the Centre election campaign, given the genuine grievances of Catholics as Catholics, the strongly anti-Catholic tenor of the opposition campaign and the importance of the local clergy in the electoral machine.

The importance of bread-and-butter issues in 1895 has, in fact, been unduly overshadowed by the political caesura which the election seemed in retrospect to constitute. But contemporaries were in no doubt as to the powerful undercurrent of economic discontent in the years before the election. One sign of this was a recrudescence of

142. Ibid, 31 January 1895.
143. Ibid, 29 January 1895.
144. Meeting of 13 January 1895, reported ibid, 17 January 1895.

anti-semitism as a by-product of hard times.[145] Among the *Mittelstand* the pre-election mood of truculence was marked by the founding in 1892 of the Württemberg *Schutzverein für Handel und Gewerbe*;[146] and the finance minister, drafting a new law in 1894 on itinerant trade (*Hausierhandel*), noted the hostility which this form of trade was arousing in the *Mittelstand*.[147] Above all, agricultural distress and the bitterness felt on the land over the Caprivi trade treaties were facts which required the attention of all the parties in the 1895 election. It was a source of embarrassment to the Centre itself that Gröber, unlike his Reichstag colleagues from Württemberg, the Centre deputies Wengert and Alfred Rembold, had voted for the Russian trade treaty. While Wengert laid great stress on his pro-agrarian vote, Gröber was faced by a government attempt to convince his peasant electorate of the Centre leader's essentially anti-agriculture standpoint.[148] However, this problem was more severe for the VP. The VP deputy Maurer later claimed that his party's support for the Caprivi treaties had been the argument most frequently used against them in 1895,[149] and the importance of this issue was revealed in the large amount of trimming on the part of the VP. Friedrich Haussmann told an election audience at Nesselbach that he was in favour of retaining the duties on agricultural products at the Caprivi level,[150] although this contradicted official VP policy. Similarly, the Reichstag VP deputy Schnaidt, a Landtag candidate in Ludwigsburg, claimed that he had voted for the Caprivi trade treaties only 'in order to prevent in the long run any further lowering of the grain duties'.[151] This bending of VP principles was commented on ironically by *Germania*, which wrote of the VP need to accommodate itself to agricultural discontent and thus to 'water down its free trade pure wine'.[152]

In appealing to peasant and *Mittelstand* grievances, as well as to a

---

145. HStaASt, E 130a, Bü 406, Nr. 11: 'Antisemitische Hetze' (1892). Press reports indicated also how widespread anti-semitism was in the campaigns of both the Centre and the agrarians. See also above, n. 113.
146. Gellately, *The Politics of Economic Despair*, p. 115.
147. HStaASt, E 130a, Bü 576, Nr. 6.
148. Pfälzische LB Speyer, Ernst Lieber Papers, G. 12, Gröber to Lieber, 7 June 1894.
149. *33 LT, PB 1*, p. 126, 10 Sitz., 8.3.1895.
150. *Deutsches Volksblatt*, 6 February 1895. Nesselbach was in the Oehringen constituency, which was nevertheless lost by the VP to the agrarian *Bauernbund*. On this, and the result at Crailsheim, where the agrarians polled over 40% of the vote at their first attempt, see Simon, *Die württembergischen Demokraten*, p. 42. The two seats were very similar in social structure and type of agriculture to the Centre-won seats in the same area, Neresheim and Ellwangen.
151. *Deutsches Volksblatt*, 5 February 1895.
152. Cited ibid, 9 February 1895.

more general sense of parochial suspicion among Württemberg Catholics, the Centre was in effect putting itself forward as the true heir to the spirit of 1848. Politically radical but socially conservative, it attacked the government for its Olympian indifference while at the same time attacking the VP for its 'doctrinaire' laissez-faire policy. On the one hand, therefore, it was able to exploit the widespread anti-governmental feeling. In Mergentheim, for example, the Centre candidate stood against Prime Minister von Mittnacht and directed his fire at official complacency in the face of popular distress (Mittnacht himself did not campaign). The candidate, a small businessman, demanded 'defence of the small man against large capital, better protection against profiteers and unfair competition, as well as against abuses of itinerant trade'. Luxury taxes and a pledge by the government that its own institutions would buy domestic agricultural produce were also included in the attacks on current official policy.[153] On the other hand, in a manner which was to become characteristic of the Centre crusade against liberalism in subsequent years, the party's campaign concentrated on showing that the VP was unfitted to represent the groundswell of popular resentment against the government. Typical was the speech of Dr Dreher on behalf of the Centre candidate in one of the struggling Oberschwaben agricultural and small business communities, Saulgau. At a meeting in Mengen he referred to the development of the Centre out of the difficulties of the *Kulturkampf* years into a party 'which through its handling of protective duties, stock exchange taxation, the usury question, unfair competition and itinerant trade, has protected the well-being of the people, while the "Volkspartei", out of clear regard for Jewish big money, has vacillated or frowned upon these genuinely popular demands'.[154]

In 1895 the Centre entered the Württemberg Lower House for the first time, represented by eighteen deputies. It had been successful in the election in appealing directly to the sense of material and non-material neglect among the Catholic population of the state.[155] In

153. Ibid, 18 January 1895.
154. Ibid, 31 January 1895.
155. As part of a proposal in 1886 to reform the lower house by replacing the *Privilegierten* who sat there with twenty-four deputies elected from among the highest tax-payers in the state, the government collected statistics on the distribution of such tax-payers. 4,124 (56%) of the 7,278 who paid more than 150 Marks in state taxes in the year 1885–6 lived in the twenty-seven towns with more than 5,000 inhabitants. Only seven of those towns had a majority of Catholics, and together they provided only 428, or slightly over 10%, of the 4,124 highest tax-payers in towns (HStaASt, E 41, Anhang II, Bü 4, copy of a reply by the government to a request for information from the President of the Lower House, 3 February 1888).

a manner which was markedly demagogic, the Centre both subsumed traditional anti-governmental resentments and insisted that the nostrums of the VP 'lawyers from Stuttgart' were, at best, irrelevant to the real economic and social problems. Both of these strains of Centre policy continued to be apparent in the following two decades, as Centre leaders sought after 1895 to maintain the allegiance of their often volatile supporters.

CHAPTER 3

The Centre Party in Württemberg
1895–1914:
Structure and Organisation

I

The Centre Party in Württemberg, as in other southern and western regions of Germany, was an organisational hybrid. It was clearly not a party of notables (*Honoratiorenpartei*); but neither was it a membership party like the VP or SPD. On the one hand, Centre leaders constituted a narrow group which determined the line taken by the party both inside and outside the Landtag: they decided policy and tactics, and were obliged to submit neither these decisions nor themselves as leaders to a party membership for approval. On the other hand, the absence of a formal party membership or machinery for questioning and changing measures and men did not mean that the Centre was immune to popular pressure. If anything the party was more susceptible to such pressures at state level than nationally. The frequently heavy-handed methods adopted by party leaders were constantly being challenged, often successfully, by sectional and parish-pump interests. Opposition could never be completely disregarded by the leadership, and it expressed itself as a real threat to party unity over particular issues (like agriculture) and on particular occasions (like elections) when rebellion was politically effective. Additionally, much more than in the Reichstag, discontent of this kind extended into the parliamentary *Fraktion* itself. In examining the complicated cross-currents within the Centre, therefore, we should perhaps begin by considering the composition of the *Landtagsfraktion*.

Forty-six elected deputies represented the Centre Party in the Württemberg Landtag between 1895 and 1914.[1] They can be divided

1. Compiled from the Register of Members for the seven parliaments between 1895 and the war, as contained in: *33 LT, BB III*, pp. 1–4; *33 LT BB IV*, pp. 419–24; *33 LT, BB IX*, pp. 117–19; *34 LT, BB II*, pp. 303–6; *34 LT, BB III*, pp. 1009–12; *35 LT, BB II*, pp. 79ff; *36 LT, BB IV*, pp. 455–64; *37 LT, BB II*, pp. 217 ff; *37 LT, BB V*, pp. 627 ff; *38 LT, BB III*, pp. 329–55; *38 LT, BB IV*, pp. 181–4; *39 LT, BB II*, pp. 235–42.

100

into a number of groups. The real leadership of the *Fraktion* was in the hands of a small number of men: six state officials in high legal positions, mostly judges (Bolz, Gröber, Kiene, Mohr, Nieder and Walter), and two lawyers in private practice (the brothers Alfred and Viktor Rembold). A second group consisted of state officials and members of the free professions who mostly did not belong to the leadership of the *Fraktion*: three district architects (Vogler, Schmid and Rapp); four local administrators (Speth, Nessler, Schlichte and Kohler); one district veterinary surgeon (Dentler); one agricultural inspector (Schmidberger); four teachers (Egger,[2] Klaus, Nussbaumer and Weber); and two newspaper editors (Eckard and Hanser). Of these, Eckard (social questions) and Weber (educational questions) may be regarded as major party spokesmen, and a number of others sometimes acted as spokesmen on day-to-day parliamentary matters. The majority were essentially back-benchers, some of whom (most notably Egger) clearly identified themselves with a third group which made up the largest single bloc in the *Fraktion*. This group was petty-bourgeois by occupation or orientation. It consisted of seven village mayors, who were usually artisans or peasants or both (Dambacher, Krug Maier, Rathgeb, Schick, Schweizer and Sommer); three peasants (Betzer, Beutel and Kessler); a publican (Schach); a small businessman (Kuen); an artisan who combined his craft with a plot of land (Herbster); and four priests (Eggmann, Keilbach, Schwarz and Späth).

We can therefore see in microcosm, in the *Landtagsfraktion* of one state, some of those features which we have seen characterised the Centre Party group in the Berlin Reichstag. There was, first, the absence of strong aristocratic leadership. The fact that the Centre emerged locally only in the 1890s meant that it never experienced in Württemberg an aristocratic phase of leadership; and the nature, as well as the timing, of the party's emergence made the likelihood of such a phenomenon remote. Many Catholic aristocrats were hostile to the new party, and it was reported that in Oberschwaben they inclined more to *Deutsche Partei* (National Liberal) candidates who had opposed the *Kulturkampf* than to more democratically-minded Centre men.[3] On the other side, it seems very likely that aristocrats were in fact deliberately

---

Further details from the *Hauptregister über die Verhandlungen der Stände des Königreichs Württemberg und der Landtagen von 1856 bis 1906*. Centre deputies elected at by-elections were traced in the *Literarische Beilage des Staats-Anzeigers für Württemberg (Chronik des Jahres)*, where by-election details are given at the end of each annual volume.

2. Egger was, in fact, a retired schoolteacher.

3. Egelhaaf, *Lebenserinnerungen*, pp. 84–5.

excluded from assuming Landtag candidacies. Gröber's antipathy towards them was well known, while there is evidence that aristocratic hopefuls for Reichstag constituencies were rejected. Thus in 1898, when Alfred Rembold wished to resign his Reichstag seat on health grounds, another Centre deputy from Württemberg, Gebhard Braun, reported to Lieber how two aristocratic applicants had been turned away by the party leadership before Rembold could finally be persuaded to stand again.[4]

Secondly, there was no upthrust of Catholic industrialists and commercial men in the Centre. Both Braun and Mauser were businessmen who represented Württemberg constituencies in Berlin, but such men were largely absent from the *Landtagsfraktion*. Over a period of twenty years the *Fraktion* contained only one merchant (Bueble), one rentier (Braunger)[5] and one factory owner (Locher), whose initial election was achieved in special circumstances as an unofficial candidate.[6] Finally, the Catholic working class in the state received no representation commensurate with its size, even when internal migration increased the so-called Catholic diaspora in the towns and cities. Between 1895 and 1914 only three secretaries of workers' associations (Andre, Graf and Gross) represented this interest. While it is true that both Bueble and Andre acted as party spokesmen and sat on Landtag committees, the narrowness of the capitalist middle-class and the working-class presence in the *Fraktion* remains noteworthy.

The main division in the Centre *Fraktion* was therefore between a group of largely legally-trained 'natural leaders' on the one hand, and a group orientated towards the problems of agriculture, *Mittelstand* and local community on the other. In Berlin this latter interest made itself felt by indirect pressure on the party leadership; at the state level the relative ease and cheapness with which they could travel to Stuttgart enabled representatives of these interests to assume a physical presence on the back benches of the *Fraktion*. It is in the tension and interplay between the attitudes of these two potentially antagonistic groups that much of the policy of the Centre in Württemberg is to be understood. It will therefore be useful to try and identify these sets of attitudes more closely.

4. Pfälzische LB Speyer, Ernst Lieber Papers, B. 35, Braun to Lieber, 30 May 1898.
5. Braunger is a difficult man to categorise. He is variously described in newspaper reports as a publican and a 'former brewer'. He certainly was the chairman of the *Wirtsverein* in Leutkirch, founded in 1894 (report in *Waldse'er Wochenblatt*, 3 January 1895). He nevertheless consistently gave his status for official purposes as *Privatier*. As there seems to be no reference to him after 1900 as a publican, and as he appears to have owed his adoption in 1900 to the fact that he stood 'above the interests', I have refrained from including him in the *Mittelstand* group in the *Fraktion*, and followed his own self-estimation.
6. See below, p. 117.

The *Honoratioren* leaders had in common a university education and legal training, and closely resembled the Centre leadership in the Reichstag. Members of the educated middle class, they emphasised the gravitas of the political calling and expected members of the parliamentary club to follow the written and unwritten rules of procedure. For all their party's exploitation of anti-governmental feelings, Centre leaders were institutional conservatives. This was true of Gröber, even if his acerbic, Swabian manner of speech and his striking, Old-Testament-prophet appearance helped to give him a reputation for radicalism among some parts of the Right in Berlin.[7] Among his colleagues, Gröber's reputation was rather one for parliamentary rectitude and an almost excessive diligence in the minutiae of committee work.[8] The deputy leader, Hans Kiene, was still more conservative in these respects: even in the turbulent and fluid situation which followed war and revolution in Württemberg, he was unwilling to take a post in the provisional all-party government until assured that this was the wish of his exiled monarch.[9]

It is significant that most of the Centre Landtag deputies who did not reside in the constituencies they represented were to be found among these men. Gröber, for example, represented the Riedlingen constituency where he had been born, but lived in Heilbronn. Alfred Rembold was a lawyer in Ravensburg who sat for Gmünd. Both men, in addition, spent much of their time in Berlin. Their perspectives were self-consciously 'statesmanlike' in placing state or national considerations over narrow constituency concerns; and they considered themselves 'above the interests' in acting as the guardians of the Centre policy of balanced justice, rather than on behalf of petty local or sectional interests. In its desire to preserve such an outlook this group was also relatively closed and self-perpetuating. While many Centre deputies sat uninterruptedly on the back-benches from 1895 onwards but were never considered as leadership material, the inner group regularly coopted new recruits with the necessary education, means and *Honoratioren* pedigree. The pattern was a common one among the bourgeois political parties; but in the Centre it was

---

7. See, for example, the letter of von Roesicke to von Böcklin, 2 June 1912, on the dangerous radicalism of Gröber. Cited, Stegmann, *Die Erben Bismarcks*, p. 324.
8. StA Cologne, Karl Bachem Papers, 7: Bachem memorandum on the Civil Code, which alludes to Gröber's 'exaggerated conscientiousness'. Karl Trimborn commented in his diary, 24 February 1902, that Gröber 'works like a horse and lives like a saint'. Cardauns, *Trimborn*, p. 72. See also Cardauns, *Gröber*, p.110.
9. T. von Pistorious, *Die letzten Tage des Königreichs Württemberg* (Stuttgart, 1936). pp. 37–8. See also Hagen, *Gestalten*, III, pp. 150 ff. Hagen also comments that Kiene's 'basic position was conservative', that he was 'above all a jurist' whose 'oath of service was sacred to him'. Kiene's main interests in the Landtag were legal and procedural questions.

especially marked. A good example is that of the Rembold brothers, Alfred and Viktor. Born into a prominent Catholic legal family, both went into private legal practice and ultimately into politics, while their two younger brothers, Siegmund and Robert, entered the medical profession.[10] Viktor, after studying in Munich and Tübingen, rose quickly in the legal world to the highest position in the corporate Bar Association (*Anwaltskammer*) of the state. He held elevated views about the dignity of station, praising what he rather extravagantly called the 'reputation for integrity' (*Titelkeuschheit*) of the advocate; and he brought the same sober sense of duty to his political career when he entered the Landtag as deputy for Aalen in 1895 and 'immediately found himself called upon as one of the leaders of the Centre'.[11] His brother Alfred was already a prominent Centre politician and Reichstag deputy when he was imposed on the safe Centre seat of Gmünd in 1900, despite fierce local opposition. He, too, immediately assumed a leading position in the *Landtagsfraktion*.

The entry of the young assistant judge, Eugen Bolz, into the leadership group in 1912 proceeded along similar lines. Bolz's father was a lawyer and three of his sisters married lawyers. His father advised the boy to follow the same career, in preference to taking orders ('They'll always need lawyers').[12] Educated in Tübingen, Bonn and Berlin, Bolz entered enthusiastically into the life of the Catholic student corporations, and in Berlin met an important contact for his future political career, the Silesian Centre leader Felix Porsch.[13] By his twenties Bolz already possessed the attributes of a natural leader of the party, and in 1911 was accepted as Reichstag candidate for the safe Centre seat of Aalen–Ellwangen–Neresheim–Gaildorf on Gröber's recommendation of him as a man standing above sectional interests.[14] Despite his youth he was also adopted as candidate for the Landtag constituency of his home town, Rottenburg, in 1912. Entering the inner group of the *Fraktion* leadership after the election, Bolz was to rise in a handful of years to the undisputed leadership of the Württemberg party. Like other successful candidates in safe Centre seats, he was the beneficiary of a determination by party leaders to bolster the expertise in the parliamentary group by encouraging men of their own kind.

In practical terms, the hold of this inner group over the *Fraktion* as a whole was expressed and consolidated by their virtual monopoly on

10. J. B. Kiene, *Viktor Rembold, Rechtsanwalt und Landtagsabgeordneter in Schwäbisch Hall* (Stuttgart, 1920), pp. 46–7.
11. Ibid, pp. 48–9.
12. Miller, *Eugen Bolz*, p. 39.
13. Ibid, pp. 49–52.
14. Ibid, p. 71; Hagen, *Gestalten*, III, pp. 205–6.

membership of key committees. Viktor Rembold, for instance, sat at different times between 1895 and 1916 on six important Landtag standing committees; on both *ad hoc* committees dealing with the reform of local government; on both dealing with educational reform; on the committee charged with adapting Württemberg law to the new civil code; and on the one dealing with new standing orders (drafted mainly by Gröber). He acted as parliamentary reporter on no less than 115 separate subjects, and shared with Gröber, Kiene, his brother and a few others the major speeches on new legislation brought before plenary sessions of the Landtag.[15] By maintaining its hold in this way, the inner group sought to exclude or neutralise the more inchoate sectional or local values which prevailed in the constituencies and found expression among a significant back-bench group in the *Fraktion*.

Representative of this group, where the values of a sometimes contradictory petty-bourgeois radicalism were foremost, was the octogenarian deputy from Ravensburg, the retired schoolteacher Theophil Egger. A member of the Left group in the Landtag before the founding of the Centre Party in Württemberg, Egger typified in his attacks on lawyers, politicians and government officials the suspicion felt by those who were excluded from the centre of power in Stuttgart. He arraigned the government bitterly for its isolation from the people, by printing for example in the *Landwirtschaftliches Wochenblatt* 'long learned articles which no peasant will read'; and for the indulgence shown by the élite towards its own kind ('They hang the small-time thief, but let the big one go').[16] He also accused the government and the political establishment of élitism in its agricultural subsidies; of favouritism towards the rich man's sport of fishing, and of concentrating (after the English pattern) on awarding prizes for cattle breeding only to the very best and most exclusively-bred animals, often from larger estates, so that 'the middling man goes away empty-handed'.[17]

If all this sat uneasily with the values of his *Fraktion* leaders, Egger was no less out of line with his anti-semitism, for since the *Kulturkampf* the great majority of important Centre leaders had followed Windthorst in rejecting anti-semitism on both principled and tactical grounds.[18]

15. Kiene, *Viktor Rembold*, pp. 52–3.
16. *33 LT, PB I*, pp. 374–7, 21 Sitz., 7.5.1895.
17. *33 LT, PB IV*. p. 2274, 107 Sitz., 24.3.1897; *33 LT, PB I*, p. 377, 21 Sitz., 7.5.1895.
18. E. Heinen, 'Antisemitische Strömungen im politischen Katholizismus während des Kulturkampfs', E. Heinen and H. J. Schoeps (eds), *Geschichte in der Gegenwart. Festschrift für Kurt Kluxen zu seinem 60. Geburtstag* (Paderborn, 1972), pp. 288, 299; K. Bachem, *Zentrumspartei*, III, p. 421; P. G. J. Pulzer, *The Rise of Political Anti-Semitism in Germany and Austria* (New York, 1964), pp. 88, 273–6.

Centre leaders in Württemberg were certainly typical in claiming to detect an imbalance between the emancipation of the Jews and the non–emancipation of Catholics, but they avoided any open expression of anti-semitism.[19] Egger, however, represented a more powerful current of feeling. For him, Jews were the instigators of a plot to subert the popular will and manipulate the honest peasant and artisan. He made perennial demands that the Württemberg authorities purchase horses directly from the peasantry and not from 'the Jews', and even brought on to the floor of the Lower House as a political issue the case of a Jewish horse dealer in Ravensburg who had been convicted of fraud.[20] On other issues like department stores, Egger saw Jewish money manipulating politicians behind the scenes.[21] This strain of petty-bourgeois radicalism was shared, if less virulently expressed, by probably a quarter to a third of the Centre *Fraktion*. As we shall see, it was to prove most dangerous to the leadership when it interlocked with broader differences over policy, particularly policy towards agriculture;[22] but there was always a gulf between the Centre leaders and back-bench critics.

This division was reinforced by the continuing parish-pump nature of politics in Württemberg.[23] If the perspectives of the leadership group were those of Stuttgart, the roots of the back-bench members of

19. A common 'outsider' status made Centre leaders unwilling to attack the Jewish minority with the weapon of exceptional legislation (just as, after 1890 at least, they opposed an anti-socialist law). But they commonly alluded to the Jewish role in 'anti-Christian' freemasonry, left liberalism, socialism and avant-garde art, as well as to the wealth of individual Jews. The residual dislike of Jews, combined with a lukewarm expression of formal tolerance, is well caught by Cardauns' comment on Gröber, that 'he was no friend of the Jews (*kein Judenfreund*), but opposed restrictions on kosher slaughtering . . .'. Cardauns, *Gröber*, p. 152.
20. See *33 LT, PB I*, p. 131, 11 Sitz., 9.3.1895; *33 LT, PB IV*, pp. 2313–14, 107 Sitz., 24.3.1897. The dealer, Salomon Einstein, had been convicted of selling a lame horse, knowing it to be lame, and sentenced to four weeks in gaol plus costs. Egger was, however, venting his spleen over rather stale news: Einstein's case and the appeal had both been heard eighteen months earlier. Report in *Waldse'er Wochenblatt*, 8 September 1895. In his speeches Egger made it clear that it was the racial rather than the criminal aspect of the case which he considered politically important. The small-town Centre newspaper made the same thing clear when they printed the names of Jews involved in criminal or bankruptcy cases in bold type and placed exclamation marks in parentheses after them. To back-benchers like Egger and papers such as the *Ipf-Zeitung*, there were few questions, whether the plight of agriculture and the *Mittelstand*, the credit system, education, art, the socialist threat, public morality or crime, in the analysis of which 'Jewish power' did not play a role.
21. *35 LT, PB IV*, p. 2676, 122 Sitz., 5.7.1902.
22. See below, Chapter Seven.
23. The residual tendency for politics in the small towns to be conceived in terms of the locality and the character of the local political representative is perhaps conveyed by the phrase which was popularly used to describe the home of Joseph Herbster, master shoemaker in Wiesensteig and Centre deputy for Geislingen: 'Bei Landtags'. Information from Fräulein Anna Herbster, of Wiesensteig, in a letter of 31 January 1975.

the *Fraktion* were firmly in their constituencies. This was true even of many of the state officials at district level. Thus Franz Xaver Nessler, an official in the Heuberg, was far removed from a man like Gröber, who divided his time between a home in Heilbronn, his constituency in Riedlingen and parliamentary obligations in Stuttgart and Berlin. Nessler was a man of the local community. His job, involving accounting and book-keeping work in eight to ten villages in the Heuberg, was the same one which his father had performed before him. He was the mayor (*Schultheiss*) of Wehingen from 1905–28 and a well-known local patron of the Wehingen gymnastic club. His election as a Centre deputy in the marginal seat of Spaichingen owed much to his championing the cause of a local railway branch line, the Heubergbahn; his part in bringing about its construction was later described in an appreciation of his life as the high-point of his political career. Until his death in 1953 he remained a man for whom the narrow Heuberg region provided the background for civic and political activity.[24]

Much the same was true of his fellow district official, Franz Speth, deputy for Wangen. He could trace his family back through four generations of estate managers, carpenters and bakers in the Kisslegg and Dietenheim villages which formed part of the constituency. He too was a mayor, in Kisslegg.[25] The basic allegiance to immediate constituency concerns was naturally even more pronounced among those who themselves sprang from the peasantry and *Mittelstand* or saw themselves as their representatives: men like Egger, whose main electoral strength was in the rural parts of the Ravensburg constituency,[26] and who was secretary of the local agricultural association;[27] Frank Xaver Krug, mayor and chairman of the agricultural loan bank in Biberach;[28] Johann Sommer, peasant, cartwright and mayor of Beizkofen in the Saulgau constituency; or Georg Maier, deputy for Rottweil, who was a peasant and mayor of Dietingen.

There was thus a wary tension between the two most important groups in the Centre *Fraktion*: between those more or less pro-governmental; between those with a Stuttgart-based and those with a constituency-based outlook; between those who wanted a

24. *Heuberger Bote*, 26 June 1953 and 25 November 1953. These newspaper cuttings and additional information provided by Herr Franz Faitsch of Wehingen, in a letter of 3 February 1975.
25. Information provided by Herr Adrian Speth of Wangen, in a letter of 25 January 1975.
26. The rural basis of Egger's support in the elections of 1895 and 1900 is specifically stressed in *Deutsches Volksblatt*, 5 February 1895, and *Schwäbischer Merkur*, 31 October 1900.
27. *33 LT, PB I*, p. 374, 21 Sitz., 7.5.1895.
28. *33 LT, PB I*, p. 143, 11 Sitz., 9.3.1895.

Fraktion with sufficient experts to man the committees and maintain a balance of class interests, and those who articulated directly the demands of a particular social group or groups. This division within the *Fraktion* was, moreover, only a reflection of the broader problems of organisation and party discipline, especially at election times, which the Centre faced in Württemberg. It is to these we shall now turn.

II

Before looking at the organisation of the Centre itself, it is important to consider what part the Catholic Church played in maintaining party discipline. Catholics lived in closed communities, particularly in small towns and villages where education and large areas of social life remained under the control of the clergy. The local priest would normally be a supporter of the Centre and use his general authority and the pulpit to discourage and hinder speakers from other parties like the SPD, especially if they came from outside the community. The Centre never denied that this occurred, arguing however that the priest was entitled to defend the Church against political attacks. Since explicit campaigning on behalf of the Centre from the pulpit would have made a priest liable to two years imprisonment under the criminal code,[29] they normally proceeded indirectly with their recommendations; telling their parishioners, for example, that they must support the candidate who upheld 'Christian principles'. There seems usually to have been little ambiguity in these pastoral directives, and there were some notorious cases of clerical influence being brought to bear in the marginal constituencies of Geislingen and Spaichingen.[30] In circumstances when Catholics felt themselves under attack — during the Landtag elections of 1906 and the Reichstag elections of 1907, for instance — the resort by both clergy and party press to defence-of-the-Church slogans became particularly shrill.[31]

29. H. Bodewig, *Geistliche Wahlbeeinflussungen in ihrer Theorie und Praxis dargestellt* (Munich, 1909), p. 56.
30. Ibid, pp. 158–60.
31. See, for example, the *Rottumbote* (Ochsenhausen), 29 November 1906: 'Are religion and the cross to be removed from the school, or should our children be brought up in the faith of Him who says "Suffer them to come unto me"? Should parents sacrifice their freedom, their faith and their children to the state which claps them increasingly into slaves' shackles? Is the Catholic ever to receive his freedom and his rights in the state which enslaves him with its taxes?' See also the appeal in Biberach of the Centre candidate, Krug, who urged electors to 'save Christian schools'. *Anzeiger vom Oberland*, 3 December 1906. Wolfgang Schulte has argued that the defensive Catholic struggle of 1907 was particularly important in the Centre's mobilisation of voters in the religiously-mixed areas of Württemberg: W. Schulte, *Struktur und Entwicklung des Parteisystems im Königreich Württemberg*, dissertation (Mannheim, 1970), pp. 120–33, esp. p. 131.

Centre campaigning tended at all times, however, to identify the interests of Church and party, an identity which was fully realised at local elections in at least one municipality where, instead of a list of Centre candidates, voters were offered a list from the Catholic *Piusverein*.[32] In addition to all this the Centre attempted, in a manner familiar to anti-clericals in all European countries, to influence the voting intentions of the enfranchised male through awakening the apprehensions of the female members of his household about the threat to the Church.[33]

Perhaps more important than overt appeals of this kind was the way in which the Church helped the Centre indirectly by creating for Catholics a distinct world within a world. Attendance at mass; reports of missionary activities overseas; the consecration of a new church organ; the rhythm of the year as it was marked out by the religious calendar; membership of Catholic charitable and social associations like the *Piusverein, Bonifatiusverein* or *Kolpingsfamilie*: these heightened the self-consciousness of Catholics in a way which cannot be overestimated. As part of the fabric of local life they established a basic community of sentiment, helping to create a parallel Catholic version of the hermetically-sealed proletarian inner world of the Social Democratic and labour movement.

The cohesiveness of this world within a world was greater in small communities than in the towns, but even here it was not complete. It frequently expressed itself at the political level, moreover, in solid opposition to an unpopular official Centre candidate. This is an indication of the difficulty involved when the importance of the religious impulse is considered in isolation. The active political role of the Church probably appeared greater and more sinister from the outside than it actually was, just as Catholics tended to exaggerate the monolithic, conspiratorial power of freemasonry. A significant number of Catholics, after all, never voted for the Centre.[34] Nor was the Church able, in disputes such as the one which broke out between

32. HStaASt, E 150, Bund 2045, Nr. 288: report from the Jagstkreis administration to the Ministry of the Interior, 23 January 1896, on the activities of the SPD and its opponents in the previous year. See also the report in *Der Oberländer*, 9 December 1896, which makes it clear that this practice was a regular one.
33. See HStaASt, Conrad Haussmann Papers, Q 1/2, 104: Centre election pamphlet, Schramberg, 22 July 1908, 'Ein ernstes Wort an unsere christlichen Frauen'.
34. The proportion of Catholics voting for the Centre Party in Reichstag elections in Württemberg was a follows: 1893, 72.2%; 1898, 80%; 1903, 82.1%; 1907, 75%; 1912, 55.2%. Schauff, *Die deutschen Katholiken*, pp. 174–5. For a discussion of how many Catholics voted for the Centre in the Landtag election of 1895, see *Deutsches Volksblatt*, 13 February 1895. The VP claimed it was only 65%; the *Deutsches Volksblatt*, after adjusting for the lower Catholic turnout and the number of virtually uncontested seats in Oberschwaben, put the figure at about 80%.

Church and Catholic teachers, to impose its own political line.[35] It is doubtful, indeed, if one can speak of the Church or the clergy having a unified political line. Not only did many parish priests have little in common with the unctuous conservatism professed at Rottenburg, but the parish clergy itself was divided along political lines, as their frequent disagreements over the selection of candidates at election times clearly showed. In this they simply mirrored the state of the Centre as a whole.

Both the unity and disunity within the Centre were ultimately the responsibility of the party itself. Like the national leaders of the Centre Party, Württemberg's Centre leaders, above all Gröber, saw the need to create modern organisational support for the party, and not to rely on the Church to convince the voter. The auxiliary organisations they helped to bring into being mobilised the energy of the local clergy on behalf of the party, not as servants of the Church but as active members of their local communities, sharing the social background and interests of the peasants and artisans among whom they lived.[36] They helped the Centre by presiding over local meetings and by their work at election times; they also contributed to keeping these social groups within the party fold by addressing themselves to practical grievances. The work of a man like Georg Dasbach in Trier, a priest who organised the local Peasant Association, had its counterpart in Württemberg in the activities of Anton Keilbach. Keilbach, founder of the newspaper *Der Schwäbische Bauer* and Centre deputy for Waldsee from 1904, was a radical parish priest who agitated on behalf of the Catholic peasantry against the holding of army manoeuvres at harvest time, organised peasant sales cooperatives and led the struggle against the organisers of rings and price-fixing among groups like the fertiliser manufacturers.[37] Keilbach's work among the peasantry, like that of Eckard and Erzberger in artisan circles and the contribution of the parish clergy who provided much of the local personnel of the *Volksverein*, helped to nurture the mass base of the Centre Party in the state.[38] The

35. See below, Chapter Four, pp. 172–3, 181.
36. The role of priests in both the local life of the community and Centre politics is illustrated by the following example. At Bellamont, the annual general meeting of the village savings and loan bank was held in December 1912, and was followed immediately by a Centre Party meeting at which a local priest exhorted those present to go to the polls in the forthcoming election. A collection for party funds then realised the sum of 18 Marks. *Anzeiger vom Oberland*, 17 December 1912.
37. *Politische Zeitfragen*, 20(Stuttgart, 1912), pp. 58–9, 65–9. See also the detailed reports on Keilbach speeches at *Volksverein* meetings in Waldsee on 3 November 1895, and Schussenried on 11 May 1897, in *Waldse'er Wochenblatt*, 5 November 1895 and 13 May 1897.
38. The extent of this mass base can be seen from the fact that one small village in the *Oberamt* of Saulgau, Herbertingen, claimed over 100 *Volksverein* members by the end of 1895. *Der Oberländer*, 4 January 1896.

proliferation of auxiliary organisations of this kind, like the growth of the party press, whose circulation in Württemberg increased from 47,300 in 1890 to 87,500 in 1903,[39] constituted a victory for Gröber's conception of political organisation over the clerical conservative conception.

Gröber's reaction to the financial plight of the newspaper *Germania* is indicative of his general attitude. Writing to Lieber, he argued that if conservative aristocrats continued to exert political pressure on the paper in exchange for their backing, and if Catholic businessmen failed to produce adequate funds in their place, the necessary money could be raised from the 'small man', with collection centres organised on a diocesan basis. For Gröber this was not just a matter of money-raising: the mobilisation of the ordinary Centre supporter by the leadership had for him a kind of moral value in itself, although in his opinion the harnessing of such support was too infrequently attempted. Gröber concluded: 'The Catholic people is much, much better than we bad sorts (*wir schlechten Kerle*) believe.'[40] This view underlay the organisation of the Centre in Württemberg: party unity and discipline were to be achieved by turning the Centre electorate into an 'army of the people', modelled closely on the SPD rather than on the more loosely organised liberal parties. The military metaphor was captured well by one Centre newspaper prior to the 1912 elections:[41]

Already in connection with [the coming election] the political and social struggle is beginning along the whole front, conducted according to the rules and with all the means of the modern age. Organisation, agitation, the press and, as a precondition of everything, the spirit of self-sacrifice, personal and in hard cash: that is the substance of the political and social techniques of war which are to be used.

The modernity of the Centre Party in terms of technical organisation took many forms. It could be seen in the attention paid by one party newspaper to the absence from the electoral register of

39. Gottwald, *Zentrum und Imperialismus*, p. 51. There was, however, considerable competition from the new commercial newspapers to what some regarded as the too-complacent Centre small-town press. See R. Richardy, 'Zur Stellung der Zentrums-Kleinpresse', *Allgemeine Rundschau* (1906), pp. 148–9. In Württemberg, the major competition came from the 1907–established *Württembergische Zeitung*: in a state where most local papers sold a few thousand copies, it had a circulation of 58,000 by 1914. Bruns, *Württemberg unter der Regierung König Wilhelms II*, p. 347.
40. Pfälzische LB Speyer, Ernst Lieber Papers, G. 24, Gröber to Lieber, 20 June 1894.
41. *Rottenburger Zeitung und Neckarbote*, 10 January 1911.

agricultural servants who changed their jobs at a particular time of the year.[42] It was evident, too, in the production and sale of three-*Pfennig* postcards which satirised political opponents like Conrad Haussmann while raising money for the party.[43] It found expression above all in what one government report described as the 'brisk activity'[44] of organisations like the *Volksverein*; a judgment confirmed by the reports appearing regularly in the local press. This level of organisation became more intensive still during election campaigns. In the sixteen days prior to the 1906 Landtag elections, for example, Franz Xaver Krug addressed thirty-one meetings in different parts of the Biberach constituency.[45] Six years later the candidate for Waldsee, Josef Mohr, exceeded even this with an itinerary of two to three daily meetings.[46] All this was very far removed in substance and style from the conservative concept of *Honoratioren* politics, in which patronage provided what support was needed for a loose party organisation, while deputies were automatically elected by virtue of their station, without having to go through the vulgar motions of campaigning.

Nor was organisation just a matter of reaching down to the localities. The structure of the Centre Party demonstrated also the importance attached by the inner leadership group to the placating of sectional grievances. In a process which began in the Rhineland and quickly found acceptance in southern and western states like Württemberg, Centre leaders realised the need to incorporate the different interests within the formal organisational structure.[47] The object was to ensure that no single group could complain of being neglected. Thus the full state committee of the Centre in Württemberg had 264 members: 39 priests, 35 officials, 24 teachers, 23 members of the free professions, 88 representing the interests of artisans, small businesses and workers, and 55 for the agricultural interest.[48] The size and composition of the constituency committees similarly reflected the desire to build in the broadest possible range of interests. In Leutkirch, 130 *Vertrauensmänner* were present to select an election candidate in

42. *Anzeiger vom Oberland*, 6 December 1906.
43. See report in the *Schwäbische Tagwacht*, 30 November 1906.
44. HStaASt, E 150, Bund 2046, Nr. 92. Report from Jagstkreis administration to Ministry of Interior on activities of SPD and its opponents in previous year. Ellwangen, 23 January 1903.
45. *Anzeiger vom Oberland*, 7 and 23 November 1906.
46. Ibid, 9 November 1912.
47. See Nipperdey, *Organisation*, pp. 268–9.
48. *Waldse'er Wochenblatt*, 5 February 1895. The representatives from Waldsee itself were two priests (one of them Keilbach), a teacher, a master shoemaker, a painter, a businessman, a publican and two peasants.

1900,[49] while four years earlier 92 men 'from all classes and all parts of the constituency' had turned out before a by-election in Saulgau for a similar purpose.[50] This was actually a smaller number than normal for a safe Centre seat. Evidence from constituencies such as Laupheim, Neresheim and Ravensburg suggests a range of attendance of 100 to 150 *Vertrauensmänner* with voting rights.[51] The number was less in seats where the Centre was a minority party: only 66 were present at a Neckarsulm meeting in 1912 which was described as 'well-attended'.[52] On the other hand, the same year saw a turn-out of over 200 *Vertrauensmänner* in Biberach for a particularly hard-fought candidate selection.[53] In Reichstag constituencies, moreover, which were roughly four times as large, this figure was usual.

There can be no doubting the scale and intensity of the political mobilisation achieved by the Centre. Nevertheless, one cannot speak of a democratisation of the party: while broad social groups were formally incorporated within the party organisation, real power remained in a few hands. This was true even at constituency level, and the previously mentioned selection of a candidate at Biberach in 1912 offers a good illustration.[54] The decision to drop the sitting deputy, Krug, and put up Eugen Graf in his place was in line with the Stuttgart leadership's desire to achieve greater balance and expertise in the *Fraktion*. The decision was made by the eighteen-man executive of the constituency committee and strongly backed by the local Centre newspaper, which echoed Stuttgart in speaking of the need for a candidate who did 'not simply pursue parish-pump politics'.[55] The vote of the 200 assembled *Vertrauensmänner* was therefore an endorsement of a prior decision taken at a higher level. This procedure seems to have been common. Moreover, what was true of the ordinary member of a constituency committee applied still more to rank-and-file Centre supporters as a whole. They were expected to vote loyally, but not to take any initiatives. In one sense, of course, all parties demanded political discipline; but in the case of the Centre the assumption that natural

---

49. *Schwäbischer Merkur*, 8 November 1900. In 1912 the number was 120: *Deutsches Volksblatt*, 2 October 1912.
50. *Der Oberländer*, 5 September 1896.
51. There were 134 at Laupheim in 1912 at a 'well-attended' meeting; Neresheim had 152 in 1906, 104 in 1912; Ravensburg 112 in 1912. See *Schwäbische Tagwacht*, 6 November 1906, 23 October 1912; *Deutsches Volksblatt*, 8 October 1912.
52. *Deutsches Volksblatt*, 26 August 1912.
53. At the two major meetings of *Vertrauensmänner*, there were aggregate voting figures of 179 and 219.
54. The account which follows is based largely on reports in the *Anzeiger vom Oberland*, 13–15 November 1912.
55. Ibid, 15 November 1912.

leaders should be followed was greater. While the VP appealed to its supporters as citizens and the SPD addressed its followers as comrades, the Centre significantly saw its voters as a dutiful flock to be kept within the fold.[56] As we shall see, chiding and exhortation were by no means always a sufficient guarantee of loyalty. But when they worked and were combined with a high standard of technical organisation, they produced a remarkable degree of electoral discipline. The following figures for three districts of the Biberach constituency in the 1900 Landtag election give an illustration of this:[57]

District	Enfranchised	Number who voted	Centre votes
Altheim	131	115	115
Ingerkingen	115	96	96
Lingenschemmern	109	93	93

Even more striking was the electoral pattern at Riedlingen in 1912, when every enfranchised male went to the polls in 33 out of 53 electoral districts and every one voted for the Centre candidate, Gröber, who collected 97 per cent of all votes cast in the constituency as a whole.

For all their insistence on the value of organisation, the Centre's 'natural leaders' in Stuttgart sought to modernise the politics of deference rather than to abolish them. Significantly the party did not hold conferences but assemblies (*Landesversammlungen*); and an analysis of one of these assemblies, at Gmünd in November 1900, illustrates well the respective roles of leaders and led.[58] The principal speakers were the assembled leaders: Gröber, Eckard, the Rembold brothers and two senior clergyman in the state, the latter being members of the *Fraktion* who represented the Catholic Church among the unelected 'privileged' deputies (*Privilegierten*) in the Lower House. In addition, two local priests sat with the platform leadership for the occasion. The accounts and explanations of the party's policy having been delivered, the assembly was then addressed by five local supporters of the Centre: a bookbinder who was secretary of the Gmünd *Volksverein*, a cabinet maker, a smallholder and local village mayor, a silversmith and an engraver. The role of these speakers was clear: it was acclamatory, a formal expression of satisfaction with the pronouncements of the state leadership. The pattern of the assembly corresponded to the way in which the Centre had acquired its broad-based organisation, from

56. On the greater 'feeling for authority' among Catholic voters, and on the natural leadership assumed by the priest and village mayor, see the remarks in Egelhaaf, *Lebenserinnerungen*, p. 81.
57. *Anzeiger vom Oberland*, 10 December 1900.
58. Details taken from *Politische Zeitfragen*, 5(Stuttgart, 1903): 'Landesversammlung der württembergischen Zentrumspartei zu Gmünd vom 11. November 1900'.

the top downwards; it also reflected the broader, non-democratic reality of the relationship between party and supporters. The Centre had no actual members. Those who were its natural supporters — attending meetings, reading the party press, voting — had no institutionalised means by which they could work to enforce their own views.

III

As we have seen at Reich level, however, the Centre was particularly susceptible at election times to the threat of double candidacies in safe seats, and this factor also operated at the state level, tempering the concentration of power held by party leaders within the Centre. This was a recurring problem for the leadership in successive Landtag elections in Württemberg. In 1895 the official Centre candidates were opposed by unofficial ones in Ellwangen and Saulgau.[59] In the 1900 elections there were double candidacies in no less than six constituencies, while in 1906 and 1912 there was further trouble in the constituencies of Biberach, Ehingen (Kiene's seat), Horb, Laupheim, Neresheim, Rottenburg and Saulgau.[60] By-elections also provided an opportunity for

59. In Ellwangen the unofficial candidate, Dambacher, polled 933 votes to the 2,241 for the official candidate, Rathgeb. See *Deutsches Volksblatt*, 5 and 7 February 1895. The double candidacy in Saulgau in 1895 is mentioned in *Der Oberländer*, 19 November 1896.
60. On the opposition to the Centre's decision to put up Graf in place of Krug in Biberach, *Anzeiger vom Oberland*, 12–15 November 1912. Earlier reports, which turned out to be accurate, can be found in *Schwäbische Tagwacht*, 26 July, 16 August 1912. In Ehingen, Kiene was opposed in 1906 by a group of 'Free Catholics' who had also contested the 1900 election: *Deutsches Volksblatt*, 4 December 1906; *Schwäbische Tagwacht*, 8 November 1906. In Horb in 1912 the sitting deputy, Kessler (the election winner in 1900 as an unofficial candidate) campaigned against the official candidate, Schweizer. *Schwäbische Tagwacht*, 23 October 1912; *Deutsches Volksblatt*, 24 October 1912; *Anzeiger vom Oberland*, 16 November 1912. On the background to the dropping of Kessler as Centre candidate, *Schwäbische Tagwacht*, 25 July, 6 August 1912. In Laupheim the official candidate in 1906, Schick, was faced by an unofficial candidate, Hetzel. *Deutsches Volksblatt*, 30 November 1906. In 1912 Schick's son was adopted officially by the Centre, but local opposition led to the substituting by the party of a new official candidate, Kohler. He was then the victim of opposition from the aggrieved Schick. *Schwäbische Tagwacht*, 27, 31 July 1912; 23, 29 October 1912; *Deutsches Volksblatt*, 2 November 1912. In Neresheim, the sitting deputy, Vogler, was dropped by the *Vertrauensmänner* in 1906, probably on the grounds of age (he was 76). Schmid was selected in his place, but Vogler seems to have made some desultory attempts to campaign unofficially. *Schwäbische Tagwacht*, 7, 20 November 1906; *Deutsches Volksblatt*, 4 December 1906. In Rottenburg, the sitting deputy, Schach, was allegedly forced to sign a statement prior to the selection of a candidate saying that he would not allow himself to be considered. As in a number of other cases, this was probably a rather heavy-handed attempt to drop an ageing deputy. *Schwäbische Tagwacht*, 1 July 1912. On apparent divisions in Saulgau, see ibid, 7, 8 August 1912.

regular local revolts: at Gmünd and Saulgau in 1896, Ravensburg in 1902, Waldsee in 1903 and Wangen in 1905.[61]

A closer examination of the widespread revolt in 1900 indicates both the attempts made by the leadership to influence the choice of candidates, and the way in which this was resisted and often overturned in practice by the recalcitrance of local Centre voters. The 1900 election followed a period of indiscipline within the *Fraktion* and the growing activity of extra-parliamentary interest groups. The leadership, in trying to control the composition of the newly-elected Centre deputies, had a number of particular concerns: to provide a social balance in the *Fraktion*; to assert the balanced justice of the Centre programme against specific interest groups' demands; and to secure sufficient experts to represent the Centre on Landtag committees.[62] They worked on the selection of candidates accordingly. In Ravensburg the Centre seems to have tried to depose the awkward Egger.[63] In the Tettnang constituency Kiene, who was holidaying at nearby Lake Constance at the time, met in the village of Hemigkosen with a handful of local *Vertrauensmänner*, mostly priests, to impress on them the value of the sitting deputy, Bueble, in the discussion of financial and tax questions. At a full constituency meeting a few days later his advice was followed.[64] In Leutkirch a letter from Gröber was read out at the meeting to select a candidate, asking that someone be elected who would be able to work in committee. This strengthened the hand of a local group which wished to see the election of Braunger rather than the sitting deputy, Eggmann; and on a close second ballot Braunger received seventy-one votes to his opponent's fifty-seven at a full constituency committee meeting.[65] In Wangen, the claims of a local small businessman, Kuen, were passed over in favour

61. On Gmünd, see HStaASt, E 14, Fasz. 538, Nr. 3316: election report, 11 December 1896; also reports in *Der Oberländer*, 2 and 9 December 1896. On Saulgau there is a series of reports in *Der Oberländer*, 26 August, 15 September, 18–19 November, which provide details of the double candidacy. On Ravensburg, Waldsee and Wangen, see HStaASt, E 14, Fasz. 538, Nr. 3071, 3411, 1355: election reports of 29 October 1902, 21 November 1903 and 15 June 1905 respectively. In all of these cases the unofficial candidate polled a considerable number of votes, and in Wangen in 1905 the unofficial candidate, village mayor Speth (who did not even campaign), beat the official candidate Metzler, an Ulm lawyer, by 1,503 votes to 1,245.
62. See the speech by Gröber to the members of the *Fraktion*, in the Stuttgart Europäischer Hof hotel on the eve of the election campaign, drawing attention to the dangers of sectionalism and interest politics. Reported in *Gmünder Tagblatt*, 11 November 1900. On the comparable Centre practice in neighbouring Baden of imposing 'committee experts' on local constituencies, see J. Becker (ed), *Heinrich Köhler 1878—1949. Lebenserinnerungen* (Stuttgart, 1964), pp. 28–9.
63. *Schwäbischer Merkur*, 31 October 1900.
64. Ibid, 4 and 6 October 1900.
65. Ibid, 7 November 1900; *Heuberger Bote*, 17 and 21 November 1900.

of the priest, Hofmann (already a Reichstag deputy), a decision apparently influenced by the hostility of the Stuttgart leadership to Kuen on account of his past political record.[66] Finally, in Gmünd, where internal squabbles had characterised the party throughout the 1890s, the leadership disregarded both likely local candidates and recommended to the constituency committee a man of proven reliability, the Ravensburg lawyer and Reichstag deputy, Alfred Rembold.[67]

This exercise in heavy-handed leadership rebounded badly. It was widely seen as a transparent favouring of 'outside' candidates and a snub to local interests: the outcome was a storm of protest from the constituencies. In Ravensburg, Egger relied on his rural popularity to resist attempts to unseat him.[68] In Tettnang, the decision to put up Bueble produced two unofficial Centre candidates: the factory owner Locher from Friedrichshafen, where Bueble was unpopular for his opposition to the Friedrichshafen–Markdorf railway line; and Schmid, a village mayor. In the first ballot of the election Bueble only narrowly held off this double challenge, polling 1,369 votes against 1,131 for Locher and 583 for Schmid. In the second ballot, however, Locher was able to beat the official candidate.[69] In Leutkirch, the decision to run Braunger rather than the sitting deputy of twenty-two years standing, Eggmann, produced 'opposition among large parts of the electorate'. At a meeting in Rossberg, Eggmann was put up as an unofficial candidate and at a further meeting in Wurzach, attended by over two hundred people, it was resolved by those present 'under no circumstances' to support Braunger. In the following weeks the Centre Party in Leutkirch was entirely split, and at the election Eggman showed the strength of feeling in the constituency by polling 1,000 of the 3,000 votes cast.[70]

In Wangen, the success of the rebels was much greater. The favoured local candidate, Kuen, was put up unofficially against Hofmann and the latter bowed to the weight of hostile opinion by standing down, leaving Kuen with an unopposed victory in the election.[71] In Gmünd, despite the energy with which the press and local party organisation supported Rembold, the rival candidacy of

66. *Schwäbischer Merkur*, 6 and 10 December 1900.
67. *Heuberger Bote*, 4 December 1900.
68. *Schwäbischer Merkur*, 31 October, 1 December 1900.
69. Ibid, 8 November, 6 December 1900.
70. *Heuberger Bote*, 17, 20, 21 November and 4 December 1900; *Schwäbischer Merkur*, 7, 8, 15, 26 November and 6 December 1900; *Gmünder Tagblatt*, 19 November 1900.
71. *Heuberger Bote*, 20 November and 4 December 1900; *Ipf-Zeitung*, 13 November 1900; *Schwäbischer Merkur*, 10, 17 November and 6 December 1900.

Klaus was announced by a group which resented the imposition of an outside lawyer on the constituency:[72]

> As there is in our area in truth no lack of fitting and capable persons, we shall under no circumstances give our votes to anyone other than a resident of the district . . . we oppose categorically the slogan put about here that Gmünd must of necessity send off another lawyer to the Landtag, just to provide it with another committee member. If necessary, we can point to a sensational example where this practice by the dominant party was resisted (Karle-Streich). Moreover, were this to become general, it would lead to the Landtag, where all classes should be represented, being turned into a monopoly, a domain of the lawyers, from which may God preserve us.

The anti–Rembold opposition argued that a lawyer with a practice in Ravensburg and a Reichstag seat in Berlin would have little opportunity to represent his constituents' views if elected to the Landtag. They contrasted the success in lobbying for local branch lines achieved by a railway-conscious deputy in Pforzheim (on the Baden–Württemberg border) with what they might expect from an outsider in Gmünd. After an extremely bitter campaign, Klaus achieved 1,465 votes on the first ballot against 2,447 for Rembold, and it required a second ballot before the official Centre candidate eventually won.[73] In two other constituencies the local electorate also reacted strongly against the official Centre candidate. In Waldsee, Beutel was opposed first by a teacher, Schätzle, then finally in the election by a village mayor, Feuerstein, who polled 1,225 votes to Beutel's 2,012.[74] In Horb, an unofficial Centre candidate, Kessler, was more successful: he polled 1,719 votes, while the official candidate Nussbaumer could secure only 1,264.[75]

In an election which clearly showed the limits of the leadership's power, the Centre was therefore faced with three men — Locher, Kuen and Kessler — who had successfully come through as unofficial candidates. The leading party newspaper, the *Deutsches Volksblatt*, commented ruefully on the lack of party discipline among 'broad sections' of the Centre electorate.[76] Nevertheless, after this

72. *Gmünder Tagblatt*, 24 November 1900; *Schwäbischer Merkur*, 26 November 1900.
73. *Gmünder Tagblatt*, 28 November, 1 and 5 December 1900; *Schwäbischer Merkur*, 6 December 1900.
74. *Schwäbischer Merkur*, 8 November and 6 December 1900.
75. *Heuberger Bote*, 15 November and 4 December 1900: *Gmünder Tagblatt*, 16 November 1900; *Schwäbischer Merkur*, 8, 14 November and 6 December 1900.
76. *Deutsches Volksblatt*, 6 December 1900.

demonstration of popular disaffection, the Stuttgart leadership showed itself strikingly pragmatic in conceding defeat. All three unofficial election victors were accepted into the *Fraktion*; indeed, four years later one of them — Locher — was chairman of the party's state assembly in Ravensburg.[77] In the same way the leadership on a number of occasions accepted as official Centre candidates men who had previously stood unofficially against the party.[78]

Many contemporary political commentators noted the capacity of the Centre Party to absorb and incorporate the pressure of various interest groups. This was one of the characteristics which gave the party its reputation for unreliability and cynicism. The behaviour of the Stuttgart leadership both before and after the 1900 Landtag elections is one example of how a belief in strong leadership was always tempered in the Centre by a willingness to placate and accommodate special interests, whether local or economic. This sponge-like quality enabled the Centre to avoid an open break with any part of its electorate in Württemberg, just as at the Reich level it prevented the secession of the agrarian or Bavarian wing of the party. Short-term party stability was guaranteed in this way, but at some cost to political consistency. For, as we shall see, it was not just at election times but in its whole political conduct that the Centre Party was coloured by an awareness of the tactical needs of the moment which often bordered on demagogy; and this mode of politics was itself produced by that tension which always existed between the outlook of the leadership in Stuttgart and its electorate in the localities.

77. *Politische Zeitfragen*, 8(Stuttgart, 1905): 'Landesversammlung der württembergischen Zentrumspartei zu Ravensburg vom 8. und 9. Januar 1905'.
78. This happened with Dambacher in Ellwangen, unofficial candidate in 1895, official in 1900; with Sommer in Saulgau, unofficial candidate in 1895 and 1896, officially adopted in 1900; and with Speth in Wangen, successful unofficial candidate in a 1905 by-election, official candidate the following year.

CHAPTER 4

The Centre Party
and the Era of Reform
in Württemberg

I

1895 was a great political climacteric in Württemberg. The elections to
the Landtag in that year saw the belated emergence of a party system
appropriate to the late nineteenth century, while the decade and a half
which followed were a period of profound institutional transformation
in the state. It is the role of the Centre Party in this process of
institutional change — the *Reformära* — which this chapter seeks to
elucidate.

In the years prior to the dissolution of the Württemberg Landtag for
the 1895 elections, the party system was an archaic one, an expression
of the political divisions of the mid-century or the 1860s rather than
those of the 1890s.[1] There were three main political groupings. Two
of these reflected the political alignments of 1848: a pro-governmental
Landespartei, consisting of many of the non-elected *Privilegierten* of the
Lower House and some other elected conservative deputies, both
Protestant and Catholic; and a largely anti-governmental Left, based
on the core of the VP but also containing a number of
democratically-minded Catholics. The third group was the *Deutsche
Partei* (DP), the Württemberg branch of the National Liberal Party,
whose political cohesion was based largely on its members' common
acceptance of the 1871 solution to the German question. Other aspects
of Württemberg politics prior to 1895 also emphasised the archaic
character of this system of loose party groupings: the continuing
presence of independents who belonged to no party; the number of
uncontested seats at elections; and the use of government influence at
elections on behalf of the *Landespartei* and the usually pro-
governmental DP.

1. On the pre-1895 party system, see Grube, *Der Stuttgarter Landtag*, p. 545; Simon, *Die
württembergischen Demokraten*, p. 55.

Changes in the first half of the 1890s had already shown the inadequacy of this system to reflect the real political and social divisions of the time. The VP, under the new leadership of the Haussmann brothers and Friedrich Payer, began to conduct itself politically less like a party of simple anti-governmental 48ers.[2] The DP adopted a more modern programme, its new departure symbolised by the adoption of the name National Liberal Party in its full title.[3] Finally, two new political forces appeared in the state, the Centre Party and the *Bauernbund*, while the SPD became significantly more active after the lifting of the anti-socialist law. At the 1895 elections the old mould was finally fractured. Both Left and *Landespartei* disappeared, the former splitting up into its constituent parts, the latter reduced to a Conservative rump. The VP returned to the Landtag as the strongest political party, replacing the former hegemony of the pro-governmental grouping; and SPD, Centre and *Bauernbund* were formally represented in the Lower House for the first time.[4]

The break constituted by 1895 was in some ways as decisive as that of 1848. On both occasions reforming members were elected on a wave of political and economic dissatisfaction, after a period of stalemate under a supine governmental majority in the Landtag; on both occasions the king and his ministers absorbed popular feeling by making concessions to the demand for reform; and on both occasions the unity of the reformers was soured by increasing conflict and bitterness between its different wings. Despite the great differences already noted between VP and Centre, these two parties, the largest in the new Landtag, represented a common groundswell of popular dissatisfaction with governmental apathy. Both styled themselves parties of the people (*Volksparteien*) and their programmes had in common demands for constitutional, economic, fiscal and local government reforms, and more generally for an end to recalcitrance in high places.[5] After the election the Centre demonstrated its commitment to reform by voting for the VP leader, Payer, as president of the Lower House, while the VP reciprocated by supporting the Centre deputy leader, Kiene, for the post of vice-president.[6] In the first three years following the election, Gröber and Kiene cooperated with VP leaders in the Landtag, as the

2. Menzinger, *Verfassungsrevision und Demokratisierungsprozess*, p. 142; Simon, *Die württembergischen Demokraten*, pp. 14–17.
3. Menzinger, *Verfassungsrevision und Demokratisierungsprozess*, p. 145; Egelhaaf, *Lebenserinnerungen*, p. 79.
4. Generally on the climacteric of 1895: Grube, *Der Stuttgarter Landtag*, pp. 549–50; Egelhaaf, *Württembergische Vierteljahrshefte für Landesgeschichte* (1916), pp. 606 ff.
5. Burkart, *Die Zusammensetzung*, p. 113.
6. Payer, 'Mein Lebenslauf', p. 38; Simon, *Die württembergischen Demokraten*, p. 56.

negotiations went on between ministers and party leaders over a programme of reforms.

Reforms did, indeed, materialise. In the decade and a half after 1895, positive cooperation between government and parties in the Landtag brought about far-reaching changes in the state's institutional fabric: revision of the constitution, changes in the educational system (the first major change since 1836), the introduction of income tax and reforms in local government.[7] This process of reform was concentrated particularly in the legislative sessions between 1900 and 1906 (subsequently known as the *Reformlandtag*) when the most important measure of all, revision of the constitution, was carried through. The Lower House became a purely elected chamber, its twenty-three *Privilegierten* removed to the Upper House. No comparable substitute was created for these excluded non-elected members, although successive governments had always insisted on the need for such a creation. Instead, the number of members elected directly in constituencies was increased from seventy to seventy-five, with Stuttgart providing the extra number; and these were to be joined, under the new constitutional rubric, by a further seventeen deputies elected from the state as a whole (divided into two large 'constituencies') from party lists, on the principle of proportional representation. For these elections, as for those in the single-member constituencies, the suffrage was to be direct, universal for males over twenty-five, and secret.[8] Charles James Fox had cited Württemberg nearly a century before as the only state in Europe possessing a constitution comparable with that of England:[9] by 1910 it had consolidated its reputation as the foremost democratic state in Germany.

In this process of democratisation, with its high point in the reform of the constitution, the VP took the leadership.[10] The reforms which it helped to achieve were a rehearsal for the later attempts made by its leaders, Payer and Conrad Haussmann — as leaders of the nationally-based *Deutsche Volkspartei* — to transform similarly the structure of the Reich, and for their attempts, as major participants at

---

7. On the measures of the *Reformära* as a whole, see Egelhaaf, V. Bruns (ed), *Württemberg unter der Regierung König Wilhelms II*, pp. 28–42.
8. Menzinger, *Verfassungsrevision und Demokratisierungsprozess*, p. 168; Grube, *Der Stuttgarter Landtag*, p. 552.
9. Burkart, *Die Zusammensetzung*, p. 3.
10. Marquardt, *Geschichte Württembergs*, p. 348; Menzinger, *Verfassungsrevision und Demokratisierungsprozess*, p. 143. The VP, of course, made much political capital out of their leadership of the reform movement. See T. Liesching, *Zur Geschichte der württembergischen Verfassungsreform im Landtag 1901–1906* (Tübingen, 1906).

the Weimar Constituent Assembly, to establish a German state based on democratic principles.[11] Their contribution to reform at the state level consisted partly in the constant pressure they exercised on the government through interpellation, debate and popular meetings, but also in a willingness to accept compromise where necessary. The rhetorical gifts of the Haussmann brothers and other VP tribunes thus complemented the mediating talents of Payer.[12] Following the lead given by the VP, other parliamentary groups supported the reform movement, including the DP and the comparatively flexible local SPD.[13]

The government itself also played an important role by responding positively to the overtures from the parties and by applying its constitutional prerogatives with reserve. The leading ministers, headed by successive Prime Ministers (von Mittnacht, von Breitling and von Weizsäcker), worked with the party leaders in drafting new legislation. Other ministers, like von Pischek, von Zeyer and von Fleischhauer, were favourably disposed towards the current of reform.[14] Even when the government had misgivings it was often prepared to accept a particular measure of reform if harmonious dealings with the parties would otherwise be jeopardised. A good example concerns the election of deputies by proportional representation. During the 1897 negotiations over constitutional reform this was clearly a proposal which aroused governmental concern: it was feared that elections via party lists in large constituencies would incorporate into the constitution the principle of representation of 'mere numbers'; that it would undermine the position of the individual deputy and his close ties with constituents, with corresponding accretions of power to highly-disciplined party organisations; that it would go too far towards removing the *de facto* advantages enjoyed by rural over urban voters; and that it would tend to weaken Württemberg's reputation among the other German states, who would brand her a dangerous innovator. But for tactical reasons, and to maintain good relations with the political parties (who by 1897 overwhelmingly favoured proportional representation), the government accepted the measure.[15] Finally, Wilhelm II, the theoretical head of government to whom ministers were accountable, did not interfere with the reforming course of his appointees. His restraint was later praised by all,

11. Simon, *Die württembergischen Demokraten*, pp. 98 ff.
12. Ibid, pp. 16, 63 ff.
13. Schlemmer, *Die Rolle der Sozialdemokratie*, pp. 46–50, 56 ff.
14. Menzinger, *Verfassungrevision und Demokratisierungsprozess*, pp. 152–3, 159 ff. All the sources note what Simon (p. 67) calls the 'atmosphere of cooperation'.
15. HStaASt, E 41, Anhang II, Bü 4: 'Votum des Staatsministeriums', pp. 1–13.

including arch-reformer Conrad Haussmann and Social Democrat Wilhelm Keil.[16]

Until 1898 the Centre Party went along with the movement for reform, but after that date was increasingly unwilling to do so. Despite broad agreement with the VP after 1898 on measures such as local government reform, the anger generated on both sides by conflict over constitutional and educational revisions so poisoned relations that common political action of a sustained kind was not possible for the two parties until after the war.[17] In 1898 the VP was in sharp disagreement with the refusal of the Centre, as the second largest party in the Lower House, to meet the challenge of the Upper House to tax reforms drawn up by Finance Minister von Zeyer. The Upper House demanded a *quid pro quo* for its support of income tax, one which constituted an effective extension of its budget rights. The Centre balked at an outright constitutional trial of strength, the reform was shelved and the two largest parties in the Lower House exchanged mutual charges, on the one side of pusillanimity, on the other of reckless bravado.[18] The reforms eventually found their way on to the statute book through a compromise solution devised by von Zeyer; but by that time the issue of constitutional reform itself had come between the two parties as a more serious quarrel.

After supporting the constitutional draft bill in its first reading in 1897, the Centre announced abruptly in April 1898 that its future support would be conditional on obtaining 'as a substitute for the protection of the confessional minority provided by the First Chamber [Upper House], a precise stipulation of the rights of the Bishop [of Rottenburg] guaranteed in Article 78 of the constitution'.[19] The Centre sought, in fact, a permanent anchoring of episcopal rights as a means of counteracting the proposed changes in the Upper House, which would have robbed the latter of its natural Catholic majority. The claim entailed, however, not only a confirmation of the bishop's control over education in Catholic schools but an essential shift in Church–State relations, for the amendment the party introduced claimed for the bishop the right to establish clerical orders in Württemberg.[20] On the predictable failure of the Centre to achieve a parliamentary majority for such a concession it voted against the

16. Grube, *Der Stuttgarter Landtag*, p. 548; Simon, *Die württembergischen Demokraten*, pp. 48–9. Conrad Haussmann was later to call Wilhelm II 'the most democratic king in Germany'.
17. Simon, *Die württembergischen Demokraten*, p. 56.
18. *33 LT, PB VIII*, p. 5388, 254 Sitz., 22.12.1898.
19. *33 LT, PB VI*, p. 4322, 198 Sitz., 5.4.1898. The *Initiativantrag* to this effect is in *33 LT, BB IX*, p. 190, Beilage 284. See also Grube, *Der Stuttgarter Landtag*, p. 550.
20. *33 LT, PV VI*, pp. 4631 ff, 214 Sitz., 11.15.1898.

reform proposals in their entirety on subsequent readings and played the chief role in denying them a majority.[21]

When inter-*Fraktion* talks were held on VP initiative prior to the introduction of a new constitutional bill in 1904, only the Centre was not represented.[22] The issue had by that stage been complicated by Centre intransigence over educational reform, and the other parties had reacted by coupling the two measures together and passing a Lower House resolution calling on the government 'to reform the state supervision of schools by introducing constitutional revision'.[23] The seeming arrogance of the Centre had produced a result in party-political terms which was a paradigm of its position in the Reich as a whole. The party was attacked for wilful and single-minded abuse of its key parliamentary position, and the VP was able to construct an anti-Centre majority in the Lower House which carried both educational and constitutional reforms.[24] These events, which preceded the Landtag elections of 1906, anticipated the formation of the Bülow Bloc, when common opposition to the Centre as an unscrupulous clerical party exploiting its key position became the basis of an electoral alliance of National Liberals, Conservatives and Progressives in 1907. Local conflicts in Württemberg therefore both reinforced and were a part of the broader pattern of Wilhelmine politics; and the reasons why the Centre did not support the VP-led era of reform in Württemberg illustrate the broader contours of the mutual antipathy of Centre and Progressives in the Reich.

II

The VP led the accusations made by the other parties that the stubbornness of the Württemberg Centre was grounded in its primary allegiance to the Church, its policy simply the opportunist pursuit of narrow confessional interest. Thus it attacked the 'predominance of clericalism',[25] and Conrad Haussmann's election committee in 1907 warned: 'The Centre pursues in an unscrupulous manner its egoistic . . . ultramontane ends and carries on a degrading horse-trading

---

21. *33 LT, PB VIII*, p. 5364, 253 Sitz., 21.12.1898; Burkart, *Die Zusammensetzung*, p. 114.
22. Liesching, *Zur Geschichte*, pp. 6–8; Menzinger, *Verfassungsrevision und Demokratisierungsprozess*, pp. 160–1.
23. *35 LT, PB VIII*, p. 5283, 230 Sitz., 16.6.1904.
24. Menzinger, *Verfassungsrevision und Demokratisierungsprozess*, pp. 161–2; Burkart, *Die Zusammensetzung*, p. 119.
25. HStaASt, Conrad Haussmann Papers, Q1/2, 104. The phrase is taken from the electoral address of the VP state committee for the 1906 Landtag election.

(*Kuhhandelspolitik*) with the most vital interests of the people and the nation.'[26] There were many attacks along the same lines from the other political parties. The government took a similar view. It argued that the Centre would never support a constitutional revision which weakened or diluted the power of the Catholic aristocracy in the Upper House; and, in considering the effects of proportional representation, saw as one of its drawbacks the prospect of being delivered into the hands of the 'clerical' Centre.[27]

Confessional motives certainly played a significant part in the formulation of Centre policy on the major reform issues. It is a telling sign that the Centre was able to compromise with the government and the other parties over measures of local government and fiscal reform, and that it was the two central issues where the position of the Church was at stake — the constitution and education — where it dug in its heels. As we have seen, Centre support for constitutional reform was made conditional on a very specific concession to the Church; and while the Centre (like the other parties) modified its position on the constitutional question over the years, this demand was a constant after 1898. There seems little doubt also that the Centre's position by 1905 had changed markedly from that of 1894 or 1897, and that some of the reasons it advanced on the later occasion for opposing reform were used, at least partly, as a means of justifying an opposition actually based on a simple defence of Church interests.

It is true that one of these later reasons given for opposition — the absence of any corporate representation of economic interests in the re-cast Lower House[28] — was by no means a sudden and alien intrusion into traditional Centre thinking.[29] The idea was present, in an extreme conservative form, in the unofficial Oberdörffer programme devised by the Centre right wing in the 1890s.[30] More in the mainstream of the party, it was a favourite theme — almost a hobby-horse — of Franz Hitze, the Centre expert on social policy and

---

26. Ibid. VP pamphlet to 'Die Wähler des IX Wahlkreises', before the second ballot contest between Centre and VP. A more detailed critique of the Centre's position on constitutional reform can be found in D. Saul, *Die Verfassungsrevision in Württemberg* (Frankfurt/Main, 1899), pp. 17–32.
27. HStaASt, E 41, Anhang II, Bü 4: 'Votum des Staatsministeriums', pp. 2, 8–10.
28. *36 LT, PB IV*, pp. 2630–1, 2643–6. 100 Sitz. 14.6.1905.
29. Compare, however, the Centre demands of 1898 and after with their initial response to the government proposals in 1897, when no mention was made by the party of corporate representation: HStaASt, E 41, Anhang II, Bü 4, Kiene (on behalf of Centre *Fraktion*) to the government, 16 March 1897.
30. On the Oberdörffer programme, see StA Cologne, Karl Bachem Papers, 14: 'Oberdörffer'sches Programm'.

a *Volksverein* leader.[31] The concept had also received encouragement in the past from Gröber himself.[32] Moreover, as Hans Kiene pointed out in attempting to counter charges of Centre inconsistency and hypocrisy, things had changed since the Centre first took up its position on constitutional reform in 1894: legislation in the Reich (supported by the party) on agriculture and artisan chambers had, by 1905, made the idea of the corporate representation of economic interests a working reality and a commonplace.[33] By the same token it is possible to maintain that another of the apparently new reasons adduced by the Centre to explain its hostility to reform — the threat from the SPD — was more valid in the political circumstances of 1905 than it would have been ten years earlier. This, and the issue of economic interest group representation, will be discussed shortly. Generally, however, the evidence still suggests that the fundamental reason for the original volte-face in 1898 was the Centre's insistence on extracting concessions for the Church, and that this motive continued to play a part in its later opposition to constitutional reform, even though other misgivings genuinely existed.

Over education, too, despite more broadly-based grounds for the Centre's negative position, clerical motives certainly played an important part. One of the major stumbling blocks to Centre agreement over the educational bills of von Breitling (1902) and von Weizsäcker (1908) was the proposal to dent the clerical monopoly of school supervision and inspection which existed in Württemberg. These functions were held to be incompatible in large urban districts with part-time clerical supervision and were henceforth to be exercised only on a full-time professional basis (although this by no means took control out of the hands of clerically-trained teachers, and certainly not away from believing Catholics and Protestants). In 1908 this principle was to be extended to all offices at district level. Both bills included also clauses which facilitated the setting up of non-denominational schools in areas where industry and the influx of labour had broken down the residential basis of confessional separation.[34] The Centre refused to compromise on either of these two principles. It conducted

31. Hitze foresaw a society organised politically as well as occupationally into seven 'estates' (*Stände*), which would be the central institutions and decision-making bodies of society. See P. Jostock, 'Der soziale Gedanke im deutschen Katholizismus', R. Hebing and M. Horst (eds), *Volk im Glauben* (Berlin, 1933), pp. 143–4. See the comments on Hitze's position by Hertling, *Erinnerungen*, II, pp. 182–5.
32. See the speech by Gröber, reported in *Deutsches Volksblatt*, 6 June 1894.
33. *36 LT, PB IV*, p. 2645, 100 Sitz., 14.6.1905.
34. Details in Egelhaaf, V. Bruns (ed), *Württemberg unter der Regierung König Wilhelms II*, pp. 34–6, 40–2; Menzinger, *Verfassungsrevision und Demokratisierungsprozess*, p. 161.

a fierce rearguard action at each parliamentary stage, painting non–clerical control and non–denominational schools as the first step towards un–Christian education, and appealing (largely in vain) for Protestant Conservative support against radical anti–clericalism and masonic intrigue as the harbingers of revolution.[35] This lack of response by Protestant Conservatives indicates the strong identity between the interests of the Catholic Church and the policy of the Centre Party. So, too, does the fact that when the Catholic teachers' associations announced their support for the educational reforms the Centre followed the Bishop of Rottenburg in denouncing this revolt.[36] As in its standing demand for the return of banned teaching orders, the Centre took up the concerns of the Church as its own in the policy adopted towards the educational bills of 1902 and 1908.

The importance of the era of reform nevertheless far transcended its effects on the Catholic Church, and the motives behind Centre policy were a good deal more complex than simple clericalism. One component of the party's reaction to the whole body of reform legislation was its hostility towards the means used by the VP to push forward the democratisation of Württemberg. We have already seen how the legally-trained local leaders of the Centre were similar in their sense of sobriety and institutional conservatism to the party's national leadership. For them the VP was breaking the rules of the parliamentary game by fomenting popular feeling as a means of pressing the government for political concessions. Certainly direct appeal to 'the people' had its part in VP tactics; so, too, did the deliberate formulation of a maximum programme as a means of securing at least a minimum one. Thus the VP maximum programme actually called for constitutional revision to be determined by a constituent assembly called under a provision which still existed from 1849; and also for the complete abolition of the Upper House.[37] In fact, as we have seen, the verbal radicalism of a man like Conrad Haussmann and of the maximum programme were complementary to the diplomatic gifts of Friedrich Payer and the realism of the minimum programme. Ultimately the VP was prepared to make substantial concessions. But an uneasiness about the tactics of the VP was a motif of Centre policy, from the clash in 1897 over how to deal with the problem of the Upper House and tax reform, through to the period before the 1906 Landtag elections, when VP popular meetings

---

35. See, for example, Dr Späth for the Centre Party, in response to the 1908 bill: *37 LT, PB III*, pp. 3081–5, 116 Sitz., 1.7.1908.
36. See below, p. 137.
37. Simon, *Die württembergischen Demokraten*, p. 58.

were organised and a heated campaign was mounted to mobilise public opinion for reform and against 'clerical reaction'.[38] This was evidence for Centre leaders of the danger of revolution from above, in which the people were led astray by irresponsible agitation and delivered into socialist hands. It seemed to confirm that strain in VP politics which Gröber had earlier dismissed disdainfully as the VP's 'protest ballyhoo' (*Protestrummel*).[39]

Now the Centre itself had benefited electorally from appeals to anti-governmental sentiment in 1895; and, as we shall see, it consistently used appeals over the heads of government and parliamentarians when it came to social and economic issues. But this was precisely the point of its hostility towards the VP and the political reform movement. The Centre cast itself in a role similar to that of the peasant and artisan rebels of 1848 rather than the politicians of the Paulskirche, attacking the VP for fomenting political unrest while ignoring real social problems. And in this attitude it was consistent, from the 1895 election campaign through to the years of the era of reform. The VP leaders, it maintained, were out of touch with ordinary opinion, particularly that in the countryside and small towns, in their insistence on the primacy of political over social reform.[40]

In addition to misgivings about the kind of political mobilisation which accompanied the VP's crusade for reform, the Centre also had reason to doubt the effects of reform legislation on what might be called its party interest. Just as the Catholic Church faced particular difficulties in maintaining the church-going habits of those who left the land, so the Centre could expect a net disadvantage from the extra weight given by constitutional reform to the urban electorate. The party's strength was in the relatively over-represented small-town and rural constituencies. Prior to reform, Ellwangen (population 5,000) and Stuttgart (population 250,000) enjoyed equal representation as 'good towns' under the 1819 constitution.[41] Now Stuttgart was to have six deputies rather than one, a piece of natural justice with worrying

---

38. Liesching, *Zur Geschichte*, pp. 11–14; Menzinger, *Verfassungsrevision und Demokratisierungsprozess*, p. 162; Simon, *Die württembergischen Demokraten*, p. 64; Schlemmer, *Die Rolle der Sozialdemokratie*, pp. 53–7, 104–5.
39. *36 LT, PB IV*, p. 2625, 108 Sitz., 28.6.1905.
40. See, for example, Viktor Rembold's major speech at the Centre's 1906 state assembly in Rottweil, reported in *Anzeiger vom Oberland*, 13 November 1906. The Centre did receive backing for this view from the Conservatives and agrarians. See the *Schwäbischer Landmann*, 1 December 1906, editorial entitled 'Auf zur Wahlarbeit'. Cited in *Oekonomierat Rudolf Schmid. Ein Lebensbild eines württembergischen Bauernführers nach seinen Aufsätzen, Worten und seinem Wirken für die Landwirtschaft* (Stuttgart, 1927), p. 153.
41. On the bias in favour of rural constituencies generally, see Burkart, *Die Zusammensetzung*, p. 100.

implications for a party like the Centre, which found the organisation and costs of mobilising an urban electorate onerous.[42]

It was true that one feature of the reforms was likely to give some benefit to the Centre: whatever the imponderabilia of proportional representation, it seemed likely — as the government realised — to weaken the Conservatives, DP and VP, and to strengthen the generally more tightly organised SPD and Centre.[43] For the Centre, above all, proportional representation in large constituencies was ideal as a means of maximising the electoral impact of scattered voters in the Catholic diaspora. It was a matter of clear self-interest that the Centre should have been an early and consistent supporter of this system.[44] Given the truth of this, the Centre's opponents naturally asked why the party opposed reform in Württemberg which benefited itself and the SPD, while it accepted and actually encouraged similar reforms with similar effects in neighbouring Baden and Bavaria. Their conclusion was that the Centre's demand in 1905 for corporate economic representation as a dam against the SPD was a piece of hypocrisy disguising clerical objectives.[45] There were, however, very real differences between Baden and Bavaria on the one hand and Württemberg on the other in the effects of electoral reform on the Centre and SPD. In both Baden and Bavaria Catholics constituted a majority. Prior to Centre–SPD cooperation to achieve reform, not only had the system discriminated against SPD representation, but the Centre's own electoral expectations were denied by a system which favoured the traditionally dominant National Liberals.[46] The movement towards electoral reform in Baden and Bavaria around the turn of the century benefited the SPD, but it also benefited the Centre, as the tables below indicate:[47]

---

42. See *Deutsches Volksblatt*, 8 February 1895, on the cost involved in urban election campaigning. On the financial problems of mass campaigns, see also ibid, 14 August 1911, and *Waldse'er Wochenblatt*, 28 August 1911.
43. HStaASt, E 41, Anhang II, Bü 4: 'Votum des Staatsministeriums'.
44. Ibid. See also the response of the Centre *Fraktion* to the 1897 bill, cited in n. 29 above, where the party's preoccupation with the principle of proportional representation is made clear.
45. *36 LT, PB IV*, p. 2646, 108 Sitz., 28.6.1905.
46. On Baden, see J. Schofer, *Erinnerungen an Theodor Wacker* (Karlsruhe, 1921), pp. 84–5; and on Bavaria, Möckl, *Die Prinzregentenzeit*, pp. 497–9.
47. In Baden the increase in Centre and SPD seats followed changes in the suffrage; in Bavaria it was the demand for changes — bringing Centre and SPD together in electoral alliances against the National Liberals — which first crucially altered the relative strength of the parties. The reform of the suffrage, when it came, merely confirmed these changed strengths.

Bavaria					Baden		
	1893	1899	1905	1907		1903	1905
National Liberal	58	44	22	25	National Liberal	25	23
Centre	74	83	102	98	Centre	23	28
SPD	5	11	12	20	SPD	6	12

In Württemberg Catholics were a minority and the unreformed electoral system was at worst neutral in its effects on the Centre. The reforms were not likely to strengthen the Centre greatly; but they would strengthen the SPD, already stronger in the state than it was in Baden or Bavaria (in Württemberg the SPD had over 20 per cent of the vote in 59 per cent of Reichstag constituencies, in Baden in 29 per cent, in Bavaria 27 per cent).[48] By maintaining its advocacy of proportional representation, but demanding as it did in 1905 the application of this system to large constituencies made up of corporate economic interests (agriculture, industry and trade), the Centre could expect to maximise its own advantages but to trim those of the SPD. Such a system, if it had been accepted, would have benefited Centre voters especially, along with Conservative supporters, because the proportion of deputies allotted to the three economic interests was to be calculated on the basis of the outdated 1895 census of occupations.[49] The demand for the corporate representation of economic interests, denounced by the Centre's opponents as a smokescreen, would in fact have served its party interest very well.

III

Analysis of the Centre's attitude towards reform just in terms of confessional motivation, tactical considerations or party-political advantage, however, gives too little weight to the transformation which the era of reform constituted. What in the end made reform necessary was a basic shift of economic, social and demographic forces, and the *Reformära* and attitudes towards it can only properly be judged against this backdrop of change. In 1890 two-thirds of the Württemberg population lived in rural communities; by 1910 more than half the population was living in less than 10 per cent of the state's *Gemeinden* (administrative districts).[50] The number of urban

48. *36 LT, PB IV*, p. 2650, 108 Sitz., 28.6.1905; HStaASt, E 41, Anhang II, Bü 4: 'Votum des Staatsministeriums'.
49. *36 LT, PB V*, p. 3087, 130 Sitz., 25.1.1906.
50. Bruns (ed), *Württemberg unter der Regierung König Wilhelms II*, p. 66.

Gemeinden actually doubled between 1891 and 1916, the result of a net loss of population from the rural areas which reflected the accelerating drift from agriculture to industry as a source of livelihood.[51] In 1895 45.1 per cent of the population was still dependent on agriculture for its means of support, compared with 42.9 per cent dependent on industry. The following years witnessed a radical change: by 1907 agriculture provided the livelihood of only 38.5 per cent of the population, industry for 49 per cent; and the proportion dependent on trade (12.4 per cent in 1907) also rose.[52] Looked at broadly, the era of reform marked an adaptation of the institutional structure of Württemberg to the changing balance of economic, social and demographic forces. Underlying the argument amongst the parties over reform lay an argument about the changing character of the state.

The VP leaders were men of the middle classes, heavily involved personally in industry, commerce and the free professions.[53] They welcomed the need and opportunity for reform which the changes in the years after 1895 presented. In Württemberg, unlike the Reich, the Progressives were a strong political force: in 1895 the VP was the largest single party in the Lower House. In Württemberg, also unlike the Reich, it was realistic to cast von Breitling, or even von Mittnacht, in the role of a Peel. Changes in the fiscal system after 1895 were, for VP leaders, a sign that industry and commerce were becoming the backbone of state finances (as they were of VP finances).[54] This seemed evidence to them of a gratifying shift from an agricultural to an industrial state. Its corollary was a more direct government recognition of the social and political role of the business and professional middle classes, and the VP looked for such a sign of recognition in the other legislation which made up the *Reformära*.

This was the essence of VP demands that constitutional reform include the removal of unelected representatives of the aristocracy, the

51. *Die Landwirtschaft und die Landwirtschaftspflege*, pp. 4, 192.
52. Bruns (ed), *Württemberg unter der Regierung König Wilhelms II*, pp. 811–12.
53. See above, Chapter Two, pp. 91–2. See also Molt, *Der Reichstag*, p. 200, referring to the VP leaders in their capacity as members of the *Deutsche Volkspartei*: 'One could almost say that their parliamentary representatives were either modest entrepreneurs or lawyers.'
54. HStaASt, Conrad Haussmann Papers, Q 1/2, 104: letter of Carl Bollinger, chairman of the Spaichingen district branch of the VP, to Haussmann, 13 November 1911. Bollinger complained that the money the party could raise locally for the forthcoming Reichstag election campaign (about 200 Marks) 'falls a long way short. If we are to campaign in the way you have proposed, the election in the constituency will cost us 1000 Marks, and I would ask you to obtain the necessary sum, perhaps through the Hansabund, or shall I perhaps write direct to the Hansabund?' The VP did, in fact, receive backing from the Hansabund. Ibid, letter of Riesser, president of the organisation, to Conrad Haussmann, Berlin, 23 January 1912.

Churches and the State University from the Lower House.[55] It also lay behind their insistence that social change and population movements be recognised in the allocation of seats.[56] This overall view informed VP attitudes to educational reform in particular. This they supported enthusiastically as a move away from an educational system appropriate to a corporate society of *Stände* towards one more in keeping with a mobile society. Greater educational opportunity, a modernised syllabus, the teaching of modern languages, the provision of ethical as well as religious education and the principle of a professional corps of teachers and inspectors: together, these constituted for VP leaders a challenge to conservative, deferential social relations and provided a means of training men and women for citizenship rather than merely fitting them for a pre-ordained place in society.[57]

The government was not concerned with the value of reform as an end in itself, but if institutional adjustments to new economic and social forces were necessary in the interests of stability it was prepared to make them. We have already seen how the emergence of a pioneering government statistician like Losch signified a change in the official mind, an acceptance that the industrial state set the conditions under which governments operated.[58] The same attitude could be seen in von Zeyer's tax reforms, designed to tap the new sources of wealth created by industrialisation and more fruitful to the state exchequer than the ramshackle assortment of taxes, duties and fees on which it subsisted prior to reform.[59] Similarly, changes in the constitution and the educational system were an official acknowledgement that new

55. On the opposition of the 'propertied liberal middle class' to the strengthening of the upper house, and their objections to a replacement (*Ersatz*) in the lower house which would favour landowning and bureaucratic elements, see Menzinger, *Verfassungsrevision und Demokratisierungsprozess*, pp. 138–9.

56. The VP deputies Schmidt (in 1895) and Friedrich Haussmann (in 1905) actually called for the abolition of the Ellwangen-*Stadt* seat, which by 1906 had only 994 registered voters. Simon, *Die württembergischen Demokraten*, p. 61, n. 21.

57. For details of the educational reform proposals, see Egelhaaf, V. Bruns (ed), *Württemberg unter der Regierung König Wilhelms II*, pp. 35, 40–2. Representative of the VP's nineteenth-century liberal emphasis on the free play of ideas as a parallel to the free play of economic forces was the speech of the VP education spokesman, Dr Elsas, who included Adam Smith among the witnesses he called to testify in favour of the government bill: *37 LT, PB III*, pp. 3186–7, 120 Sitz., 4.7.1908.

58. See above, Chapter Two, p. 85.

59. Details from O. Trüdinger, 'Finanzwesen und Steuern', V. Bruns (ed), *Württemberg unter der Regierung König Wilhelms II*, pp. 187 ff; E. Schremmer, 'Zusammenhänge zwischen Katastersteuersystem, Wirtschaftswachstum und Wirtschaftsstruktur im 19. Jahrhundert. Das Beispiel Württemberg: 1821–1877/1903', I. Bog et al (eds), *Wirtschaftliche und soziale Strukturen im säkularen Wandel: Festschrift f. Wilhelm Abel z. 70 Geburtstag*, vol. III, *Wirtschaft und Gesellschaft in der Zeit der Industrialisierung* (Hanover, 1974), pp. 690–1.

social forces were at work.[60] A striking example of the extent to which the government had abandoned its role of maintaining the customary economic and social order came in its response to overtures from the *Gesellschaft für wirtschaftliche Ausbildung*.[61] This was an organisation backed by major commercial and banking interests — including the Diskonto, Deutsche and Dresdner banks — which aimed to further understanding of commercial needs through propaganda and educational courses at its *Akademie für Sozial- und Handelswissenschaften*, situated appropriately in Frankfurt. In 1904 it approached the Württemberg government with a number of requests: that one representative of each major department of state sign a statement publicly endorsing the aims of the Society; that information about the organisation be circulated to interested junior officials; and that suitable officials be released on paid leave to attend courses at the Frankfurt academy. The overall response was warm. A statement was duly signed by six high-ranking officials and appeared in the *Schwäbischer Merkur*; and the departments generally welcomed the scheme of releasing officials, although they requested further detailed information from the Society. The most lukewarm department (the *Verkehrsabteilung* of the Foreign Office) was sceptical only because it felt its officials already had adequate command of economic and commercial matters from their university studies. The government's response to this approach is indicative of its more general position. It may not have taken the lead in bringing about institutional reforms; but in the interests of sound administration it was prepared to follow where a lead was given, whether by the *Gesellschaft für wirtschaftliche Ausbildung* or by the VP.

The Centre Party was able to agree with the VP over what the era of reform represented. Neither saw the move towards reform as concerning just the position of the Church or party-political fortunes: these effects were merely symptomatic. But where the VP welcomed reform as an instalment of liberal modernisation, the Centre feared it as a potential solvent of established social relations. Centre leaders distrusted the social forces and movements brought into being by industrialisation, an attitude which was curiously at odds with their complaints that Catholics were under-represented in the ranks of entrepreneurs, public officials and professional men. Men like Gröber, himself the beneficiary of upward social mobility, argued on the one hand that Catholics should assert themselves and play a more positive

60. There was explicit acknowledgement of this, as far as the reforms of the constitution were concerned, in HStaASt, E 41, Anhang II, Bü 4: 'Votum des Staatsministeriums'.
61. The account which follows is taken from HStaASt, E 130 II, Bü 486, Nr. 12–23: the reactions of the different government departments.

role in public affairs; it was even a common argument among the Catholic élite that too many intelligent young Catholics were being lost from business and the professions to the priesthood.[62] Yet faced with the concrete reality of institutional reforms which encouraged, for example, broader educational opportunity, the reaction of Centre leaders was the traditional conservative one. Rural society and social relations were, they maintained, the repositories of virtue and social order; and freethinking professors, doctrinaire liberals and masonic schoolteachers were undermining this social order from the towns.[63]

Therefore, while those at the head of the Centre pointed out that Catholics were over-represented in poor rural areas and were educationally under-privileged,[64] they were largely unwilling to pay the price of Catholic social emancipation. Greater social mobility was linked in their minds to the undermining of belief, the dissolution of the family, an increased crime rate and immorality in general, which tended to be regarded as an urban phenomenon.[65] The result was that Gröber, Kiene and others were very active in articulating the grievances which emanated from Catholic communities, but were unwilling to endorse reforms which might have ameliorated some of those grievances. Their attitude towards the measures of the era of reform, which they identified with the nostrums of laissez-faire liberalism, was therefore one of suspicion.

At the root of these apprehensions lay the view that the measures

62. Rost, *Die wirtschaftliche und kulturelle Lage*, pp. 181, 201.
63. See Gröber's panegyric to the conservative good sense of the rural population: *36 LT, PB V*, p. 3087, 130 Sitz., 25.1.1906. Of the many other speeches in a similar vein, a typical one was made by Dr Späth, Centre educational spokesman: *37 LT, PB III*, pp. 3081–5. 116 Sitz., 1.7.1908. At the local level, Centre newspapers were much more direct than party leaders in parliamentary debates, complaining (like the *Neckarbote*, 20 October 1904, in an article entitled 'Jüdische Moral') of 'mass poisoning' morally by urban Jews; or (like the *Waldse'er Wochenblatt*, 7 March 1897) rhetorically asking readers if education should be in the hands of the clergy, or 'given over to the Jews and freemasons'.
64. So, for example, Späth, *37 LT, PB III*, p. 3084, 116 Sitz., 1.7.1908, where the allusion to relative Catholic poverty is given an anti-semitic twist; and Viktor Rembold, *37 LT, PB III*, pp. 3195–6, 120 Sitz., 4.7.1908. The objective fact of Catholic educational under-privilege is not in doubt. In the *Donaukreis*, which contained 16 *Oberämter*, there were 7 *Vollanstalten*: 4 were in the 6 predominantly Protestant *Oberämter*, only 3 in the 10 predominantly Catholic ones. Rost, *Die wirtschaftliche und kulturelle Lage*, p. 180.
65. See Kiene, *37 LT, PB IV*, pp. 3969–71, 148 Sitz., 9.2.1909, on the 'moral and intellectual poisoning of the springs', and a full-blooded attack on immorality, satire, contraception and the undermining of authority, associated for him with the loss of customary constraints. Like other Centre leaders, Kiene made much play of the national 'weakness' and low birth-rate in France, where moral and intellectual license had allegedly won the upper hand in the liberal Third Republic. He warned of the supposed dangers in Germany: 'A people which is not sexually healthy is not physically healthy or strong, its ability to defend itself is weakened.' Späth, similarly, claimed a connection between 'moral education' in France and a rising rate of crime.

most favoured by the VP tended to destroy traditional social ties, atomise society and play into the hands of the SPD.[66] This view was evident in Centre criticism of the earlier liberalisation of commercial codes and marriage laws. In the post-1895 reform measures it can be seen in fears that constitutional change would benefit the SPD, and in the argument that some parts of the tax reform conferred undue benefits on aggressive and socially divisive forces like business and commerce at the expense of forces which allegedly represented social harmony — Church charities and the *Mittelstand*, for example.[67] Centre apprehensions emerge most clearly, however, on the issue of education. For the Catholic élite education had traditionally been regarded as a major battle-field against the Enlightenment: industrial development and the rise of modern class society sharpened its significance. The Centre viewed with concern the political education of the working class by the trade unions and the SPD. It was symptomatic of attitudes among the party leadership that when Gröber attacked an openly repressive piece of anti-working-class legislation like the *Zuchthausvorlage* he did so on the grounds of its preoccupation with symptoms rather than causes. The real problem, he argued, lay in social atomisation, in revolutionary ideas being inculcated in the working class from above, and in faulty education.[68] Hence the concern with which the Centre looked at the proposals for educational reform in Württemberg.

First, the state announced its willingness to assume the responsibility for education in areas where pressure of numbers had exposed the inadequacy of clerical resources. For the Centre, more than clerical control was at stake here. The spread of public educational provision weakened the rights of the head of family over his children and gave tacit official approval to full-blooded industrialisation: education divorced from the family and the Church encouraged and made it

66. The 'organic versus atomistic' metaphor of which German conservatives were so fond was explicitly brought into the constitutional debate by Gröber (*36 LT, PB V*, pp. 3085–9, 130 Sitz., 25.1.1906) and by Viktor Rembold, who argued that 'the people is an organic whole divided into occupational estates' (*36 LT, PB V*, p. 3119, 108 Sitz., 28.6.1905). Rembold traced his attachment to this idea back to Wilhelm Riehl. See also Kiene's speech to the Centre Party's 1906 assembly in Rottweil, where the organic metaphor is emphasised. Report in *Deutsches Volksblatt*, 23 November 1906. On the context of these corporative ideas, see R. H. Bowen, *German Theories of the Corporative State, with Special Reference to the Period 1870–1919* (New York, 1947).
67. Gröber, *33 LT, PB V*, p. 3173, 145 Sitz., 10.6.1897; Viktor Rembold, *33 LT, PB V*, p. 3188, 146 Sitz., 11.6.1897.
68. For a Reichstag speech of this kind by Gröber, on the *Zuchthausvorlage*, see reports in the *Deutsches Volksblatt*, 10, 11 January 1895. For a similar expression of Gröber's views, see his attitude towards the Lex Heinze: R. J. V. Lenman, 'Art, Society and the Law in Wilhelmine Germany: the Lex Heinze', *Oxford German Studies*, 8 (1973–4), esp. p. 91.

possible for husband and wife to entrust their offspring to the state and go off to the factory.[69] Rather than maintaining a balance between classes and interests, the state appeared to be giving its imprimatur to a philosophy of economic and social ferment. The Centre feared a similar ferment from changes in the school syllabus which raised childrens' expectations and made them dissatisfied with the social milieu in which they had been brought up.[70]

Secondly, the proliferation of state schools and training colleges for teachers, together with teachers' rising salaries, brought a further problem for the Centre: it promoted conflict between Catholic teachers, who increasingly tended to see themselves as members of a professional body, and a clerical control over many parts of education which seemed to block their avenues to promotion. As early as 1901 a meeting of the Catholic Teachers Association at Ravensburg passed a set of 'theses' deploring the frustrations which attended the efforts of its members to rise in the profession.[71] Despite the public intervention of both the Centre and the Bishop of Rottenburg this revolt was never properly subdued.[72] The anti-clerical organ of the non-Catholic teachers in Württemberg, the *Lehrerheim*, continued to be widely read by Catholic members of the profession, and in 1909 one local meeting of the Catholic Teachers Association was so incensed by the continuing clerical block to professional advancement that it voted its full support to the VP spokesman on education. The man in question, Löchner, was not only a schoolteacher himself but also a freemason.[73] To Centre leaders, this kind of sectional interest demand was disturbing and symptomatic. It illustrated that 'war of all against all' which VP liberalism provoked, which a major instalment of reform would exacerbate and from which only the SPD could ultimately benefit.

69. As early as 1899, Gröber was sounding a warning about this tendency to 'educational socialism' (*Erziehungssozialismus*): *34 LT, PB III*, pp. 2012–14, 88 Sitz., 29.11.1899. See also J. B. Kiene, *Die Zwangserziehung Minderjähriger Gesetz vom 29. Dez. 1899* (Stuttgart, 1900). For similar Centre views on the von Weizsäcker bill: *37 LT, PB III*, pp. 3081–3, 116 Sitz., 1.7.1908.
70. *37 LT, PB III*, pp. 3084–5, 116 Sitz., 1.7.1908.
71. *Politische Zeitfragen*, 9 (Stuttgart, 1906), p. 144.
72. See the editorial attack on the *Vereinsbote*, organ of the Catholic Teachers Association, in *Deutsches Volksblatt*, 17 March 1903. On the opposed positions of Rottenburg and the teachers themselves over the von Weizsäcker bill, see Egelhaaf, *Lebenserinnerungen*, p. 124. In 1906, the *Württembergischer Volkslehrerverein* considered putting up its own candidate for the Landtag election. They were concerned especially with achieving official (*Beamter*) status, and with the establishment of new ground-rules for relations between the clergy and themselves. See *Schwäbische Tagwacht*, 9 January 1906.
73. This vote followed a considerable amount of pro-VP opinion expressed in the *Vereinsbote*. Thus, for example, in the *Vereinsbote*, 6 December 1908, cited in *Deutsches Volksblatt*, 9 January 1909.

IV

Educational reform provides a good example of how the Centre Party opposed institutional change which might have helped redress the balance between relatively advanced urban areas and relatively backward rural ones, which would thus in the long run have benefited Catholic communities especially. This is true of the way the Centre backed clerical control against the wishes of Catholic professional teachers, and thereby — at least indirectly — helped to perpetuate the under-representation of Catholics in the occupations of industrial society. It is true as well of Centre opposition to the reformers' proposals to add an extra year to the school leaving age.[74] There was therefore some tension between the attitudes of Centre leaders and the objective long-term interests of many Centre voters. But the party's policy, in fact, commanded much support in rural and small-town Catholic communities, where educational reform aroused apprehensions which were different from those of the leadership, but could nevertheless be exploited by them. The burden of taxation was already, as we have seen, a sensitive issue in such areas, and educational reform would entail either new expenditure for indebted districts or the removal of control along with the financial burden from the local community.[75] The general education favoured by government and reform parties alike was also widely feared: subjects like foreign languages were thought to raise childrens' expectations and incite them to desert practical pursuits on the farm or in the workshop in favour of a white-collar job in the town.[76] This was a general problem for the German peasantry and *Mittelstand* around the

---

74. *37 LT, PB IV*, p. 3407, 128 Sitz., 19.12.1908.
75. *37 LT, PB IV*, pp. 3407–9, 3419, 128 Sitz., 19.12.1908. The indebtedness of the communes was especially severe in rural areas. Discussing the subject in the context of agriculture's misfortunes, one contemporary wrote: 'It is a well-known fact that in many communes, as a result of the accumulation of communal burdens, the weight of taxes has exceeded the resources of the tax-payers.' M. Rapp, *Die Einfuhr von landwirtschaftlichen Produkten und deren Einfluss auf die Lage der Landwirtschaft* (Stuttgart, 1900), p. 18.
76. See the contributions to the education bill debate by the Centre 'agrarian' back-benchers, Kessler and Maier: *37 LT, PB III*, p. 3180, 120 Sitz., 19.12.1908. The *Waldse'er Wochenblatt* probably had its finger on the pulse of local feeling when it talked of the 'much exaggerated cultivation of intellect (*Verstandsbildung*)', 10 January 1897. Nor do the local priests seem to have encouraged the peasantry to set a high value on education. Curate Pfaff, at a *Volksverein* meeting in Schussenried, objected that 'the Democrats [i.e. VP] want to bring everyone who leaves school to the point where he can deal with every need and not fall into the hands of the Jew. But against this it must be said that already well-educated peasants have fallen victim to the usurious Jews.' Reported in *Waldse'er Wochenblatt*, 13 May 1897.

turn of the century[77] and the evidence suggests that it was present among rural communities in Catholic Württemberg. There is, for example, the literary evidence from *Meine Steinauer*, a *Heimatsroman* set in Oberschwaben and written by a school friend of Matthias Erzberger, which depicts the family tension in a peasant household where a son has left home to train as a teacher.[78] More concretely, the local Centre press in this period contained many complaints from artisans antagonised by another unwelcome sign of social mobility: the fact that apprentices were being attracted to skilled and well-paid factory jobs after enrolling in government-sponsored courses in technical education.[79]

The proposal to raise the school leaving age by a year therefore aroused two objections: it would stretch local financial resources; and it would strike hard at the Catholic petty bourgeoisie and peasantry by diminishing the supply of family labour on which, with labour costs rising, they were increasingly dependent.[80] An enquiry in 1904 showed that out of 308,160 children of school age in Württemberg, 67,456 worked in some kind of paid agricultural employment, nearly half as domestic servants.[81] When this is added to the number of children of both sexes working unpaid, the common pattern in Oberschwaben because of the size of holdings, it can be seen how powerful an interest the larger and medium-sized peasant proprietors had in restricting educational expansion.[82] It is significant that the Centre's alternative proposal to raising the school leaving age, formulated in a motion by Johannes Weber, was a re-casting of general secondary

---

77. See, for example, R. Engelsing, *Zur Sozialgeschichte deutscher Mittel- und Unterschichten* (Göttingen, 1973), pp. 101–5; Wernicke, *Kapitalismus und Mittelstandspolitik*, pp. 174, 179, 182–4, quoting reports from artisan chambers around the turn of the century; K. Scheffler, *Der junge Tobias. Eine Jugend und ihre Umwelt* (Leipzig, 1927), pp. 35–7, 170; W. Hofmann, *Mit Grabstichel und Feder. Geschichte einer Jugend* (Stuttgart and Tübingen, 1948), pp. 125–6.
78. W. Schussen, *Meine Steinauer. Eine Heimatsgeschichte* (Stuttgart and Leipzig, 1908). Schussen's real name was Wilhelm Frick. Details on him in Bruns (ed), *Württemberg unter der Regierung König Wilhelms II*, pp. 519–20; K. Epstein, *Matthias Erzberger and the dilemma of German Democracy* (Princeton, 1959), p. 7.
79. See, for example, the complaints aired at the annual general meeting of the Rottenburg *Gewerbeverein*, reported in the *Neckarbote*, 1 March 1904.
80. *Die Landwirtschaft und die Landwirtschaftspflege*, p. 5, arguing that the supply of family labour was particularly important from around the 1890s.
81. Ibid, p. 195, n. 4.
82. There was a precedent for peasant resistance to compulsory schooling. In Austria, after liberal educational reforms in 1867, peasant opposition led to a restriction of the obligatory school law in rural communes. E. Bruckmüller, 'Bäuerlicher Konservatismus in Oberösterreich. Sozialstruktur und politische Vertretung in einem österreichischen Kronland', *Zeitschrift für bayerische Landesgeschichte*, 37 (1974), I, p. 139.

schooling, to pay particular attention to 'the training of young men in agricultural and of young women in household matters'.[83]

Where the Centre's opponents saw only cynical confessional opportunism, they might in fact have done better to examine the party's very worldly political opportunism. The position of the Centre during the era of reform is an example of the leadership's dexterity in exploiting popular discontent and using it to overcome the latent tension which existed between themselves and Centre supporters in the localities. The issue of educational reform, especially, reveals how Centre leaders were able to harness the currents of agrarian and petty-bourgeois dissatisfaction in Catholic communities to their own more conservative apprehensions. Major items of legislation like educational and constitutional reform, however, show only a limited part of the Centre leadership's political repertoire. In matters of this kind they were necessarily on the defensive, justifying themselves against attacks by parties like the VP that the Centre was dragging its heels over reform. The political skills and the opportunism of the Centre were most in evidence on economic and social issues, where the party took a more aggressive role in articulating grassroots grievances and using them as a stick with which to beat both the government and the VP. It is to this aspect of Centre policy, and in particular to its demagogic exploitation of *Mittelstandspolitik* and parish-pump resentments, that we shall now turn.

83. *37 LT, PB IV*, p. 3409, 128 Sitz., 19.12.1908.

CHAPTER 5

The Centre and the Volkspartei after 1895:
Economic Policy and
the Uses of Mittelstandspolitik

I

We have seen how the emergence of the Centre as a major political force in Württemberg in the 1890s owed much to the party's ability to harness and articulate the apprehensions of the traditional *Mittelstand*; and that, conversely, the adherence of the VP to laissez-faire economic views was a source of weakness when it addressed itself to these groups. This continued to be the case after 1895, and the Centre found in its *Mittelstandspolitik* — whatever the contradictions of such a policy — an effective weapon against both the government and the VP. Before discussing the relationship of VP and Centre to the *Mittelstand* and its problems, however, it will be useful to examine the background of the economic and social policies over which the parties disagreed.

The previous chapter has shown how the balance between agriculture and industry in the Württemberg economy shifted decisively in the years after 1895. The state which for so much of the nineteenth century had languished behind other parts of Germany enjoyed, from the 1890s, a reputation for industrial growth and stability which it still retains. This apparently sudden change of fortune was, in fact, consistent with the peculiar development of Württemberg. Lack of mineral deposits, geographical factors and transportation problems had caused the state to lag behind in the first, heavy-industrial phase of German economic growth; but the traditional, decentralised, artisan-based economic structure gave it an advantage during the 'Second Industrial Revolution' at the end of the century. The production of a wide range of finished producer and consumer goods became a Württemberg characteristic, and this 'quality industry of great variety and healthy decentralisation' became the basis of what Walter Grube has called the state's 'enviable stability' in economic terms.[1]

In the twenty years up to the war Württemberg still lacked an important iron and steel industry and possessed only a limited textile sector, but it became increasingly noted for sophisticated manufactured products with clear origins in the artisan's workshop: engineering products, precision instruments, toys, musical instruments.[2] The advantages of delayed industrial take-off, enjoyed by Germany as a whole when compared with Britain, were of particular importance in Württemberg, where characteristic branches of the 'Second Industrial Revolution', like chemicals and motor vehicles, were prominent. Statistics indicate the leading sectors of the state's tardy but rapid industrialisation. Württemberg made up only 3.8 per cent of the total Reich population in 1907, and it is a sign of the nature and above all the breadth of its economic advance that it boasted over 6 per cent of the total German labour force in more than fifty different branches of industrial production, including harmonica and accordion manufacture (37.9 per cent), cigarette-lighting apparatus (30.8 per cent), corsetry manufacture (30.4 per cent), felt toys (27.2 per cent), firearms (25 per cent), linoleum, bleach and dyestuffs (22.3 per cent), motor vehicles (20.8 per cent), timekeeping and surgical instruments (19.8 per cent and 18.8 per cent), coffee surrogates (15.1 per cent), galvanised plate ware (14.9 per cent), varnish and lacquers (13.6 per cent) and distillery and brewery equipment (10.4 per cent).[3] It was through its superiority in industries of this kind that Württemberg made good the gap which had opened up in the course of the nineteenth century between it and earlier industrialised German states.

One by-product of this industrial growth led by sophisticated goods from expanded workshops was the existence of some spectacular cases of artisans-made-good. Erhard Junghans rose from master watchmaker to entrepreneur with a world market, combining the quality of production of the artisan with the business acumen he had acquired in the United States.[4] Jacob Sigle, shoemaker's apprentice from a small peasant family, established the Salamander shoe company in the Kornwestheim suburb of Stuttgart and by 1916 employed 3,400

1. W. Grube, 'Staat und Wirtschaft im Königreich Württemberg', *Festgabe für Max Miller zur Vollendung des 60. Lebensjahres, Der Archivar*, 14 (Düsseldorf, 1961), pp. 348, 344.
2. Hoffmann, *Landwirtschaft und Industrie in Württemberg*, pp. 1–3; Ehmer, *Südwestdeutschland*, p. 11; Bartens, *Die wirtschaftliche Entwicklung des Königreichs Württemberg*, pp. 9–13.
3. Bruns, *Württemberg unter der Regierung König Wilhelms II*, pp. 814–15.
4. Ehmer, *Südwestdeutschland*, p. 55.

workers.[5] Gottfried Daimler achieved a similarly meteoric rise from Cannstatt baker's son to head of the Daimler-Motoren-Gesellschaft in Stuttgart–Untertürkheim.[6] Even in the sphere of armaments the motif of quality goods produced by the enterprising and expanded artisan concern was evident: to the steel battleship-plating of Stumm and Krupp, Württemberg could reply with the Mauser brothers, small-scale rifle makers in Oberndorf, who succeeded in having the German army adopt their *Mausergewehr*, based on a model of the French *chassepot* captured at the battle of Champigny.[7]

Men like Sigle and the Mausers remained exceptional, however. The lack of commercial sense and dislike of written records commonly found amongst artisans often inhibited expansion where the conditions for it clearly existed. Even in a relatively advanced and successful concern this could be a problem: in the Walcker family's organ-building business in Ludwigsburg it took the combined efforts of the younger Karl and Oskar Walcker to overcome the reluctance of Paul and Eberhard to adopt modern ' business methods and, for example, submit tenders for large, non-local contracts.[8] More important still, in the conditions of increasingly heavy-industrial and commercial concentration which resulted from the Great Depression, even the possibility of expansion was denied to the majority of small artisan producers. Between 1895 and 1907 the number of males employed in manufacturing increased by 100,000, but this increment was very unevenly spread. The total number of concerns actually fell by 25 per cent during that period and the share of labour employed by concerns of different sizes altered markedly. While the share taken by medium-sized concerns (six to twenty employees) remained almost constant, large concerns (over twenty-one employees) increased their share greatly at the expense of small ones employing five or less people. Small businesses accounted for 49.3 per cent of the labour force in 1895, only 33.6 per cent twelve years later; large concerns accounted for 38.7 per cent in 1895, but 53.4 per cent twelve years later.[9] This transformation was proceeding more rapidly than in Germany as a whole; and the changing pattern of allocation of labour

5. Ibid, p. 53.
6. W. Zorn, 'Typen und Entwicklungskräfte deutschen Unternehmertums', K. E. Born (ed), *Moderne deutsche Wirtschaftsgeschichte*, p. 36.
7. Blos, *Denkwürdigkeiten*, I, p. 82.
8. O. Walcker, *Erinnerungen eines Orgelbauers* (Kassel, 1948), pp. 14–16.
9. Bruns, *Württemberg unter der Regierung König Wilhelms II*, pp. 821–2. In Ehingen in 1880 there were 2,552 business concerns with a total taxable return of 532,874 Marks. By 1905 there were only 2,066 concerns with a total taxable return of 1,195,748 Marks. This change was the result, according to the official account, of a 'decline of artisan branches'. *KW* (1907), IV, p. 96.

was most strikingly evident in the dominance of the labour market by the growing number of limited and public companies: in 1907 they constituted less than 10 per cent of all businesses, but accounted for 44.5 per cent of the total labour force in the state.[10]

In general, therefore, the position of artisan producers in the years after 1895 was an increasingly difficult one. The structure of industry in Württemberg was changing so quickly that small manufacturers could not expect to retain their position simply by standing still. While a minority made the qualitative as well as quantitative leap from master craftsman to entrepreneur, the movement towards concentration ruthlessly thinned the ranks of the smallest producers, forcing them into the position of dependent workers. At the same time, medium-sized concerns which struggled to maintain their independence faced the full force of competition with more efficient larger rivals.[11] They were mostly unable to take advantage of economies of scale, their share of the available capital stock was shrinking[12] and they frequently had problems competing for raw materials and outlets. These factors, together with the increasing application in industry of machinery and new sources of power like electricity, had the effect of widening the gap between the most rationalised concerns and the rest.[13]

The result of these developments was a continuing demand from artisan producers, like that already voiced before the 1890s, for government intervention in the economy to redress the imbalance between large and small concerns, and to modify in favour of the latter the terms on which they competed. Modification of the taxation and tender systems, the ending of work in state prisons which competed with artisan producers, and the provision of credit were among the measures called for; support by the Württemberg repesentatives in the *Bundesrat* for the introduction of a revived guild

10. Bruns, *Württemberg unter der Regierung König Wilhelms II*, pp. 828–9.
11. On the way that the fiscal system worked in favour of technically progressive, capital-intensive concerns, see E. Schremmer, I. Bog *et al* (eds), *Wirtschaft und Gesellschaft in der Zeit der Industrialisierung*, pp. 679–86.
12. There developed, it is true, a network of smaller trade, savings and loan banks designed to service the *Mittelstand*. By 1914 Württemberg possessed 124 such banks, 55 with limited liability. But the terms on which these banks lent money were set by conditions in the wider capital market, especially by the fluctuations in interest rates. The Spaichingen *Handwerkerbank*, in its report for the year 1899, spoke of the 'enormously high discount and bank interest rate', and noted its need to balance the demand from customers for cheap money against its own risks, bearing in mind the 'quite exceptional demands being made on our resources'. Report in *Heuberger Bote*, 6 February 1900.
13. A. Gemming, *Das Handwerkergenossenschaftswesen in Württemberg* (Stuttgart, 1911), pp. 1–9; Bruns, *Württemberg unter der Regierung König Wilhelms II*, p. 872. Generally, Wernicke, *Kapitalismus und Mittelstandspolitik*, pp. 160 ff.

system was also demanded.[14] The call for government action was echoed by small retailers, whose local organisations and pressure groups became more vociferous from around the last decade of the century in response to the quickening tempo of change in the retail sector. Department stores had aroused hostility before the 1890s; their enormous expansion in the following years — one commentator in 1899 said that they were 'springing up like mushrooms'[15] — brought demands from the retailers' protective associations and other organisations for controls over this 'unfair competition'.[16]

Throughout Germany the process of concentration in manufacturing and retailing which became marked from the 1890s added a new word to the political vocabulary: *Mittelstandspolitik*.[17] This concept, that the state should protect artisans and retailers because they (like the peasantry) formed the kernel of a healthy society, was seized upon by the parties of the right and centre as an alternative both to traditional liberal economic thinking and to the programme of the SPD. Changes in the Conservative and National Liberal programmes in these years testified to the new centrality of *Mittelstandspolitik*;[18] and the Centre, which had always included references to the importance of the *Mittelstand* in its programmes, sharpened its emphasis on the theme.[19] In Württemberg, where the process of concentration like that of industrialisation itself, was more modern and telescoped, *Mittelstandspolitik* had considerable relevance. It was a touchstone of economic and social policy, a means of measuring the distance between political parties; and it divided the Centre and VP even more than the issues of the reform era.

II

The VP was unsympathetic to *Mittelstandspolitik*. This was consistent with the changing nature of the party: by the 1890s it was certainly no

14. Bruns, *Württemberg unter der Regierung König Wilhelms II*, pp. 870–8; *50 Jahre Handwerkskammer Stuttgart* (Stuttgart, 1951), pp. 17–21.
15. H. Crüger, *Vortrag über gewerbliches Genossenschaftswesen, Warenbazare und Grosswarenhäuser gehalten auf dem 41. Verbandstag Württ. Gewerbevereine in Calw im Oktober 1899* (Stuttgart, 1899), p. 13.
16. See, for example, the attack on 'unfair competition' at the Württemberg *Schutzverein für Handel und Gewerbe* annual general meeting, June 1899, reported in *Ipf-Zeitung*, 14 June 1899.
17. On this, see especially Winkler, W. Rüegg and O. Neuloh (eds), *Zur soziologischen Theorie und Analyse des 19. Jahrhunderts*, pp. 163–79; and on *Mittelstandspolitik* and the political parties, Wernicke, *Kapitalismus und Mittelstandspolitik*, pp. 416–46.
18. F. Salomon, *Die deutschen Parteiprogramme*, 3 vols (Leipzig and Berlin, 1907–20), II, pp. 73, 83–4.
19. See above, Chapter One, pp. 53–7.

longer the party of the small man that it had been at the time of its founding. Its leaders and deputies in the Landtag now tended, as we have seen, to be recruited from business and the professions. The same was true of the party's inner committee and full state committee. The social composition of the latter organisation continued to change in the years up to 1914. Liberal artisans, it is true, remained a significant and constant group, but the largest-growing social groups on the committee were those of middle class professionals (doctors, lawyers, editors, engineers and, above all, teachers, who constituted 13 per cent of the total committee membership by 1914), officials and white-collar workers; and they were increasing their share at the expense of groups like publicans and small businessmen.[20] A lack of sympathy for the objectives of *Mittelstandspolitik* therefore found expression in a changing organisation, which in turn reinforced this outlook.

The particular nature of industrialisation in Württemberg also reinforced the 'Manchester' liberalism of the VP. The instances of artisans-made-good which it afforded seemed to demonstrate the benefits of laissez-faire coupled with entrepreneurial initiative. Paradigmatic was the case of Robert Bosch,[21] a friend of Conrad Haussmann and politically close to the VP. Bosch, himself of rural petty-bourgeois stock, not only seemed to prove by his own example the opportunities for social mobility provided by a liberal economic system: by the direct provision of employment in his modern works and indirect provision of benefits to society through large-scale private philanthropy he was a symbol of all that was deemed best in the canons of Cobdenite economic orthodoxy. Liberal beliefs of this kind were also underlined by a further general aspect of industrialisation in the state. Men like Bosch were able to prosper partly because markets for their kind of product remained relatively buoyant even at periods of economic recession. This, and the fact that Württemberg's sophisticated finished goods were heavily export-orientated and could be sold to pay for food imports,[22] tended to confirm liberal VP men in their belief in the general benefits to be obtained from free trade internationally as a corollary to laissez-faire at home.

The VP was therefore hostile to the idea of state intervention on

20. Simon, *Die württembergischen Demokraten*, pp. 28–31.
21. HStaASt, Conrad Haussmann Papers, Q 1/2, 78, has correspondence relating to various canal projects in which Haussmann was directly concerned, including a three-way exchange of letters between Haussmann, Bosch and a Prussian official in the Ministry of Public Affairs, in which Haussmann was an intermediary between the pro-canal official and Bosch, who was anxious to get official support for canal projects dear to his heart.
22. Ehmer, *Südwestdeutschland*, p. 43; Bruns, *Württemberg unter der Regierung König Wilhelms II*, pp. 817–18.

behalf of either the working class or the *Mittelstand*. The deputy for Tuttlingen, Christian Storz, expressed his party's economic philosophy well when in 1895 he wrote as follows on the subject of guilds:[23]

The guilds are antiquated, obsolete organisations which have long since been pruned away and which can be of no use in our times. We have large-scale industry and we should be happy that we have it, for otherwise we would have no industry at all. When a man with money builds a factory near small-scale, guild-organised artisans then they have no choice, guild or no guild, than to go into the factory. The social problem will never be solved with outmoded organisations of that kind.

The free play of economic forces, in short, provided the motor of material progress and social reconciliation.[24] The active state role called for by the SPD and the advocates of *Mittelstandspolitik* was dismissed as mischievous: government was to restrict its activity to the creation of a sound business climate and the provision of posts, railways and technical education; industrial concentration and the ruin of small concerns should not trouble it. Although supporting the progressive taxation of personal income the VP was thus in favour of the preferential treatment of dividends. It consistently voted down the progressive taxation of department stores, and it opposed a Landtag motion calling on the Württemberg government to move in the Bundesrat for an extension of the law on 'unfair competition'. Conrad Haussmann stated the underlying philosophy clearly when he argued: 'It does not appear to me to be the duty of the state to burden concerns which are rationally managed only in order to procure an easier livelihood, supposed or real, for other, smaller enterprises.'[25]

Now it is true, as Klaus Simon has pointed out, that from around 1900 the VP made some verbal concessions towards the idea of

23. *Grenzboten*, 1 February 1895, cited in *Deutsches Volksblatt*, 6 February 1895.
24. It is noteworthy that Storz applied very similar ideas to Germany's colonial possessions in West Africa. His account of journeys there contains high praise for the energies of the businessmen active on the spot, coupled with condemnation of officials, whom he charges frequently with being too 'bureaucratic' and too impractical in business matters. Once again, Storz read a social message into this. With less heavy-handed, unimaginative bureaucracy and more dynamic development of natural resources through improved communications, the 'terrible colonial war' in South-West Africa would, he argued, not have occurred. In the colonies, as at home, the moral was a Cobdenite one: it was the free unfolding of economic energies, not the actions of governments, which would bring peace and prosperity. See C. Storz, *Reisebriefe aus Westafrika und Beiträge zur Entwicklung der deutschen Kolonien in Togo und Kamerun* (Stuttgart, 1906), esp. part II, pp. 53–75.
25. *33 LT, PB V*, p. 3171, 145 Sitz., 10.6.1897.

economic interventionism, including the idea of *Mittelstandspolitik*.[26] The handling of the problems of the *Mittelstand* at party conferences after the turn of the century was one sign of this. But the actual policy of the VP underwent no discernible change. Hans Hähnle was still able, in 1902, to dismiss state interference in the retail sector on the classic liberal economic grounds that it was 'demoralising'.[27] The VP still continued to insist that artisans and small businesses generally should help themselves rather than call on the government for aid, just as it lectured the working class on the dangers of 'collectivism'. This contributed to the VP's steady loss of Landtag seats, the number of which fell from 31 out of 70 in 1895 to only 19 out of 90 after the election of 1912, as the party was squeezed between the Centre and Conservatives' successful courting of *Mittelstand* (and peasantry) on the one hand, and the winning over of the working class by the SPD on the other.[28] The striking emphasis placed by the VP on purely political rather than economic and social issues, best exemplified in its leadership of the reform movement, was in fact a commentary on the party's weakness.[29] This political emphasis served partly to distract attention from its vulnerability to attack on its economic and social policies.[30] More than that, it reflected the optimistic and even ingenuous mid–nineteenth-century Cobdenite categories in which VP leaders thought. In this respect entirely true to the VP's traditions, they still looked to a world where political parties were based on voluntary association not economic pressure groups,[31] and where the encouragement of unfettered economic development was a policy to undermine privilege and win political popularity. The VP's austere eschewing of *Mittelstandspolitik* was the mirror image of its espousal of political reform.

The Centre stood the policy of the VP on its head: reluctant to

26. Simon, *Die württembergischen Demokraten*, esp. p. 43.
27. *35 LT, PB IV*, p. 2687, 123 Sitz., 8.7.1902. The occasion was a debate over department stores.
28. On the slowness of the VP to modify its 'Manchester' views, and the political implications of this, see Simon, *Die württembergischen Demokraten*, pp. 38 ff.
29. Friedrich Payer himself noted how by the time of the 1906 Landtag election, with the growing importance of economic issues, the VP lacked a relevant and topical (*aktuelles*) programme. Payer, 'Mein Lebenslauf', p. 42.
30. This was especially true of the way the VP 'played the clerical card' at the height of the reform movement to isolate the Centre, particularly by trying to drive a wedge between the Centre and Conservatives. See Burkart, *Die Zusammensetzung*, pp. 115, 119.
31. In a very significant speech, Conrad Haussmann compared the Centre, as the corporate representative of Church interests, and the SPD, representative of the corporate interest of the working class, with the VP, the party of no particular corporate group but of the 'general interest'. This was not simply party-political rhetoric: it was indicative of the VP's Cobdenite views of voluntarism and the middle class as 'general class'. *37 LT, PB I*, p. 94, 6 Sitz., 16.2.1907.

support the measures of the reform era, it backed whole-heartedly the demands for an interventionist government role in the economy which emanated from *Mittelstand* circles. In this the Centre pursued the kind of policy with which it had appealed to its electorate prior to 1895. It responded, for example, to the demands of artisan producers by helping to bring about a change in the tender system used by public authorities, so that large firms with the lowest tenders were not automatically to be awarded contracts.[32] It welcomed the introduction in Württemberg in 1897 of the Reich law partially restoring the guild system, which it had itself helped through the Reichstag together with the Conservatives. The object in both cases was to confer on the craftsman a special protection from the impact of competition in the free market; and the same intention underlay support for Württemberg's master bookbinders, who were trying to maintain their craft monopoly in the binding of school books, hymn books and religious calendars against interlopers such as schoolteachers, school inspectors and sacristans.[33]

Characteristic of the Centre's solicitude for *Mittelstand* concerns was the attempt to prop up the traditional brewing industry in the state. In this branch of production concentration was far advanced, the market dominated by a number of large firms utilising technical innovations beyond the reach of the smaller brewer. Stuttgart was a major centre for the manufacture of sophisticated brewery equipment like copper cooling vats, and this helped to consolidate the position of the great Stuttgart brewing cartels like the Siegelberger Aktienbrauerei-Wulle, with its total share capital in 1906 of 3.75 million Marks.[34] The Centre electorate included two important groups which wanted to see the taxation system altered in their favour. There were, first, the family brewers, peasants or artisans with a small plot of land who produced enough beer domestically for their own needs, with a little extra. In the party's Oberschwaben heartland there were 700 such family brewers in Gröber's constituency of Riedlingen, 556 in Biberach and 372 in Leutkirch. Two other predominantly Catholic areas represented by the Centre contained the largest numbers of family brewers in the state: Neresheim, with over 700, and Ellwangen, with more than 1,000.[35] The main area of concern for this group was the lack of

---

32. *Politische Zeitfragen*, 4 (Stuttgart, 1900), p. 194; Bruns, *Württemberg unter der Regierung König Wilhelms II*, p. 877.
33. *Politische Zeitfragen*, 4 (Stuttgart, 1900), pp. 199–200.
34. On the Siegelberger Aktienbrauerei-Wulle, see *Deutsches Volksblatt*, 3 December 1906.
35. See the speech of Caspar Vogler, Centre deputy for Neresheim: *33 LT, PB II*, pp. 1071–2, 50 Sitz., 21.6.1895. On the traditional strength of brewing in the Laupheim and Waldsee areas, see Schwab, Weiss and Holtermann (eds), *Handelskammer Ravensburg*, p. 157.

exemption in the malt tax for *Weissbier*, the main domestically-brewed beer. The second group was made up by medium-sized businesses which were finding it difficult to survive in competition with larger rivals. In Ehingen, for example, where 'beer brewing [had] always been an important concern', an official report recorded a large fall in the number of independent breweries.[36] The main demand from this interest was for favourable differentials in the incidence of the malt tax and a ban on the use of surrogates like rice in the preparation of beer: these afforded advantages of cost over malt barley, but only to the large enterprises which could raise the initial capital to invest in their application.[37]

Centre deputies from the constituencies concerned were active in bringing these grievances before the Landtag. In 1895 a Centre bill incorporating the brewers' demands, and an interpellation of the government along the same lines, were instrumental in the drawing up of a government bill which banned the use of malt surrogates entirely and fixed a scale of tax liabilities advantageous to middle-sized concerns.[38] In the years up to 1906 the party could claim with some justification that its efforts had slowed down the 'swallowing up of small concerns' (*der gewerbliche Aufsaugungsprozess*): in that time the number of breweries diminished by only 287, compared with the figure of 463 in the same length of time prior to the introduction of the new law in 1899.[39] In 1909, when tax levels in the state had to be adjusted to the Reich financial reforms and both government and Landtag committee decided to remove the differentials, it was the Centre which led the eventually unsuccessful opposition in committee and on the floor of the Lower House.[40]

The interests of the retailing *Mittelstand* also played an important part in the shaping of the Centre's economic policy; and few groups were more vociferous in the period from the 1890s, as direct pressure was brought to bear on the political parties through threats of organised election boycotts. In 1895, for example, the Centre candidate in Waldsee, Anton Beutel, was faced with claims for special attention both from the highly-organised butchers and from publicans looking

36. *KW* (1907), IV, p. 97.
37. For the brewers' demands, see the report of the 1899 annual general meeting of the Württemberg brewers in Biberach, *Ipf-Zeitung*, 7 June 1899.
38. *33 LT, BB III*, p. 529, Beilage 53: motion of Dentler (Wangen) to ban malt surrogates; *33 LT, BB III*, p. 491, Beilage 42: 'Initiativantrag Vogler und Genossen'; *33 LT, PB VII*, pp. 4559–61, 209 Sitz., 4.5.1898: Kiene's interpellation.
39. *37 LT, PB VI*, p. 6167, 227 Sitz., 9.8.1909.
40. In committee, the party's representatives repeated the demand of family brewers for exemption, and asked for a 10% reduction in the malt tax for producers in the 25,000–50,000 kg band: *37 LT, BB VII*, p. 70, Beilage 433.

for repeal of a special tax levied in Württemberg on sales of wine.[41] This latter demand was part of a campaign by a group whose vigorous sectional pressures were frequently alluded to by contemporaries. The Centre did not accede to the publicans' wishes on this issue; but the party did take up another of their complaints — the sale of bottled beer by non-publicans.[42] The Centre also paid considerable attention to the demands of ordinary shopkeepers. The party introduced a bill the passing of which enabled the removal from station platforms of automatic vending machines, a serious irritant to local tradesmen. Its implementation led to the removal of machines from 116 sites.[43] After years of lobbying the Centre also succeeded in bringing on to the statute book a progressive tax on the turnover of all stores and companies with subsidiary branches.[44] This was not the only initiative taken by the party against large retail outlets. We have already seen how the Centre was a strong supporter of the Reich law of 1896 which substantially enlarged the concept of 'unfair competition'. When this failed to prevent local complaints about advertising, free offers and the ubiquitous travelling salesman with his order book,[45] the party ran a press campaign in Württemberg on the evils of modern commercial methods, and took the issue up politically at state level. It interpellated the government for statistics on the abuse of the law, asked that the existing powers be more strictly used and divided the Landtag on a motion calling on the Württemberg delegation in the Bundesrat to move for even tighter restrictions on travelling salesmen — the 'itinerants in patent leather shoes', as one Centre politician contemptuously described them.[46] Here, as in the sphere of education, the conservative morality of Centre leaders reinforced, and was reinforced by, the economic resentments of the party's supporters. Men like Gröber and Kiene could agree with directly-affected shopkeepers in the localities on the evils of the

41. *Waldse'er Wochenblatt*, 26 January 1895.
42. See, for example, *35 LT, PB II*, pp. 1211–12, 52 Sitz., 25.5.1901; *37 LT, PB I*, pp. 626–8, 26 Sitz., 17.5.1907; *37 LT, PB I*, p. 723, 30 Sitz., 1.6.1907.
43. *Politische Zeitfragen*, 4 (Stuttgart, 1900), p. 180.
44. Details of the law, which came into effect on 8 August 1903, in Wernicke, *Kapitalismus und Mittelstandspolitik*, pp. 639–40. In the final committee stage the motion was defeated 8–6, with the six Centre representatives in the minority: *35 LT, BB III*, pp. 434–5, Beilage 159. But the Centre put the motion for a progressive tax again in the final reading in the lower house (*35 LT, BB III*, p. 700, Beilage 185), and it was carried — with Conservative help — in the final vote: *35 LT, PB IV*, p. 2705, 123 Sitz., 8.7.1902.
45. For four examples among many, see *Waldse'er Wochenblatt*, 13 February 1897 ('Vom Oberland, February 6') and 7 April 1898 (report of *Gewerbeverein* meeting); *Ipf-Zeitung*, 14 June 1899 (report of *Gewerbeverein* meeting) and 2 June 1900 (Rottweil Chamber of Commerce meeting report).
46. The phrase is that of Karl Walter: *37 LT, PB I*, p. 621, 26 Sitz., 17.5.1907.

travelling salesman or department store, even if their perspective differed.

In its pursuit of *Mittelstandspolitik* the Centre paid great attention to the day-to-day details of government activity. A decision by the government to sell off land formerly used by the army to a Rhineland bank, for example, met opposition from a Centre motion that the sale should be permitted only after a guarantee that no department store be built on the site. This contingency was considered by government, VP, DP and SPD alike as an insufficient cause to forgo the large profit to the state; but the incident allowed the Centre, in its election guide of 1906, to contrast its own zeal for the *Mittelstand* cause with the recalcitrance of the government and the other parties, in particular the VP:[47] 'The *Volkspartei* man Henning was an enraged advocate on behalf of the department store and large concerns. He even established that if our motion was accepted the *Mittelstand* would be endangered. His more than curious proof of this was understood by nobody, however. The *Volkspartei*'s intercession on the side of the department stores will be noted.' The warning note struck here was significant. We have already commented a number of times on the political dexterity of the Centre leadership, and the skilful use of Landtag debates for 'outside consumption' furnishes a good example. For it was not so much in its measures on behalf of the *Mittelstand* that the Centre was successful: as we shall see, *Mittelstandspolitik* was shot through with contradictions. The real Centre success was in the realm of appearance rather than substance, in the way it managed to persuade its followers of the party's solicitude for the cause of the small man by a public stance of support for economic measures which often had only a cosmetic effect.

III

The likelihood of economic measures to protect the *Mittelstand* succeeding was limited in the first place by the contradictions within *Mittelstandspolitik*. Centre politicians frequently talked as if an identity of interest between different parts of the traditional *Mittelstand* was axiomatic. This was not actually the case, and even historically such an assumption involved a strong element of myth. The relationship, for example, between the baker and the peasants and craftsmen among whom he lived was not one of timeless rural harmony, but one of achieved social differentiation. If it was true that the small baker was

47. *Politische Zeitfragen*, 12 (Stuttgart, 1906), p. 450.

being threatened by larger concerns, it was also true that his existence in the first place was founded on a decline in home bread-making among fellow members of the *Mittelstand*. The same applied to other groups like brewers, millers, butchers and tanners. These sectional differences had their origins in the guild system. But there is little doubt that the advent of tariff protection and the intensified activity of particular pressure groups in the late nineteenth century greatly increased the potential area of conflict.[48] Appeals to the grievances of individual groups within the *Mittelstand* could certainly be a potent political weapon, as the Centre showed; but orchestrating these grievances was more difficult. The problem of sectional demands was tacitly acknowledged by one party newspaper which attacked butchers and publicans at the 1895 election for pursuing 'special economic interests'.[49] It noted with approval the comments of a Munich newspaper that[50] '. . . through the agitation of these and other interest-groups the campaign in some constituencies has taken on a regrettable giddiness. The agitation is frequently conducted not in the light of major political considerations, but of special interests, local wishes and inclinations.' Yet the Centre itself was prepared to support the special demands of groups like the brewers and dignify them with the name *Mittelstandspolitik*, even when such measures clearly benefited one section of the *Mittelstand* only at the expense of others.

As a programme rather than a slogan, therefore, *Mittelstandspolitik* was suspect from the start in its demagogic disregard of conflicting interests. This is readily apparent in the attempts made by its advocates to gloss over differences between artisan manufacturers and retailers. The rhetoric of Centre leaders implied that both groups were common victims of liberal business codes (*Gewerbefreiheit*). The claim had, indeed, a certain plausibility: both artisans and retailers were affected by businesses which were able to expand and destroy the comfortable *Nahrungsprinzip*, whereby a fixed circle of customers provided a secure livelihood. But the *Nahrungsprinzip* itself was older

48. For the conflict of interest between millers and the peasantry, see the petition of Württemberg millers calling for the raising of the tariff of flour and the lowering of the tariff on grain: *34 LT, BB III*, p. 483, Beilage 167. Significantly, it was reported in 1903 how much millers were enjoying their respite from competition with larger rivals as a result of the cheaper grain prices then prevailing: *Der Bürgerfreund*, 8 March 1903. For the adverse effect of the 1902 rise in agricultural tariffs on the price of the raw materials of artisan groups like butchers (who were particularly hard-hit), bakers, tanners and millers, see the reports of artisan chambers in Wernicke, *Kapitalismus und Mittelstandspolitik*, pp. 162, 167–9.
49. *Waldse'er Wochenblatt*, 26 January 1895.
50. *Münchener Neuesten Nachrichten*, cited ibid. This tendency was well described in the later memoirs of two conservatively-minded Württemberg politicians: Egelhaaf, *Lebenserinnerungen*, p. 125; Pistorius, *Die letzten Tage*, pp. 156–9.

and more entrenched among artisans as a result of the guild system, which had guaranteed master artisans a legally enforced degree of exclusivity not possessed by shopkeepers.[51] In fact, in the great mid-century debates over *Gewerbefreiheit*, retailers had often been found on the side of liberal reformers, fighting via the destruction of guild privileges for a share of the trade which artisans wished to keep a direct matter between producer and consumer.[52] A conflict continued to exist between these two groups within the *Mittelstand*, however much the presence of supposedly common enemies served to obscure the fact. In the latter part of the nineteenth century, for example, bakers (who belonged to a traditionally strong and self-conscious guild) were complaining that retailers in various branches — grocers, greengrocers, milk sellers, even *Schnapps* sellers — were robbing them of a living by selling bread.[53] As rents rose and artisan producers were forced off the front streets into attics and back rooms, away from direct contact with customers, their antagonism was directed not only against the factory which undercut them, but also against the retailer who had usurped the artisan's traditional position and stepped into the growing gap between producer and consumer. The measures which the Centre supported in the interests of shopkeepers were bound to harm the interests of artisans, if only indirectly.

On the other hand, the enactment in Germany of conservative, protectionist legislation such as that supported in Austria by the Christian Social Party, where the shopkeeper's right to repair certain goods was curtailed in the interests of artisans, would no doubt have produced as hostile a reaction among German retailers as it did among Austrian ones.[54] Certainly by the 1890s retailers themselves had a number of new sectional grievances against artisans. As shopkeepers became increasingly uneasy about the competition of large retail outlets like the department stores, it was artisan producers patronising such concerns who appeared to shopkeepers to be lacking in a sense of *Mittelstand* solidarity. There can be little doubt that such stores were attractive to artisan families,[55] and the exhortations from politically

---

51. For an account of the differences between artisans and retailers, see Gellately, *The Politics of Economic Despair*, pp. 22–5.
52. As, for example, in Bremen: Branding, *Die Einführung der Gewerbefreiheit in Bremen*, pp. 31–2.
53. P. Arnold, *Das Münchener Bäckergewerbe* (Stuttgart, 1895), p. 50.
54. J. Wernicke, *Der Mittelstand und seine wirtschaftliche Lage* (Leipzig, 1909), pp. 56–7.
55. The clientele of the Tietz department stores was, in the early years of their existence, composed largely of artisans. See Tietz, *Hermann Tietz*, p. 30. The agrarian academic Suchsland noted that it was 'unfortunately largely members of the active *Mittelstand* itself who are among the best customers of the department stores'. Cited Wernicke, *Kapitalismus und Mittelstandspolitik*, p. 562.

pro-*Mittelstand* circles that artisans should see through the 'swindle' of the stores testifies to this. In Württemberg the powerful slogan campaign in the Centre press, urging artisans not to desert the local tradesman, to 'hold together more', to 'buy at home, not from the Jew', suggests how seriously disunity in the *Mittelstand* undermined Centre claims.[56] Artisans were also supporting large retail outlets in another way: as deliverers. Theodor Heuss noted a typical case of the master carpenter in Heilbronn at the turn of the century whose major work was the manufacture of cupboards for a furniture store.[57] The extensive researches of the *Verein für Sozialpolitik* into artisan circumstances in Württemberg and other states suggest that such practices were widespread.[58] Given the situation in which most artisans were forced to earn a living, this is hardly surprising; but it casts some light on the contradictions involved in pursuing in an advanced industrial society a *Mittelstandspolitik* which had as its premise the existence of a unified, or at least harmoniously interdependent, *Mittelstand* with common interests as well as common bogeymen. *Mittelstandspolitik* was in fact a gloss on truculent and sectional interest-group pressure; and it was often self-defeating, for the gains of one group cancelled out those of another.

There was another, even more important reason why the measures which the Centre supported on behalf of the *Mittelstand* could not, in the long run, succeed. This was the attitude of the Württemberg government, which, like the governments of the Reich and the other states, only concerned itself with the survival of the *Mittelstand* as long as this did not conflict with its own interests.[59] At two crucial points there was such a conflict. First, as we have seen, state finances depended increasingly on revenue from large-scale industry and commerce. In order to finance its growing expenditure — on pro-*Mittelstand* measures amongst others — government had an interest in these concerns continuing to flourish and thus, for example, in the gradual transfer of labour and capital resources from marginal concerns to larger ones which were more rationally managed and

56. See, for example, *Waldse'er Wochenblatt*, 9 November 1897 and 2 July 1898; and *Ipf-Zeitung*, 20 March 1899.
57. T. Heuss, *Preludes to Life. Early Memoirs*, transl. M. Bullock (London, 1955), p. 87. Crüger, *Vortrag* (p. 28) also notes small masters working for stores in Württemberg.
58. *Schriften des Vereins für Sozialpolitik*, 62–70 (Leipzig, 1895–7), containing detailed reports on artisan conditions in different parts of the Reich. On artisans as deliverers, see vol. 64 (1895), p. 246, on shoemakers in Württemberg; also vol. 63 (1895), p. 80 and vol. 70 (1897), pp. 302, 318.
59. Winkler, W. Rücgg and O. Neuloh (eds), *Zur soziologischen Theorie und Analyse des 19. Jahrhunderts*, p. 175. Winkler, however, perhaps gives less weight to this than it merits.

more profitable.[60] Secondly, the state's larger role in economy and society from the end of the century also gave it a growing direct interest in the siphoning off of labour from comparatively unproductive, marginal concerns. Where its labour requirements had previously been modest, to run the state forestries for instance, they now had to take into account the construction and maintenance of railways and canals; and the municipalities needed a growing number of employees to maintain public transport, gas and other utilities. Furthermore the rise in the number of white-collar officials at both levels, in welfare, state abattoirs, public libraries and so on, more than kept pace with this rising need for manual labour; and this labour force tended to be prised from the *Mittelstand*, or at least from the sons and daughters of the *Mittelstand*.[61]

While the Württemberg government, like all governments of the Wilhelmine period, paid lip-service to the special qualities of the *Mittelstand*, the measures which were enacted on behalf of these groups frequently had little effect, or served merely — like the differentials in the malt tax — to slow down the process of industrial and commercial concentration. The department stores, for example, continued to grow, and the special taxes imposed on them were either passed on to deliverers, to the ultimate detriment of all retailers, or compensated for by further increases in turnover.[62] The revitalised guilds (over which, like the artisan chambers established in 1897, the government retained ultimate control) lacked the crucial power to fix prices, and without this sanction were effectively unable to shield their members from market competition.[63] The true position of the government was perhaps indicated by the short shrift it gave to a petition from the pro-*Mittelstand Centralvereinigung deutscher Vereine für Handel und Gewerbe*, on the subject of state officials' consumer cooperatives and the damage they allegedly caused to independent retailers: the analysis of the *Centralvereinigung* was dismissed as 'superficial' and its recommendations disregarded.[64]

Certainly, where pro-*Mittelstand* legislation was on the statute book

---

60. Schmidt, I. Bog *et al* (eds), *Wirtschaft und Gesellschaft in der Zeit der Industrialisierung*, p. 728, refers to small businesses 'hoarding' labour.
61. Bruns, *Württemberg unter der Regierung König Wilhelms II*, pp. 823–4, 782. In the railway and postal services of the state the numbers employed rose from 12,000 in 1895 to 19,500 in 1907. By 1914 23,000 were employed by the railways alone.
62. Wernicke, *Der Mittelstand*, pp. 44–5. This was something about which sympathisers with the shopkeepers' cause had warned. See Crüger, *Vortrag*, p. 14. See also Gellately, *Politics of Economic Despair*, pp. 43–4.
63. Bruns, *Württemberg unter der Regierung König Wilhelms II*, p. 870; *50 Jahre Handwerkskammer Stuttgart*, p. 20.
64. HStaASt, E 130 II, Bü 486, Nr. 84.

it was often not acted upon, or its operation made to serve another purpose. Thus state authorities continued to be reluctant to grant contracts to artisan workshops; and when the artisan chambers proposed more radical changes than the revised contract/tender system the government did not comply. The changes it instituted in 1912 by decree, by-passing the Landtag where the Centre and Conservatives then had a majority, did not include the demands most valued by artisans.[65] The educational subsidies provided by the state to artisans were also, in practice, used to help train a labour force consistent with the complex industrial society which was emerging in Württemberg. The bulk of the newly-established educational institutions were in technical, engineering and electrical trades rather than in traditional artisan crafts. The government stipulated, too, that the examining committees of the artisan chambers should examine not only craft products but also the work of factory apprentices; and exhibitions of work organised by the chambers and receiving official support were similarly obliged to include work from the factory bench as well as the artisan workshop.[66]

The kind of economic measures supported by the Centre undoubtedly did help to modify the operation of the laissez-faire system, slow down the disappearance of artisans and retailers and contribute towards the 'reinsurance of the *Mittelstand*'. *Mittelstandspolitik*, however, often had only a marginal or cosmetic effect, as a result both of its own contradictions and the attitude of government. The element of demagogy which the advocacy of such a policy entailed in fact attracted considerable criticism from contemporaries. Hans Crüger, for example, an organiser of artisan cooperatives himself, spoke at the annual meeting of the Württemberg *Gewerbevereine* (trade associations) in 1899 and attacked the 'so-called *Mittelstandspolitiker*' who 'believe they have found a special programme on the basis of which the *Mittelstand* can be maintained and helped'.[67] He denied that the interests of members of the *Mittelstand* could be so easily identified, and that the interests of its different constituent groups were necessarily identical. Most of all he deplored the way in which the word *Mittelstand* had been 'thrown into artisan circles',[68] as demagogic politicians took the line of least resistance by encouraging the most negative and ultimately most hopeless policies in order to preserve the support of these struggling groups. Some of Crüger's strictures certainly applied to the policies put forward by the Centre.

---

65. Bruns, *Württemberg unter der Regierung König Wilhelms II*, pp. 877–8.
66. Ibid, pp. 858–9, 880–1.
67. Crüger, *Vortrag*, p. 10.
68. Ibid.

In a sense, though, this was precisely the usefulness of such a stance to the party: by articulating the grievances of artisans and retailers the Centre addressed itself successfully to a widespread sense of neglect among demoralised social groups. The success of this tactic lay more in the sphere of politics than the sphere of economics; and its use was not confined only to the complaints of artisans and retailers. Just as the Centre made political capital out of *Mittelstand* discontent, so it seized more generally on small-town complaints about bureaucratic *hauteur* and liberal indifference. In the process it forged a powerful political weapon to be used against both the government and the VP.

IV

Like *Mittelstandspolitik*, the appeal to parish-pump resentments contained a considerable element of demagogy. We have seen how the Centre Party in Württemberg contained real differences between Stuttgart leadership and small-town supporters, differences which extended to the *Landtagsfraktion* itself. Men like Gröber, Kiene and the Rembolds were part of the parliamentary fraternity, sharing with leaders from the other parties a concern with matters like budgetary propriety; and for all their frequent appeals to parochial distrust they were certainly not always averse to supporting prestigious projects in the capital which would be unlikely to meet with small-town approval. When the Centre courted popularity by expressing doubts about the proposed re-building of the Stuttgart main station at a preliminary estimated cost of 8 million Marks,[69] this must be set against its support for the re-building of the capital city's Court Theatre at a cost of 3.3 million Marks. The correspondence of Kiene with the intendant of the theatre and the mayor of Stuttgart indicates that the deputy leader of the Centre was a principal parliamentary force in helping to bring about the rebuilding.[70]

The argument over the Stuttgart main station should not be seen as an isolated incident. It belonged to a consistent style of Centre politics in the state, characteristic of which was the development by the party of the technique of using plenary and committee sessions in the Landtag to speak for the benefit of an outside audience. It this way the Centre was able to emphasise, at no real cost, its solicitude for the interests of the little man. Now it is true that in a period when

---

69. *37 LT, PB I*, p. 40, 4 Sitz., 14.2.1907. On the cost of the re-building, Bruns, *Württemberg unter der Regierung König Wilhelms II*, p. 49.
70. HStaASt, Hans Kiene Papers, Q 1/5, 4: 'Hoftheater'. Mayor von Gauss and theatre intendant to Kiene, 17 December 1905 and 29 January 1906.

parliamentary debates and the details of committee sittings were very fully reported even in the local press, this was not something unique to the Centre.[71] But contemporaries noted how the Centre made particularly widespread use of the technique;[72] and thorough perusal of the Landtag proceedings reveals numerous occasions when attitudes were struck by Centre leaders which would have been merely jejune if not intended for outside consumption. Such, for example, was the suggestion by the financial expert Hans Kiene that a conversion of state loans in 1895 would benefit the Rothschilds against the interests of small savers.[73] Moreover, in one respect at least, the Centre was tactically ahead of the other bourgeois parties. This was in the production of edited reports of parliamentary debates for electoral consumption, a practice later developed at Reich level by Matthias Erzberger, but learnt by him in Württemberg from his mentor Joseph Eckard.[74] From as early as 1895 the latter's professionally edited pamphlets, buttressing reports in the local press and at *Volksverein* meetings, served as a means of keeping the Centre in touch with its electorate and reassuring them of its concern. For a party addressing itself to a comparatively sealed–off Catholic world these techniques were especially useful.[75]

The skill of the Centre leadership consisted in the way they were able to re-work the old small-town, petty-bourgeois bogeys of 1848 into a new idiom which could articulate the grievances of such people at the turn of the century; and at the same time, disguising the shortcomings and contradictions which we have already noted in Centre policy, could marry together the different but related concerns of leaders and led. Thus the city, for a man like Kiene a potentially

---

71. On this subject, see the sour comments of Pistorius, *Die letzten Tage*, pp. 156–9.
72. This tendency on the part of Centre leaders was something which all the other parties were agreed in detecting. Wilhelm Keil, for example, was later to write: 'The representatives of all the *Fraktionen* were very concerned in committee to agitate "out of doors". By long-standing tradition all motions and counter-motions in the committee sittings were published in the newspaper reports. Thus, as many motions as possible were put. If we Social Democrats came up with motions putting particular demands to the government, then there would normally follow motions from the other parties, above all the Centre, calling on the government to "consider", "examine" or do "as soon as possible" or "if possible" this, that or the other.' W. Keil, *Erlebnisse eines Sozialdemokraten*, 2 vols (Stuttgart, 1947–8), I, pp. 237–8. Similar charges were made over the conduct of the Centre in plenary sessions by Friedrich Haussmann (*33 LT, PB I*, p. 128, 10 Sitz., 8.3.1895), and by the *Schwäbischer Merkur* (27 April 1903), a paper which stood close to the DP.
73. *33 LT, PB I*, p. 211, 15 Sitz., 26.4.1895.
74. Hagen, *Gestalten*, III, pp. 165 ff; and on Erzberger's early career generally as a pamphleteer and journalist: Epstein, *Erzberger*, pp. 10–17.
75. There was, again, a parallel here, like that noted at the level of party organisation, between the Centre and the SPD. Both paid great attention to the press and propaganda, and both were dealing with a relatively closed, sealed-off constituency.

dangerous centre of immorality, 'alien' literature and social unrest, could be depicted to Centre voters as a parasite on the countryside. In this the party built its demonology of solid foundations, for Stuttgart especially had, as we have seen, traditionally been regarded in this light because of the institutions most strongly identified with it: court, army, bureaucracy and finance. The figures standing for exploitation and spendthrift luxury needed only to be brought up to date: in place of high expenditure on the civil list, the amount of state resources devoted to the education of a prodigal élite; in place of the chancellery official, the administrator of posts or railways; in place of the money-lender, the Stuttgart branch of a big Berlin bank.

A good illustration of the Centre technique can be seen in the long fight of the party against the state Veterinary High School, which it considered an unnecessary waste of financial resources. In 1910 the Centre was able, with Conservative and some DP help, to obtain a Landtag majority for the closure of the High School, which occurred two years later.[76] Prior to that, Kiene had argued forcefully against moving the High School to Stuttgart, portraying the issue as a battle between frugal, small-town taxpayers and an indulgent élite. He asked rhetorically if it really served the interests of agriculture to 'transfer the veterinary students to the State University, with all the raised pretensions and trimmings of university life that the future veterinary surgeons will be given there'.[77] Kiene himself was concerned by the costs involved, and perhaps by the spectre of a further swelling of student numbers in the relatively turbulent atmosphere of the capital city. For a former student at Freiburg, Tübingen and Heidelberg, and a life-long member of the Guestphalia student corporation, the posture adopted was somewhat disingenuous. The issue had the advantage that it could be made popular, particularly as a high proportion of the veterinary students had not been born in Württemberg;[78] and Kiene was able to quote a peasant who had allegedly complained to him about the new type of 'over-educated' veterinary surgeon, 'the gentleman with the top hat and kid gloves' whose practical knowledge was supposedly deficient.[79] In the combination which it brought into

76. The Centre motion for the 'abolition of the High School, with the retention if possible of the Horse Clinic', was passed in the lower house by 47–33. *Literarische Beilage des Staatsanzeigers für Württemberg*, 24 and 25, 31 December 1910, p. 381. It should be noted, however, that later VP attempts to make political capital out of the closure of the school were scornfully dismissed by the SPD. See *Schwäbische Tagwacht*, 25 September and 30 October 1912.

77. *36 LT, PB IV*, p. 2483, 100 Sitz., 14.6.1905.

78. In 1900, 37 out of the 114 students were non-Württembergers, in 1909 53 out of 129. *Politische Zeitfragen*, 20 (Stuttgart, 1912), p. 84.

79. *36 LT, PB IV*, p. 2483, 100 Sitz., 14.6.1905.

play, of conservative apprehensions among the leadership and more basic suspicions among party followers, this issue produced an echo of the Centre position on more general educational concerns.

On a wide range of other matters too the Centre exploited widespread feeling about biased institutional arrangements in the state, turning apparently neutral issues into matters of principle. Joseph Nieder took up complaints about the neglect of the *Jagstkreis* and about administration from 'outside', when the government reorganised its agricultural inspectorate.[80] The centralisation of forestry administration was criticised on similar grounds, while Gröber entered a routine debate on the reorganisation of state postal rates to support the claims of back-bencher Theophil Egger that the changes (which removed the differential favouring local post) were regarded with 'disapproval and dissatisfaction' on the land, as 'purely a favouring of the large towns, especially Stuttgart'.[81] Gröber himself thundered that towns like Stuttgart, Heilbronn and Reutlingen were not paying their way; that they constituted a burden on rural districts:[82] 'I maintain . . . that the new rate means principally a greater burdening of the rural population against the urban. . . . Furthermore, large businesses will now be favoured over smaller ones . . . and now large businesses with their oppressive competition will enter the markets of small businesses in our small towns and localities.'

Of all the issues of this kind out of which the Centre made electoral capital, perhaps the most significant was railway politics. This lent itself particularly to the Centre's mode of politics. The railway network in Württemberg radiated out from Stuttgart, a natural communications centre.[83] Furthermore, the 2,500 km of main line completed by 1891 contrasted sharply with the less than 100 km of

---

80. When the state decentralised its agricultural inspectorate, a step welcomed by the Centre, it provided inspectors in only three of the four *Kreise*. Nieder put forward a Centre motion that a fourth inspector be found for the *Jagstkreis*, regretting that areas like Neresheim would otherwise continue to be badly served and the peasantry would still have to travel to Ulm and be dealt with 'from outside'. *35 LT, PB VI*, pp. 3943–4, 177 Sitz., 20.5.1903. Eventually the *Jagstkreis* did receive its inspector, with his base at Ellwangen. *Die Landwirtschaft und die Landwirtschaftspflege*, p. 127.
81. *33 LT, PB II*, p. 1004, 47 Sitz., 18.6.1895.
82. Ibid, p. 1011. Note, too, Kiene's speech along similar lines referring to the alleged unfairness to rural areas of the state building regulations (*Bauordnung*), which he claimed were geared to urban conditions. Report in *Deutsches Volksblatt*, 23 November 1906.
83. 'Stuttgart is to a quite marked extent the political, cultural and commercial centre of the state (one needs only to glance at a map of communications to recognise that Stuttgart is the hub of the state around which everything else is orientated).' Hoffmann, *Landwirtschaft und Industrie in Württemberg*, p. 4. On the pattern of Württemberg railway construction in general, see G. von Morlok, *Die Königlich württembergischen Eisenbahnen. Rückschau auf deren Erbauung während der Jahre 1835–89* (Stuttgart, 1890); O. Supper, *Die Entwicklung des Eisenbahnwesens im Königreich Württemberg* (Stuttgart, 1895).

branch line.[84] The flow of competitive goods into the state was thus facilitated, while small-town and rural producers were kept at a disadvantage because of their isolation. In 1890 only 45 per cent of the population had access to the railway network, this had risen to only 57 per cent by 1903 and was estimated even by 1916 at only 70 per cent.[85] While urban communities and the growing number of suburban commuters were offered special services and reduced rates, outlying areas complained bitterly of injustice. In addition to this, financial retrenchment meant that local authorities had to meet the cost of most of the twenty-seven branch lines constructed between 1891 and 1915.[86]

This was grist to the mill for the Centre, and the party made it very clear how strongly it supported such expressions of neglect. Its opposition to the costly rebuilding of the main station in Stuttgart must be seen in this context. Centre back-benchers repeatedly stressed the injustice done to peripheral areas and took railway officials to task for their arrogance (as, for example, the official who wrote to Laupheim 'near Ulm', although Laupheim was an administrative district in its own right).[87] The party also courted local popularity by obtaining better rates for agricultural workers travelling by rail.[88] Above all, the Centre programme called more explicitly than that of its VP opponents for more branch line construction, and its deputies identified themselves closely with this issue.[89] As we have seen, Franz Xaver Nessler's election at Spaichingen in 1906 (the first occasion the Centre had won the seat, although it was overwhelmingly Catholic) owed much to his championing of the cause of the Heubergbahn, which had long been desired by local voters.[90] There was also the case of

84. Bruns, *Württemberg unter der Regierung König Wilhelms II*, p. 757.
85. Ibid, p. 67.
86. The nature of the terrain in Württemberg also made the costs of new track greater than in most states; and this, together with the absence of a traffic in heavy industrial goods like coal or iron, made the Württemberg railways less profitable than elsewhere. These considerations in themselves made for official caution about opening new lines. In addition, the government seems to have felt by the beginning of the twentieth century that the network had perhaps been extended in too rash and cavalier a fashion. It noted especially the time-lag before the 'economically slumbering' regions which had been brought into the network began, through industrialisation, to generate a financial return to the state exchequer. HStaASt, Hans Kiene Papers, Q 1/5, 6: printed official material on state railways and their profitability.
87. The issue was raised by Schick (deputy for Laupheim), *33 LT, PB IV*, p. 2737, 126 Sitz., 30.4.1897.
88. *Politische Zeitfragen*, 20 (Stuttgart, 1912), pp. 72–3.
89. *Politische Zeitfragen*, 4 (Stuttgart, 1900), p. 129; J. Andre, *Zentrum und Landwirtschaft* (Stuttgart, 1918), p. 4. Andre was able to point to the suggestion of the VP leader, Theodor Liesching, that railway petitions (which Centre deputies were extremely zealous in backing) should be more carefully examined. *33 LT, PB IV*, p. 4034, 151 Sitz., 12.2.1909.
90. See above, Chapter Three, p. 143.

Caspar Vogler, Centre deputy for Neresheim, whose role as an architect — in both the technical and broader senses — of the Härtsfeldbahn, constructed in 1899 to link Aalen and Ballmertshofen via Neresheim, was a major one. The importance to the local communities of such branch lines is illustrated by the fact that the small town of Dillingen made Vogler an honorary citizen when the line from Ballmertshofen was extended to Dillingen in 1904.[91]

Issues of this kind could, of course, rebound and work against the Centre. We have already seen how dissatisfaction over railway branch lines played a part in the revolt of 1900 in the constituencies of Gmünd and Tettnang, as it did in local discontent with Kiene in Ehingen.[92] The case of the Rottweil by-election of 1913 could also be cited, where the Centre candidate Glüther was chairman of the local railway committee. A VP election pamphlet attacked Glüther vigorously. It attributed to an inhabitant of Dunningen (which was part of the constituency) the statement that 'we have finally had enough of being led around by the nose for fifteen years by the Rottweil Centre over our railway'. The pamphlet contrasted the unsuccessful local railway scheme with the successful completion of lines at Herrenberg–Tübingen and Gerabronn, which were VP strongholds. If the Centre was not going to represent local interests, it continued, electors should vote for the liberal candidate, who would do so.[93] It is difficult to assess the final importance of this issue, but the Centre certainly lost the Rottweil seat after holding it for thirteen years.[94]

The history of one other Württemberg constituency also suggests how Centre tactics could be successfully turned against the party. This was Spaichingen, 90 per cent Catholic and won for the Centre by Nessler in 1906. But in 1895 and 1900, alone of constituencies in the state with such a preponderance of Catholics, it returned a VP man, Schumacher. Part of the reason for this undoubtedly lay in the fact that Schumacher was a Catholic, even though this factor did not appear to have the same weight in other seats.[95] But Schumacher's

---

91. Information provided by Herr Dr Karl Setz of Neresheim, in a letter of 10 February 1975. I am also grateful to Herr Wilfried Vogler of Neresheim for his help in locating this information.
92. See above, Chapter Three, pp. 117–8. Discontent over a local branch line also seems to have played some part in the 1900 election in Biberach. See *Anzeiger vom Oberland*, 3 December 1900.
93. HStaASt, Conrad Haussmann Papers, Q 1/2, 104: 'Wahlaufruf an die Wähler von Rottweil'.
94. The victory was, however, a very narrow one. Müller, a DP man with VP support, gained 4,551 second ballot votes, against 4,443 for the Centre candidate, Glüther.
95. It should be noted, however, that the VP was able to win the Oberndorf Landtag seat from the Centre in 1900 fielding a Catholic candidate.

political style was also very similar in its populist rhetoric to that normally employed by the Centre against liberal opponents, and this must provide at least one of the reasons why the VP retained the Spaichingen seat for so long. In 1900, for example, Schumacher released an election pamphlet denouncing the 'outside' (*fremd*) Centre candidate, and urging the value of electing a local man like himself: 'For we already have too many *Stuttgart gentlemen* in the House, *who are inclined to represent the interests of the city of Stuttgart more than those of the country.*'[96] It was a classic, and successful, piece of parish-pump politics; but it was exceptional in coming from the VP, for more commonly it was the Centre which exploited feelings of this kind against both the government and the VP itself.

96. *Heuberger Bote*, 4 December 1900. The italicised words were printed in bold type in the original.

CHAPTER 6

The Centre and the Polarisation
of Politics in Württemberg:
Relations with the Social Democrats

As we have seen, the election of 1895 marked a fundamental change in Württemberg politics, away from loose party groupings of the pro- and anti-governmental kind and towards parties based on economic interests or social class. The *Landespartei*, and to a lesser extent the National Liberal DP, were the chief victims of this process in 1895. But the changed nature of politics in that year was not a once-for-all event: the alignment of parties along class lines became more marked in the following years and the parties of the middle, above all the VP, lost ground electorally to those of the Left and Right, the SPD and the agrarian Conservatives. The years after 1900 saw a succession struggle over an important part of the former VP electorate, and this placed the Centre in a curiously ambiguous position. On the one hand it had won its political position in the state by exploiting the grievances of outlying Catholic areas and of groups like the *Mittelstand* and peasantry against the liberal capitalism espoused by the VP; and it continued after 1895, as we have seen, to maintain its position vis-à-vis the VP by making political capital out of such grievances. It was in this respect a 'successor party'. On the other hand the Centre was itself threatened from Right and Left by the increasing polarisation of politics, as both the Catholic peasantry and Catholic working class became more aware of their particular economic interests. It is to the uneasy relations of the Centre with the rising force of Social Democracy that we shall therefore now turn.

I

In 1895 the electoral performance of the SPD in Württemberg was modest: while the VP secured thirty-one of the seventy elected Landtag seats, the SPD won only two, reduced shortly afterwards to one on the death of the deputy for Cannstatt. It was in 1900 that the

VP was first shaken by the SPD challenge. The party chairman, Schnaidt, lost his seat in Ludwigsburg, and the SPD was also successful in Stuttgart, Cannstatt and Göppingen. Even Conrad Haussmann was taken to a second ballot contest by the SPD in an election which saw the overall vote of the latter party nearly double, from 30,000 to 58,000. In the 1903 elections to the Reichstag the VP again lost votes, while the SPD increased its strength enormously, from 60,000 to 100,000 votes. The real vulnerability of the VP was clear by the time of the 1906 Landtag elections, when it dropped to only twenty-four seats out of ninety-two in the newly enlarged Lower House and the SPD tripled its representation from five to fifteen. Six years later, at the state elections of 1912, the SPD had nearly drawn level with the VP, having risen to seventeen seats while the VP dropped again to nineteen.

At one level the Centre welcomed the victories of the SPD as a confirmation of its own views on the bankruptcy of liberalism. As early as the 1898 Reichstag elections, when the drift from VP to SPD was apparent, one Centre newspaper argued that the results had shown the preference of the electorate for parties with clear views on the social question; and the general 'turn to the left' with which the VP sought to draw comfort from its defeat was dismissed as 'gallows humour'. The paper noted that on issues such as anti-militarism and indirect taxation the VP would always be outflanked on the left, and concluded that its emphasis on political issues and its empty general appeal to traditional liberal feeling were no longer capable of marshalling significant social forces behind the VP. The Centre and the SPD, it argued, were the two great parties of the future.[1] Critical analysis of this kind was an attempt to score off the VP; and it was consistent with the scorn reserved by all Centre politicians and leader writers for liberal politicians and their 'uncommitted' (*farblos*) allies in the press, who allegedly tried to ignore or gloss over the social question. This sort of analysis also suggested, however, a greater degree of complicity and common interest between Centre and SPD, both of which had entered the Landtag in 1895 and gained strength at VP expense. Beyond this shared situation of being 'successor parties', Centre and SPD certainly had much in common. As in the Reich generally they recruited their support from the poorest parts of the population and saw themselves as mass parties. They also had a common dislike of exceptional legislation and repressive bureaucracy. Adolf Gröber was one of the most vigorous opponents of the *Zuchthausvorlage* (Penitentiary Bill), characteristically blaming social

---

1. *Waldse'er Wochenblatt*, 2 June 1898.

unrest on liberal and free-thinking professors rather than on the working class; and the SPD motion in the Württemberg Landtag objecting to Bülow's Law of Association (a measure defended by Friedrich Payer) could be largely withdrawn as the Centre had already tabled one which made the same points.[2] Moreover, the attacks of the Social Democrats on privileged bourgeois society found their counterpart in Centre attacks on horse racing, duelling and car rallying as the self-indulgences of a selfish and decadent ruling élite.[3]

Centre and SPD also shared common ground in their specific attacks on liberalism and the VP. They were able to agree on the dehumanising effects of industrial capitalism, and SPD concern with factory conditions was echoed by Centre objections to certain kinds of female labour and to the unwillingness of employers to recognise popular holidays. In contrast to the recalcitrant VP, the Centre and SPD cooperated in pressing for workers' chambers to be set up, and for greater provision to aid the unemployed.[4] Both parties, too, propagated a world-view which denied the exclusive benefits of liberalism in economic or social spheres and indicted its values as partial and historically limited. While the SPD noted that the VP had become, as one of them put it, a party of 'bourgeois and capitalist interests',[5] the Centre constantly attacked the VP on the similar grounds that it was dominated by 'Manchester men'. Indeed, in its critical observations on changing economic and social relations the Centre was often strikingly close to the marxist terms of the SPD. The Centre newspaper with the largest Württemberg circulation, the *Ipf-Zeitung*, described in the following terms the significance of urban class segregation and the division of labour:[6]

> The urban population is split into many more, and more unequal, occupations than the rural population; one man can no longer judge another man's job, and the differences between the labour of the hand and brain in particular are more pronounced. . . . Beyond the differences of occupation, social conflicts are also sharper in the towns; alongside the relatively small number of 'owners' is the vast army of 'workers' who frequently look upon the former solely as exploiters . . . between the 'better' and lower classes a gulf has

2. Schlemmer, *Die Rolle der Sozialdemokratie*, p. 110.
3. On horse-racing, *Deutsches Volksblatt*, 15 June 1895; on duelling, *Deutsches Volksblatt*, 30 January 1895 and *Waldse'er Wochenblatt*, 15 January 1898, and generally, Rost, *Die wirtschaftliche und kulturelle Lage*, p. 6; on car rallying, see the Centre contributions to the debate in *35 LT, PB IV*, p. 2739, 125 Sitz., 10.7.1902.
4. *Politische Zeitfragen*, 17 (Stuttgart, 1912), pp. 30 ff.
5. Blos, *Denkwürdigkeiten*, II, p. 67.
6. *Ipf-Zeitung*, 6 March 1899.

opened up which is becoming increasingly permanent. On the land the connecting doors between the public *Gastzimmer* and the *Herrenstüble* are seldom completely closed. In the towns the 'better public houses' are separated from the 'inferior' ones; even the districts of the town are developing a socially distinct character. One half no longer knows how the other half lives and dwells.

Yet for all these attitudes held in common, the Centre and the SPD were able to come to no sort of sustained political understanding in Württemberg. In circumstances which were different from either Baden or Bavaria they did not even cooperate tactically over electoral reform,[7] and despite the apparent affinities of the two parties the Centre tended to ally with the Conservatives on the Right and the SPD with the VP on the Left. The 1907 election showed clearly that while the Centre and SPD were the common official 'enemies of the Reich', these divisions between Left and Right cut across the divisions of the Bülow Bloc.[8] By 1912, when the Centre fought both Landtag and Reichstag elections in formal alliance with the Conservatives, and the SPD and VP gave mutual electoral undertakings in a number of seats, the distance between the two parties was as great as it had been since 1895. This fact poses problems of explanation similar to those already considered at national level. The argument that religion divided the two parties can, again, be only a partial explanation. Certainly it was a source of mutual hostility, particularly when — as in questions concerning education or sexual morality, for example — differences over religion were reinforced by differences over the role of the family.[9] But attitudes on both sides were more muted than in a state like Prussia. It is significant that in the great scandal caused by allegations after the 1906 Landtag elections of clerical influence in the Geislingen constituency, the SPD took an extremely moderate stance.

---

7. There were, however, local officials — such as those in Leutkirch — who feared that the Centre and SPD would collaborate politically 'at the first good opportunity'. But these fears were dismissed by the Ministry of the Interior in Stuttgart. HStaASt, E 150, Bund 2045, Nr. 291, report from the *Donaukreis* administration on the activities of the SPD in 1895, Ulm, 28 January 1896.

8. K. Jakob, 'Landtagswahlen und Reichstagswahlen in Württemberg', *Süddeutsche Monatshefte* (1907), I, pp. 517 ff.

9. The *Waldse'er Wochenblatt* (15 October 1895) argued that it was not so much the hatred of the SPD for religion which made it a threat to the Catholic peasant, but 'even more' its 'planned destruction of the entire social order, marriage, the family and property'. Kiene included in his indictment of non-denominational schools, which the SPD advocated, not just the alleged threat to religious instruction, but the alleged danger to moral health and the rights of Christian parents. The charge that the SPD was bent on the destruction of family life by the advocacy of free love and contraception was an extremely common one at all levels of the Centre Party and press.

A priest in Wiesensteig, the part of the constituency from which the successful Centre candidate came, admitted threatening his parishioners with the prospect of divine retribution if they voted for any other candidate. His actions, criticised even by the Centre leader Kiene as injudicious and 'tasteless',[10] brought a furious response from the VP, which demanded the annulment of the result. But the SPD, which provided the chairman of the Landtag committee investigating the affair, voted down this demand on the grounds that the priest's actions could not be equated with more obvious and direct forms of election bribery.[11] The incident sheds light on the fact that it was the VP, in its increasingly vulnerable political position, which made most use of the anti-clerical card, not the SPD. More generally, it suggests that the religious factor alone — although it would clearly always play a role — cannot explain the growing acerbity of Centre–SPD relations.

There remains the argument that feelings of outraged rectitude on the part of Centre leaders, and of contempt for Centre pusillanimity on the part of SPD leaders, worked to divide the parties. If the proposition were true it might explain why the two parties generally found cooperation easier after the war than before it. By the later period the SPD had given ample demonstration during the war, and even more during the revolutionary situation which followed, that its sometimes revolutionary vocabulary was not going to be matched by corresponding actions. This was certainly so in Württemberg, where the Centre for its part, after initial concern, reconciled itself to the situation and saw in support for the SPD a means of averting chaos and a further move to the left.[12] In the years from 1918 to 1923 both Centre and SPD were able to contribute to legislation and provide ministers, losing in the process some of the animosity fostered by mutual suspicion.

But this argument is more difficult to apply to Württemberg than to Germany as a whole, and not simply because it was a southern state where even prior to 1914 the relatively democratic political tradition softened relations between all the parties. In Württemberg, unlike the Reich or even a state like Bavaria, where the Centre had an overall parliamentary majority for almost all the period 1881–1914, the Centre was not a 'party of government'; nor was the SPD recalcitrantly anti-governmental. The leaders of the Centre, precisely because of their conservatism, frequently attacked the government for

10. Bodewig, *Geistliche Wahlbeeinflussungen*, p. 163.
11. Ibid, pp. 160–1.
12. Morsey, *Zentrumspartei*, pp. 86, 172.

enacting legislation which it was claimed would encourage social ferment and unrest: as we have seen, educational reform and many aspects of government economic policy were viewed in this light.[13] The SPD, on the other hand, was often to be found on the side of the government: its positive approach to legislation was clearly shown in the *Reformlandtag*, when it held the balance in the Lower House between the VP and DP liberals and the Centre–Conservative bloc which was beginning to emerge.[14] Just as the SPD group in the Stuttgart council supported the progressive measures of mayors like von Rümelin and von Gauss, so the SPD *Landtagsfraktion* was prepared to support the progressive measures of ministers like von Fleischhauer and von Breitling.[15] Encouraged by a government which allowed trade union buildings to fly the red flag openly and which permitted the first international socialist congress on German soil (even lending public buildings for the occasion), the SPD conducted itself politically in a very different way from the pariah SPD parties of Prussia and Saxony which attracted so much Centre hostility. After 1907 Württemberg SPD deputies voted for an annual budget, took part in Landtag opening ceremonies, swore the oath of allegiance, went to ministerial dinners and even took part in parliamentary outings.[16] Indeed, it was precisely this behaviour which led to Württemberg SPD men like Keil and Hildenbrand being reviled as reformists by the Left.[17]

Even Keil, however, the post-war apostle of better relations with the Centre, was not willing to go beyond personal friendship with Centre politicians. Nor was he able to induce the Centre itself to cooperate with the SPD prior to 1914. And the most important single reason for this was neither division over religion nor different attitudes towards government. The clearest dividing line between Centre and SPD, evident in Württemberg and more generally in the Reich, was the one which divided them over what sort of society was to develop out of a liberal capitalism and political liberalism which were both clearly on the retreat. In Württemberg the Centre and the SPD were both 'successor parties' to the VP, and to a lesser extent to the National Liberal DP; but they differed fundamentally in the way they regarded the legacy. The striking similarities we have seen in the attitudes of the Centre and SPD towards industrial capitalism

13. See above, Chapter Four.
14. Schlemmer, *Die Rolle der Sozialdemokratie*, p. 102.
15. Keil, *Erlebnisse*, I, p. 158; Schlemmer, *Die Rolle der Sozialdemokratie*, pp. 54, 103–6.
16. Schlemmer, *Die Rolle der Sozialdemokratie*, p. 113.
17. The attitude of the 'conciliatory' SPD group on the Stuttgart municipal council — Kloss, Mattutat, Fischer, Heymann — was attacked by the party left on similar grounds. See the long report in the *Schwäbische Tagwacht*, 23 November 1906.

extended, in fact, only to their analysis of its immediate effects. When it came to more long-term views the two parties drew opposite conclusions and offered antithetical solutions.

The politicians of the Centre saw in laissez-faire not so much an inequitable system of production as a morally and socially disagreeable force, and they viewed the ferment of classes which it created not as the premise of a new order but as an aberration of the old. While they continued to bemoan Catholic backwardness and under-representation in modern branches of production, they nevertheless, in their attacks on the social system which 'Manchesterism' had allegedly brought about, looked backwards for inspiration: to an idealised period when '*Stand* consciousness' outweighed class consciousness; when the city and the factory did not exert their magnetic appeal on the sons and daughters of the peasantry and *Mittelstand*; and when liberalised marriage laws, female factory labour and revised educational syllabuses had not undermined the basis of customary family authority. The SPD, for its part, attacked liberal capitalism from a very different standpoint, one which — despite the reformism of the Württemberg party — reflected the mechanistic marxist stages theory of SPD ideologue Karl Kautsky.[18] It affirmed the free movement of labour, commodities and ideas as a necessary break with the customary order, in which productive capacity was cramped and the lower classes not yet freed either from material necessity or paternalist control. In short, while the SPD attacked both the short-term abuses and long-term irrationality of capitalism, it saw the laissez-faire measures with which the VP was identified as a precondition of the socialist society which would transcend the capitalist one when the latter achieved its fullest maturity, not simply (the 'undialectical' Centre solution) replace it at a historically arbitrary point in time. Hence provisional support for liberalism and capitalism was construed as the role of the SPD, in so far as this helped to accelerate the logic of historical development and capitalism's own demise.[19] The reformism of the SPD in Württemberg simply made this two-stage theory of the road to socialism easier to follow, since relations with the liberal VP in everyday matters were closer.

Rather than an anti-liberal alliance of Centre and SPD, there thus developed in Württemberg an informal coalition of VP and SPD, sharing with the Great Coalition in neighbouring Baden a common hostility to the Centre. The SPD supported the VP in calling for

18. See Ritter, *Arbeiterbewegung*, pp. 97 ff, for an account of Kautsky's Marxism.
19. See the article 'Der Kapitalismus als Revolutionär', *Schwäbische Tagwacht*, 20 August 1912.

constitutional and educational reforms,[20] and in these and more general cultural issues attacked the Centre sharply as the party of 'reaction' and *Bildungsfeindlichkeit* (hostility to education).[21] In few German cities were the links between socialist and liberal intellectuals as close as in Stuttgart. Wilhelm Keil achieved for the SPD's major newspaper in the state, the *Schwäbische Tagwacht*, a reputation for liberality and high cultural standards among liberal middle-class circles. Socialist intellectuals like Wilhelm Blos became part of the radical cultural circle around Conrad Haussmann and Herman Hesse.[22] In supporting advanced liberal demands the SPD naturally saw them only as a preliminary assault on *ständisch* society: the party wished for a more radical break with the old order than the VP could countenance or thought politically possible, for fully non-denominational schools, for example, and the exclusion of all aristocrats from parliamentary institutions. But the VP, fearing more lost votes or the withdrawal of SPD support from the parliamentary reform programme, allowed itself to be pushed to the left; and the SPD for its part was prepared to accept a minimum programme and give its backing to compromise reforms.[23] The common action of the two parties extended therefore over a wide range of issues.

II

The SPD also supported the VP rather than the Centre on many economic issues. The Centre, as we have seen, developed out of its anti-laissez-faire stance a policy which called for state intervention on behalf of the *Mittelstand*. The SPD, with its primary interest in low prices for the consumer, would have no truck with such a policy. It rejected efforts, such as those backed by the Centre, to shelter small producers from the effects of the market. These efforts to 'save' the *Mittelstand* were scornfully dismissed by the SPD as an attempt 'to

20. Schlemmer, *Die Rolle der Sozialdemokratie*, pp. 53–7, 104–6; Simon, *Die württembergischen Demokraten*, p. 58.
21. See the speech of the SPD education spokesman, Heymann, on the *Bildungsfeindlichkeit* of the Centre: *37 LT, PB II*, p. 3072, 116 Sitz., 1.7.1908. See also the SPD's defence — alongside the VP — of the satirical magazine *Simplizissimus* against Centre attacks: *Politische Zeitfragen*, 15 (Stuttgart, 1912), p. 69.
22. Both Wilhelm Blos and Wilhelm Keil mention in some detail in their memoirs the close relations which existed between liberal and socialist intellectuals. The progressive mayor of Stuttgart, Emil von Rümelin, who moved in the best circles but prided himself on being a 'state socialist', was a friend of Blos. Like many others in government and high office he was a reader of the *Schwäbische Tagwacht*.
23. Schlemmer, *Die Rolle der Sozialdemokratie*, pp. 104, 106.

re-erect old barriers to trade and return to medieval economic conditions'.[24] The SPD deputy Tauscher, in line with the two-stage theory of economic development we have already noted, actually cited the American trusts as a model form of rational economic development;[25] and on questions of this sort the SPD aligned itself unhesitatingly with the VP and the captains of industry in its ranks.

Conflict between the Centre and SPD was particularly great at the point where the interests of *Mittelstand* and working class were most sharply divergent: the problem of the retail sector. The existence of a large number of small shopkeepers, whom the Centre sought to keep afloat, made little sense economically. Even Centre leaders admitted that this group contained a large penumbra of inefficient members;[26] and their chronic lack of competitiveness was tacitly conceded when the Centre press was obliged to attack artisans and other members of the *Mittelstand* for patronising department stores because of the price advantages they offered.[27] Those shopkeepers who travelled into the towns, bought up stock from larger outlets and re-sold it at a higher price in the small towns further underlined this point.[28] The Centre, as a long-term solution, advocated the encouragement of purchasing cooperatives in which retailers pooled their resources, just as it called for sales cooperatives among artisans. As we shall see, these ventures were largely to prove a failure;[29] but there can be little doubt that where they were successful — especially among butchers and bakers — the result was higher prices for the consumer. In Schramberg, for example, a bakers' cooperative was reported as being so successful that it 'prepared the way for a rise in prices which would not have been possible for the individual [baker]'.[30] It was hardly surprising that this provoked SPD hostility. Karl Kloss, SPD deputy for Stuttgart, singled out the independent bakers as a group by whom the consumer was 'milked in an outrageous way'.[31] The party also sided with the VP

24. *35 LT, PB IV*, p. 2699, 123 Sitz., 8.7.1902.
25. *35 LT, PB IV*, p. 2698, 123 Sitz., 8.7.1902.
26. Thus, Kiene: *35 LT, PB IV*, p. 2678, 122 Sitz., 5.7.1902. Kiene, however, implied that the problem of 'overcrowding' was principally among concerns in newly built-up urban areas, whereas in fact it applied also to smaller towns. There were Centre politicians who recognised the full extent of the problem. Karl Trimborn, for example, spoke in 1905 of the 'extraordinary glut of small retailers'. Wernicke, *Kapitalismus und Mittelstandspolitik*, p. 422. August Engel, a party expert and pamphleteer on the subject, shared Trimborn's view.
27. See above, Chapter Five, p. 155.
28. *35 LT, PB IV*, p. 2695, 123 Sitz., 8.7.1902. For SPD criticism of the small retail sector as inefficient, see *Schwäbische Tagwacht*, 13 August 1912.
29. See below, pp. 179–81.
30. Gemming, *Das Handwerkergenossenschaftswesen*, p. 79.
31. *33 LT, PB III*, p. 1736, 80 Sitz., 9.5.1895.

against the Centre in defending the advantages of large stores and attacking those who helped to raise the price of goods in the shop. In the debate over a turnover tax on department stores, for example, Wilhelm Keil explicitly aligned the SPD with the arch laissez-faire VP deputy Oskar Galler in rejecting such a measure.[32]

The well-organised butchers and bakers were prominent, too, in the clash between *Mittelstand* interest groups and working-class consumer cooperatives in Württemberg, a struggle which also embroiled the Centre and SPD on opposite sides. The cooperative movement in the state, which stood as a symbol of growing economic and social conflict, had two distinct wings: the producer and sales cooperatives (including peasant cooperative ventures) of the independent *Mittelstand*, which grew out of the efforts of Schulze-Delitzsch; and the cooperatives of the working and white-collar classes, pioneered in Württemberg by Eduard Pfeiffer.[33] In the early years the two movements had remained uneasily together under the same umbrella organisation, but as a more clearly differentiated class society emerged the conflict between producer and consumer grew sharper and the pressure increased for a formal separation of the two wings. In 1902 the Reich consumer movement seceded and began to grow rapidly in size. By 1913 it numbered 100,000 members in Württemberg and had moved from its original distributory role to become a large-scale producer in its own right, especially of bread, other foodstuffs and shoes.[34] Early German socialists like Lassalle had been suspicious of the petty-bourgeois character of the cooperative movement. But the secession of 1902 quickened an already growing SPD interest in the consumer cooperatives and led to an increasing interlocking of socialist party and cooperative movement.[35] To the SPD deputy and consumer

---

32. *35 LT, PB IV*, p. 2694, 123 Sitz., 8.7.1902.

33. On the difference in character of the two wings of the cooperative movement, see K. Bittel, 'Eduard Pfeiffer und die deutsche Konsumgenossenschaftsbewegung', *Schriften des Vereins für Sozialpolitik, Untersuchungen über Konsumvereine*, 151 (Leipzig, 1915).

34. Membership figures in F. Feuerstein, *Geschichte des Verbandes württembergischer Konsumvereine 1904–1929* (Stuttgart, 1929), p. 14. In 1889 the Stuttgart cooperative had 15 food shops, in 1914 38. In 1902 it opened its first shoe shop, and added a second in 1908. But its bakery showed the most spectacular expansion: in 1900 the new, enlarged premises on the Schlosserstrasse were using 1.8 million kg. of flour annually; by 1905 this had risen to 2.8 million, and by 1913 to 4 million. E. Hasselmann, *Und trug hundertfältige Frucht. Ein Jahrhundert konsumgenossensch. Selbsthilfe in Stuttgart* (Stuttgart, 1964), pp. 71–2, 77.

35. The growing acceptance by the SPD of the political role of the consumer cooperatives had sound doctrinal support from Marx, who at Geneva in 1865 praised the movement as an important stage in the development of working-class consciousness. F. Feuerstein, *Denkschrift über die Bedeutung des Genossenschaftswesens für die Entwicklung der Gemeindewirtschaft. Mit besonderer Berücksichtigung der Konsumgenossenschaften* (Stuttgart, 1920), pp. 21–2.

cooperative chairman in Württemberg, Franz Feuerstein, the organisation, like the trade unions, provided evidence of the growing self-consciousness and strength of those 'consuming masses'[36] who had been reduced to selling their labour.

The scale of cooperative turnover soon provoked opposition from the *Mittelstand*: the working-class and white-collar workers' cooperatives became for petty retailers a symbol of their oppression as potent as the Jewish-owned department store. In Württemberg the *Schutzverein für Handel und Gewerbe*, the artisan chambers and especially the bakers' association (the *Bäckerverband*) were active in petitioning the government, running press campaigns and lobbying sympathetic parties in order to achieve a curtailment of cooperative business.[37] The Conservatives supported these demands; and the Centre, so diligent in its efforts to establish producer and sales cooperatives among *Mittelstand* groups, was also a consistent supporter of measures designed to obstruct the consumer movement. In 1896 Centre and Conservatives obtained legal restrictions on consumer cooperative operations, and in the following years the two parties worked together in the Württemberg Landtag against the SPD and VP to broaden the campaign.[38] The issue pointed up the very real conflict between the *Mittelstand*-orientated Centre and the working-class-based SPD.

Centre support for *Mittelstand* economic interests against the SPD was in part, of course, a response to pressure from below: it made sense for the Centre to address itself to the material grievances of those who were so strongly represented among its supporters. In this respect the 'defence of the *Mittelstand*' against the collectivism of the SPD ran parallel to the 'defence of the *Mittelstand*' against VP liberal capitalism. There was, however, the important difference that the Centre was on the offensive against the VP, winning and securing votes by appealing to anti-capitalist sentiment, whereas it was on the defensive against the SPD, fearful that with the decline of the independent petty bourgeoisie would come a further polarisation of classes and political allegiances from which the Centre could only lose in the long term. It would therefore be a mistake to see Centre policy just as an accession to material pressure. Here, as in other spheres, such pressure reinforced a prior concern on the part of Centre

36. Feuerstein, *Geschichte*, p. 4.
37. Hasselmann, *Und trug hundertfältige Frucht*, p. 68; Feuerstein, *Geschichte*, p. 4. In 1912 the *Schutzverein für Handel und Gewerbe* organised a boycott of the candidates from parties which refused to support its aims. *Deutsches Volksblatt*, 4 November 1912.
38. *Politische Zeitfragen*, 4 (Stuttgart, 1900), pp. 180 ff; *Politische Zeitfragen*, 16 (Stuttgart, 1907), pp. 94 ff.

politicians about the social, political and moral ferment which accompanied rapid industrialisation.

Like many politicians and intellectuals of a conservative persuasion in the Wilhelmine period, Centre leaders looked for ways to slow down this development, and *Mittelstandspolitik* was an appropriate instrument. An idealised *Mittelstand* of moderately prosperous, frugal, independent and conservative men was of great symbolic importance to the Centre. If nurtured, it would supposedly act as a healthy bulwark against both the abuses of plutocracy and the dangerous urges of a 'dependent' working class with no real stake in the social order.[39] In stressing the independence and conservative good sense of the *Mittelstand*, Centre politicians endowed it in effect with the qualities of a general class: if the state sustained the *Mittelstand*, the *Mittelstand* would sustain the state.[40] In this, too, the SPD and Centre were at odds. For the SPD had, in the proletariat, its own general class. While the Centre tended to see the worker as a degraded artisan, the SPD viewed the artisan as a potential proletarian. The political conflict between the two parties was therefore more than a clash over rival economic interest groups: behind the immediate question of whether the *Mittelstand* could be preserved as an independent force lay the broader question of whether the Centre or the SPD conception of the future development of society would prevail.

We have already noted how the sense of a need to 'defend' or 'save' the *Mittelstand* permeated Centre thinking on a wide range of issues, from the desirability of postal rates not harming smaller local businesses, to arguments that the educational structure should not favour the factory system at the expense of the family economy of farm and workshop. It was also one element of Centre solicitude for the 'unorganised' in the fight over constitutional reform, and it informed party attitudes on fiscal change.[41] A telling example of how arguments about the social desirability of preserving the *Mittelstand* could affect party policy is provided by Centre attitudes on the payment of allowances to elected public representatives. At national level the payment of Reichstag deputies, a long-standing radical

39. For one clear statement of this, among very many, see the 1903 Reichstag election address of the Centre, printed in *Deutsches Volksblatt*, 2 May 1903: 'Against the efforts of Social Democracy and the advance of large capital, we are striving for the preservation and the strengthening of the *Mittelstand* amongst artisans and small business. We will not give up their futures as lost.'
40. On this trade-off, or 'mutual reinsurance', see Winkler, W. Rüegg and O. Neuloh (eds), *Zur soziologischen Theorie und Analyse des 19. Jahrhunderts*, pp. 163–79.
41. See above, Chapters Four and Five. It is noteworthy that over the tax brackets to be applied to the levying of income tax, Gröber differed with spokesmen from the other parties in calling for a lighter tax liability for middle incomes, with a correspondingly higher rate for those above and below. HStaASt, E 130a, Bü 588, Nr. 45a, 46c.

demand, was taken up by the Centre and explicitly justified by politicians like Adolf Gröber as a means of strengthening the representation of the *Mittelstand*.[42] In Württemberg, too, such arguments were strong enough to outweigh other considerations such as budgetary frugality. Whereas, for example, all but five of the Centre *Landtagsfraktion* voted in 1907 against reimbursing the costs of the presidents of Upper and Lower Houses, the entire party accepted the case for allowances to be given to local councillors under the new municipal code. The reason for this was made clear: it was, in Gröber's words, in order to enable people 'from the *Mittelstand* in particular'[43] to seek election. The hoped-for effect of allowances was spelled out in greater detail still by Viktor Rembold:[44] 'We work on the assumption that nobody will reasonably want to see just the Social Democrats and plutocracy sitting in the town hall and competing amongst themselves for the seats . . . our main reason for supporting moderate payment of costs is to prevent that. It should be made possible for small and middling men to take up a seat on the council.'

We have seen in a different context how the economic measures subsumed under the head of *Mittelstandspolitik* were often self-contradictory and ran up against both the currents of economic change and the interests of government.[45] How realistic was it, therefore, for the Centre to cast the *Mittelstand* as a buffer between SPD and plutocracy: how real were the independence and conservatism of groups like artisans and shopkeepers? One obvious sign that the *Mittelstand* was not equipped with the sturdy independence the Centre wished upon it was the very existence of a need for *Mittelstandspolitik*. While the Centre on the one hand articulated complaints from this group that its members were being ground between organised capital and organised labour, and that government assistance was required to alleviate the situation, it argued on the other hand that the *Mittelstand* was a repository of economically independent men, the antithesis of dependent wage-slaves. This really highlighted the critical problem: by the turn of the century, under the impact of economic and social change, groups like master artisans and shopkeepers had already lost many of those attributes of security and self-reliance with which they were still being credited by parties such as the Centre. About 55 per cent of both artisan and small retailing

---

42. See Gröber's Reichstag speech of 20 February 1901: 'One should above all be concerned with the *Mittelstand*, which has not received the representation it deserves.' Molt, *Der Reichstag*, pp. 43–4, n. 16.
43. *34 LT, PB III*, p. 2271, 101 Sitz., 23.12.1899.
44. *34 LT, PB III*, p. 2283, 101 Sitz., 23.12.1899.
45. See above, Chapter Five, pp. 152–8.

businesses, for example, were one-man (in the case of the latter often one-woman) concerns, many of which simply did not enjoy an income sufficient to maintain a family.[46] There were also indications that the social status of the *Mittelstand* was being eroded. There seems to have been a decline in the number of servants employed by such families; a decline, probably, in the level of participation in civic activities like membership of the local fire-brigade, art association or gymnastic club; and an unmistakeable decline, finally, in the technical standards and qualifications among small retailers.[47] It is consistent with this picture that one account of Württemberg in the two decades before the war should have spoken of the 'pessimism which was dominant in artisan and small business circles for many years'.[48]

By the beginning of the twentieth century, in fact, the idealised view of the *Mittelstand* had been overtaken by events. Growing insecurity was testified to by the sons of artisans who rejected the opportunity to take over the family patrimony, preferring a career as a white-collar worker or minor official, and by the parallel behaviour of the daughters of *Mittelstand* families, who increasingly were taking jobs as shop assistants, stenographers and typists, winning a measure of economic security on their own account and marrying outside their own social milieu into the families of white-collar workers.[49] This tendency was noted and often condemned by Centre politicians, who saw it as a further symptom of unwelcome social change. The 'new' *Mittelstand* of white collar workers was itself dismissed as the 'so-called' or 'pseudo' *Mittelstand*, whose members were not authentically independent.[50] But this attitude was in many ways blinkered and disregarded the real advantages which the 'new' *Mittelstand* possessed over the 'old': it was expanding rapidly (more rapidly than the labour force as a whole), it offered a vastly greater range of skilled and specialised occupations than the small shop or workshop, and it provided a secure income together, often, with some

---

46. Wernicke, *Kapitalismus und Mittelstandspolitik*, p. 341. Among artisans, Gustav Schmoller put the proportion of *Alleinmeister* (unassisted master craftsmen) at about three in four, but this is probably an exaggeration. A Reich survey of 1895, based on a cross-section of 61,000 masters, produced the figure of 55%, and this seems a likely one for artisans in general. The figure for retailers was similar. See Gellately, *Politics of Economic Despair*, p. 33.
47. For further details, and references, see D. Blackbourn, 'The *Mittelstand* in German Society and Politics, 1871–1914', *Social History*, 4 (1977), pp. 409–33, esp. pp. 421–3.
48. Bruns, *Württemberg unter der Regierung König Wilhelms II*, p. 824.
49. Blackbourn, *Social History* (1977), pp. 423–4.
50. See, for example, Herbster: '. . . let us take care that the artisan remains independent, that an independent *Mittelstand* remains in existence, not this modern *Mittelstand* which is no longer independent'. *37 LT, PB V*, p. 4565, 170 Sitz., 23.4.1909; and also Gröber, *36 LT, PB III*, p. 1721, 71 Sitz., 28.4.1905.

kind of pension. In public service, as in the private sector, similar advantages existed, amounting to real opportunities for 'respectability' and a tangible measure of security. Indeed, by contrast with the old *Mittelstand*, not only white-collar workers but the proletariat itself, earlier a symbol of dependence and insecurity, constituted an expanding class enjoying increased real wages and a growing proportion of skilled workers among its numbers. Through trade unions and the consumer cooperatives the working class had also shown its capacity to create strong organisations to protect its own interests. It was, in fact, partly this organisational élan which made it possible for the SPD to think of the proletariat as a general class, and to anticipate confidently the day when the votes of the working class would provide it with political power through the ballot-box.

Centre efforts to nurture the *Mittelstand* as a counter-weight or buffer against such a contingency did not entirely leave out of account the despondency and pessimism which we have noted. Recognising these weaknesses, it was one of the objects of Centre policy to try and imbue the *Mittelstand* with renewed confidence and impart to it something like the class consciousness which the efforts of the SPD and trade unions had helped to create among the working class; to bring about the 'raising of *Stand* consciousness without which no *Stand* as such can exist'.[51] But like other aspects of *Mittelstandspolitik*, this too was in many ways unsuccessful, a lack of success which can be clearly seen when the spectacular growth of the working-class consumer cooperatives is compared with the failure of the parallel producer, credit and sales cooperatives in which the Centre tried to interest the *Mittelstand*. There was, in the first place, a marked failure to stimulate cooperatives at the point of contact with the consumer: among retailers themselves, and among artisans in the form of sales cooperatives. Among small and often technically backward shopkeepers the problems of organisation involved in establishing cooperative purchasing often proved insuperable.[52] This was compounded by individual jealousies and an unwillingness to recognise the value of common action, symptoms of what one leader of the cooperative movement called the *Mittelstand*'s 'lack of interest in its own interests'.[53] Sales cooperatives also developed very slowly:

51. *Waldse'er Wochenblatt*, 3 December 1895, 'Zur Handwerkerfrage'. See also Joseph Eckard, on the need for artisans to become more conscious of *Stand* interests: *33 LT, PB VII*, p. 4538, 208 Sitz., 3.5.1898.
52. On the slow development of these, and the widespread scepticism of shopkeepers, see Gellately, *Politics of Economic Despair*, pp. 64–7.
53. The cooperative organiser, Rodegast, speaking at the cooperative *Verbandstag* in Frankfurt/Main in 1908, cited Gemming, *Das Handwerkergenossenschaftswesen*, p. 102.

there were only five in Württemberg in 1907.[54] The basic problem was not just the fear of something new, or even the initial capital outlay, but the permanent suspicion among actual or potential cooperative members that secrets would be given away or an advantage lost to competitors. This was why there were such frequent instances of sales cooperatives breaking down or encountering difficulties even after the initial problems had been overcome. It was reported at the 1905 meeting of the Federation of Württemberg Artisan Cooperatives, for example, that one member of a sales cooperative had refused to pay his contributions simply because someone else's goods had been sold before his: he left the cooperative and advertised his business independently in the press.[55] All commentators noted the frequency of such problems, and the Centre itself condemned the petty business envy which prevented common action.[56]

The Centre also failed to interest artisans in raw material cooperatives and producer cooperatives. In the period 1897–1900, when Reich legislation was passed encouraging the creation of such ventures, only two were formed in Württemberg.[57] In 1907 there were still only thirty raw material and twenty-two producer cooperatives in the state. Most of these, moreover, were accounted for by a few highly-organised groups with particular reason to pool their resources. Of the total of fifty-six cooperatives of all kinds among artisans in 1907, fifteen had been formed by bakers (who faced particular competition from consumer cooperatives) and ten by butchers (for similar reasons, and perhaps also in response to the problems caused by state abattoir regulations). Woodworkers were also a partial exception to the general apathy. Certainly, despite government subsidies and the exhortations to solidarity of Centre and Conservative politicians, the number of artisans organised in cooperatives remained tiny in most branches of production. In 1907 it amounted to only 13 out of 5,983 tailors (0.3 per cent), 26 out of 5,018 locksmiths and blacksmiths (0.5 per cent), 153 out of 10,598 joiners and carpenters (1.5 per cent) and 15 out of Württemberg's 966 glaziers (1.6 per cent). The average for all crafts in the state was a meagre 3 per cent. Catholic areas were no exception to this: the total number of organised craftsmen in Ravensburg was a mere sixty-one, in Ehingen sixteen.[58]

The baleful history of shopkeeper and artisan cooperatives undercut

54. Gemming, *Das Handwerkergenossenschaftswesen*, p. 69.
55. Ibid, pp. 95–6.
56. See, for example, Kiene: *35 LT, PB IV*, p. 2678, 122 Sitz., 5.7.1902.
57. Gemming, *Das Handwerkergenossenschaftswesen*, p. 18.
58. Ibid, pp. 69–74.

Centre claims on behalf of the *Mittelstand* and illustrated how difficult it was to encourage such groups to pool their resources and 'move with the current', as one Centre deputy put it.[59] But Centre politicians themselves were partly responsible for this widespread apathy: while emphasising the need for self-help and cooperatives, they had nevertheless, often in a highly demagogic manner, encouraged the *Mittelstand* to blame its problems on a free-for-all economic order, and thus contributed to the attitude among artisans and shopkeepers that negative solutions to their problems would be more efficacious than positive action. In other words, measures like department store taxation, limitations on consumer cooperatives and other forms of state intervention were presented as panaceas; and members of the *Mittelstand*, having been flattered that they were pillars of the social order, naturally looked for government action to preserve their livelihoods. In the 1890s, as artisans awaited the results of conservative, guild-orientated revisions in the imperial business code, their wary, truculent mood was pronounced; and when the 1897 legislation, like changes in the tender system and other pro-*Mittelstand* measures, failed to meet the expectations which had been aroused, the Centre found itself severely handicapped, since further attempts to nurture artisan organisations had to be made against a background of profound and continuing disillusion.

Shortly after the 1897 legislation had been passed, the Centre expert on artisan affairs, Joseph Eckard, admitted that in Württemberg at most only a sixth of artisans were organised in guilds or equivalent bodies. He spoke of the 'lethargy' among them and their insufficient awareness of *Stand* interests.[60] To rectify this, the Centre launched a programme designed to prepare the artisan for his new, more self-conscious role. Injunctions to organise filled the party press and both Eckard and Matthias Erzberger worked hard to add backbone to the artisan movement. One of Erzberger's achievements was the founding of the *Schwäbischer Handwerkerbund*.[61] In 1898 he was also designated *Volksverein* specialist in artisan affairs in Württemberg,[62] and throughout this period was undertaking a peripatetic lecturing programme to persuade artisans to form guilds and support the new artisan chambers more than they had supported the existing chambers of commerce and trade associations. Here too, though, the Centre was disappointed in its expectations: Erzberger's tour was met with cynicism and indifference. In Waldsee, for example, after outlining the

59. *37 LT, PB I*, p. 680, 28 Sitz., 19.5.1907.
60. *33 LT, PB VII*, p. 4538, 208 Sitz., 3.5.1898.
61. Epstein, *Erzberger*, pp. 12–13.
62. *Waldse'er Wochenblatt*, 20 November 1898.

possibilities of the new institutions created by the law of 1897, he found his closing appeal for greater organisation answered by the local trade association chairman, the shoemaker Konrad Binder, who 'explained that he could not enthuse over the law [of 1897] and argued in a masterly speech that the artisan was languishing because here a Jew, there a large capitalist and over the road yet another was selling goods at give-away prices, goods produced not by hand but by machine'.[63] Binder's response was all the more significant for his being a Waldsee delegate on the Centre's full state committee. When Erzberger spoke in February 1899 at Riedlingen he was received in the same manner when debating whether artisans should organise themselves or join a trade association. The report of the meeting commented that 'the artisans here will have nothing to do with the latter and very little to do with the former'.[64]

Erzberger's failure could be seen in the first report of the local artisan chamber in 1901, which showed the membership of the *Schwäbischer Handwerkerbund*, even after a considerable propaganda campaign, at only 683, a size dwarfed by the trade associations in which practising artisans constituted a minority.[65] The continuing failure to overcome the demoralised attitude on the part of artisans was marked by the almost negligible increase after 1901 in the number of artisans belonging to associations other than the trade associations. In compulsory and voluntary guilds together the number of members rose by 1914 to only 15,000, a small proportion of all artisans. The *Fachvereinigungen*, voluntary guild-type associations, increased their membership over the same period only from 2,672 to 3,017, while the number organised in all *Handwerkervereine* actually dropped from nearly 6,000 to just over 4,000.[66]

III

The bolstering up of independent artisan businesses was the core of a Centre policy designed to preserve the *Mittelstand* generally as a counterweight to the working class and the growing strength of the SPD. In the light of the precarious economic position of artisans, and the failure of Centre *Mittelstandspolitik* to improve their position more than marginally, it is instructive to put the question: how did so many artisans manage to survive at all without recourse to cooperatives or

63. Ibid, 14 April 1898.
64. Ibid, 2 February 1899.
65. *50 Jahre Handwerkskammer Stuttgart*, p. 69.
66. Bruns, *Württemberg unter der Regierung König Wilhelms II*, p. 872.

membership of the guilds? Certainly this is a question which the Centre seems never to have asked itself, for the party's view allowed only the two clear-cut alternatives of solidarity or oblivion for the *Handwerkerstand* as a whole. In the years just before the war the party press was still repeating the rallying cries of the 1890s, 'fellowship', 'cooperation' and the need for '*Stand* consciousness': there was no indication given as to how the artisans enumerated by census and inquiry had weathered the storm. This lack of curiosity perhaps reflects the fact that the likeliest explanation was the one least palatable to the Centre. The failure of cooperatives, as all observers agreed, had as one of its major causes the unwillingness of larger, more successful craftsmen to join such ventures. If they succeeded it was because they had effectively become small entrepreneurs. But what of the much greater number of small masters whose fate was more problematical? It will be argued that many of them, in fact, abandoned their increasingly spurious claims to independence and resigned themselves to a more secure life as part of the 'dependent' labour force; that despite attempts by the Centre, the Conservatives and others to preserve the *Mittelstand*, many members of it were actually being proletarianised as the SPD predicted, and to the SPD's advantage.

There were a number of ways in which those who were nominally independent artisans became dependent workers. They might become direct suppliers of either finished goods to the wholesaler or part-finished goods to the factory. An example of the first kind is the master carpenter in Heilbronn, whom we have already noted, who produced cupboards for a furniture store.[67] An example of the second type is the master turner to whom Wilhelm Keil was apprenticed near Hamburg, whose small workshop produced only ladies' umbrella handles for a factory.[68] He was apparently characteristic of very many in the Hamburg area, and almost certainly in Württemberg too. By the end of the nineteenth century a third of all master craftsmen were tailors, shoemakers and joiners, and among the first two branches at least there was an average of less than one assistant per master.[69] Given the process of concentration and the negligible participation of such craftsmen in cooperatives, it seems likely that many had relinquished any real independence and worked on much the same lines as the carpenter and turner already mentioned: tailors as outworkers for the clothing industry; shoemakers simply sewing on the soles of factory shoes; and joiners — together with glaziers, masons, locksmiths and

---

67. See above, Chapter Five, p. 155.
68. W. Fischer, *Quellen zur Geschichte des deutschen Handwerks* (Göttingen, 1957), p. 171.
69. Wernicke, *Kapitalismus und Mittelstandspolitik*, p. 138.

painters — hiring out their skills to building contractors. Certainly, evidence of the changing nature of the building and construction industry suggests the likelihood of this.[70] There was also growing scope for groups like shoemakers and tailors, as well as for watchmakers and others, as repairers: if they could not compete with Junghans or Salamander as independent producers, it was still possible to make a living by acknowledging their status as the servicing auxiliary of the large-scale factory.

If significant numbers of artisan members of the *Mittelstand* were in fact beginning to accept an effectively dependent status as workers, one might expect to see them represented in the consumer cooperatives. And this was the case. In 1907, 15.3 per cent of the Stuttgart cooperative's members were from economically 'independent' groups, and of the 33,000 members in 1914 over 5,000 were classified as 'independent' in either business or agriculture.[71] This, again, was part of a national pattern: in Breslau the number of 'independents' in the consumer cooperative was still larger.[72] In the Catholic areas of Württemberg, too, while the producer and sales cooperatives petrified, the consumer organisations made great progress: regional branches were opened in Gmünd (1871), Aalen (1894), Wasseralfingen (1898), Oberndorf (1900), Rottweil (1903), Ravensburg (1906), Rottenburg (1907), Spaichingen (1910), Laupheim (1912) and Ehingen (1913).[73] Many of these branches were in towns where the factory proletariat was small; and here it is plausible to suggest that the consumer movement attracted members of the *Mittelstand* who saw themselves at least as much as workers and consumers, rather than primarily as independent producers.

It would be going too far to argue that the artisan *Mittelstand* was proletarianised in the years up to 1914; that, as the SPD predicted and hoped, it had simply dropped into the ranks of the 'general class' of the workers. But it would also be wrong to assume that the policy adopted by the Centre Party and the Conservatives, of building up the *Mittelstand* as a buffer against the proletariat, had met with any great success. The process on which both Left and Right put their political

---

70. For an account of the changing nature of the building industry, see A. Winnig, *Der weite Weg* (Hamburg, 1932), pp. 246–7; Scheffler, *Der junge Tobias*, pp. 187–90. The traditional artisan modes of working were being altered, as architects and contractors increased their role; and the period prior to 1914 was also one of great technological change in the various branches of the construction industry, with the introduction of reinforced concrete, the electric saw and metal scaffolding.
71. Hasselmann, *Und trug hundertfältige Frucht*, p. 66.
72. Naumann, *Demokratie und Kaisertum*, p. 79. In all, 9% of the half-million members of the *Zentralverband deutscher Konsumvereine* at the beginning of 1904 belonged to the independent *Mittelstand*. Wernicke, *Kapitalismus und Mittelstandspolitik*, p. 487.
73. Feuerstein, *Geschichte*, pp. 84–5.

glosses was a complex one: of upward and downward changes in income and independence, of adaptation, above all of increasing internal stratification within the *Handwerkerstand*. What is clear is the ability of the SPD to recruit support among those whom the Centre still saw as independent and conservative.[74] We know from the history of the SPD at Reich level that it drew upon this group for votes and leadership: from the start of the socialist movement had been fuelled by the presence of artisans who saw themselves as workers, and in the period from 1893 to 1914 one-quarter of all the SPD *Fraktion* members in the Reichstag still had a petty-bourgeois occupation (and more than half were still practising artisans — printers, tailors, cigar makers and joiners especially).[75] In Württemberg, where craft traditions were strong, this feature was pronounced. Karl Kloss, the first SPD deputy in the Landtag, had this background; so did Wilhelm Keil and the veteran Heilbronn militant, Gustav Kittler. The SPD in the state consistently addressed itself not only to the 'wretchedly vegetating small craftsmen',[76] but also to nominally more independent artisans. Even craftsmen who employed two assistants, so the party argued, 'could not be distinguished by income or by social circumstances from the wage earner'.[77] The SPD found a response from both groups. Craftsmen who had effectively forfeited their independence looked to the trade unions and SPD for support during industrial disputes such as those in the building industry. The extent of the party's strength here was indicated by the publication of socialist trade-union newspapers aimed at these branches, like *Der Zimmerer* and *Der Grundstein*.[78] At the same time, the way in which identification with the working class by apparently more substantial artisans could develop even where traditional ideas and values remained was shown

74. Winkler, who is arguing precisely about the attempt by the Right to forge the *Mittelstand* into a bloc against large capital and the proletariat, notes the ability of the SPD to recruit among proletarianised artisans. Winkler, W. Rüegg and O. Neuloh (eds), *Zur soziologischen Theorie und Analyse des 19. Jahrhunderts*, pp. 173–4. Mention should also be made of the shopkeepers, many of them actually refugees from the working class following depression or victimisation, who were locked firmly within the subculture of Social Democracy; and of the SPD publicans, the *Parteibudiger*, who in some places made up as much as 5% of party membership. R. Michels, *Political Parties. A Sociological Study of the Oligarchical Tendencies of Modern Democracy*, transl. E. and C. Paul (New York, 1968), pp. 266–9. The Württemberg SPD seems to have been aware of these trends, see *Schwäbische Tagwacht*, 13 August 1912.
75. Molt, *Der Reichstag*, p. 212.
76. *Schwäbische Tagwacht* leading article, 27 November 1906, prior to 1906 Landtag election.
77. Ibid.
78. In elections to the Biberach commercial court in 1906, the Free Trade Union list apparently did well as a result of the many unemployed local craftsmen in the building industry. *Schwäbische Tagwacht*, 1 December 1906.

by the group of master joiners in Schramberg, who set up a guild and elected the local SPD Landtag candidate to the position of *Obermeister*.[79]

There was a further aspect of the changing structure of the *Handwerkerstand* which undercut Centre hopes while aiding the SPD. This was the growing distance between masters on the one hand and journeymen and apprentices on the other. The relations between masters and men from the 1890s were in many cases worse in workshops than in larger factories. At the tactical level, trade union organisers could see the advantage of undertaking industrial action against smaller employers who lacked the resources to resist a long dispute.[80] But there were deeper reasons for the increase in tension. On the one hand, employees in the workshop resented the characteristic long hours, low wages and heavy-handed discipline; while on the other hand the masters complained that the growth of courses in technical education was robbing them of labour at critical times, and — like other parts of the reform legislation directed against the *ständisch* social order — tended to loosen customary loyalty to the master and tempt journeymen and apprentices away to the factory.[81] It was part of the Centre attachment to the preservation of the *Mittelstand* that it should have condemned this conflict, stressing the supposed community of interest between all members of the *Handwerkerstand* and calling for the return to an idealised past of harmony and fellowship in the workshop.[82] In practice, though, when the Centre spoke of artisans it was very much the interests of masters it supported. The legislation of 1897 was aimed at restoring some of the paternalistic discipline and self-government within the guild which had been abandoned in the liberal business codes of the previous decades; and the introduction of the *kleiner Befähigungsnachweis* (the so-called 'little certificate of qualification'), in order to improve the position of masters, entailed closing the door on the ambitions of

---

79. *Deutsches Volksblatt*, 26 October 1912. An administrative report of 1896 from the *Jagstkreis* to the Ministry of the Interior, on the activities of the SPD in the previous year, made a similar point. It stressed that most of the SPD members in Gmünd were goldsmiths whose conduct was exemplary in its 'respectability'. HStaASt, E 150, Bund 2045, Nr. 288, report dated Ellwangen, 23 January 1896.

80. K. Saul, *Staat, Industrie, Arbeiterbewegung im Kaiserreich. Zur Innen- und Sozialpolitik des Wilhelminischen Deutschland 1903–1914* (Düsseldorf, 1974), pp. 61, 84, 99. It was, for example, not possible for small workshops to operate a blacklist in the way that larger concerns could.

81. Bruns, *Württemberg unter der Regierung König Wilhelms II*, pp. 867–8. See the complaints aired on this subject at the 1904 annual general meeting of the Rottenburg trade association, reported in the *Neckarbote*, 1 March 1904.

82. See the *Waldse'er Wochenblatt*, 3 December 1895, 'Zur Handwerkerfrage'. See also Joseph Eckard, *33 LT, PB VII*, p. 4548, 208 Sitz., 3.5.1898.

journeymen and apprentices.[83] Centre policy was at best irrelevant, at worst hostile, to the interests of journeymen and apprentices.

The SPD, though, made significant inroads into the labour force of the workshops. We have many examples of this from other parts of Germany: from Bremen, where 'Social Democracy had many supporters among journeymen, of whom few could hope to become independent'; from Liegnitz, where Paul Löbe was part of a socialist discussion group established by apprentice compositors, turners and joiners; and from Herford, where the young apprentice locksmith Carl Severing was introduced to the metal workers' trade union and the SPD by a journeyman in his workshop.[84] Apprentices seem commonly to have been converted by journeymen, who themselves often came into contact with both trade union and socialist ideas when on the tramp (*auf der Walze*).[85] The pattern was similar in Württemberg, where the Centre, like the government in its reports, noted the particular appeal of the SPD to young workers. Industrial organisation among apprentices and journeymen naturally did not always lead straight to the SPD. Karl Schirmer, for example, was apprenticed to a locksmith in Aulendorf, converted to trade union activity and was later active as a trade union leader in Munich.[86] Schirmer's career, however, was in the Christian rather than the Free trade unions, and his allegiance stayed with the Centre rather than the SPD.[87] But as Centre condemnation of class divisions in the workshop indicated, the tendency of journeymen to see themselves as workers was a long-term trend that was worrying to the party. Like the failure of

83. The 1897 revision of the *Reichsgewerbeordnung* (RGO) did not go far enough for many master artisans, who continued to demand changes in article 129 of the RGO, to allow only those with the title of master to supervise apprentices. A concession to this demand was made with the introduction in 1908 of the *kleiner Befähigungsnachweis*. This measure, fully supported by the Centre, was a further shift away from the concept of freedom of trade, although it still failed to satisfy extreme master artisans' demands. See Wernicke, *Kapitalismus und Mittelstandspolitik*, pp. 834 ff.

84. Branding, *Die Einführung der Gewerbefreiheit in Bremen*, p. 91; P. Löbe, *Der Weg war lang. Lebenserinnerungen* (Berlin, 1954), p. 19; C. Severing, *Mein Lebensweg*, I (Cologne, 1951), p. 21.

85. Tramping had traditionally been a way in which radical ideas spread. Hermann Smalian, *Ein Leben im Dienst der Buchdruckerkunst* (Leipzig, 1919), pp. 8–9, recounts how he went on the tramp in the 1860s, having been given notice for participating in a strike of journeymen printers in Berlin, and took part in wages struggles in other towns. He noted, significantly, that south Germany especially contained many radical print journeymen from Leipzig, spreading their ideas after finding it difficult to obtain employment in their home town.

86. Schirmer, *50 Jahre Arbeiter*.

87. Note, however, that Schirmer was thought by many in the Centre to be close to the SPD in his politics. As a prominent and self-consciously working-class member of the left wing of the Bavarian Centre, he was always a potentially difficult figure. Möckl, *Die Prinzregentenzeit*, esp. pp. 467–71.

Mittelstandspolitik at other levels, it undermined the belief that the class polarisation of society could be reversed. It also exposed the Centre to competition with the SPD at one of its weak points: the ability to organise and harness the political support of Catholic workers.

IV

It was partly their adherence to the idea of nurturing the *Mittelstand* that made it difficult for Centre politicians, especially in south Germany, to come to grips with organising Catholic workers. The frequent description of the working class as the *Arbeiterstand*, for example, betrayed an approach geared to a less fluid society than the one which actually existed in the two decades before the war. At Reich level this ingrained discomfort at the idea of the working class informed even the 'realist' views of the Centre's social expert, Franz Hitze, whose ideal was a society divided into seven estates (*Stände*), with production rigidly controlled: there would be no rootless proletariat and the worker would be 'conservative and happy again' within his own self-governing *Stand*.[88] A similar strain was revealed in the thinking of the Württemberg Centre, when the party's support for employment exchanges was coupled with the hope that they could be used to channel the urban unemployed back to the land, to take jobs in the labour-starved sectors of agriculture and domestic service.[89] It is significant that one of the Württemberg Centre politicians who was prepared to lend his voice to this, with reservations, was Joseph Andre, a workers' secretary in Stuttgart, elected from the Oberndorf Landtag constituency in 1906. Andre belonged to a group of younger Centre men in the state — others were Matthias Erzberger and Eugen Graf — who had received their political education in classes organised by Joseph Eckard, editor of the *Deutsches Volksblatt* and a recognised Centre expert in south Germany on social policy.[90] As party and press functionaries, these men certainly did not belong to the world of traditional notable politics; but as we have seen already, while the Centre in Württemberg was never conservative in this sense, its leaders did not embrace the ideas of modern class society as readily as they embraced modern methods of party-political struggle and propaganda. Just as for a previous editor of the *Deutsches Volksblatt*, Konrad Kümmel, 'the working class took second place to the

88. Jostock, R. Hebing and M. Horst (eds), *Volk im Glauben*, p. 144. As Jostock points out, Hitze's root idea was de-proletarianisation.
89. *Politische Zeitfragen*, 17 (Stuttgart, 1912), pp. 6–9.
90. Hagen, *Gestalten*, III, pp. 142, 165.

peasantry and artisans',[91] so Joseph Eckard placed more emphasis on the need to rescue the dignity of the artisan than on the problems of the dependent labour force; and so Andre and Erzberger, in turn, imbibed a similar outlook.

It is not surprising, therefore, that when a workers' secretariat was established by the Centre in Stuttgart in 1897 and run (part-time) by Erzberger, it was 'eventually made use of more by artisans than workers'.[92] An uncomfortable paternalism and unwillingness to accept the worker on his own terms characterised attempts to organise Catholic workers in bodies like the *Arbeiterwohl* (Workers' Welfare) and Catholic workers' associations.[93] Allied to this was a tendency among Centre politicians to differentiate in principle between organising apprentices and journeymen ('single men') and factory workers ('married men'), even when this flew increasingly in the face of social realities.[94] Paternalism, a latent attachment to the *Mittelstand* rather than the working class and a general prejudice against the realities of class society were all noted by one Christian trade union leader as reasons why the Centre found it difficult to organise Catholic workers in southern states like Württemberg.[95]

In the 1880s only eight Catholic workers' associations were founded in the state, with a total membership probably under 1,000.[96] The following decade saw an improvement, so that by September 1896 there were twenty-five such organisations with about 3,500 members in all.[97] After the turn of the century the work of founding new associations continued, and a high level of organisation was achieved in certain places. A government report from Gmünd in 1902 noted that there were Catholic apprentices', journeymens' and workers' associations with their own libraries in almost every parish of the constituency.[98] The *Deutsches Volksblatt* was nevertheless driven to make a rueful contrast between the Catholic workers' associations on the one hand, and the organisation, energy and financial self-sacrifice of SPD-organised workers on the other.[99] On the Catholic side

91. Hagen, *Gestalten*, II, p. 450.
92. Hagen, *Gestalten*, III, p. 167; M. Gasteiger, *Die christliche Arbeiterbewegung in Süddeutschland* (Munich, 1908), p. 131.
93. Gasteiger, *Die christliche Arbeiterbewegung*, pp. 43 ff.
94. Ibid, p. 44.
95. Ibid, pp. 58–9.
96. Ibid, p. 66.
97. Report of workers' secretary Neumaier to a September 1896 *Volksverein* meeting in Stuttgart, reported in *Der Oberländer*, 28 September 1896. Gasteiger, *Die christliche Arbeiterbewegung* (p. 89) gives slightly lower figures.
98. HStaASt, E 150, Bund 2046, Nr. 85. Report on the activities of the SPD and its opponents for 1901, dated Ellwangen, 17 February 1902.
99. See, for example, *Deutsches Volksblatt*, 9 July 1912.

paternalistic attitudes remained an obstacle. It is revealing, for example, that when a Catholic workers' association was set up in Wangen it had only forty-five members but twenty-five honorary members.[100] Up to the war the associations continued to be organised on a diocesan basis, with a clerical *Präses* in charge. Workers were exhorted to be 'oaks' in their family life and 'apostles' for their faith.[101] The tone is well captured by a song written for Catholic workers' associations celebrating the name-day of their *Präses*:[102]

> . . . Laßt im Herzen widerhallen
> Unsrer Liebe Hochgesang!
> Gilt's doch den zu ehren heut',
> Der uns Vater ist und Freund;
> Der uns treulich steht zur Seite,
> Uns in Glück und Leid stets eint.
>
> Nimmer müd' im edlen Streben
> Führt er uns der Tugend Bahn,
> Stets bereit, für uns zu leben
> Spornt er uns zum Streben an;
> Ernst und ratlos fortzuschreiten
> Auf des Lebens rauhem Pfad;
> Und für unsern Stand zu streiten
> Wider düst'rer Lehren Saat . . .

Even when, in response to pressure from Catholic workers, Centre leaders came round to an acceptance of the need for Christian trade unions, the first ones were organised on the old lines, as craft sections (*Fachabteilungen*) of the workers' associations. Membership of the trade union craft section automatically lapsed when membership of the local workers' association lapsed (or membership of the local journeymens'

100. *Waldse'er Wochenblatt*, 26 September 1897.
101. See the reports on the Twentieth Conference of the South German Catholic Workers Associations (and Seventh Conference of the South German Catholic Womens' Workers Associations) in Gmünd, August, 1912: *Deutsches Volksblatt*, 26–29 August, 1912.
102. Let the hymn of our love and acclamation echo in the heart! For today we honour the one who is our father and friend; who stands loyally at our side and unites us always in good fortune and adversity.

Never tiring in the noble endeavour, he leads us into the path of virtue. Always ready to live for us, he spurs us on to endeavour; to advance with proper dignity and without guidance on the hard road of life; and to fight for our *Stand* against the seed of false teaching.

A. Keilbach, *Lieder für Katholische Arbeitervereine Württembergs* (Stuttgart, 1907), p. 95.

association, or even *Volksverein für das katholische Deutschland* branch, where no workers' association existed).[103]

It was only at the beginning of 1900, as Catholic workers themselves began to organise, that independent Christian trade unions emerged on any significant scale in the construction, metal-working, wood-working and textile industries, and among state railway and postal employees.[104] But after initial successes the progress of these unions was also sluggish. The Württemberg Postal Union, for instance, had slightly fewer members and branches in 1907 than two years earlier. Among metal workers, the Free trade union recruited much more heavily than its Christian counterpart in Catholic towns like Friedrichshafen, Leutkirch and Ravensburg.[105] The flaccid development of the Christian trade unions was a product not so much of dissatisfaction with the kind of paternalism that was formerly evident in the workers' associations, but of a growing awareness on the part of Catholic workers (even *within* the Christian trade unions) that Centre Party policy was in many ways antipathetic to working-class interests. The identification of the Centre with the cause of propping up small, uneconomic businesses and retailers, and even more — as we shall see in the next chapter — with the peasantry and high agricultural tariffs, led to widespread resentment. This was the cause of a fierce dispute between Centre and Christian trade unions over the tariffs of 1902 (the 'neutrality debate').[106] It is useful to compare the figures for the respective growth of Christian and non-Christian trade unions in Württemberg in the period 1909–10, in the immediate aftermath of the Centre's support for the agrarian-orientated Reich financial reforms of 1909, a measure unpopular with all parts of the working class. In this period, while the Free trade unions increased their membership from 57,500 to 74,500 and the Hirsch–Duncker unions from 2,000 to 10,000, the Christian trade unions increased theirs only from 6,000 to 7,000, and the workers' associations even more marginally from 12,561 to 12,927.[107] This may, perhaps, be seen as an organisational parallel to the local election results of 1909 in neighbouring Baden, where the Centre

103. Gasteiger, *Die christliche Arbeiterbewegung*, p. 235.
104. Ibid, pp. 236–7.
105. Ibid, table pp. 406–7; *Schwäbische Tagwacht*, 15 July 1912.
106. At the second Christian Trade Union congress at Frankfurt/Main in 1900, the 'neutrality' idea was supported by Eugen Roth, editor of *Der Schwäbische Eisenbahner*, the organ of the Christian Federation of Württemberg Railway and Steamship Employees which Eckard had played a major part in founding. Gasteiger, *Die christliche Arbeiterbewegung*, pp. 305 ff.
107. Figures given in the *Rottenburger Zeitung*, 24 May 1911.

sustained heavy losses to the SPD in the aftermath of its support for the financial reforms.[108]

The Centre Party in Württemberg also lost Catholic working-class support at the polls in the years before the war. In both Württemberg and Baden, however, this loss was less immediately apparent than in cities like Cologne, Düsseldorf and Munich, where the disaffection of Catholic workers resulted in the loss of actual Reichstag seats to the SPD. The real Centre electoral strongholds in Württemberg, as in Baden, remained the countryside and small towns, and here the SPD enjoyed very limited success. The party made hardly any headway in rural Catholic areas, as numerous government reports testify. The clergy and village mayors usually proved hostile when SPD speakers did make an appearance, and as the party press itself admitted there was genuine hostility from local inhabitants as well to such 'outsiders'.[109] The fact that a large number of SPD Landtag and Reichstag candidates lived in Stuttgart or its suburbs can hardly have helped matters.[110] In the expanding small and medium-sized towns of Oberschwaben and other Catholic areas the SPD achieved a greater impact: meetings could be held more easily and local party branches were established. Even here progress was uneven and the level of activity sustained by a local branch was often dependent on the initiative of a small number of men, in at least one case on the part of a worker who had moved into the district from outside. It is a measure of the SPD's weakness in such towns that its growth seems to have been noticeably held up in Tettnang and Neckarsulm simply by the formation of active Christian workers' associations.[111] The party was increasing its vote as the social structure of these towns changed. Generally speaking, however, its share of the vote was low and its membership small, and the Centre Party remained dominant. It was in recognition of this problem that the SPD, in March 1912,

108. The Centre share of the poll dropped from 46.5% to 39% between the Landtag elections of 1905 and 1909. In one urban constituency, Mannheim–Weinheim, its share dropped by 10%. A. Rapp, *Die Parteibewegung in Baden 1905–1928* (Karlsruhe, 1929), pp. 6, 48.

109. See, for example, *Schwäbische Tagwacht*, 29 November 1906.

110. The SPD Landtag candidates in 1906 for the 68 non-Stuttgart seats included 31 who were themselves resident in the capital. The figure becomes over half of the total if one includes candidates who were resident in towns which effectively belonged to Greater Stuttgart, like Cannstatt, Degerloch, Feuerbach and Zuffenhausen. *Schwäbische Tagwacht*, 17 November 1906, which carries a list of SPD candidates. The pattern was similar in 1912: ibid, 26 October 1912.

111. On Tettnang, see the very detailed progress report for 1912 of the SPD Württemberg state executive, in *Schwäbische Tagwacht*, 27 August 1912. On Neckarsulm, HStaASt, E 150, Bund 2046, Nr. 82: report on the activities of the SPD and its opponents in the *Neckarkreis* during 1901. Report dated 1 February 1902.

established a regional party secretariat in Oberschwaben aimed at 'systematic agitation in the domain of the Centre'.[112]

The SPD posed a much greater threat in those Catholic towns which were industrialising more rapidly. Aalen and Gmünd, neighbouring constituencies which were closer than other Catholic towns to the economic life of the Neckar valley, provide a good example. In Aalen the SPD established a foothold on the local council in the 1890s, with help from the radical Aalen VP.[113] By 1901 there were four SPD branches in the constituency, the largest boasting ninety members, and the location of the party's political and recreational activities included both the more industrialised Aalen and Wasseralfingen and the smaller surrounding communities of Abstgmünd and Unterrombach.[114] This base among the craft and factory labour force made it possible for the SPD in Aalen to run the Centre close in elections if it had second-ballot support from the VP and DP.[115] The threat to the Centre was also considerable in Gmünd. Here the SPD was able to attract 200 people to one of its meetings as early as 1896 and maintained a high level of political activity in subsequent years. Government reports indicated the party's particular appeal to gold and silver workers and wood workers.[116] The SPD's growth was all the more impressive, given the organisational efficiency of the Centre Party in the constituency and its network of associations for apprentices, journeymen and workers. It is a sign of the Centre's concern that a group of Alfred Rembold supporters should have tried in 1906 to obtain positions on the supervisory board of the SPD-dominated Gmünd consumer cooperative. The attempt was a failure.[117] Indeed, in the final years before the war the Centre seems to have lost control over a significant part of the Catholic working class in Gmünd. The SPD increased its vote considerably in the Reichstag election of 1907 in a number of predominantly Catholic electoral districts, where the Centre call for abstention had clearly been

---

112. *Schwäbische Tagwacht*, 27 August 1912.
113. HStaASt, E 150, Bund 2045, Nr. 288: report on the activities of the SPD in the *Jagstkreis* in 1895. Report dated Ellwangen, 23 January 1896.
114. Ibid, Bund 2046, Nr. 85: report on the SPD in the *Jagstkreis* in 1901. Report dated Ellwangen, 17 February 1902.
115. In the Aalen Landtag election of 1895, when the SPD candidate received second-ballot support from former VP and DP voters, the party came within 17 votes (2,633 to 2,650) of defeating Viktor Rembold. *WJbb* (1895), III, pp. 186–7.
116. HStaASt, E 150, Bund 2045, Nr. 288; Bund 2046, Nr. 1, 85, 92, 183. Reports on the activities of the SPD in the *Jagstkreis* in 1895, 1896, 1901, 1902 and 1907. The *Schwäbische Tagwacht* for November 1906 gives a good idea of the level of political activity sustained by the SPD in the area.
117. *Schwäbische Tagwacht*, 30 November and 3 December 1906.

defied;[118] and Catholic workers in Gmünd featured early and prominently in the 1912 meat boycott organised by the SPD.[119]

Further evidence of the Centre's weakness among Catholic workers is furnished by the party's failure in the so-called diaspora, areas where internal migration had created large Catholic enclaves in towns with a Protestant majority. There were some striking examples in other parts of the Reich of towns where there was heavy Catholic migration but no corresponding political success for the Centre. In Dortmund, for example, the Catholic proportion of the population rose steadily in the Wilhelmine period, but the Centre lost ground equally steadily to the SPD as the Catholic working class defected to the latter.[120] The same was true in Nürnberg, where the Catholic population increased from 14,000 in the 1870s to 90,000 in 1911 (when they constituted nearly 30 per cent of the total), but the seat was dominated by the SPD.[121] In Württemberg the Centre sustained a serious loss of votes among Catholic workers — manual and white-collar — who had migrated to the growing towns, especially Reutlingen, Heilbronn, Ulm and Stuttgart.[122] While the Catholic proportion of the population in the relatively rural *Donaukreis* and *Schwarzwaldkreis* fell between the end of the 1860s and 1905, the Catholic part of the industrialised *Neckarkreis* rose from 7.84 per cent to 11.2 per cent;[123] and the Catholic minority was not only growing through continuing internal migration, but through a higher rate of natural increase. Yet the Centre vote here remained insignificant, while SPD support increased greatly. It is a telling sign of Centre weakness among the Catholic work force of large urban centres that in Stuttgart, 20 per cent Catholic by 1907, the Centre had to form an alliance with the Conservatives in order to stand any chance of obtaining even one of the six seats which were distributed on the basis of proportional representation.[124]

Between 1898 and 1912 the Centre share of the votes cast by Catholics at Reichstag elections in Württemberg fell from 80 per cent to 55 per cent.[125] This loss can be accounted for partly by the general

---

118. Schulte, *Struktur und Entwicklung des Parteisystems*, pp. 121–2.
119. *Schwäbische Tagwacht*, 25 September 1912.
120. H. Graf, *Die Entwicklung der Wahlen und der politischen Parteien in Gross-Dortmund* (Hanover, 1958), p. 24.
121. Rost, *Die wirtschaftliche und kulturelle Lage*, p. 207; A. Klöcker, *Konfession und sozialdemokratische Wählerschaft. Statistische Untersuchung der allgemeinen Reichstagswahlen des Jahres 1907*, dissertation Erlangen (M–Gladbach, 1913), table 3, p. 27.
122. Schulte, *Struktur und Entwicklung des Parteisystems*, p. 116. On the creation of a Catholic diaspora in these towns between 1890 and 1914, see Bruns, *Württemberg unter der Regierung König Wilhelms II*, p. 380.
123. Rost, *Die wirtschaftliche und kulturelle Lage*, p. 133.
124. *Deutsches Volksblatt*, 30 November 1906.
125. Schauff, *Die deutschen Katholiken*, pp. 174–5.

weakening of the confessional bond; disaffection among both peasantry and *Mittelstand* must also have played a role. But the evidence suggests that it was not so much here as among Catholic workers in the diaspora and the industrialising Catholic towns that the Centre was most vulnerable. The Centre's weakness politically among Catholic workers resulted from the party's preoccupation with the *Mittelstand* and from its failure to do more than slow down the polarisation of both society and politics along class lines. The inability to appeal strongly to Catholic workers was also, in turn, both cause and effect of the Centre's growing adherence to agrarian policies, and the simultaneous forging of closer links with the agrarian Conservatives. It is to this process that we shall now turn.

CHAPTER 7

The Centre and the Polarisation of Politics in Württemberg: Relations with the Agrarian Conservatives

I

The growing strength of the SPD on the Left was paralleled by the increase in support for the agrarian Conservatives on the Right. The gains of these two parties in the years between 1895 and 1912 pointed up the continuing tendency of the political parties to align themselves along sharper class lines. As we have seen, this posed problems for the Centre as well as for the other 'middle parties' of the VP and DP. Given the difficulties it faced in maintaining the allegiance of Catholic workers, the Centre found its rural vote very necessary. As in the Reich, the peasantry made up a disproportionately large part of the Centre constituency. In Württemberg as a whole the number of those employed in agriculture fell from 45.1 per cent to 38.5 per cent between 1895 and 1907; but in the Catholic areas of the *Jagstkreis* and *Donaukreis* the figure was still around 50 per cent at the latter date.[1] The Centre had to pay a price, however, to maintain this electoral reservoir. While the party continued after 1895 to talk of the need for a balance of class interests, its policy actually underwent a shift in the direction of the agrarians.

At the same time, the alienation of the Centre from the VP, DP and SPD over the politics of the reform era and other issues coincided with a change in the nature of the Conservatives. From a pro-governmental party of aristocrats, the Conservatives became increasingly popular, demagogic opponents of both the liberal capitalist system and of government reform policy. As the Centre drew apart from the VP and SPD, the Conservatives drew apart from their former allies in the DP: the two parties' policies began to converge in a common opposition to the government and a defence of agriculture laced with *Mittelstandspolitik*. The years 1900 to 1906

1. Bruns, *Württemberg unter der Regierung König Wilhelms II*, p. 924.

196

marked a period of political change similar in some ways to the years prior to 1895. Out of these years was forged a new set of political alignments: on the one side a hardening Left bloc of SPD and VP, with the DP towed along; and on the other side increasingly close cooperation between the Centre and agrarian Conservatives, culminating in the *Schwarz-Blau-Block*.

The problems of agriculture and the realignment of parties continued, therefore, to interlock in the last two decades before 1914, as they had in the first half of the 1890s. The attitudes adopted towards the peasantry by the different parties remained an important touchstone of politics, for rural claims to attention were sharpened rather than dulled by fear and uncertainty. Change in the countryside produced on the whole a contradictory picture. On the one hand, there was a steady modernisation of agriculture: yields rose, state encouragement was given to more effective and scientific means of arable farming, hop-growing, market-gardening and animal husbandry; educational institutions were extended, along with the agricultural inspectorate; and land was reclaimed and improved, with nearly 10,000 acres of arable and 5,000 acres of meadow drained between 1881 and 1906.[2] Alongside this modernising infrastructure was the development of cooperative ventures among the peasantry itself, especially among dairy farmers. In 1907 the United Cheese-Dairies of the Württemberg Allgäu produced 26,241 *Hektoliter* of milk, 4,348 *Zentner* of cheese and 591 *Zentner* of butter, with a total value of 377 million Marks. Württemberg could boast a total of nearly 500 dairy cooperatives by 1907.[3]

On the other hand, these developments frequently met with a flaccid or even truculent response. Government initiatives over scientific farming were criticised for showing too little regard for practicalities, the agricultural inspectorate was attacked for being too remote from the peasantry, and the railway network was accused of neglecting rural, agricultural areas.[4] Attempts to encourage the use of artificial fertiliser met the argument that the cartels of fertiliser manufacturers were providing low-quality produce at inflated prices.[5] The response to cooperatives was also by no means wholly positive. The *Rottenburger Zeitung*, for example, noted in October 1898 that an

2. Ibid, pp. 943–4.
3. *WJbb* (1907), II, pp. 83 ff.
4. See above, Chapter Five, pp. 160–2. While most of the grievances noted here were very real, the form of expression they were couched in was often personalised and atavistic. The *Waldse'er Wochenblatt* (13 February 1898) reported the case of three women being denounced as witches and turned over to the local exorcist after cattle grew thin and began to milk badly.
5. See, for example, the letter to the *Waldse'er Wochenblatt*, 29 May 1898, on this subject.

extraordinary meeting of the local agricultural loan bank called to discuss a grain-selling cooperative was 'very thinly attended'.[6] Other newspapers noted the lack of cooperative spirit in such matters,[7] while a government report in 1909 commented that it would require a long time for the peasantry to recognise the usefulness of sales cooperatives.[8] Together with suspicion towards official initiatives, there were continuing complaints of the kind so widespread earlier. Prices were thought too low, especially before the Bülow tariffs of 1902, middlemen and the stock exchange were blamed for taking an unfair profit and manipulating prices, and the growing hostility of urban consumers was resented. Finally, costs continued to rise. Government taxes and insurance contributions took a growing proportion of peasant income, while labour costs moved steadily upwards.[9] By 1912, taking board, lodging and money wages together, male farm labourers were being paid between 900 and 1,200 Marks a year, female labourers between 700 and 960 Marks. The cost of both male and female labourers also rose by just over 40 per cent between 1898 and 1909: by the time of the war, male day labourers in agriculture could earn 3.40 Marks a day in summer, as high as the prevailing local rates for general day labour.[10]

This background of material discontent, and a growing rural self-consciousness vis-à-vis consumers and advocates of the fully-fledged industrial state, helps to explain the rise of the *Bauernbund*, the Württemberg branch of the *Bund der Landwirte*. In 1896 this organisation had 2,050 members, and had increased to around 20,000 by 1914.[11] Agrarian feeling was also something the Centre Party could not ignore. In 1895 it had successfully exploited peasant discontent: now it was faced with the task of fulfilling its pledges and keeping the Catholic peasantry satisfied with Centre representation. The Centre did, in fact, continue to address itself to the

---

6. *Rottenburger Zeitung*, 5 October 1898.
7. *Waldse'er Wochenblatt*, 16 January 1898: 'There is no *Stand* in which working together in cooperatives proceeds more slowly and with more difficulty than among the peasantry. It holds fast to the traditional and out-moded system of selling, etc., and it has very often been said that in no *Stand* is the lack of public spirit and solidarity so lacking.' On the slow growth of agricultural loan banks in Oberschwaben, see *Waldse'er Wochenblatt*, 22 May 1898; *Ipf-Zeitung*, 23 January 1899.
8. *Die Landwirtschaft und die Landwirtschaftspflege*, p. 223.
9. It is interesting that a petition of Württemberg tenant farmers (*Gutspächter*) to the government in May 1897 (concerning the effects of tax revisions) talked gloomily of 'present agricultural conditions' and listed particular grievances in the following order: 'The continuously rising wages, the expenditure on insurance and low grain prices'. HStaASt, E 130a, Bü 578, Nr. 54.
10. Bruns, *Württemberg unter der Regierung König Wilhelms II*, p. 929.
11. *Oekonomierat Rudolf Schmid*, p. 18. The *Bauernbund*'s own figures are not precise. See, also, the figures in Hunt, *The People's Party in Württemberg* p. 93, n. 22.

peasantry. The party's 1895 election programme called for a variety of measures to alleviate the problems of agriculture, and in its first five years of Landtag activity the Centre attempted to win government support for them. On Centre initiative the state paid 200,000 Marks to a north German hail insurance company so that peasant premiums could be lowered; and the Centre also demanded the creation of local agricultural insurance associations, with voluntary contributions and state financial support.[12] In the re-casting of the regulations governing servants (*Gesindeordnung*), Centre policy was to demand longer periods of notice from domestic servants in agriculture and to impose greater penalties on those who allegedly encouraged breach of contact.[13] The party also supported the construction of rural railway branch lines, the provision of more rural credit, free travel for harvest workers on the railway, state insurance for losses incurred by peasant cattle-raisers when their animals were rejected by the abattoirs, and alterations in the building regulations (*Bauordnung*) to reflect peasant interests.[14]

Up to 1900, though, the Centre remained moderately agrarian in its policy. The official line of the party was one of support for all social groups, and it branded the more one-sidedly agrarian demands of the *Bauernbund* as selfish sectionalism.[15] As in other parts of the Reich, however, the Centre faced a challenge in the 1890s from its volatile peasant constituents. The unofficial Centre candidate at the Gmünd by-election of 1896, for example, was able to address himself particularly to rural discontent.[16] There were, in addition, a number of indirect signs of rural volatility. The Anti-Semitic Reichstag deputy, Paul Förster, received a large and enthusiastic audience when he spoke in 1895 in Biberach, while during the 1898 election campaign for the XVI Reichstag constituency (which included Biberach) the Centre candidate had his address interrupted by anti-semitic hecklers.[17] The Centre also had to bear in mind the situation in neighbouring Bavaria, where the agrarian policy and radical petty-bourgeois egalitarianism of

12. Andre, *Zentrum und Landwirtschaft*, p. 3.
13. *34 LT, PB I*, pp. 804–5, 37 Sitz., 10.5.1899; *34 LT, PB I*, p. 829 ff, 38 Sitz., 12.5.1899; *Politische Zeitfragen*, 4 (Stuttgart, 1900), p. 163. Just as there was a parallel development in Austria over the restriction of education in rural areas because of harvest needs (see above, Chapter Four, p. 139, n. 82), so there was also pressure in Austria, at the end of the nineteenth century, to tighten up the *Dienstbotenordnung*. For the debate on this in the Upper Austrian Landtag, see Bruckmüller, *Zeitschrift für bayerische Landesgeschichte* (1974), I, p. 136.
14. *Politische Zeitfragen*, 4 (Stuttgart, 1900), pp. 129, 163–77.
15. See, for example, the Centre's 1900 programme, printed in *Schwäbischer Merkur*, 6 November 1900.
16. *Der Oberländer*, 2 December 1896. See also earlier reports in this newspaper during September 1896.
17. *Waldse'er Wochenblatt*, 10 August 1895 and 14 June 1898.

the *Bayerischer Bauernbund* formed an important alternative focus for the allegiance of the Catholic peasantry.[18]

Dissatisfaction with the Stuttgart Centre found expression in the smaller Centre newspapers, which transmitted rural opinion more directly and tended to adopt a clearer agrarian line than the Stuttgart-based *Deutsches Volksblatt*. Here, the latent tension between Centre leadership and the rank-and-file appeared in an anti-agrarian versus agrarian form. The *Waldse'er Wochenblatt*, for example, which generally called for more agrarian measures, also spoke of the great division in the Centre as that between 'those more, and those less favourable to government'; and it firmly identified itself with the latter.[19] Clearer still was the case of the *Ipf-Zeitung*. While the Centre leadership called for a balance of classes, the *Ipf-Zeitung* followed the *Bauernbund* in demanding the retention of an agriculturally-based state: it argued that the census of occupation returns was misleading, that many classed as belonging to industry were actually engaged part-time on the land, and that industry and trade very often had their living provided for them by agriculture:[20] 'So in judging and handling the major aspects of tariff, trade and economic policy, one should certainly not start with the assumption that we in Germany should always subordinate the interests of agriculture to those of industry. For the great strength of the German people still rests on the former.' Agrarian writers like von der Goltz were cited to demonstrate that Germany was still capable of agricultural self-sufficiency;[21] stock exchange speculation and Jewish money were blamed for the problems of both consumers and peasant producers. With such general statements of the agrarian case went a regular stream of practical suggestions and demands on the most sensitive agrarian issues: for higher tariff protection, tougher control over meat imports, a

18. Möckl, *Die Prinzregentenzeit*, pp. 450 ff. The *Ipf-Zeitung*, 24 March 1899, printed a political fable of the 'war of the bees and wasps', in which the dissatisfied bees allowed themselves to be led astray by their mortal enemies, the wasps, who proceeded to steal their honey. Although *Ipf-Zeitung* was consistently more agrarian than the Stuttgart leadership of the Centre, it nevertheless attacked the efforts of the 'wasps' from the *Bayerischer Bauernbund* to win the peasantry away from the Centre. The article closed with an appeal to the peasantry not to allow itself to be misled by such agrarian blandishments.

19. *Waldse'er Wochenblatt*, 2 March 1895. The paper mentioned especially the difficulty of reconciling the interests of agriculture and industry. The *Waldse'er Wochenblatt*, however, also attacked the propaganda of anti-Centre agrarians (25 July, 4 September 1897, 10 May 1898). Like the *Ipf-Zeitung*, and like George Heim and his agrarian supporters within the Bavarian Centre, the paper stood at one point of a triangle, the local Centre leadership and the non-Centre agrarians making up the other two.

20. *Ipf-Zeitung*, 15 September 1899.

21. *Ipf-Zeitung*, 11 August 1899. On von der Goltz, see R. Drill, *Soll Deutschland seinen ganzen Getreidebedarf selbst produzieren?* (Stuttgart, 1895), pp. 7-8.

reduction in the number of imported horses and measures to keep young men working in agriculture rather than allowing them to leave for the towns.[22]

The differing perspectives between moderate and more full-blooded agrarians also extended to the Centre *Fraktion*, where the line of division not surprisingly corresponded to that between the leadership and the back-benches. The latter represented largely rural, parish-pump interests, which in turn were mostly agricultural. If one examines the Landtag speaking records of deputies like Max Dentler (Wangen), Xaver Rathgeb (Ellwangen), Kaspar Bueble (Tettnang), Johannes Sommer (Saulgau), Simon Schach (Rottenburg), Anton Beutel (Waldsee), Franz Xaver Krug (Biberach) and Caspar Vogler (Neresheim), it emerges that the majority of their contributions to debate dealt with directly agricultural matters. They called, among other things, for greater allowances for particular groups of producers in the annual budget allocations; for legal barriers against butter, hop and malt surrogates, and against wine produced with artificial substances; for action against horse- and cattle-dealing middlemen; and for measures to alleviate the rural labour shortage. While many of these demands were either merely routine, or had official party backing, such an intense preoccupation with narrowly material and parochial concerns was potentially disturbing, both to the government[23] and — because of its clear sectionalism — to Centre leaders. The best example of this group and its latent threat is perhaps provided by Theophil Egger, the retired schoolteacher from Ravensburg already noted as the most striking of the radical petty-bourgeois back-benchers in the Centre.[24] Egger claimed in 1900 to have spoken three hundred times in the Landtag in the preceding five years,[25] and in his violent agrarian postures and disrespect for authority Egger represented a position far removed from that of the Centre leadership in Württemberg. To the extent that a man like Egger was a maverick, his views were an embarrassment rather than a threat to the *Fraktion* and party leaders. Thus Egger's complaint during a department store debate that too little was being done because 'so many gentlemen are directly or indirectly dependent on

22. Thus in the course of three weeks in September 1899, taken at random, *Ipf-Zeitung* turned its attention to the following: grain prices (5th), agricultural labour shortage (12th, 23rd and 25th) and the import of horses (14th).
23. The government, in considering the effects of the *Proporz* elections, noted that 'these might create a counterweight which is not to be underestimated against the influence of the limited viewpoints of many elected from the narrow confines of the district constituency'. HStaASt, Anhang II, copy of a memorandum by von Sarwey.
24. See above, Chapter Three, pp. 105–6.
25. *Schwäbischer Merkur*, 3 December 1900.

Jewish money' was neutralised by Kiene's urbane pronouncement that Centre policy was dictated only by considerations of fiscal and social justice.[26] Similarly, when Egger campaigned idiosyncratically for corporal punishment as a sanction against gipsies and itinerant unemployed workers, and against the bicycle as a threat to the horse and the stability of rural life, party leaders swiftly intervened to dissociate themselves and the Centre from this individual expression of views.[27] Nevertheless, when Egger's private campaigns interlocked with broader dissatisfaction on the Centre back-benches, this agrarian group within the *Fraktion* could place the leadership in a difficult position.

This group of deputies began its analysis of economic and social policy from the classic agrarian standpoint: *'Hat der Bauer Geld, hat's die ganze Welt'* ('If the peasant has money, so has the whole world'). To a considerable extent this position was compatible with official Centre policy, which itself emphasised the community of interest between peasant, artisan and shopkeeper, and the interdependence of the traditional *Mittelstand* in town and country.[28] Yet there were real conflicts of interest between primary producers demanding a high price for their produce, and *Mittelstand* families in town and country made up primarily of consumers. These conflicts were heightened in the case of groups like butchers, millers and bakers, who not only experienced high agricultural prices directly as consumers, but indirectly through the demands of journeymen for higher wages and through the drop in custom as they necessarily passed these higher prices on to their customers.[29] In these cases the agrarian group in the Centre *Fraktion* was not always prepared to compromise over the primacy of agriculture. Thus, dealing with a request by millers for heavier duties on flour and a reduction of those on grain, the back-benchers Kaspar Bueble and Franz Xaver Krug came out firmly against the millers, and followed Hans von Ow, agrarian president of the *Zentralstelle für die Landwirtschaft*, in putting the interests of agriculture higher. Bueble argued that the small miller and the peasant

---

26. *35 LT, PB IV*, pp. 2676–9, 122 Sitz., 5.7.1902.
27. On the question of the bicycle, see the speech of Egger, followed by that of Gröber, in *35 LT, PB IV*, p. 2739, 125 Sitz., 10.7.1902. On corporal punishment, Egger, *35 LT, PB I*, p. 521, 25 Sitz., 17.4.1901; and Viktor Rembold's statement of official party policy, which was opposed to corporal punishment in such cases, during the following sitting: *35 LT, PB I*, p. 548, 26 Sitz., 18.4.1901.
28. The supposed interdependence, for example, of the peasant and rural craftsmen was one of the grounds used by Alfred Rembold to justify the propping up of the local brewing industry in Württemberg. See above, Chapter Five, pp. 149–50.
29. See above, Chapter Five, pp. 152–3.

had much in common, but that in the case of conflicting interests the latter was in greater need of tariff protection.[30]

The most serious revolt against the Centre leadership came over tax revisions which formed part of the general fiscal reorganisation of the late nineteenth and early twentieth centuries in Württemberg. This was a focus of agrarian interest, for the tax system in the state had long favoured the owners of buildings and businesses over those with an income from agricultural land. Under the *Kataster* (register of assessment) system of arriving at tax liability, it has been shown that by 1863 agriculture was burdened with 70 per cent of the land, buildings and business tax, although it contributed only 49.5 per cent of Württemberg's gross product.[31] Business, by comparison, paid only 12.5 per cent, despite accounting for 43.5 per cent of gross product. The revised law of 1873, with effect from 1877, adjusted this imbalance very markedly: the burden on agriculture was reduced by 24 per cent, that on business increased by 88 per cent. However, the drop in agricultural prices in the last two decades of the century meant that the notional profit on which the *Kataster* for agriculture was based was in fact about 20 per cent above actual profits in the 1890s. In the debate over fiscal revision, this element of seeming injustice was a spur to agrarian indignation.[32] Throughout the tax debates the Centre leadership attempted to secure a reconciliation between agricultural and business interests, to avoid what the reporter for the Landtag committee, Sachs, called the 'struggle of interests' of earlier years.[33] This was a delicate manoeuvre when the land, buildings and business tax had to be brought into line with the introduction of a personal income tax, for the logical measure — the simultaneous introduction of a property tax (*Vermögenssteuer*) — not only presented practical difficulties, but encountered opposition both generally among agrarians and in the Cente itself, on the grounds that in Prussia and elsewhere such a tax had worked to the detriment of agriculture. The *Kataster* for the business tax, however, included personal earnings as well as fixed capital: its continuation along with income tax would have involved an element of double taxation. The Landtag committee therefore proposed to re-cast the business tax, taking out a fixed percentage to offset the tax already paid on personal income. But this

30. *34 LT, PB IV*, p. 2620, 117 Sitz., 16.5.1900. See the similar reaction of the agrarian Centre back-bencher Johannes Sommer, when the conflict reappeared six years later over a millers' petition: *Politische Zeitfragen*, 12 (Stuttgart, 1906), p. 400.
31. Schremmer, I. Bog *et al*(eds), *Wirtschaft und Gesellschaft in der Zeit der Industrialisierung*, p. 688.
32. Ibid, pp. 689–91.
33. *33 LT, .PB VI*, p. 3800, 174 Sitz., 15.12.1897.

led to a demand from Hans von Ow and other agrarians, including Centre deputies, that in view of the drop in agricultural prices since 1873, agriculture too should be allowed a decrease in the *Kataster* assessment of that year. In the committee's bargaining, Centre leaders advocated a 40 per cent reduction for business and a 20 per cent reduction for agriculture: this was actually a favourable bargain for agriculture, since to take full account of the double taxation element, the reduction for business might well have been 60 per cent rather than 40 per cent. In fact, the reduction of 40 per cent proved unsatisfactory to committee members of other parties, particularly the VP, and the compromise eventually agreed on was 50 per cent for business, 20 per cent for agriculture. It was this compromise which Viktor Rembold recommended to the full Centre *Fraktion* for acceptance.[34]

The agrarian group in the Centre was dissatisfied with the agreement and a number of them approached Rembold, stating their refusal to vote for his recommendations. Rembold admitted in the Landtag that since the Centre members of the committee had agreed to the compromise, 'anxieties had made themselves felt, to which a part of our own *Fraktion*, as of other *Fraktionen*, could not shut its eyes'.[35] To Conrad Haussmann's charge that an agrarian tendency was making itself felt, Rembold could only confess the Centre leadership's inability to control and dictate the vote of its own rebels: Kiene was obliged to resign himself to a temporary deadlock and to move in the Landtag to pass on to the discussion of itinerant trade, where the party was less divided.[36] Only after further concessions had been wrung from the committee could the deadlock be broken and the support of agrarian back-benchers in the Centre once more be relied upon.

The back-bench revolt over tax reform, along with sentiment in the small-town press and in the constituencies generally, was one of many signs which alerted Centre leaders to the strength of agrarian feeling. As the 1900 election year opened, the Centre and VP both found themselves in the position of 'middle parties', with the buoyant SPD and agrarian Conservatives making the pace and forcing a polarisation of opinion on the issues of town versus country, producer versus consumer and, above all, the symbolic issue of tariff revision, on

34. For the progress of the debate generally, see *33 LT, PB VI*, 174 Sitz, 15.12.1897, and 175 Sitz, 16.12.1897; *33 LT, PB VII*, 179 Sitz., 22.12.1897.
35. *33 LT, PB VI*, p. 3834, 175 Sitz., 16.12.1897; *33 LT, PB VII*, p. 3934, 179 Sitz., 22.12.1897. For anxieties in the Centre outside the *Fraktion*, see the *Waldse'er Wochenblatt*, 27 June 1897.
36. *33 LT, PB VI*, p. 3836, 175 Sitz., 16.12.1897. Although *Politische Zeitfragen*, 4 (Stuttgart, 1900), pp. 15–16, 104 ff, reported these debates very comprehensively, no mention was made of the differences within the *Fraktion*.

which an official committee had already been appointed in Berlin. The fact that the Reichstag would debate the tariff issue shortly after the Württemberg Landtag election cast a long shadow over the campaign. At the VP's annual conference in Stuttgart, for example, the official line of opposition to protectionism prevailed, but as in 1895 there was an element of trimming by candidates in agricultural constituencies: the candidate for Crailsheim addressed the conference on the 'plight of agriculture' and declared himself a supporter of 'moderate protective tariffs'.[37] The Centre also looked to protect its flank against the agrarian danger. In a major speech before an audience of 500 in his Riedlingen constituency, Gröber catalogued all that the party had done for agriculture and 'warned against giving credence to the scions of the north German *Bund der Landwirte*; when they spoke of the interests of agriculture they meant the interests of east Elbian agriculture'.[38] Gröber dwelt conspicuously on the Centre support for protective tariffs in the Russian trade treaty, its support for the abolition of the sliding scale which served east Elbian Junker interests, its part in banning futures trading in grain and its support for meat quotas and restrictions on imports. Gröber went out of his way to emphasise the Centre's services to agriculture at state level, too, in contrast to the 'east Elbians' of the *Bauernbund*. In 1900 the full apparatus of Centre auxiliary organisations was mobilised in a drive for party unity against the parties of allegedly selfish sectional interests, especially the agrarian Right. The peasant was approached directly with detailed accounts of the Centre's solicitude, the artisan and worker reassured about the 'balance justice' of Centre policy.

As the Centre *Fraktion* dispersed for the election campaign at the beginning of November 1900, fears of disunity and of the assertion of naked class interest were the leading motifs of Gröber's speech to the *Fraktion* at its farewell dinner in Stuttgart. 'Differences', he warned 'should not be aired in public. As soon as a *Fraktion* campaigns with divided views, even if those views may be good in themselves, it ceases to have the success of a united *Fraktion*. So always together and united as the *Fraktion* of the minority.[39] The appeal to confessional unity was a sign of the problem the Centre leadership faced in 1900 with the demands of economic interest groups. The wish to put an end to indiscipline from the *Fraktion*'s agrarians in particular was one of the motives behind the rather heavy-handed drive by the party leaders to vet Centre candidates for the 1900 elections. As we have seen, however, this manoeuvre rebounded, as intra-party disputes and

37. *Heuberger Bote*, 13 January 1900.
38. Ibid.
39. *Gmünder Tagblatt*, 2 November 1900.

unofficial candidates revealed instead the true state of dissatisfaction with the leadership. Agrarian discontent was one of the prime factors in this dissatisfaction. The attempts to remove the obdurate octogenarian Egger from the Centre candidacy in Ravensburg were abandoned, for example, when the local *Vertrauensmänner* backed down under Egger's threats to fight the seat anyway; and this capitulation, according to one newspaper, occurred 'exclusively out of regard for rural voters'.[40] In the double candidacies of Gmünd and Tettnang the issue of branch lines was prominent, a matter traditionally connected closely with agrarian agitation. There is also other evidence in Gmünd that the strength of the unofficial candidate, Klaus, was in agricultural parts of the constituency.[41] It is certainly the case that the *Bauerbund* candidate in the Gmünd constituency, Joseph Rupp, collected around 250 votes in former Centre-voting areas.[42] The strength of local feeling among Centre voters on the tariff, rural labour shortage and similar issues was indicated by the success of the unofficial candidate in Horb, the tenant farmer Franz Kessler, who beat the official candidate Nussbaumer on an extreme agrarian programme and was afterwards rumoured to have been financed by the *Bauernbund*.[43] It was indicated, too, by the success of a number of official Centre candidates, like Franz Xaver Krug, Johannes Sommer and Joseph Dambacher, who were demanding firm measures in the defence of primary producers, including in some cases tariffs even higher than those called for by the *Bauernbund*.

The Centre débâcle in 1900 was in part a problem of party discipline, and analysed in those terms by the *Deutsches Volksblatt*.[44] The elections also, however, presented the Centre with a further problem: how should it react to the changed strengths of the political parties in Württemberg, and to the sharpening antagonism between agrarian and anti-agrarian forces which partly underlay these changed strengths?

---

40. *Schwäbischer Merkur*, 31 October 1900.
41. See the advertisement in the *Gmünder Tagblatt*, 1 December 1900, from 'many rural voters', who claimed they were 'in the happy position of being able to give our votes to a man who, himself from the country, is more familiar with rural conditions than his rival'. The reports in the same paper generally indicated that Klaus was strongest in the rural areas.
42. *Gmünder Tagblatt*, 6 December 1900.
43. See *Der Beobachter*, 11, 18 January 1901, and the *Deutsches Volksblatt*, 14, 21 January 1901. Kessler denied, rather unconvincingly, that he had attended a *Vertrauensmänner* meeting of the Conservatives, under the chairmanship of party secretary Friedrich Schrempf. It is certainly the case that Kessler was treated by the Centre Party as a hostile agrarian candidate throughout the campaign, and only accepted into the *Fraktion* when he had beaten the official candidate, Nussbaumer.
44. *Deutsches Volksblatt*, 6 December 1900.

II

The elections of 1895 represented a basic shift of the party-political constellation in the Landtag; the elections five years later marked a shift hardly less significant.[45] In 1895 the VP, Centre and DP dominated the Landtag, with sixty-three of the seventy elected members. In 1900 the two parties of economic sectionalism and protest, The SPD and *Bauernbund*-Conservatives, increased their strength at the expense of the 'middle parties'. On the one hand, as we have seen, the SPD began to put serious pressure on the VP. At the same time, the VP lost the Neckarsulm seat to the agrarians and others were saved only by the campaigning of transparently agrarian VP candidates.[46] Within the *Kartell* of DP, Conservatives and *Bauernbund* there was also an altered balance in favour of the pure agrarians. In 1895 there had been fourteen DP deputies, only one official Conservative and a number of independents with agrarian leanings, whose separate voice was lost within the loose coalition of the pro-governmental DP, Conservatives, *Privilegierten* and independents, who together constituted the *Freie Vereinigung*. But in 1900 the DP representation sank to eleven, for the party had been obliged to let agrarians contest former DP seats. The *Bauernbund* and Conservatives now numbered six, and sat in the Landtag as a self-consciously distinct, agrarian group.[47] The change from loose groupings of a pro-governmental and anti-governmental kind, where independents still played a role, to more strictly defined parties aligned on the basis of social class was a feature of the 1895 election results. The process was taken a stage further in 1900.

The polarisation of interests which this sharper party definition reflected was important not just for the DP and VP, but for the Centre as well. As both Catholic working class and Catholic peasantry saw before them the example of growing parties enunciating sectional interests, the Centre could expect pressure on its electoral base from both directions. The danger of losses to the Left was evident from the strength of the SPD in industrialising areas like Aalen and Gmünd,

45. For the full results in 1900, see *WJbb* (1900), III, pp. 208–11.
46. Candidates like Johannes Schock, for example, himself a peasant, who is claimed to have said that he could 'subscribe to the programme of the *Bauernbund* from A to Z'. See *Deutsches Volksblatt*, 21 January 1901; and J. C. Hunt, 'The "Egalitarianism" of the Right: The Agrarian League in Southwest Germany, 1893–1914', *Journal of Contemporary History* (1975), p. 518.
47. On the swallowing up of DP seats by the Bauernbund, see Hunt, *Journal of Contemporary History* (1975), pp. 514–15, 526. On this pattern elsewhere, particularly Baden and the Pfalz, see Molt, *Der Reichstag*, pp. 136–7.

while the strong agrarian component in the 1900 election débâcle illustrated the competition on the Right. The heightened agitation of Left and Right after the 1900 elections, over the revision of tariffs, forced the Centre to take sides; and both the strength of agrarian feeling within the Centre and the changing nature of the agrarian Conservatives led the party into closer alliance with the Right in subsequent years.

Prior to 1900 relations between the Centre and the Right had been cool. This was partly because the Conservatives at that time were more closely allied with the DP, and thus identified with those policies which were anathema to the Centre: vigorous anti-Catholicism, an anti-Polish policy and a nationalist, Protestant-based throne-and-altar outlook which the Centre detected in the political thrust of *Sammlungspolitik*.[48] But Centre antipathy towards the Conservatives in Württemberg before 1900 was not based solely on the fact that they were tarred with the DP brush. The Conservatives and independent conservatives within the *Freie Vereinigung* were also attacked by the Centre for their own brand of *étatiste* and pro-Junker politics. Conservative militarism was widely unpopular in the lower reaches of the Centre, and the party leaders had to take note of feeling among the Catholic peasantry that the army took labour from the land while increasing taxes, that manoeuvres interfered with the harvest, and that war might devastate the land and would carry off first the sons of the peasantry.[49] In addition, the Centre accused the Conservatives of favouring east Elbian agriculture rather than the peasant farmer, in their attacks on the hegemony of industrial and commercial capital.

This charge had much truth in it and separated Centre and Conservatives on a number of issues prior to 1900. When the Centre asked the Württemberg government to move in the Bundesrat against

48. There was another aspect of *Sammlungspolitik* which was widely unpopular in the Centre: the building of the battle fleet. Kiene himself was critical of what this would cost, and the unpopularity of the fleet among the peasantry was reflected in the anti-naval stance of newspapers like *Ipf-Zeitung*, *Waldse'er Wochenblatt*, *Rottumbote* and *Anzeiger vom Oberland*, which were as hostile as their Bavarian counterparts.

49. On manoeuvres and labour for the harvest, see *Die Landwirtschaft und die Landwirtschaftspflege*, p. 194. An outbreak of foot-and-mouth disease, like those of 1891 or 1911, always produced an angry call for the cancellation of manoeuvres; but even the general problem of labour shortage on the land was sufficient to bring regular demands for the non-call-up of reservists and the cancelling of manoeuvres during harvest time. See *Waldse'er Wochenblatt*, 17, 25 July 1911. The local clergy reinforced anti-military feeling among the peasantry. Curate Kappler, for example, used to deliver a set speech to *Volksverein* meetings on 'The Five Wounds of Europe', identifying one of the wounds as militarism (the others were unbelief, self-indulgence, capitalism and socialism). See Kappler's talks to meetings in Steinach and Wolfegg, reported in *Waldse'er Wochenblatt*, 16 June, 3 August 1895.

a re-introduction of the pro-Junker sliding scale, for example, the Conservatives voted against the motion.[50] Similarly, while the Conservative von Hermann dismissed the entire fiscal reform connected with the introduction of income tax as 'the first step . . . on the road which ends in state communism',[51] the Centre sought to achieve advantages for the *Mittelstand* and peasantry and to attack the profits not only of big business, but of the big estates. Thus one motion presented by the *Freie Vereinigung* as a means of providing tax relief for agriculture was quickly dismissed by Viktor Rembold as a 'gift' for large estates, along with large-scale commerce and industry. They alone would benefit, he argued, 'not agriculture in general'.[52] On the same issue, which dealt with relief from communal taxation, Gröber and Bueble reasoned from similar pro-*Mittelstand* and pro-peasant premises: out of 5,000–6,000 families in his Tettnang constituency, Bueble claimed that only about twenty stood to gain from the *Freie Vereinigung* amendment.[53]

It is significant that in voting down this motion the Centre found itself aligned with the sole SPD deputy and an important part of the VP which included both Haussmann brothers and Schnaidt, against the aristocrats of the *Freie Vereinigung* Right. At this time, the summer of 1897, for all the latent and open conflict between the Centre on the one side and the VP and SPD on the other over the issues of reform and *Mittelstandspolitik*, these parties could still unite in their opposition to those like von Hermann, whose interest in protecting agriculture was directed to securing advantages for the larger landowner. The Centre campaign in both the Reichstag election of 1898 and the Landtag election of 1900 against the class-interest of pro-Junker Conservatives was indicative of the antagonism felt in the Centre towards politicians of that kind. Even in the years before 1900, however, if von Hermann stood for traditional Conservatism, there were others on the Right whose politics were closer to those of the Centre; who appealed directly to the peasant proprietor, attacked the government, and — like the Centre — identified liberal capitalism as the enemy of peasantry and *Mittelstand*. Indeed, it was the presence of these elements on the Right which gave the campaign of 1900 much

---

50. *Politische Zeitfragen*, 4 (Stuttgart, 1900), p. 174. For the background to the sliding scale and its repeal, see Nichols, *Germany after Bismarck*, pp. 297–8.
51. *33 LT, PB III*, p. 1479, 69 Sitz., 11.12.1895. It is noteworthy that von Hermann was a deputy with whom Theophil Egger clashed over the subsidies to cattle breeding: von Hermann was an admirer of the English system of breeding on large estates. See above, Chapter Three, p. 105.
52. *33 LT, PB V*, p. 3229. 147 Sitz., 12.6.1897.
53. *33 LT, PB V*, p. 3442, 148 Sitz., 15.6.1897.

of its agrarian tone. One sign of the growing weight of more violent agrarians within the Conservatives was the change in the leadership of the *Bauernbund* in 1896, when von Gaisberg-Helfenberg was succeeded by Rudolf Schmid, a wealthy tenant farmer who leased land belonging to the Hohenlohes.[54] Schmid, who remained chairman of the *Bauernbund* for twenty-one years, was a fierce opponent of government and bureaucracy, accusing them in the same way as the Centre of raising taxes to finance institutional changes which benefited only commerce and industry.[55] As the *Bauernbund* and Conservatives became formally allied after 1900, with the former setting the tone, the affinities between Centre and Right became more pronounced.

After the elections of 1900 the loose coalition of the *Freie Vereinigung* dissolved. The DP and the Conservatives became increasingly estranged, while the Conservatives and *Bauernbund* became virtually indistinguishable organisations. Friedrich Schrempf, for example, the party secretary of the Conservatives, was also a leading official in the *Bauernbund*; leading *Bauernbund* publicists like Dr Wolff and Theodor Körner had close personal and political ties with the Conservatives; and the Conservative *Deutsche Reichspost* was not only printed on Körner's own presses but also appeared as the local agrarian *Württembergische Landpost*.[56] Within the newly-consolidated Conservative–*Bauernbund* group it was not the traditional conservatism of men like von Hermann, but the radical demagogy of men like Schmid, Körner and Wolff, angled at the small and middle peasant, which was dominant. Schmid asked rhetorically who had benefited from canal and railway building, and concluded that it was only trade and industry, while the 'small man' and the peasant had borne the cost.[57] In a manner strikingly similar to the Centre, the Conservatives also scorned the measures of the era of reform, arguing that the *Mittelstand* and peasantry had little interest in constitutional or educational reform, but were looking to the political parties to solve their economic problems.[58]

In this way the politics and the political style of the Centre and the Conservatives began to converge, as both defined themselves in the era of reform against a government which they claimed was in the

---

54. Hunt, *Journal of Contemporary History* (1975), pp. 516–17.
55. *Oekonomierat Rudolf Schmid*, p. 153.
56. Hunt, *Journal of Contemporary History* (1975), p. 516.
57. *Oekonomierat Rudolf Schmid*, p. 49.
58. Ibid, p. 153.

hands of the VP and the reforming Left.[59] Both parties called for an active *Mittelstandspolitik*, comprehensive agricultural protection (not just for grain), the building up of local transportation, special taxes on department stores and a curtailment of consumer cooperative operations. Both attacked the abuses of 'mobile capital', called for less governemt attention to reform and demanded an end to luxury expenditure. Both, finally, saw in the rise of the SPD a long-term threat against which the *Mittelstand* and peasantry should be mobilised. Differences remained, of course. Over the proposal to set up agricultural chambers (*Landwirtschaftskammer*), for example, where the Conservatives favoured the creation of just one central chamber elected through the machinery of the existing agricultural associations, the Centre argued strongly for four separate chambers. Their reasons revealed the differences they still had with the agrarian Conservatives: not only would one chamber have tended to leave unrepresented the peculiar interests of Oberschwaben agriculture, but it would probably have led to an accretion of power in the hands of larger landowners, at the expense of small and middle peasants.[60] On this issue the parish-pump orientation of the Centre and the more *étatiste*, traditional approach of the Conservatives were very clearly at odds and produced considerable mutual acrimony. But in general these differences were becoming more muted after the turn of the century. On the one hand, as we have seen, the Conservatives and *Bauernbund* were turning more and more into a single demagogic party appealing directly to the small man. On the other hand, the Centre was itself being forced by the logic of its policy to subscribe to a more *étatiste* outlook. This was particularly true of the party's *Mittelstandspolitik*, which required considerable subventions from the state. But it was also true of agriculture; for although the Centre liked to stress the need for self-help on the farm, as in the workshop, the party was committed in practice to an expensive and extensive apparatus of government intervention. In fact the Centre called for a level of expenditure which the government was unable to countenance: the Centre proposal,

59. It is significant that the Right, as well as the Centre, singled out the government minister Johann von Pischek as especially 'radical' and pro-VP. For one of the many stern rebukes which von Pischek issued to those who made far-reaching agrarian demands, see his speech in Geislingen to the 44th Assembly of Württemberg Agriculturalists on Whitsuntide Monday, 1903: *Der Bürgerfreund*, 6 June 1903. On the hostility of the agrarian Conservatives to von Pischek, see Hunt, *Journal of Contemporary History* (1975), p. 520; and on the antagonism of the Centre, *Politische Zeitfragen*, 16 (Stuttgart, 1912), p. 19.
60. *Politische Zeitfragen*, 20 (Stuttgart, 1912), pp. 22–37; and on the background, *Die Landwirtschaft und die Landwirtschaftspflege*, pp. 26–7.

supported by the *Bauernbund* and Conservatives, to pass the cost of meat inspection fees on to the state would have added 500,000 Marks annually to the budget.[61]

The growing sense of identity between agrarian Right and Centre was recognised on both sides. It was given expression by the *Bauernbund* even before the 1900 elections at their annual state conference in November 1900, where Rudolf Schmid spoke of the need to 'lay aside all political and religious quarrels' in order to preserve the *Mittelstand* in business and agriculture, and drew particular attention to the fact that Centre economic policy was 'national not international'.[62] The compliment was returned by the Centre in actions rather than words, for as the new parliamentary session opened after the elections the party began to outbid the agrarians on their own terms. When the new Landtag met, the Centre immediately tabled a motion asking the government if it was prepared to move in the Bundesrat for a 'satisfactory increase' in import duties, not only on rye and wheat but also on oats and barley.[63] Even before this contentious motion reached the Lower House for debate at the end of January 1901, the common ground shared by the Centre and Conservatives had been shown in a number of heated exchanges with the SPD. In the third session of the Landtag, for instance, Gröber replied to a fierce attack on his party by the SPD for its 'dear bread' policy with an equally hostile speech on the neglect of agriculture by the Left, accusing the latter of exaggerated concern for the consumer.[64] This exchange was to be representative of those which followed the 1900 elections. In the Landtag there was a rapid polarisation into two groups, with the VP and SPD advocates of political reform and cheap bread building a bloc on the Left, the Centre and Conservatives forming a *de facto* parliamentary alliance on the Right, and the DP caught uneasily between the two. With the tariff debates in Berlin pending, it was the issue of import duties and agriculture versus industry, rather than political reform, which principally divided the parties in this way. It is thus all the more noteworthy that it was the Centre, rather than the *Bauernbund*–Conservatives, which seized the initiative in putting the agrarian case against the constant attacks of the SPD. In replying to the anti-agrarian philippics of the Social Democrats, Viktor and Alfred Rembold, Gröber and Kiene were the main protagonists, earning praise for their views from the *Bauernbund*

61. *Politische Zeitfragen*, 20 (Stuttgart, 1912), pp. 82–3.
62. Report in *Schwäbischer Merkur*, 12 November 1900.
63. *Politische Zeitfragen*, 12 (Stuttgart, 1906), p. 296.
64. *35 LT, PB I*, pp. 22, 27–8, 3 Sitz., 19.1.1901.

deputy Haug, who expressed delight that his party had found 'allies' in the Centre.[65]

When debate opened on the Centre's motion concerning increases in the grain tariff, the party's acceptance of the agrarian outlook became clear. Alfred Rembold, making the opening speech on behalf of the motion, invoked the spectre of unlimited grain imports, depressed prices and an intensified flight from the land ruining German agriculture and turning the country more and more into a purely industrial state. Perhaps most significant was the method he used to counter arguments that such developments might actually benefit the small peasant and the *Mittelstand*, by cutting feedstuff prices and increasing consumption of meat, dairy produce, fruit and vegetables. Rembold based his case on two classic agrarian arguments. First, he maintained that all agricultural producers had a common interest in the continuing profitability of grain, for otherwise a growing emphasis on more diversified agricultural produce would in turn deflate their market prices. He added that many small peasants also owed their livelihood to part-time work on large estates. Secondly, he put forward the autarkic view which had been argued by the *Sammlung* parties at the 1898 Reichstag elections: a protectionist system best served the interests of both agriculture and industry, for the survival of the former not only assured German self-sufficiency in food production, but would also provide industry with a secure home market at the same time that industrial tariffs protected it directly.[66]

In discussing the importance of agriculture, Centre leaders had commonly stressed the value to family life and social stability of attachment to the soil. These arguments it continued to put forward, as did Centre back-benchers of a more pronounced agrarian stamp like Krug and Sommer, who both entered the debate during the further two days allowed for it. But a sharper emphasis by both front-bench and back-bench speakers on specifically economic agrarian demands was now added to these arguments. Particularly noteworthy were the contributions to the debate of two new Centre deputies from overwhelmingly agricultural constituencies, Joseph Dambacher and Franz Kessler, whose stance was indistinguishable from that of the *Bauernbund*. Kessler, in fact, demanded a grain tariff of 7 Marks across

65. *35 LT, PB I*, p. 54, 5 Sitz., 23.1.1901. The Centre motion was finally debated in the tenth sitting of the new parliament, on 30 January 1901. Almost all the first nine sittings contained parliamentary sparring over the tariff issue, mostly between the Centre and SPD.

66. *35 LT, PB I*, pp. 172–76, 10 Sitz., 30.1.1901. Cf. the arguments put forward by the agrarian Conservative, Theodor Körner: *Die Zollfrage. Volkswirtschaftliche Flugschriften*, 3 (Stuttgart, 1911).

the board, a figure viewed as 'regrettably high' by the government and at least as high as the figures being flourished at *Bauernbund* meetings.[67] The overall effect of the Centre contribution to the debate was, as the DP agrarian deputy Aldinger[68] and press commentators pointed out, to leave the Conservatives and *Bauernbund* largely without arguments of their own to put forward. As one newspaper remarked:[69]

> The tactics of the Centre were very skilful: the most effective material for agitation was wrested from the *Bauernbündler* with effortless ease; indeed, the parliamentary clumsiness of the *Bauernbündler* and Conservatives . . . was so great that their two spokesmen only got a hearing in an utterly exhausted House after the last of a series of *redelustige Landboten*, and with the best will in the world were not in a position to put forward any new points of view, let alone demands of their own.

At the same time, it should not be forgotten that the January debate was also an indication of how 'middle parties' like the Centre and VP were being forced to take up positions on the tariff question by the public agitation of both agrarian Right and SPD Left.[70] In the spring and summer of 1901, for example, the SPD not only used interpellations in the Landtag to raise the issue, but tried to organise a broader public against the proposed tariff increases, putting the question up for debate throughout the state in municipal councils where it enjoyed representation. Pressure from the agrarians also continued throughout 1901: even the chambers of commerce and the official *Zentralstelle für die Landwirtschaft* saw themselves required to take up a position in favour of moderate increases in agricultural tariffs.[71] Part of this pressure revealed itself in the activities of *Bauernbund* members of the local agricultural associations. At a meeting of the Ulm association in Niederstotzingen, for example, where the chairman moved a resolution accepting the moderate rise in

67. *35 LT, PB I*, pp. 200, 209, 11 Sitz., 31.1.1901.
68. *35 LT, PB I*, p. 184, 11 Sitz., 31.1.1901.
69. *Tägliche Rundschau* (Berlin), 4 February 1901, cited in *Deutsches Volksblatt*, 12 February 1901.
70. Official reports to the Ministry of the Interior from Waiblingen (for 1901) and Göppingen (for 1902) argued that the agitation of the *Bauernbund* was serving to increase the appeal of the SPD. HStaASt, E 150, Bund 2046, Nr. 82, 93.
71. The Stuttgart Chamber of Commerce, although less enthusiastic than its opposite number in Ravensburg, had decided in July 1900 that 'in the light of the political position' it would not come out against raising the grain tariffs. It hoped to head off even wilder agrarian demands which, it feared, would isolate Germany from world markets and prevent the conclusion of any new trade treaties. This stance was confirmed in the chamber's meeting of March 1901. *Deutsches Volksblatt*, 8 March 1901.

tariffs supported by the Württemberg government, the *Bauernbund* deputies present agitated for a stronger stand: one proposed a tariff of 6.50 Marks for wheat and spelt (in place of 6 Marks), another a common tariff of 7.50 Marks for all grains, a demand for which the great majority at the meeting voted. In Catholic Gmünd, where agrarian issues had figured in the recent Landtag election and where, according to one newspaper, 'the grain tariff question [had] given rise in the Gmünd area to demonstrations on the land', the chairman of the Iggingen agricultural association cautioned the peasantry to be content with moderate increases in the tariffs and not allow themselves to be made the plaything of politically-interested parties.[72] It was indicative of local feeling, however, that in early 1902 the former *Bauernbund* Landtag candidate, Joseph Rupp, acquired a seat on the committee of the Gmünd association.[73]

Under cross-fire from Right and Left, the VP found itself in some political difficulty. Although the VP *Beobachter* attacked the Centre for passing under 'the yoke of the agrarians',[74] the Landtag majority which had passed the Centre motion on tariff increases actually included six VP deputies, while two others with agrarian sympathies were absent from the final vote.[75] In the debate, only Carl Betz, deputy for the Heilbronn constituency where the SPD was strong, maintained the traditional vituperation formerly reserved by the VP for answering agrarian demands. Oskar Galler and Conrad Haussmann, well-known free-traders, accepted the case for a temporary tariff of modest proportions, and even the proposed increase was criticised largely for the effect it would have on the renewal of the Caprivi trade treaties. In municipal councils where the SPD raised the tariff question there was also evidence of VP embarrassment in the face of the agrarian challenge: in Tuttlingen the council refused to allow the subject on the agenda at all; in Geislingen VP men voted against an SPD motion condemning tariff increases, supporting instead a 'moderate raising of the duties' in the light of the 'continuing, serious plight' of agriculture; and in Göppingen the VP councillor Hermann Speiser, owner of a family business dealing in agricultural implements, voted against his party colleagues and in

72. *Deutsches Volksblatt*, 15 March 1901.
73. *Gmünder Tagblatt*, 11 February 1901.
74. *Der Beobachter*, 2 February 1901.
75. *35 LT, PB I*, p. 226, 13 Sitz., 1.2.1901. The six deputies who supported the motion were Beurlen, Hartranft, Münzing, Rath, Schmid and Schock. The absentees were Maurer and Stockmayer. Four of the six VP supporters of the motion (Beurlen, Münzing, Hartranft and Rath) had faced serious agrarian opposition in the previous Landtag election. See *Deutsches Volksblatt*, 4 February 1901.

favour of a higher tariff.[76] Despite these compromises, however, the VP still found itself drawn towards the SPD. The political reform programme brought the parties together, and on a broad range of economic issues they cooperated in the Landtag. VP and SPD also cooperated in municipal elections,[77] and with the DP badly split between left and right, the VP saw in the SPD a likely ally in the coming Reichstag elections of 1903.

While the VP was drawn to the Left, the Centre moved with the agrarian current, as it had in the January tariff debate, while clinging to its theoretical commitment to a balance between classes in economic legislation. The *Deutsches Volksblatt* ran editorials attacking grain speculators as the cause of high prices, supporting an upward movement of agricultural tariffs, and criticising the Bülow government in Berlin for not acting more decisively against liberal attempts to block such a revision.[78] In agricultural association and *Volksverein* meetings, the Rembold motion and the Centre contribution to the January debate were publicised and the electorate assured of the party's solicitude for agriculture.[79] In the constituencies the harder agrarian stance of the Centre seems to have been popular. At a meeting in Günzkofen, for example, a unanimous resolution on the tariff issue was passed:[80]

1. The assembled agricultural producers acknowledge gratefully the efforts of the imperial government to help out the peasantry through increased tariffs on agricultural products.
2. They express the hope, however, that in the interests of an agriculture with more spending power, it will succeed in a) making more equal the tariff rates on the various grains, and b) raising the minimum tariff. It was further confirmed by all the agriculturalists present that each was in a position to sell grain, and each would benefit from increased tariff protection.

The issue of agricultural tariffs therefore contributed to a convergence of Centre and *Bauernbund*–Conservative policy, and this was reinforced by common hostility to large-scale capital and to department stores when the question of tax reform once more came

76. *Deutsches Volksblatt*, 9 April, 6 April and 16 March 1901.
77. On the continuing cooperation of VP and SPD in Stuttgart, see Keil, *Erlebnisse*, I, p. 158; on Heilbronn, see Kittler, *Erinnerungen und Erlebnisse*, p. 138.
78. See, for example, *Deutsches Volksblatt*, 11 February and 5 June 1901.
79. In one issue of the *Deutsches Volksblatt* (13 April 1901) three *Volksverein* meetings of this kind were reported, in Neuhausen, Massenbackhausen and Dormettingen.
80. *Deutsches Volksblatt*, 27 November 1901.

before the Landtag. Differences nevertheless remained in relations between the Centre and the Right. The Centre was concerned about the shrill agrarian tone of the *Bauerbund*–Conservatives,[81] while continuing to harbour suspicions that this disguised a basic allegiance to pro-Junker policies. The position of the Right on Catholic schools and the repeal of anti-Jesuit legislation was also considered at best unreliable, at worst openly anti-Catholic. The Right, in turn, shared a considerable part of the general non-Catholic view that the Centre was untrustworthy. For congruent policies to be translated into actual political alliance between Centre and Right, distrust on both sides had to be broken down. This began to occur as a result of electoral cooperation from 1903 onwards.

III

In February 1903, shortly before the Reichstag elections, a crucial by-election took place in the Landtag seat of Münsingen, an election which Matthias Erzberger considered to be 'one of the most interesting for a long time'.[82] It came after Centre–Conservative cooperation at the Reich level over the Bülow tariff revisions, and in the same month as the national *Bund der Landwirte* at its annual meeting in Berlin had put out a clear signal of friendly intent to the Centre, von Wangenheim claiming that 'We should not fight the Centre. We must urge our Catholic associates (*Berufsgenossen*) to ensure that the interests of agriculture are represented in the Centre in a manner which corresponds to their importance.'[83] In the Münsingen election the Württemberg *Bauernbund* was able to give an earnest of its good intentions and thus set under way locally the process of political alliance which was to culminate in the *Schwarz-Blau-Block*.

The by-election was necessitated by the death of the former VP deputy, the agrarian-inclined Rath, but in a strongly agricultural seat the chances of the VP retaining it were reduced by the agrarian mood of the electorate. Erzberger, working in the constituency for the Centre, remarked that:[84] 'A striking phenomenon is apparent here:

81. One effect of *Bauernbund* agrarianism was to encourage a political climate in which the Centre was put under pressure by its own peasant voters. At the Ravensburg by-election of 1902, caused by the death of Theophil Egger, an unofficial candidate 'was put up by the agriculturalists of the constituency' and collected nearly 1,000 votes. HStaASt, E 14, Fasz. 538, Nr. 3071, report on by-election, Stuttgart, 29 October 1902.
82. *Deutsches Volksblatt* 19 February 1903.
83. Report on von Wangenheim's speech of 9 February 1903, at the Zirkus Busch in Berlin, in *Deutsches Volksblatt*, 10 February 1903.
84. *Deutsches Volksblatt*, 19 February 1903.

people who were firm supporters of the VP a few years ago are now rabid supporters of the *Bauernbund*. The VP has become highly displeased. Its conduct over the tariff question and the schools question has taken the ground away from under it.' The confessional balance in Münsingcn gave the Centre a good chance of winning the seat if it could resist the pressure of the buoyant *Bauernbund* in Catholic areas, a pressure also noted by Erzberger. The Centre therefore fought an independent campaign aimed at convincing its natural electorate of the superfluity of the *Bauernbund* on agrarian issues, and its unreliability on those which concerned Catholics as such. On the eve of the election it stated its determination to reach the second ballot and give the *Bauernbund* the 'opportunity, by supporting the Centre, to take the seat away from the VP'.[85]

The three major parties finished very close together in the first ballot, with the Centre at the top and the *Bauernbund* just squeezed out of second place by the VP candidate, Reihling.[86] Just over a week later the local committee of the *Bauernbund* decided unanimously to recommend second-ballot support for the Centre candidate, Schmid, in view of the affinities which existed between Centre and Right, and the danger of a growing rapport on the Left between VP and SPD:[87]

> On the questions of *Schutz der nationalen Arbeit*, and in particular the protection of our agriculture and *Mittelstand*, the Centre takes a recognisedly positive position. If this party unfortunately still does not give its full support to our efforts, it nevertheless stands a great deal closer to them than the Democrats [i.e. the VP]. The Centre stands with us on the basis of the Christian world-view. Confessional differences must recede into the background when set against the Democrats and their confessional characterlessness. The wishes and needs of the rural population receive much firmer and more reliable consideration from the Centre than from the Democrats.

This decision by the *Bauernbund* was followed by the Conservative *Deutsche Reichpost*, which also saw the Centre as an ally in the struggle for a policy favourable to agriculture and the *Mittelstand*.[88] The seat was, in the end, saved for the VP, although only by blatant use of the

---

85. Ibid.
86. Result, with 1900 Landtag election figures for the parties in parentheses: Schmid, Centre, 1,663(1,192); Reihling, VP, 1,556(1,962); Hermann, *Bauernbund*, 1,447(1,191). *WJbb*(1903), 'Chronik des Jahres', I; *Deutsches Volksblatt*, 23 February 1903.
87. Cited in *Deutsches Volksblatt*, 2 March 1903.
88. Summary of press reactions: *Deutsches Volksblatt*, 5 March 1903.

confessional weapon among the Protestant population, and the choice of a transparently agrarian candidate.[89] But the decision of the *Bauernbund* and Conservatives showed that they had come to value the common economic cause higher than traditional confessional antagonisms; and in making this clear they opened the way for further cooperation with the Centre.

This was evident in the Reichstag elections which followed. They were characterised by a further hardening of lines between Left and Right: the Centre, with its almost impregnable block of seats in Oberschwaben, succeeded in maintaining its position; but the VP was a victim of the growing polarisation between agriculture and industry, peasantry and working class. In constituency IV, for example, a former safe seat, Friedrich Haussmann failed even to reach the second ballot. The case was representative, for the constituency embraced the communities of Vaihingen, Böblingen, Maulbronn and Leonberg: close to Stuttgart, it contained both a hard core of peasants and an expanding proletariat. The same pattern repeated itself in constituencies III and V.[90] In all, the VP lost one seat and over 12,000 votes, while the SPD vote rose spectacularly from 60,000 to 100,000.[91] The VP campaign attempted to present a different face to town and country; mostly, though, it offered simply a muted version of the SPD's views, for the SPD had threatened to withdraw its support if the VP did not dissociate itself from a concessionary attitude towards the agrarians. Hence the VP tried to stiffen its flagging free trade principles, and fought on a platform of opposition to all 'extremism' in economic demands, but above all against the 'extremism' of the agrarian Right.[92] Accordingly it supported the SPD in three second ballots (constituencies III, IV and V), and received SPD support in return in a further four (constituencies VII, VIII, IX and XII).[93]

If this marked the continuing formation of an anti-agrarian Left, events on the Right provided a mirror-image. Most striking here was the rejection by the *Bauernbund*–Conservatives of the electoral alliance with its old *Kartell* partner, the DP, and the forging instead of further links with the more agrarian Centre. In a 1902 by-election in Leonberg, the *Bauernbund* had already demonstrated that it was willing to press demands on the DP to the point of political rupture, imposing

89. Result: Reihling 2,575, Schmid 2,054. See HStaASt, E 14, Fasz. 538, Nr. 620. report on by-election, Stuttgart, 7 March 1903. Campaign details also in *Politische Zeitfragen*, 12(Stuttgart, 1906), pp. 633–6.
90. Results and analysis in *Schwäbischer Merkur*, 17 June 1903.
91. *Schwäbischer Merkur*, 22 June 1903.
92. VP (in fact, for the Reichstag election: Deutsche VP) programme, in *Der Beobachter*. Copy in HStaASt, E 130a, Bü 1426: newspaper cuttings on election.
93. *Schwäbischer Merkur*, 26 March 1903.

an unpalatable agrarian candidate on the latter.[94] In 1903 it took this a stage further, carrying its agrarian agitation to new heights and putting up candidates against the DP even in constituencies where a common *Kartell* candidate might have succeeded, and where the *Bauernbund*'s chances were — by its own admission — hopeless.[95] At the same time, the agrarians put out feelers to the Centre, put up Catholics as candidates and hinted that they might support Centre attempts to reverse the anti-Jesuit legislation.[96] The 'Münsingen pact' was still clearly valid for the *Bauernbund* and its Conservative allies. The Centre again reacted with suspicion and conducted its own robust agrarian campaign, making no first ballot concessions, and proceeding with the objective 'not to let itself be outdone by the agrarians'.[97] In its second-ballot policy, however, while confessional distrust still influenced the Centre, more general political considerations also played a part in its support for the Right. Throwing its weight behind the *Bauernbund*, the Centre helped its candidates to defeat the VP in constituency XII and the SPD in constituency III.[98]

The cooperation between Centre and Right in 1903 continued in the following years, surviving political circumstances which might have been expected to jeopardise it. Alliance between the Centre and the Right was likely to be most succesful when economic issues enjoyed primacy in political life. The years from 1904 to 1906, however, saw the peak of the reform wave in matters like the constitution and local government. This not only tended to undercut the importance of economic issues which drew the Centre and the Right together; it was also used by the VP to isolate the Centre, as the intransigent 'clerical' opponent of reform, from potential allies, including the *Bauernbund*–Conservatives. But this temporary alignment of the

94. In a constituency where agrarian feeling was pronounced, the DP had little choice but to support the candidate, Immendörfer, who in fact won the seat with a higher vote than the DP deputy had received in 1900. *Gmünder Tagblatt*, 13 March 1902.
95. Thus in constituency XIV, the *Bauernbund*–Conservatives put up a candidate, even though Dr Eugen Nübling admitted in the *Ulmer Schnellpost* (5 June 1903, cited *Schwäbischer Merkur*, 7 June) that this would bring victory to the Left by dividing the DP–Conservative vote. However, the *Bauernbund*–Conservatives also put up candidates in all but two clear Centre constituencies, although several of these were merely nominal (*Zählkandidaten*).
96. See the expression of pro-Centre feeling in the *Schwäbischer Landmann*, 1 May 1903, and the selection of a Catholic candidate, Albert Treiber, in constituency VIII, where the Centre could expect 3–4,000 first-ballot votes if it fielded a candidate. Treiber went on record before the election with various comments about his support for repeal of article 2 of the anti-Jesuit law. See *Schwäbischer Merkur*, 26, 27, 28 May 1903.
97. Centre Party assembly at Rottweil, 24 May 1903, speech by Kiene: *Schwäbischer Merkur*, 25 May 1903.
98. *Schwäbischer Merkur*, 26 May 1903. On constituency III and Centre support for the Right, see Kittler, *Erinnerungen und Erlebnisse*, p. 143.

Bauernbund–Conservatives with the reform parties was incomplete and fragile: the Right never gave any indication that it could be extended to lasting, or electoral, cooperation. Indeed, in the Mergentheim by-election of 1904 the alliance with the Centre was struck up again. This by-election was a case of Münsingen in reverse. The DP secretary, Fetzer, in accordance with the political situation in the Landtag in 1904, tried to win the *Bauernbund* for a common candidacy or joint campaign against the Centre, but this approach was rejected by the Conservative secretary, Schrempf.[99] Instead the Right put up a Catholic candidate, Valentin Mittnacht, and engaged in a 'zealous spinning of threads over to the Centre' (*eifrige Fädenspinnen zum Zentrum hinüber*).[100] This time the Centre reacted more positively: its own candidate, Pfeufer, was put up late, campaigned only nominally and directed his attack exclusively against the joint liberal candidate of the VP and DP, Keller. Pfeufer collected only 20 per cent of the first-ballot votes in a 40 per cent Catholic constituency, and only 1,063 votes against figures ranging from 1,200 to 1,600 in the previous three elections. The suspicions of the VP and DP that this was deliberate were confirmed by the Centre's own explanation of its policy. It had deliberately avoided reaching the second ballot because of the danger of a confessional campaign like that mounted the previous year in Münsingen, and preferred to be in a position where it could decide the outcome of the second ballot between the liberal Keller and the Conservative Mittnacht.[101] In the event, Mittnacht won after a turnout of Catholic voters larger than that for their own candidate on the first ballot, and the *Deutsches Volksblatt* claimed the credit on behalf of the Centre for the success of the Right.[102]

99. Details of Fetzer's negotiations with the local *Bauernbund* leader, Zainer, in *Schwäbischer Merkur*, 12 November 1904, which also printed the correspondence between Fetzer and Schrempf. The DP had also sought a common DP–Conservative–*Bauernbund* candidate in Münsingen: HStaASt, E 14, Fasz. 538, Nr. 620. Report on by-election, Stuttgart, 7 March 1903.
100. *Schwäbischer Merkur*, 19 October 1904.
101. *Deutsches Volksblatt*, 19 November 1904.
102. *Deutsches Volksblatt*, 3 December 1904. The government also attributed Mittnacht's victory to the Centre, as well as to what it sourly called the 'not particularly scrupulous agitation' on the part of the *Bauernbund*. HStaASt, E 14, Fasz. 538, by-election report, Stuttgart, 3 December 1904. Mittnacht received 2,846 votes to Keller's 2,810, on a high second-ballot turnout of 91 per cent. Significant is the Catholic community of Stuppach, which in the first ballot cast 92 Centre and 8 *Bauernbund* votes. In the second ballot, Mittnacht polled 122 votes, more than he and the Centre candidate polled together on the first ballot. *Schwäbischer Merkur*, 3 December 1904. The Mergentheim result was overturned, however, in June the following year, after complaints of irregularities. In the re-election, the sides lined up as before; but on this occasion, perhaps because of the solidity of SPD second-ballot support for the VP–DP candidate, Häffner, the previous result was reversed. See reports in HStaASt, E 14, Fasz. 538, Nr. 1536, 2225, 2379, 30 June, 31 August, 13 September 1905.

Mergentheim was only one sign that Centre and Right were becoming conscious of a natural community of interest in Württemberg. The achievements of the Reform Landtag, as Friedrich Payer later admitted, robbed the VP of a clear programme for the future:[103] this exposed the party even more to attacks on its economic policy, and thus made it easier for the Centre and Right to agree. The Centre, as we have already seen, tilted in 1906 against VP reform efforts for both tactical and principled reasons. Scorn for the 'merely' political nature of VP success was a motif of the Centre's pre-election assembly at Rottweil in November 1906. The *Bauernbund–* Conservatives, despite their temporary support for the reform parties in the Landtag, were no less harsh on the VP, and on the same grounds. Thus the pre-election editorial in the *Schwäbischer Landmann* disdainfully attacked the political achievements of the *Reformlandtag:* 'And what will all this cost us? Faced with nothing but laws, we shall soon no longer know if we're coming or going, and who benefits from all the many laws and reforms? Certainly not the respectable and hard-working citizen and peasant!'[104] Moreover, even in the period of the Centre's greatest political isolation, around 1904–6, there were heated economic controversies which served to emphasise the common ground they shared with the Right. In 1900–2 the tariff issue and the 'milk war' had divided agrarians and anti-agrarians; in 1904–5 this function was served by the issue of the shortage and high cost of meat.[105] Shifts in Centre attitudes had also taken place which added to their sense of common interest with the Right. One sign of this was the more openly agrarian temper of the Centre *Fraktion*, both leadership and back-benchers; and this was strengthened by the election in May 1904 of the radical agrarian priest Anton Keilbach into the Centre *Fraktion*, after a by-election in Waldsee. Another indication was the changed tone of the *Deutsches Volksblatt*. It had not been unknown earlier for the paper to combine an anti–capitalist outlook with attacks on the VP as the party of Jewish business; but such attacks seem to have become harsher and more regular as fears of

103. See above, p. 148, n. 29.
104. *Schwäbischer Landmann*, 1 December 1906.
105.| Both Centre and *Bauernbund* blamed the meat shortage and rise in prices during 1904–5 on the middleman, claiming that the peasant was an innocent — or even exploited — party. See the *Neckarbote*, 6 August 1904; *Oekonomierat Rudolf Schmid*, pp. 76 ff; and Hunt, *Journal of Contemporary History* (1975), pp. 518–19. On the milk war and the fight between town and country, see *Oekonomierat Rudolf Schmid*, p. 191.

political isolation lent greater stridency to their tone.[106] It was a telling sign of the extent to which Centre and Right had drawn together since the 1900 elections that in 1906 *Bauernbund* and Centre were responsible for practically identical publications, detailing the involvement of VP politicians in Jewish businesses and inviting their readers to draw the appropriate conclusions.[107]

In the proportional representation elections for Stuttgart in the 1906 Landtag elections, the Conservatives and Centre combined their lists, enabling the *Bauernbund* candidate, Hiller, to win a seat.[108] Even more significant was the extent to which the Right–Left, agrarian versus anti-agrarian polarity which had developed since 1900 cut across the lines of the Bülow Bloc in the Reichstag elections of 1907. The Bloc should have divided the VP from the SPD and the Conservatives from the Centre. In fact, the Conservatives and the *Bauernbund* disliked the liberal complexion optimistically put on the Bloc by the VP, and continued to oppose VP candidates; while the DP, which had seen its overtures to the Conservatives rejected in previous years, most spectacularly at Mergentheim, was being edged by its own Young Liberals towards cooperation with the VP and rejection of the agrarian Right.[109] The Bloc was thus incomplete and internally rent in Württemberg even at its inception, and the actual course of the election alignments brought this out. Especially significant was the struggle over constituency III (Heilbronn). Here the candidate of the VP, Friedrich Naumann, was supported by the entire Left, from the local (and radical) branch of the DP to the SPD, while the Conservatives put up the agrarian Dr Wolff as their own candidate, in open

---

106. See, for example, *Deutsches Volksblatt*, 10 January and 29 September 1906. The sense of isolation certainly had an impact on Centre attitudes in 1906. At the Rottweil state assembly of the party in that year, where Viktor Rembold referred to 'enemies all around', a Catholic priest from Weissenau criticised Conrad Haussmann in the following terms; 'It is the old story: freedom is demanded for the Jews, for the usurers, for dissolute art, for the dirty products of the press; but the demands of the Catholic and Christian people are trampled upon.' *Anzeiger vom Oberland*, 13 November 1906. Anti-semitism in the Centre Party normally became more virulent at times when Catholics and the Centre were themselves — or felt themselves to be — under external attack.
107. HStaASt, Conrad Haussmann Papers, Q 1/2, 104: *Bauernbund* pamphlet 'An die Landtagswähler des Oberamtsbezirks Münsingen' (n.d. 1906 ?); *Deutsches Volksblatt*, 3 December 1906.
108. *Deutsches Volksblatt*, 30 November 1906.
109. Conrad Haussmann was in Heilbronn, campaigning in the Landtag elections, when news came of Bülow's Reichstag dissolution. He was enthusiastic about the potential for a liberal course on the part of the imperial government, and urged once again that the DP leave its alliance with the Conservatives in local elections and form a liberal bloc. See HStaASt, Conrad Haussmann Papers, Q 1/2, 104: newspaper cuttings on 1906–7, esp. the *Heilbronner Zeitung*, 15 December 1906.

contravention of Bloc solidarity, and received the open support of their supposed opponents in the Centre.[110] Even in the adverse circumstances of 1906-7, the understanding which had been built up between Centre and Right was therefore maintained.

IV

The Bülow Bloc in Reich politics was characterised by the constant tension between Liberals and Conservatives, anti-agrarians and agrarians. The Centre — which not only resented its exclusion from the key position in the Reichstag, but also feared the anti-clerical and radical implications of the Progressives' part in the Bloc — hoped for a return to an alliance of Centre and Conservatives. It therefore welcomed the shattering of the Bloc in 1909 over financial reform. From 1909 onwards Centre and Right cooperated more closely at national level, and in 1912 this found expression in the *Schwarz-Blau-Block*. In Württemberg, as we have seen, the lines of the Bloc were never firmly adhered to by either side. Political developments in the state were much closer to those in neighbouring Baden, where the entire Left formed a *Grossblock* aimed against the coalition of Centre and Right. In Württemberg a variant of this set of alignments was clearly emerging in the years up to 1906–7; the remaining years up to 1912, when elections were held to both the Reichstag and Württemberg Landtag, saw its consolidation.

Under the pressure of the Young Liberals the DP moved towards a definitive break with the Right, and towards permanent cooperation with the VP. The growing realisation by the DP that the Conservatives were becoming more intransigently agrarian was reinforced by their dislike of the verbal concessions on clerical issues made by the Right to win Centre approval. After 1907 the VP and DP became politically closer, sharing anti-clerical and anti-agrarian views. The Herrenberg by-election of 1909, when the two parties collaborated electorally against the Conservatives as well as the Centre, demonstrated the strength of this tie.[111] Relations between the two bourgeois liberal parties and the SPD were such as to prevent a

110. Jakob, *Süddeutsche Monatshefte* (1907), I, pp. 517 ff; Kittler, *Erinnerungen und Erlebnisse*, pp. 143–4; Heuss, *Erinnerungen*, pp. 59–64.
111. On Herrenberg, see *Literarische Beilage des Staatsanzeigers für Württemberg*, 13 November 1909. On the DP's 'rediscovery' of its liberalism, see Hunt, *Journal of Contemporary History* (1975), p. 526. The tendency of the DP to move closer to the VP was certainly a source of concern to some local DP figures, whose reliability in following the leftward turn of the leadership was sometimes in doubt. See *Schwäbischer Merkur*, 18 January 1911; Egelhaaf, *Lebenserinnerungen*, p. 126.

complete replica of the Baden *Grossblock*. The growing influence of the left wing within the SPD, especially in Stuttgart and Göppingen, was a major source of alarm, particularly as the SPD *Fraktion* in the Landtag continued to increase in size.[112] Nevertheless, there was cooperation between the VP and SPD at municipal elections,[113] a reflection of the way in which, despite internal frictions, the Left as a whole was given its identity by the nakedly agrarian posture of the Right. This was especially marked after 1909. While the DP grew closer to the VP, therefore, the VP continued to cooperate with the SPD on a minimum programme which included educational reform and economic liberalism. As the VP tried to recruit electoral support among the growing white collar groups of those in state service and the private tertiary sector, its advocacy of cheap bread and consumer interests gave it much in common with the SPD.[114] The links between the VP and SPD on the one hand, the VP and DP on the other, produced a large measure of electoral cooperation in 1912.[115]

At the same time, the Centre and Conservatives drew closer together on the Right. The *Bauernbund*–Conservatives broke with their former allies in the DP: they attacked the DP for moving to the left under the influence of its young leader, Johannes Hieber,[116] and by 1909 were openly accusing the DP-orientated *Schwäbischer Merkur* of being the 'paper of the stock exchange'.[117] By 1912 the Right had fully accepted the Centre as its natural ally on economic as well as cultural issues. On the Centre side, the rightward shift evident after the late 1890s was continued. We have seen in earlier chapters how the Centre was divided from the VP and SPD on a range of issues: reform of the

112. Simon, *Die württembergischen Demokraten*, p. 58; Schlemmer, *Die Rolle der Sozialdemokratie*, p. 120.
113. At Neckarsulm in 1908, for example. See *Deutsches Volksblatt*, 7 January 1908.
114. In 1911, as the result of an exceptionally hot and dry summer, the price of various agricultural products — including potatoes, fruit and milk — rose above the normal level, and there were renewed cries of protest, particularly about the price of milk. As the SPD showed at the beginning of the year at a by-election in Heilbronn, where it defeated the VP (see *Deutsches Volksblatt*, 14 January 1911), it was in a good position to make political capital out of such developments and force the VP into a more pro-consumer stance.
115. In the 1912 Landtag elections there were formal agreements between the VP and SPD in Backnang, Oberndorf, Vaihingen, Leonberg and Waiblingen. At the same time the VP cooperated with the DP in Besigheim, Geislingen, Göppingen, Künzelsau and Sulz. HStaASt, Conrad Haussmann Papers, Q 1/2, 104: especially the undated document 'Beschlüsse des engeren Ausschusses. Für Nachwahl'. In certain local circumstances, DP, VP and SPD concluded a direct alliance. This was the case in the Biberach municipal elections of 1912. See *Anzeiger vom Oberland*, 2 December 1912.
116. See the scathing attack on Hieber and the 'turn to the left' for which he was held responsible, in *Deutsche Reichspost*, 6 February 1909 (cited *Deutsches Volksblatt*, 9 February). The DP leader Keinath was also attacked for allegedly making himself a pawn of the SPD. *Oekonomierat Rudolf Schmid*, pp. 146–7.
117. *Oekonomierat Rudolf Schmid*, p. 96.

constitution and education, the programme of institutional adaptation to the industrial state set in motion by the government, and economic policy. Despite residual confessional suspicions on both sides, cooperation with the Right presented fewer obstacles and increasingly became a reality as Centre policy was adapted to developments both inside the party and elsewhere. Agrarian pressures from its own supporters modified Centre policy in a direction which brought it closer to the agrarian Conservatives; and the change in the Conservatives themselves, from a rump of pro-governmental notables to a largely anti-governmental party with a demagogic appeal to the 'small man', made the identity of interest between the Centre and the Right more obvious both in style and substance.

The growing alliance of Centre and Right was therefore the result of a process of change on both sides. In fact, Conservatives and Centre crossed much of the same political ground in the twenty years prior to 1914. The *Bauernbund*–Conservatives in Württemberg, like the *Bund der Landwirte* nationally, represented an attempt by astute conservatives to preserve their political position by means of a popularised appeal. To maintain the backing of peasantry and *Mittelstand* they offered a demagogic package of agrarianism, radical anti-capitalism, anti-urbanism, anti-semitism and *Mittelstandspolitik*; and underpinning this, while giving the programme an appearance of support for all classes, was an insistence on autarky.[118] Centre policy, as we have seen, was also the product of an interplay between a conservative but flexible political leadership, and the aspirations of a peasant and petty-bourgeois rank-and-file. By 1906, Centre leaders had already translated and mediated these popular impulses into an affirmation of autarky, with its protectionist stress on *Schutz der nationalen Arbeit*. Thus Kiene, at the Centre's pre-election assembly at Rottweil in 1906, argued:[119]

> Germany must stand on two feet, one a strong and healthy agriculture, the other a healthy home industry. . . . Yes, it would be a national misfortune if, as is so often said, Germany became a purely industrial state, or remained a purely agricultural country. For our agriculture must be in a position such that it can largely feed our German people, in the event of a war we must be self-sufficient, we cannot allow ourselves to be dependent on neighbours with whom we may be in a state of war.

118. See, above all, Puhle, *Agrarische Interessenpolitik und preussischer Konservatismus*. On Württemberg particularly, Hunt, *Journal of Contemporary History* (1975), pp. 518 ff.
119. *Deutsches Volksblatt*, 23 November 1906.

The 'Germany must stand on two feet' speech at Rottweil was to be a motif of Centre policy and speech-making in subsequent years, and it indicated those developments in the party which brought it closer to the Right. In the 1890s, the traditional solicitude of the Centre for the peasantry and *Mittelstand*, like its emphasis on 'balanced justice' in the formulation of economic policy, had been projected backwards towards an idealised, pre-industrial harmony of classes. By 1914 this had altered. The contradictions of *Mittelstandspolitik*, and the need to accommodate agrarian interests within the party, while at the same time trying to persuade other social groups like the Catholic working class that 'balanced justice' still prevailed, led to a re-statement of this traditional concept of class harmony in a new form which brought the Centre very close to the Conservative concept of *Schutz der nationalen Arbeit*. At the level both of interest politics and the axioms of policy in which these were clothed, the Centre and the Right began to speak the same language.

This was very evident from the policies enunciated by the Centre in the approach to the Reichstag and Landtag elections of 1912. It was clear, for example, in the speech at Rottenburg of Eugen Bolz, newly-adopted candidate for Reichstag constituency XIII, in March 1911.[120] Bolz began by quoting with approval the agrarian academic Buchenberger, before going on to condemn international free trade. A certain measure of commercial interchange was necessary, he admitted, but 'not in the most indispensable foodstuffs, with bread and meat': for a country to be dependent in this way on foreign supplies was a calamity, and it was precisely Britain's dependence on foreign food imports which had led to her aggressive naval policy. The opponents of tariffs, argued Bolz, were the representatives of large capital; whereas the securing of wartime supplies, the preservation of the peasantry and the maintenance of the 'strength of the people' — moral as well as physical — depended on the existence of general tariff protection. A similar note was struck by Matthias Erzberger in a speech at the end of the same year.[121] As the Reichstag election approached, the *Deutsches Volksblatt* and other Centre papers ran numerous articles in which agrarianism and *Schutz der nationalen Arbeit*, anti-English feeling and hostility to 'mobile capital', were linked together in a manner indistinguishable from that adopted by the Right. This had its counterpart at the level of electoral cooperation. The Centre deliberately reduced the number of candidates it put up in

120. Bolz's speech given on March 5, reported in full in *Rottenburger Zeitung und Neckarbote*, 7, 8, 10 and 11 March 1911.
121. Speech in Wolfegg on 9 December 1911, reported in *Waldse'er Wochenblatt*, 12 December 1911.

hopeless Reichstag constituencies, and gave open support to the *Bauernbund*–Conservatives in constituencies III, VII, VIII, X, XII and XIV. The Right, in turn, made the gesture of putting up no candidate in the four safe Centre seats, and explicitly declared in advance in favour of Eugen Bolz in constituency XIII.[122]

The approach to the Landtag elections at the end of 1912 saw the emergence of a similar pattern, with the Centre and the Right concentrating their fire on identical targets. Typical was the attack on the government by both the *Deutsche Reichspost* and the *Deutsches Volksblatt* for its alleged failure to counter what the Centre newspaper called the 'most scandalous and frivolous inflaming of the people' by the anti-agrarians.[123] It is also significant that in October the *Deutsches Volksblatt* printed a fulsome tribute to Adam Röder, the editor of the *Deutsche Reichspost* for the previous three years, who was leaving to work for a Conservative newspaper in Hildesheim. Röder, said the *Deutsches Volksblatt*, had brought new honour to conservatism in Württemberg with his brave attacks on the 'arrogance' of the VP. In view particularly of the 'socialist tidal wave', it continued, the Centre warmly welcomed his 'exemplary work for the conservative cause'.[124] Prominent party politicians similarly continued with the line they had taken before the Reichstag elections a year earlier. Erzberger, addressing an audience of 350 in Neckarsulm, talked of British trade rivalry, the threat of encirclement and Germany's need to remain close to Austria-Hungary: the tariff policy, he argued, was a vital prop of national policy, essential for the 'preservation of the German people'.[125] The political vocabulary which was shared by the Centre and the Right was, once again, unmistakable; and, once again, the two joined forces electorally. By the summer of 1912 Centre newspapers were re-affirming the existence of the *Schwarz-Blau-Block* for the Landtag elections, and by November the party had decided to support the *Bauernbund*–Conservative candidate on the first ballot in a number of crucial constituencies, including both Münsingen and Mergentheim.[126] In the elections the *Schwarz-Blau-Block* made a net gain of six seats, giving them half of the ninety-two seats in the Landtag. As the

122. *Deutsches Volksblatt*, 11 January 1912. See also Schulte, *Struktur und Entwicklung des Parteisystems*, pp. 122–5, who suggests that declared Centre support for *Bauernbund* candidates was partly a means of maintaining the electoral discipline of its own supporters.
123. *Deutsches Volksblatt*, 24 September 1912.
124. Ibid, 2 October 1912.
125. Speech of 11 October, reported in *Deutsches Volksblatt*, 16 October 1912.
126. *Anzeiger vom Oberland*, 15, 16, 25 November 1912.

government pointed out, the alliance had brought the Centre itself no direct benefits; but it had undoubtedly helped the Right.[127]

In 1900 the Württemberg government had counted the Centre as an oppositional party like the VP and SPD, while the Conservatives were bracketed with the DP as friendly to the government.[128] This taxonomy was reasonable at the turn of the century; by 1912 it no longer applied. A fitful variant of the Baden *Grossblock* had emerged on the Left, despite radical strains within the SPD, and despite the hankerings of the DP right wing towards a 'bourgeois bloc' against the SPD. In 1913, for example, the successful DP candidate against the Centre in a by-election at Rottweil received both VP and SPD support.[129] On the other side, the government now referred automatically to the *Bauernbund*–Conservative–Centre bloc as 'the Right', in tones which showed that it did not consider this newly-consolidated force a naturally friendly one.[130] The absoluteness of the changes between 1900 and 1912 should not be exaggerated. As the party-political flux at Reich level after 1912 showed, and as the voting on a measure like the imperial property tax of 1913 confirmed, one cannot talk of a rigid Left–Right polarity on the eve of 1914. This was also the case in Württemberg. Real changes had nevertheless taken place in the party politics of the state since the 1890s. And, in fact, the process of change which made possible the formation of the *Schwarz-Blau-Block* locally illuminates the more general transformation undergone by both Conservatives and Centre in the Wilhelmine period. The *Bauernbund*–Conservatives, sustaining their political position by means of a demagogic popular appeal, changed from the *étatiste*, pro-governmental party of the 1890s to one which was both more independent and more strident. The Centre underwent a similar process in reverse, which ended with the party firmly anchored politically on the Right.

Centre participation in the *Schwarz-Blau-Block* was not fortuitous; nor was it the result of leadership by the traditional right wing of the party. Significantly, it was men like Gröber and Erzberger, universally regarded in Berlin as standing on the left of the party, who intoned Conservative slogans like *Schutz der nationalen Arbeit*. The Centre

127. HStaASt, E 14, Fasz. 538, Nr. 3749: summary of election results, Stuttgart, 17 November 1912.
128. HStaASt, E 14, Fasz. 538, Nr. 3641: summary of 1900 Landtag election results, Stuttgart, 6 December 1900.
129. HStaASt, E 14, Fasz. 538, Nr. 3122: reports on Rottweil by-election, Stuttgart, 14 and 28 September 1913.
130. HStaASt, E 14, Fasz. 538, Nr. 3583: report on 22 October 1913 by-election in Gerabronn, Stuttgart, 23 October 1913.

move to the right was partly a result of its desire to play a more positive, 'national' role in Berlin. It was also the result, as the Centre experience in Württemberg shows, of the contradictions in the party's policy; the outcome, that is, of encouraging, absorbing and orchestrating the aspirations of its own natural constituency. A strongly anti-*étatiste* party in the 1890s, the Centre — like the Conservatives — had sustained its political position by means of a demagogic popular appeal. But the party fell victim to its own demagogy. Yielding to the aspirations and interest pressures which it had itself encouraged, and unable to reconcile agrarianism, *Mittelstandspolitik* and the interests of the Catholic worker, the Centre nevertheless kept up its claim to be all things to all men. At the economic level, however, such a pledge could be redeemed only by the advocacy of autarky; and at the political level this made sense only if the Centre drew closer to the Right.

Conclusion

Historians have had considerable difficulty placing the Centre Party within the politics of imperial Germany. It has often been depicted as a special case, as a peculiarly opportunistic party which was dedicated to pure politicking. As we have seen, there is an element of truth in this. The present study has tried, however, to go beyond this view. By examining the Centre both nationally and locally, the aim has been to bring out those features of the party's attitudes which were permanent and underlying. At one level, this is a matter of explaining why the party was so consistently inconsistent — a point which perhaps deserves more consideration than it has often received. More centrally, the question has been posed: why did the Centre tend to align itself with the Right rather than the Left in the two-and-a-half decades before 1914, when it had a pivotal position in the Reichstag? In answering this question, it has been argued in the present study that the Centre, far from being a special case, was in fact a characteristic political creature of imperial Germany. And, as such, its behaviour can help to illuminate some of the wider problems of the German political system prior to 1914.

The Centre was founded as a defensive reaction on the part of German Catholics faced with a minority position in the newly-unified Reich and with a subsequent onslaught against the Church. The party's greatest electoral success was in 1874, at the height of the *Kulturkampf*. While the Centre remained almost exclusively a party of Catholics, however, it was by no means simply a Catholic or confessional party. This study has tried to show that from the 1890s in particular, under a new generation of national leaders, the Centre began to cast off the more obvious clerical and confessional attributes which had been inherited from the period of the *Kulturkampf*. Certainly, on issues like the re-admission of teaching orders to Germany, the Centre followed the line of the Church. On educational issues in general the party's policy was heavily coloured by religious

231

considerations, although (as close examination of the reform era in Württemberg shows) these were never the only ones in play. On other issues, however, where the policy of the Church was equally clear, the Centre was prepared, on political grounds, to defy the wishes both of the German hierarchy and of Rome. The attitude taken up towards the military bills of 1887, 1890 and 1893 furnishes perhaps the best example. Both leaders and supporters of the Centre continued, of course, to share a common faith. The rhythm and tenor of Catholic life undoubtedly helped to reinforce allegiance to the Centre, particularly in the countryside and small towns; and the Catholic clergy played a considerable role in the party's political machine. There were, moreover, very many instances — both national and local — when the Centre leadership appealed to basic Catholic sentiments and loyalties, especially when the party was divided. That such appeals often failed, however, indicates the extent to which the Centre had changed since the days of the *Kulturkampf*. At the Reichstag elections of 1912, nearly one-half of the Catholics who went to the polls voted for a party other than the Centre; while for those who remained loyal it was not simple piety but an intricate web of interests and aspirations which bound them to the party. In this respect, as in its parliamentary practice in Berlin and the state legislatures, the Centre was — as its principal leaders intended — a 'political party'.

The orientation of the Centre towards the Right was not the result, therefore, of the party's frequently-alleged 'confessional' nature. Nor was this alignment an outcome of the party's dominance by a traditional élite pursuing reactionary goals. While Catholic aristocrats provided successive chairmen of the Centre *Reichstagsfraktion* up to the war, the real leadership of the party was in the hands of bourgeois politicians. Lieber's victory over the Silesian aristocratic conservatives on Windthorst's death was decisive in this respect, and the 1890s generally formed a watershed as far as the nature and style of party leadership were concerned. The weight of aristocratic influence on the formulation of party policy diminished after that time; so too did the number of aristocrats in the *Reichstagsfraktion*. This was also true locally in states like Bavaria and (to a lesser extent) Silesia, where aristocratic influence had previously been considerable; and in a state like Württemberg, where this had always been much less the case, local leaders quite deliberately guarded against such a possibility. This vacuum was not filled, however, by captains of industry. The importance of businessmen like Karl Trimborn and Richard Müller should not be underestimated, of course, and their counterparts at the local level were sometimes dominant Centre Party figures (particularly in urban industrial areas like Essen and Krefeld). Largely, though, industrial and commercial men were absent from the ranks of the Centre, a reflection of continuing Catholic economic backwardness. Indeed, in the 1920s Centre leaders were still urging that a greater number of business representatives become active in the party. The new national leadership of the Centre from the 1890s was, however, thoroughly bourgeois. It consisted partly of businessmen, but much more of Catholics from the professions: academics, officials, publishers and, above all, lawyers. As this study has sought to show, it was lawyers, those quintessential political brokers of bourgeois parliamentary institutions, who set the tone of Centre leadership both in the Reich and locally. It was they, as far as 'politics from above' are concerned, who contributed most to the anti-Left orientation of the Centre Party.

The political outlook of these men had its roots in Catholic 'backwardness'. The self-conscious new generation of national Centre leaders in the 1890s embodied perfectly the aspirations of bourgeois Catholics in general. They were attempting to transcent the Catholic sense of inferiority, to erase the stigma of hostility to the Reich with which Catholics had been burdened since the *Kulturkampf*, and to make it possible for aspiring Catholics to play a larger role both in the public bureaucracy and the professions. 'Out of the Tower' (*Heraus aus dem Turm*) and the 'parity question' were the twin slogans of this generation: as the Centre 'came into its own' within the German polity, so respectable Catholics would come into their own as equals within German society. An attachment to the status quo, a powerful sense of procedural rectitude, and a desire that Catholics be allowed to prove themselves reliably 'national' went hand in hand with this position. The negative tactics and the bitterly critical tones of the Left — especially the SPD — were disliked by Centre leaders. Conduct of this kind was an uncomfortable reminder of a pariah status they themselves wished to transcend. The SPD, as they saw it, wanted to change the political rules in an irresponsible way; they wanted only to exploit them soberly. In this respect, attitudes rooted in a specifically Catholic sense of inferiority reinforced more generally bourgeois conservative anxieties.

A similar cast of mind characterised the party's leading politicians in Württemberg, also mainly lawyers. They shared with their counterparts in Berlin the position of being political parvenus; and they shared also the parvenu's unhappy mixture of assertiveness and apprehension. After 1895 there was certainly a clear assertion of the Centre presence in the Stuttgart Landtag, a desire to be seen to play a 'constructive' role. But men like Adolf Gröber, Hans Kiene and the Rembolds also nurtured an apprehensive conservatism which expressed itself over many issues. It can be seen in their suspicion of the era of reform, particularly its educational provisions, and in their fears about the social and moral effects of industrialisation. It was evident in their regret that authority in the family, as in society at large, was supposedly being eroded. It was clear, finally, in their concern about the challenge to the constitutional fabric of the state which the SPD (and at times, if only rhetorically, the VP) seemed to represent. In Stuttgart, as in Berlin, such attitudes tended to make the Centre lean towards the Right politically. As far as Centre attitudes towards the government were concerned, the similarity between national and local parties was rather less. In Berlin, Centre politicians were normally pro-governmental, although over certain issues (like the Lex Heinze) the party found itself outflanking the government on the right, in the name of morality and public order. In Stuttgart, as in Munich and Karlsruhe, this outflanking occurred more often. At many points, not least during the era of reform, the Württemberg Centre found itself defending the idea of authority against authority itself. The high-point of this Centre tendency to be *plus royaliste que le roi* was to come in 1919, when the overthrown monarch, Wilhelm II, had to persuade Hans Kiene to serve in a republican government. Centre leaders in the Reich, in Württemberg and in the other German states nevertheless shared an innate conservatism and an unwillingness to oppose government consistently from a reformist standpoint. They were ultimately more concerned with establishing their credentials as 'loyal' Catholics.

In their reactions to the stigma of Catholic inferiority, Centre leaders thus assumed positions which cut them off from the parties of the Left. Catholic backwardness, however, also helped to determine the political alignment of the party in another important respect. The retarded economic development of Catholic Germany left both the Catholic bourgeoisie and (to a lesser extent) the urban working class relatively under-represented in the Catholic population as a whole. This, coupled with the anti-urban bias of imperial Germany's electoral geography, meant that a disproportionately large part of the Centre's natural constituency was made up of peasants and members of the *Mittelstand*. Under the impact of long-term agricultural crisis, and the growing difficulties faced by small businesses, these groups began to demand legislative measures to protect their livelihoods. As the role of pressure groups within the German parties increased, the Centre therefore tended to become a vehicle for interests of this kind. Indeed, in Württemberg, it was by addressing itself to peasant and petty-bourgeois grievances that the party acquired and consolidated its mass base. There, as in the Reich generally, the 1890s were the decisive period when the Centre institutionalised its solicitude for the peasant, artisan, shopkeeper and publican. The Centre was consequently divided from both the Progressives and the SPD by its pursuit of *Mittelstandspolitik* and by its agrarian stance. These policies, at the same time, gave the Centre a good deal in common with the Right. At Reich level the *Schwarz-Blau-Block* of 1912 was the political culmination of this identity of interest; in Württemberg, the local origins of the bloc can be seen as early as the Münsingen and Mergentheim by-elections of 1903 and 1904.

The Centre was therefore a typical Wilhelmine party in the attention it paid to particular material interests. This is an aspect of the party which has usually received too little attention. It would be misleading, however, to view the Centre just as a bland and efficient clearing-house for material interests of the kind described. In the first place, the interests of the peasantry and petty bourgeoisie were often at odds with one another, and even more at odds with the interests of the Catholic bourgeoisie and working class. All of these grievances and aspirations may have had common origins in the problem of Catholic backwardness. But the grievances and aspirations themselves were by no means identical or even reconcilable with each other. Centre support for the 'national' navy was popular with the Catholic bourgeoisie, but it antagonised the peasantry. On the other hand, anti-margarine legislation mollified the peasantry, but it made many bourgeois Catholics uneasy (the local Centre agent mentioned in Chapter One, who owned a margarine factory, was not alone in this). The Catholic working class, of course, suffered twice over. They paid for both the guns and the butter. The superficial smoothness and symmetry of Centre economic policy, its constant emphasis on the need for a just balance of interests, was therefore more apparent than real. Indeed, the Centre's stress on *Mittelstandspolitik*, like its later adherence to the idea of 'protecting national labour' (*Schutz der nationalen Arbeit*) can be seen as a way of asserting an artificial harmony in the face of very real — and politically troubling — conflicts of interest.

There is a second and connected reason why it would be misleading to see the Centre as simply 'relaying' its supporters' aspirations. The party leadership was actually under severe pressure from below. The various groups whom the Centre claimed to represent not only had conflicting demands, but were often prepared to threaten the party if their own demands were not met. Bourgeois Catholic opposition was shown in the movement of 'national Catholics', abortive though this ultimately proved to be. As we have seen, particular professions — like schoolteachers — were also prepared to put pressure on the party.

More seriously, there was antagonism between the Centre and the Christian Trade Unions after the turn of the century, especially over the tariff issue. This was only one sign of the dissatisfaction within the Catholic working class over Centre policy. Above all, the Centre's rural and small-town voters were by no means the conservative and deferential force that has sometimes been assumed. They, too, frequently demonstrated their disaffection with the course followed by the party. This was perhaps most spectacularly evident in Bavaria; but parish-pump sullenness, agrarian revolt and double candidacies at elections were by no means confined to that state. As the power of the confessional bond weakened, Centre leaders thus faced a serious problem of balancing above these conflicting and often threatening pressures. As their loss of electoral support between the 1870s and 1914 shows, they often failed. This was particularly so among the Catholic urban working class, who deserted the party in large numbers. Even where the Centre was able to keep Catholics within the party fold it did so at a cost. The price paid by the Centre for its short-term successes was its adoption of a damagingly irresponsible and demagogic style of politics.

A central concern of the present study has been to reconstruct the formation of this demagogic politics. In Württemberg, with which the study has been especially concerned, this basic element in Centre politics was forged out of the leadership's uneasy relationship with the Catholic countryside and small towns where, as in the Reich overall, the party had its chief support. In the years between the 1880s and 1914 such areas were in a state of flux, caught between traditional parochialism and exposure to powerful outside forces. Some of these forces, as we have seen, were of a directly economic kind; but they were accompanied in their effect by the impact of local railways, the newly-expanding local press, and less direct influences like the return of sons and daughters from the towns. These developments were signs of an important social leavening in Wilhelmine Germany; but their effect was partial and contradictory, particularly when it came to changing political consciousness. Social changes of this kind frequently meant only that traditional expressions of rural and parochial sentiment were given a superficially new form. In 1848 the villages and small towns had argued about hawkers, the colour of the local militia uniforms and the neglect of the law-makers in Stuttgart. Fifty years later they argued about travelling salesmen, the local railway branch line and the neglect of the agricultural inspector in Ulm. At the turn of the century, no less than in 1848, political success was dependent on being able to effect a juncture between the narrow preoccupations of the local community and the broader mainstream of public life in which political leaders operated. It was here that the Centre in Württemberg succeeded with its demagogic style of politics, and did so largely at the expense of the two liberal parties. In both of these respects, developments in Württemberg were characteristic of the Reich as a whole.

By 1895 the National Liberal DP had already given signs that its hold over the Württemberg electorate was loosening, as the ties of deference broke down and were replaced neither by firm organisation nor by successful appeal to material interests. In the following twenty years the Progressive VP betrayed symptoms of becoming similarly isolated from its historic peasant and *Mittelstand* base. When its reforming energy was spent, the VP found itself badly equipped to address itself to what Conrad Haussmann once called the 'dark urges' of the people. The agrarian Conservatives were more successful. And so was the Centre. Building on the organizational zeal of the parish clergy, the party cultivated its local popular support in many different ways. Its Landtag deputies were usually men with deep roots in the local community: village mayors, secretaries of loan banks, men who went on the annual outing of the Brown Cow Insurance Society. The party press similarly transmitted very directly the currents of local feeling on matters such as the incursion of travelling salesmen or the labour shortage on the land. Most important of all, even Centre leaders like Gröber and Kiene, learning the lesson of constituency revolts, took up and gave political respectability to issues which would otherwise have remained the minutiae of parliamentary business, but were the very stuff of local politics. This was not just a matter of pressing parish-pump grievances of a material kind. The style of politics adopted by the Centre was more broadly populist. Kiene's echoing of peasant antagonism towards the veterinary surgeon with the 'top hat and kid gloves' was representative. Equally demagogic pronouncements on subjects like women's emancipation, 'degenerate literature' and the immorality of the city — the antithesis of the wholesome village or small town — came readily from prominent Centre figures. Partly, of course, these were expressions of a genuine moral conservatism; but they were also what Centre leaders thought their supporters wanted to hear. Historians have often accused the Centre of maintaining its political position by cynical manipulation of confessional loyalty. They should, perhaps, examine more closely the political success which the party achieved through a very worldly orchestration of its supporters' material and parochial resentments.

The demagogy of the Centre was destructive and damaging in a number of different ways. It discredited the party with contemporaries, reinforcing the view that the Centre was essentially unscrupulous. It was especially damaging to the party's relations with the forces of the Left. They were the particular butt of the Centre's populist pronouncements, denounced not only for their 'pro-urban' economic policies, but also for their dangerous 'free-thinking'. This produced a legacy of bitterness on the Left which persisted into the Weimar Republic, and its immediate effects were particularly felt in those areas of south and west Germany where the Centre, the Progressives and the SPD might otherwise have been expected to cooperate. The Centre, finally, was the victim of its own demagogy. Agrarian and small-town appetites were fed rather than satisfied by the party. It was, as we have seen, consequently driven into positions which made the policy of a 'just balance of interests' even harder to realise. The Centre could maintain this economic and political balance only by offering further verbal concessions to workers and other urban Catholics as well. The internal dynamics of Centre policy thus led inexorably towards a form of autarky parallel to that followed by the government itself and invoked by the Right. The Centre's support in 1912 for the ultra-conservative slogan of 'protecting national labour' was the final outcome of this dilemma.

These conclusions about the Centre re-emphasise the fruitfulness of recent approaches to the history of the *Kaiserreich*. In a number of important respects, however, reconsideration of the Centre Party raises question marks over such approaches. It may therefore be useful, finally, to draw together some of the points where this study has suggested the need for a different emphasis. These fall into two main categories: first, those points where analysis of the Centre directly affects our view of imperial Germany; secondly, those points where the politics of the Centre indirectly illuminate the workings of the imperial German political system. The paragraphs which follow will attempt to deal with both.

It is clear that the Centre fits uneasily into the familiar political landscape of the *Kaiserreich*. The evidence of this study suggests, in particular, that arguments about the diversion or blunting of reformist energies in the *Kaiserreich* — about its political immaturity — need to take account of many complicated cross-currents. Attitudes among the Catholic peasantry and petty bourgeoisie, for example, with whom this book has been closely concerned, differed considerably from the picture which is often presented of an imperial German population being manipulated and mobilised behind the status quo. The reality was a good deal more oblique than this. The rural parts of Catholic Germany seem to have been almost untouched by the blandishments of social imperialism: there was little enthusiasm for the navy (or, in many cases, the army), and the membership of associations like the Pan-German League and the Navy League was very small. There was, in fact, an instinctively radical temper in many of these communities, expressing itself at least in part against the idea of distant government and arrogant officialdom. The Centre was able to carry these supporters with it politically because the view of the world which it presented — in which liberals and socialists were equated with arrogant officials as 'outsiders' — was deftly attuned to the actual experience of rural and small-town Catholics. The demagogy of the Centre was better equipped to channel the currents of petty-bourgeois and agrarian radicalism than the blunt instrument of an overtly manipulative social imperialism.

The case of bourgeois Catholics similarly suggests that a refinement of current ideas is in order. It is commonly argued that the German bourgeoisie as a whole was diverted from the task of domestic reform by a process of feudalisation, whereby it adopted the manners and values of the Junker aristocracy, bureaucracy and officer corps. The blunting of reformist ambitions among the Catholic bourgeoisie is hardly consistent with this picture. Few bourgeois Catholics were cast in the Diederich Hessling mould. They did not share the ethos of the student duelling fraternities and, as we have seen, bourgeois Catholics found access to both the officer corps and the bureaucracy very difficult. There was, in fact, a quickly-awakened strain of resentment among middle-class Catholics against military and bureaucratic high-handedness, finding expression in Centre Party leaders like Adolf Gröber. When bourgeois Catholics indicated their desire for a domestic place in the sun, they did so as part of an urge for emancipation which made itself felt in spite of, rather than because of, the values associated with the Junker aristocracy, bureaucracy and officer corps. It is significant in this respect that Centre Party leaders, the embodiment of such aspirations, made their strongest legislative commitment not to the 'Prussian' and 'feudal' features of the status quo, but to the 'national' and 'bourgeois' ones. The support for the civil code and the navy are good examples of this. Both, by implication, were measures which looked beyond a society governed by arbitrary abuse of law and the values of the Prussian officer: both, that is, looked beyond a society in which Catholics were likely to be eternally consigned to second-class status.

In this case, as in the case of the petty bourgeoisie and peasantry, the grievances and aspirations of German Catholics should be located in the particular position occupied by Catholics in German society, not in the seamless web of social imperialism and a feudalised bourgeoisie. It is within this context, too, that the political conduct and alignment of the Centre Party can best be understood. In emphasising this, the intention is certainly not to suggest that we revert to some comfortable view of an imperial Germany innocent of social tension and political manipulation. This study has laid stress on the importance of class conflict in the *Kaiserreich*, and on the presence of often recklessly demagogic forms of politics. Both remain very much on the historian's agenda. Two important qualifying points need to be made, however. First, the demagogic manipulation of popular sentiment was by no means the exclusive preserve of the government, the traditional élite and their agencies. It had a place in the repertoire of a much wider range of political leaders, as the case of the Centre Party illustrates very clearly. Bismarck, Bülow and Bethmann have already been joined on the political stage of the *Kaiserreich* by once less familiar figures like Miquel and the functionaries of the major interest organisations: it is now perhaps time that this stage was still more fully peopled with figures like Ernst Lieber, Hans Kiene and the Rembolds. They also played important roles, whether local or national.

The second point which needs to be made concerns the real nature of that role. Bülow, Miquel and Hans Kiene had one thing at least in common: all were reacting politically 'from above' to pressures 'from below'. Such pressures should not be underestimated, for there was a powerful social and political ferment at work in imperial Germany. This took many forms. The Württemberg government referred in the 1890s to the agitation of 'the homeopaths, the anti-inoculationists, the pro-cremationists, the agrarians and the publicans'. It might have added many other social groups and sectional interests to the list, from the teachers to the shopkeepers, from the pacifists to the *nationale Verbände*. All were propelled into public life, in a period of unprecendented social change, by the spread of education, communications and the new means of political agitation. All were part cause, part beneficiary of the growing levels of political participation in the *Kaiserreich*. So, too, was that less organised but ubiquitous body of opinion which asserted with growing conviction the importance of local identity and interests in themselves, at the very time when imperial Germany was becoming increasingly more unified as a political nation.

These were forces which in different ways challenged both governments and the established political parties of all political persuasions, forces to which the latter were obliged to react. It was precisely this interaction, proceeding at different levels and intensities, which produced many of the familiar features of public life in the *Kaiserreich*: the manipulation of interests, the reckless demagogy and the generally febrile atmosphere of German politics in the years before 1914. It is one part of this intermingling of aspirations and intentions 'above' and 'below' which the present study has tried to reconstruct, rather than either politics above or politics below by themselves. It would be misleading on the one hand to view popular aspirations of whatever kind as having been simply taken up and acted upon by political leaders; and on the other hand to construe political manipulation too mechanically, without taking into account the full force of pressure from below. In the end, after all, political manipulation itself is a process, not an act. We have seen, in the case of the Centre Party, how painful and protracted this process was. It was also cumulative, for expectations which had been encouraged were not so easily satisfied. It might be argued, in this respect, that the Centre Party in particular contained within itself many of the problems and contradictions of the German Reich as a whole. The history of its instability reveals, in microcosm, the history of the Reich's instability. The government of the Reich attempted to straddle conflicting interests. It sought to turn this weakness into strength by affecting to stand above the interests, while at the same time creating a demonology of enemies to bolster its position. It raised expectations by policies which were often demagogic. And it followed an increasingly zig-zag course in the years before 1914, to be delivered finally into the hands of the army by its own failure. The trajectory of the Centre was a parallel one. It too attempted to balance above conflicting interests. It too claimed to stand above them, at the same time creating a demonology of enemies to reinforce its own position. It too raised expectations by policies which were often demagogic. And it too followed a zig-zag course, to be delivered in 1914 into the hands of the government and the Right.

APPENDIX 1

The Distribution of Catholics in Württemberg

Oberämter in which Catholics made up more than 80% of the population.

Oberämter in which Catholics made up 50–80% of the population.

242

The Distribution of Centre Landtag
Seats in Württemberg

Seats won by the Centre Party in the Württemberg Landtag elections of 1895.

Centre Party Deputies in the Württemberg Landtag, 1895–1914

	Occupation	Constituency
Andre, Joseph	Workers' association official	Oberndorf, 1906–
Betzer, Georg	Peasant	Elected through 'List', 1912–
Beutel, Anton	Peasant	Waldsee, 1895–1903
Bolz, Eugen	Legal official	Rottenburg, 1912–
Braunger, Nikolaus	Rentier, with former interest in brewing industry	Leutkirch, 1900–
Bueble, Kaspar	Merchant	Tettnang, 1895–1900
Dambacher, Joseph	Village mayor	Ellwangen(Amt), 1900–12
Dentler, Max	Veterinary surgeon	Wangen, 1895–1900
Eckard, Joseph	Editor	Oberndorf, 1895–1900
Egger, Theophil	Retired schoolteacher	Ravensburg, 1895–1902
Eggmann, Ferdinand	Priest	Leutkirch, 1895–1900
Graf, Eugen	Workers' association official	Elected through 'List', 1906–12; Biberach, 1912–
Gröber, Adolf	Legal official	Riedlingen, 1895–
Gross, Johannes	Workers' association official	Elected through 'List', 1912–
Hanser, Gustav	Editor	Elected through 'List', 1906–
Herbster, Joseph	Master shoemaker and smallholder	Geislingen, 1906–12; elected through 'List', 1912–
Keilbach, Anton	Priest	Waldsee, 1904–12
Kessler, Franz	Peasant	Horb, 1900–12
Kiene, Johann (Hans) Baptist	Legal official	Ehingen, 1895–

Klaus, Anton Bruno	Schoolteacher	Schwäbisch Gmünd, 1895–6
Kuen, Eduard	Small businessman	Wangen, 1900–5
Kohler, Alfons	Local government official	Laupheim, 1912–
Krug, Franz Xaver	Village mayor	Biberach, 1895–1912
Locher, Georg	Factory owner	Tettnang, 1900–
Maier, Georg	Peasant and village mayor	Rottweil, 1900–13
Mohr, Joseph	Legal official	Waldsee, 1912–
Nessler, Franz Xaver	Local government official and village mayor	Spaichingen, 1906–
Nieder, Joseph Anton	Legal official	Ellwangen(Stadt), 1895–1906
Nussbaumer, Pankratius	Schoolteacher	Horb, 1895–1900
Rapp, Joseph	District architect	Saulgau, 1895–6
Rathgeb, Xaver	Peasant and village mayor	Ellwangen(Amt), 1895–1900
Rembold, Alfred	Lawyer	Schwäbisch Gmünd, 1900–
Rembold, Viktor	Lawyer	Aalen, 1895–
Schach, Simon	Publican	Rottenburg, 1895–1912
Schick, Johannes	Village mayor	Laupheim, 1895–1912
Schlichte, Max	Local government official	Ravensburg, 1902–
Schmid, Michael	District architect	Neresheim, 1906–
Schmidberger, Joseph	Agricultural inspector	Ellwangen(Amt), 1912–
Schwarz, Alfons	Priest	Schwäbisch Gmünd, 1897–1900
Schweizer, Adrian	Village mayor	Horb, 1912–
Sommer, Johann	Cartwright, smallholder and village mayor	Saulgau, 1896–
Späth, Karl Joseph	Priest	Elected through 'List', 1906–
Speth, Franz	Local government official	Wangen, 1905–
Vogler, Caspar	District architect	Neresheim, 1895–1906
Walter, Karl Ludwig	Legal official	Ellwangen(Stadt), 1906–
Weber, Johannes	Schoolteacher	Elected through 'List', 1906–

APPENDIX 4

The Composition of the Reichstag, 1887–1912

Party	1887	1890	1893	1898	1903	1907	1912
Conservatives	80	73	72	56	54	60	43
Free Conservatives	41	20	28	23	21	24	14
National Liberals	99	42	53	46	51	54	45
Liberal Vereinigung }	32	66	13	12	9	14 }	
Progressives }			24	29	21	28 }	42
Volkspartei	—	10	11	8	6	7 }	
Centre	98	106	96	102	100	105	91
Guelphs	4	11	7	9	6	1	5
SPD	11	35	44	56	81	43	110
Poles	13	16	19	14	16	20	18
Danes	1	1	1	1	1	1	1
Alsatians	15	10	8	10	9	7	9
Anti-Semites	1	5	16	13	11	16	13
Others	2	2	5	18	11	17	6
Total	397	397	397	397	397	397	397

The Composition of the Württemberg Landtag, 1895–1912

Party	1895	1900	1906	1912
SPD	2	5	15	17
VP	31	27	24	19
DP	14	11	13	10
Centre	18	18	25	26
Conservatives/Bauernbund	1	6	15	20
Independent	4	3		
Total	70	70	92	92

Note: The figures for 1895 and 1900 show only elected deputies; they do not include the twenty-three *Privilegierten* who also belonged to the Lower House of the Landtag. Some of these attached themselves to a particular party grouping, although most called themselves Independents.

The Growth of Electoral Participation: Percentage Turnout at Landtag Elections in the Constituency of Rottweil, 1870–1913

Year of election	First Ballot	Second Ballot
1870	60.2	
1876	80.0	
1882	70.1	
1889	61.1	
1895	87.2	93.0
1900	83.3	
1906	90.3	
1912	88.8	
1913*	88.4	94.2
*By-election		

HStaASt, E 14, Bü 538, Nr. 3122, 28 September 1913.

Bibliography

A. Unpublished Archival Sources

Stadtarchiv Cologne
  Karl Bachem Papers
Landesbibliothek Speyer
  Ernst Lieber Papers.
Hauptstaatsarchiv Stuttgart
  E 14, Kabinettsakten IV, Fasz. 538: Wahlen, 1877–1918.
  E 41, Anhang II: Verfassungsrevision.
  E 130 II, Bü 238: Landwirtschaft.
  E 130 II, Bü 241: Handels- und Gewerbekammer.
  E 130 II, Bü 486: Handel, Industrie und Volkswirtschaft.
  E 130a, Bü 406: Antisemitische Hetze.
  E 130a, Bü 420: Sozialpolitische und sozialwirtschaftliche
  Massnahmen.
  E 130a, Bü 576–88: Staatssteuerreform.
  E 130a, Bü 1426: Wahlen.
  E 150, Bund 2041: Politische Vereine und Versammlungen:
  Allgemeines, 1861–1918.
  E 150, Bund 2045–6: Akten betr. die Bekämpfung der
  Sozialdemokratie 1890–1916.
  Q 1/2: Conrad Haussmann Papers.
  Q 1/5: Hans Kiene Papers.

B. Unpublished Sources in Family Possession

Franz Ballestrem Papers, in possession of Dr jur. Carl Wolfgang
  Graf von Ballestrem

C. Material, Information and Recollections Privately Communicated by:

Dr Hans Dentler, Ehingen.
Herr Franz Faitsch, Wehingen.
Fräulein Anna Herbster, Wiesensteig.
Herr Norbert Schlichte, Ravensburg.
Dr Karl Setz, Neresheim.
Herr Adrian Speth, Wangen.
Herr Wilfried Vogler, Neresheim.

D. Published Official Sources (Württembergische Landesbibliothek, Stuttgart)

Beschreibung des Oberamts Ellwangen. Herausgegeben von dem Königlichen Statistisch-topographischen Bureau. Stuttgart, 1886.
Beschreibung des Oberamts Gmünd. Herausgegeben von dem Königlichen Statistisch-topographischen Bureau. Stuttgart, 1870.
Beschreibung des Oberamts Tettnang. Herausgegeben vom K. Statistischen Landesamt. Stuttgart, 1915.
Das Königreich Württemberg. Eine Beschreibung von Land, Volk und Staat. Hrsg. von dem K. Statistisch-topographischen Bureau. Stuttgart, 1863.
Das Königreich Württemberg. Eine Beschreibung nach Kreisen, Oberämtern und Gemeinden. Herausgegeben von dem K. Statistischen Landesamt. 4 vols. Stuttgart, 1904–7.
Die Landwirtschaft und die Landwirtschaftspflege in Württemberg. Denkschrift Hrsg. von der K. Zentralstelle für die Landwirtschaft. Stuttgart, 1908.
Literarische Beilage des Staatsanzeigers für Württemberg.
Verhandlungen der Württembergischen Kammer der Abgeordneten. Protokoll-Bände und Beilage-Bände.
Württembergische Jahrbücher für Statistik und Landeskunde. Herausgegeben von dem K. Statistischen Landesamt. (Prior to 1885: Herausgegeben von dem K. Statistisch-topographischen Bureau.)

E. Newspapers (Württembergische Landesbibliothek, Stuttgart)

Anzeiger vom Oberland. Biberacher Tagblatt (Biberach).
Der Beobachter (Stuttgart).
Der Bürgerfreund (Mengen).

Deutsches Volksblatt (Stuttgart).
Gmünder Tagblatt (Gmünd).
Heuberger Bote (Spaichingen).
Ipf-Zeitung (Ellwangen).
Neckarbote. (Rottenburg).
Der Oberländer (Saulgau).
Rottenburger Zeitung und Neckarbote (Rottenburg).
Rottumbote (Ochsenhausen).
Schwäbischer Merkur (Stuttgart).
Schwäbische Tagwacht (Stuttgart).
Waldse'er Wochenblatt (Waldsee).

F. PAMPHLET LITERATURE, MEMOIRS AND CONTEMPORARY PUBLISHED SOURCES

Adam, P. *Lebenserinnerungen eines alten Kunstbuchbinders.* Stuttgart, 1951.
Arnold, P. *Das Münchener Bäckergewerbe.* Stuttgart, 1895.
Bachem, J. 'Wir müssen aus dem Turm heraus', *Historisch-politische Blätter.* 1906, I.
Bachem, J. *Erinnerungen eines alten Publizisten und Politikers.* Cologne, 1913.
Bartens, A. *Die wirtschaftliche Entwicklung des Königreichs Württemberg mit besonderer Berücksichtigung der Handelsverträge.* Frankfurt/M., 1901.
Becker, J. (ed.) *Heinrich Köhler 1878–1949; Lebenserinnerungen.* Stuttgart, 1964.
Blos, W. *Denkwürdigkeiten eines Sozialdemokraten.* 2 vols. Munich, 1914–19.
Bodewig, H. *Geistliche Wahlbeeinflussungen in ihrer Theorie und Praxis dargestellt.* Munich, 1909.
Braun, A. *Die Warenhäuser und die Mittelstandspolitik der Zentrumspartei.* Berlin, 1904.
Cardauns, H. *Aus dem Leben eines deutschen Redakteurs.* Cologne, 1912.
Crüger, H. *Vortrag über gewerbliches Genossenschaftswesen, Warenbazare und Grosswarenhäuser gehalten auf dem 41. Verbandstag Württ. Gewerbevereine in Calw im Oktober 1899.* Stuttgart, 1899.
Dor, F. *Jacob Lindau. Ein Badischer Politiker und Volksmann in seinem Leben und Wirken geschildert.* Freiburg i.B., 1909.
Drill, R. *Soll Deutschland seinen ganzen Getreidebedarf selbst produzieren?* Stuttgart, 1895.
Egelhaaf, G. *Lebenserinnerungen.* Edited by A. Rapp. Stuttgart, 1960.
Elben, O. *Lebenserinnerungen 1823–1899.* Stuttgart, 1931.

Gasteiger, M. *Die christliche Arbeiterbewegung in Süddeutschland*. Munich, 1908.

Gemming, A. *Das Handwerkergenossenschaftsbewegung in Württemberg*. Stuttgart, 1911.

Goetz, W. 'Die Reichstagswahlen 1907', *Süddeutsche Monatshefte*, 1907, I.

Gottron, B. *Erlebtes und Erlauschtes aus dem Mainzer Metzgergewerbe im 19. Jahrhundert*. Mainz, 1928.

Hainlen, K. C. *Gemeinfassliche natürliche Beschreibung Württembergs. Mit besonderer Beziehung auf die Landwirtschaft*. Stuttgart, 1867.

Hertling, G. von. *Erinnerungen aus meinem Leben*. 2 vols. Munich, 1919–20.

Heuss, T. *Preludes to Life. Early Memoirs*. Transl. M. Bullock. London, 1955.

Heuss, T. *Erinnerungen 1905–1933*. Tübingen, 1963.

Hofmann, W. *Mit Grabstichel und Feder. Geschichte einer Jugend*. Stuttgart and Tübingen, 1948.

Hohenlohe, C. zu. *Denkwürdigkeiten der Reichskanzlerzeit*. Ed. K. A. von Müller. Stuttgart, 1931.

Hue, O. 'Die Katholischen Arbeiter und das Zentrum', *Neue Zeit*. 1903, II.

Hüsgen, E. *Ludwig Windthorst*. Cologne, 1911.

Jakob, K. 'Landtagswahlen und Reichstagswahlen in Württemberg', *Süddeutsche Monatshefte*. 1907, I.

Jung, W. *Der Gewerbsmann und die gewerblichen Verhältnisse Württembergs*. Ulm, 1845.

Keil, W. *Erlebnisse eines Sozialdemokraten*. 2 vols. Stuttgart, 1947–8.

Keilbach, A. *Lieder für Katholische Arbeitervereine Württembergs*. Stuttgart, 1907.

Kiene, J. B. *Die Zwangserziehung Minderjähriger Gesetz vom 29. Dez. 1899*. Stuttgart, 1900.

Kittler, G. *Aus dem dritten württemb. Reichstags-Wahlkreis. Erinnerungen und Erlebnisse*. Heilbronn, 1910.

Körner, T. *Volkswirtschaftliche Flugschriften*. Stuttgart, 1911.

Liesching, T. *Zur Geschichte der württembergischen Verfassungsreform im Landtag 1901—1906*. Tübingen, 1906.

Löbe, P. *Der Weg war lang. Lebenserinnerungen*. Berlin, 1954.

Morlok, G. von. *Die Königlich Württembergischen Eisenbahnen. Rückschau auf deren Erbauung während der Jahre 1835–89*. Stuttgart, 1890.

Naumann, F. *Demokratie und Kaisertum; ein Handbuch für innere Politik*. Berlin, 1900.

Naumann, F. *Die politischen Parteien*. Berlin, 1910.

Payer, F. *Vor 50 Jahren. Aus der Entstehungsgeschichte der Württembergischen Volkspartei*. Stuttgart, 1914.

Payer, F. *Mein Lebenslauf.* Typed Ms. Stuttgart, 1932.

Pistorius, T. von. *Die letzten Tage des Königreichs Württemberg (mit Lebenserinnerungen von seinem letzten Finanzminister).* Stuttgart, 1936.

Politische Zeitfragen in Württemberg. Zwanglos erscheinende Hefte. 4–22, Stuttgart, 1900–1912.

Rapp, M. *Die Einfuhr von landwirtschaftlichen Produkten und deren Einfluss auf die Lage der Landwirtschaft.* Stuttgart, 1900.

Richardy, R. 'Zur Stellung der Zentrums-Kleinpresse', *Allgemeine Rundschau,* 1906, pp. 148–9.

Rost, J. *Die wirtschaftliche und kulturelle Lage der deutschen Katholiken.* Cologne, 1911.

Saul, D. *Die Verfassungsrevision in Württemberg.* Frankfurt/M., 1899.

Scheffler, K. *Der junge Tobias. Eine Jugend und ihre Umwelt.* Leipzig, 1927.

Schirmer, K. *50 Jahre Arbeiter.* Duisburg, 1924.

Schmidt-Buhl, K. *Schwäbische Volksmänner, 17 Lebensbilder.* Stuttgart, 1908.

Schnurre, T. *Die württembergischen Abgeordneten in der konstituierenden deutschen Nationalversammlung zu Frankfurt am Main.* Stuttgart, 1912.

Schriften des Vereins für Sozialpolitik, 62–70, 76. Leipzig, 1895–7, 1898.

Schulthess' Europäischer Geschichtskalender, 1899, 1901. Munich, 1900, 1902.

Schussen, W. (pseud. for Wilhelm Frick). *Meine Steinauer. Eine Heimatsgeschichte.* Stuttgart and Leipzig, 1908.

Seidenberger, J. *Der parlamentarische Anstand unter dem Reichstagspräsidium des Grafen von Ballestrem nebst parlamentarischem Lexikon.* Cologne, 1903.

Severing, C. *Mein Lebensweg,* I. Cologne, 1951.

Smalian, H. *Ein Leben im Dienst der Buchdruckerkunst.* Berlin, 1919.

Spahn, M. *Ernst Lieber als Parlamentarier.* Gotha, 1906.

Spahn, M. *Das deutsche Zentrum.* Mainz and Munich, 1907.

Storz, C. *Reisebriefe aus Westafrika und Beiträge zur Entwicklung der deutschen Kolonien in Togo und Kamerun.* Stuttgart, 1906.

Supper, O. *Die Entwicklung des Eisenbahnwesens im Königreich Württemberg.* Stuttgart, 1895.

Vischer, L. *Die industrielle Entwicklung im Königreich Württemberg und das Wirken seiner Centralstelle für Gewerbe und Handel.* Stuttgart, 1875.

Walcker, O. *Erinnerungen eines Orgelbauers.* Kassel, 1948.

Wernicke, J. *Der Mittelstand und seine wirtschaftliche Lage,* Leipzig, 1909.

Winnig, A. *Der weite Weg.* Hamburg, 1932.

G. OTHER WORKS

Andre, J. *Zentrum und Landwirtschaft.* Stuttgart, 1918.

Aufmkolk, E. *Die gewerbliche Mittelstandspolitik des Reiches (unter besonderer Berücksichtigung der Nachkriegszeit).* Diss., Munich. Emsdetten, 1930.

Bachem, K. *Vorgeschichte, Geschichte und Politik der Deutschen Zentrumspartei; zugleich ein Beitrag zur Geschichte der Katholischen Bewegung, sowie zur allgemeinen Geschichte des neueren und neuesten Deutschland, 1815–1914.* 9 vols. Cologne, 1927–32.

Barkin, K. *The Controversy over German Industrialization 1890–1902.* Chicago, 1970.

Bauer, C. *Politischer Katholizismus in Württemberg bis zum Jahr 1848.* Freiburg i.B., 1929.

Bauer, C. *Deutscher Katholizismus. Entwicklungslinien und Profile.* Frankfurt/M., 1964.

Bergsträsser, L. *Geschichte der politischen Parteien in Deutschland.* Munich, 1960.

Bertram, J. *Die Wahlen zum Deutschen Reichstag vom Jahre 1912.* Düsseldorf, 1964.

Bittel, K. 'Eduard Pfeiffer und die deutsche Konsumgenossenschaftsbewegung', *Schriften des Vereins für Sozialpolitik, Untersuchungen über Konsumvereine,* 151, I. Munich and Leipzig, 1915.

Blackbourn, D. 'The *Mittelstand* in German Society and Politics, 1871–1914', *Social History,* 4, 1977.

Born, K. E. 'Von dem Reichstag bis zum ersten Weltkrieg', B. Gebhardt (ed.), *Handbuch der deutschen Geschichte,* III, Stuttgart, 1960.

Bowen, R. H. *German Theories of the Corporative State, with Special Reference to the Period 1870–1919.* N.Y., 1947.

Branding, U. *Die Einführung der Gewerbefreiheit in Bremen und ihre Folgen.* Bremen, 1951.

Bruckmüller, E. 'Bäuerlicher Konservatismus in Oberösterreich. Sozialstruktur und politische Vertretung in einem österreichischen Kronland', *Zeitschrift für bayerische Landesgeschichte,* 1974, I.

Bruns, V. (ed.) *Württemberg unter der Regierung König Wilhelms II.* Stuttgart, 1916.

Buchheim, K. *Ultramontanismus und Demokratie; der Weg der deutschen Katholiken im 19. Jahrhundert.* Munich, 1963.

Bühler, M. *Die Stellung Württembergs zum Umschwung in der Bismarck'schen Handelspolitik 1878/9.* Diss., Tübingen, 1935.

Burkart, O. *Die Zusammensetzung des württembergischen Landtags in der geschichtlichen Entwicklung.* Diss., Würzburg, 1922.

Buzengeiger, W. *Die Zusammenhänge zwischen den wirtschaftlichen Verhältnissen und der politischen Entwicklung in Württemberg um die Mitte des 19. Jahrhunderts.* Diss., Munich. Ulm, 1949.

Cardauns, H. *Adolf Gröber*, M.-Gladbach, 1921.

Cardauns, H. *Karl Trimborn.* M.-Gladbach, 1922.

Clapham, J. H. *The Economic Development of France and Germany 1815–1914.* Cambridge, 1936.

Conze, W. 'Vom "Pöbel" zum "Proletariat" ', *Vierteljahrschrift für Sozial- und Wirtschaftsgeschichte,* 1954.

Demeter, K. *Grossdeutsche Stimmen 1848/49. Briefe, Tagebuchblätter, Eingaben aus dem Volk.* Frankfurt/M., 1939.

Dessauer, L. *Die Industrialisierung von Gross-Stuttgart.* Diss., Tübingen, 1916.

Egelhaaf, G. 'Württemberg in den fünfundzwanzig Jahren 1891–1916', *Württembergische Vierteljahrshefte für Landesgeschichte,* 1916.

Ehmer, W. *Südwestdeutschland als Einheit und Wirtschaftsraum.* Stuttgart, 1930.

Eley, G. '*Sammlungspolitik*, Social Imperialism and the Navy Law of 1898', *Militärgeschichtliche Mitteilungen,* 15, 1, 1974.

Engelsing, R. *Zur Sozialgeschichte deutscher Mittel- und Unterschichten.* Göttingen, 1973.

Epstein, K. *Matthias Erzberger and the dilemma of German Democracy.* Princeton, 1959.

Evans, R. J. (ed.) *Society and Politics in Wilhelmine Germany.* London, 1978.

Fassbender, M. 'Durch Kenntnis zum Verständnis unserer Landbevölkerung', F. Thimme (ed.), *Vom inneren Frieden des deutschen Volkes.* Leipzig, 1916.

Feuerstein, F. *Denkschrift über die Bedeutung des Genossenschaftswesens für die Entwicklung der Gemeindewirtschaft. Mit besonderer Berücksichtigung der Konsumgenossenschaften.* Stuttgart, 1920.

Feuerstein, F. *Geschichte des Verbandes württembergischer Konsumvereine 1904–1929.* Stuttgart, 1929.

Fischer, W. *Quellen zur Geschichte des deutschen Handwerks.* Göttingen, 1957.

Fischer, W. *Wirtschaft und Gesellschaft im Zeitalter der Industrialisierung.* Göttingen, 1972.

Fogarty, M. P. *Christian democracy in Western Europe, 1820–1953.* London, 1957.

Franz, G. (ed.) *Quellen zur Geschichte des deutschen Bauernstandes in der Neuzeit.* Darmstadt, 1963.

Franz, R. A. H. *Das Problem der konstitutionellen Parlamentarisierung bei Conrad Haussmann und Friedrich von Payer.* Göppingen, 1977.

Fricke, D. *Die bürgerlichen Parteien in Deutschland 1830–1945*. 2 vols. Leipzig, 1968–70.

50 Jahre Handwerkskammer Stuttgart. Stuttgart, 1951.

Gehring. P. 'Von List bis Steinbeis', *Zeitschrift für württembergische Landesgeschichte*, 1943.

Gellately, R. *The Politics of Economic Despair: Shopkeepers and German Politics 1890–1914*. London, 1974.

Gerschenkron, A. *Bread and Democracy in Germany*. Berkeley, 1943.

Gerschenkron, A. *Economic Backwardness in Historical Perspective*. Harvard, 1966.

Gottwald, H. *Zentrum und Imperialismus*. Diss., Jena, 1966.

Graf, H. *Die Entwicklung der Wahlen und der politischen Parteien in Gross-Dortmund*. Hanover, 1958.

Groh, D. *Negative Integration und revolutionärer Attentismus. Die deutsche Sozialdemokratie am Vorabend des Ersten Weltkriegs*. Frankfurt/M. and Berlin, 1973.

Grube, W. *Der Stuttgarter Landtag 1457–1957*. Stuttgart, 1957.

Grube, W. 'Staat und Wirtschaft im Königreich Württemberg', *Festgabe für Max Miller zur Vollendung des 60. Lebensjahres. Der Archivar*, 14. Düsseldorf, 1961.

Haering, H. 'Württemberg und das Reich in der Geschichte', *Zeitschrift für württembergische Landesgeschichte*, 1943.

Hagen, A. *Staat und katholische Kirche in Württemberg in den Jahren 1848–1862*. 2 vols. Stuttgart, 1928.

Hagen, A. *Gestalten aus dem Schwäbischen Katholizismus*. 4 vols. Stuttgart, 1948–63.

Hamerow, T. S. *Restoration, Revolution, Reaction. Economics and Politics in Germany, 1815–1871*. Princeton, 1958.

Hardach, K. W. *Die Bedeutung wirtschaftlicher Faktoren bei der Wiedereinführung der Eisen- und Getreidezölle in Deutschland 1879*. Berlin, 1967.

Hasselmann, E. *Und trug hundertfältige Frucht. Ein Jahrhundert konsumgenossensch. Selbsthilfe in Stuttgart*, Stuttgart, 1964.

Haushofer, H. *Die deutsche Landwirtschaft im technischen Zeitalter*. Stuttgart, 1963.

Heckart, B. *From Bassermann to Bebel. The Grand Bloc's Quest for Reform in the Kaiserreich, 1890–1914*. New Haven, 1974.

Heinen, E. 'Antisemitische Strömungen im politischen Katholizismus während des Kulturkampfs', E. Heinen and H. J. Schoeps (eds.), *Geschichte in der Gegenwart. Festschrift für Kurt Kluxen zu seinem 60. Geburtstag*. Paderborn, 1972.

Hippel, W. von. *Die Bauernbefreiung im Königreich Württemberg*. 2 vols. Boppard, 1977.

Hoffmann, H. *Landwirtschaft und Industrie in Württemberg*. Berlin, 1935.

Hunt, J. C. 'Peasants, Grain Tariffs, and Meat Quotas: Imperial German Protectionism Reexamined', *Central European History*, 1974.

Hunt, J. C. 'The "Egalitarianism" of the Right: The Agrarian League in Southwest Germany, 1893–1914', *Journal of Contemporary History*, 1975, 3.

Hunt, J. C. *The People's Party in Württemberg and Southern Germany, 1890–1914*. Stuttgart, 1975.

Jacobs, F. *Deutsche Bauernführer*. Düsseldorf, 1958.

Jostock, P. 'Der soziale Gedanke im deutschen Katholizismus', R. Hebing and M. Horst (eds.), *Volk im Glauben. Ein Buch vom Katholischen Deutschland*. Berlin, 1933.

Kalkhoff, H. (ed.) *Nationalliberale Parlamentarier des Reichstages und der Einzellandtage 1867–1917*. Berlin, 1917.

Kehr, E. *Schlachtflottenbau und Parteipolitik, 1894–1901. Versuch eines Querschnitts durch die innenpolitischen, sozialen und ideologischen Voraussetzungen des deutschen Imperialismus*. Berlin, 1930.

Kiene, J. B. *Viktor Rembold, Rechtsanwalt und Landtagsabgeordneter in Schwäbisch Hall*. Stuttgart, 1920.

Kircher, W.-S. *Adel, Kirche und Politik in Württemberg 1830–1851. Kirchliche Bewegung, Katholische Standesherren und Demokratie*. Göppingen, 1973.

Klöcker, A. *Konfession und sozialdemokratische Wählerschaft. Statistische Untersuchung der allgemeinen Reichstagswahlen des Jahres 1907*. Diss., Erlangen. M.-Gladbach, 1913.

Koenig, M. *Die bäuerliche Kulturlandschaft der Hohen Schwabenalb*. Tübingen, 1958.

Koselleck, R. *Preussen zwischen Reform und Revolution*. Stuttgart, 1967.

Krohn, H.-B. *Die Futtergetreidewirtschaft der Welt 1900–1954*. Hamburg and Berlin, 1957.

Lange, J. *Die Stellung der überregionalen katholischen deutschen Tagespresse zum Kulturkampf in Preussen (1871–1878)*. Frankfurt/M, 1974.

Langewiesche, D. *Liberalismus und Demokratie in Württemberg zwischen Revolution und Reichsgründung*. Düsseldorf, 1974.

Lebovics, H. '"Agrarians" versus "Industrializers". Social Conservative Resistance to Industrialism and Capitalism in late Nineteenth Century Germany', *International Review of Social History*, 1967, I.

Lenman, R. J. V. 'Art, Society and the Law in Wilhelmine Germany: the Lex Heinze', *Oxford German Studies*, 1973–4.

Marquardt, E. *Geschichte Württembergs*. Stuttgart, 1961.

Menzinger, R. *Verfassungrevision und Demokratisierungsprozess im Königreich Württemberg*. Stuttgart, 1969.

Michels, R. *Political Parties. A Sociological Study of the Oligarchical Tendencies of Modern Democracy*. Transl. E. and C. Paul, N.Y., 1968.

Miller, M. *Eugen Bolz, Staatsmann und Bekenner*. Stuttgart, 1951.

Miller, M. and Uhland, R. (eds.), *Lebensbilder aus Schwaben und Franken*, IX. Stuttgart, 1963.

Mittmann, U. *Fraktion und Partei. Ein Vergleich von Zentrum und Sozialdemokratie im Kaiserreich*. Düsseldorf, 1976.

Möckl, K. *Die Prinzregentenzeit. Gesellschaft und Politik während der Ära des Prinzregenten Luitpold in Bayern*. Munich and Vienna, 1972.

Molt, P. *Der Reichstag vor der improvisierten Revolution*. Cologne and Opladen, 1963.

Morsey, R. *Die Deutsche Zentrumspartei 1917–1923*. Düsseldorf, 1966.

Morsey, R. 'Die deutschen Katholiken und der Nationalstaat zwischen Kulturkampf und dem ersten Weltkrieg', *Historisches Jahrbuch*, 1970.

Müller, K. 'Zentrumspartei und agrarische Bewegung im Rheinland, 1882–1903', K. Repgen and S. Skalweit (eds.), *Spiegel der Geschichte; Festgabe für M. Braubach zum 10. April 1964*. Münster, 1964.

Neher, A. *Die wirtschaftliche und soziale Lage der Katholiken im westlichen Deutschland*. Rottweil, 1927.

Nichols, J. A. *Germany after Bismarck. The Caprivi Era 1890–1894*. Cambridge, Mass., 1958.

Nipperdey, T. *Die Organisation der deutschen Parteien vor 1918*. Düsseldorf, 1961.

Noll, A. 'Wirtschaftliche und soziale Entwicklung des Handwerks in der zweiten Phase der Industrialiserung', W. Rüegg and O. Neuloh (eds.), *Zur soziologischen Theorie und Analyse des 19. Jahrhunderts*. Göttingen, 1971.

Oekonomierat Rudolf Schmid. Ein Lebensbild eines württembergischen Bauernführers nach seinen Aufsätzen, Worten und seinem Wirken für die Landwirtschaft. Stuttgart, 1927.

Popp, A. *Die Entstehung der Gewerbefreiheit in Bayern*. Leipzig, 1928.

Puhle, H.-J. *Agrarische Interessenpolitik und preussischer Konservatismus im wilhelminischen Reich, 1893–1914*. Hanover, 1966.

Pulzer, P. G. J. *The Rise of Political Anti-Semitism in Germany and Austria*. N.Y., 1964.

Rapp, A. 'Württembergische Politiker von 1848 im Kampf um die deutsche Frage', *Württembergische Vierteljahrshefte für Landesgeschichte*, 1916.

Rapp, A. *Die Parteibewegung in Baden 1905–28*. Karlsruhe, 1929.

Reinöhl, W. (ed.) *Revolution und Nationalversammlung 1848. Schwäbische Urkunden (Reden, Berichte, Briefe, Tagebuchblätter, Gedichte)*. Stuttgart, 1919.

Renner, H. *Georg Heim, Der Bauerndoktor*. Munich, 1960.

Rich, N. and Fisher, M. H. (eds.) *The Holstein Papers*. 4 vols. Cambridge, 1955–63.

Ritter, G. A. *Die Arbeiterbewegung im Wilhelminischen Reich; die Sozial-demokratische Partei und die Freien Gewerkschaften, 1890–1900*. Berlin, 1957.

Röhl, J. C. G. *Germany without Bismarck. The Crisis of Government in the Second Reich, 1890–1900*. London, 1967.

Rosenberg, A. *Imperial Germany. The Birth of the German Republic, 1871–1918*. Transl. I. F. D. Morrow, Oxford, 1931.

Rosenberg, H. *Probleme der deutschen Sozialgeschichte*. Frankfurt/M., 1969.

Ross, R. G. *Beleaguered Tower: The Dilemma of Political Catholicism in Wilhelmine Germany*. Notre Dame, Indiana, 1976.

Roth, G. *The Social Democrats in Imperial Germany; a study in working-class isolation and national integration*. Totowa, N.J., 1963.

Salomon, F. *Die deutschen Parteiprogramme*. 3 vols. Leipzig and Berlin, 1907–20.

Sauer, P. *Die jüdischen Gemeinden in Württemberg und Hohenzollern*. Stuttgart, 1966.

Saul, K. *Staat, Industrie, Arbeiterbewegung im Kaiserreich. Zur Innen- und Sozialpolitik des Wilhelminischen Deutschland 1903–1914*. Düsseldorf, 1974.

Schauff, J. *Die deutschen Katholiken und die Zentrumspartei*. Colgne, 1928.

Schenda, R. *Volk ohne Buch. Studien zur Sozialgeschichte der populären Lesestoffe 1770–1910*. Frankfurt/M., 1970.

Scheuerle, A. *Der politische Katholizismus in Württemberg währen der Jahre 1857–1871*. Diss., Tübingen, 1923.

Schlemmer, H. *Die Rolle der Sozialdemokratie in den Landtagen Badens und Württembergs und ihr Einfluss auf die Entwicklung der Gesamtpartei zwischen 1890 und 1914*. Diss., Freiburg i.B., 1953.

Schmidt, K.-H. 'Die Rolle des Kleingewerbes in regionalen Wachstumsprozessen in der zweiten Hälfte des 19. Jahrhunderts', I. Bog *et al* (eds.), *Wirtschaftliche und soziale Strukturen im säkularen Wandel: Festschrift f. Wilhelm Abel z. 70. Geburtstag*. 3 vols. Volume III, *Wirtschaft und Gesellschaft in der Zeit der Industrialisierung*. Hanover, 1974.

Schmierer, W. *Von der Arbeiterbildung zur Arbeiterpolitik*. Hanover, 1970.

Schofer, J. *Erinnerungen an Theodor Wacker*. Karlsruhe, 1921.

Schremmer, E. 'Die Auswirkungen der Bauernbefreiung hinsichtlich der bäuerlichen Verschuldung, der Gantfälle und des Besitzwechsels von Grund und Boden', K. E. Born (ed.), *Moderne deutsche Wirtschaftsgeschichte*. Cologne and Berlin, 1966.

Schremmer, E. 'Zusammenhänge zwischen Katastersteuersystem, Wirtschaftswachstum und Wirtschaftsstruktur im 19. Jahrhundert. Das Beispiel Württemberg: 1821–1877/1903', I. Bog *et al* (eds.), *Wirtschaftliche und soziale Strukturen im säkularen Wandel: Festschrift f. Wilhelm Abel z. 70. Geburtstag.* 3 vols. Volume III, *Wirtschaft und Gesellschaft in der Zeit der Industrialisierung.* Hanover, 1974.

Schulte, W. *Struktur und Entwicklung des Parteisystems in Königreich Württemberg. Versuch zu einer quantitativen Analyse der Wahlergebnisse.* Diss., Mannheim, 1970.

Schwab, E., Weiss, P., and Holtermann, K. *100 Jahre Oberschwäbische Industrie- und Handelskammer Ravensburg 1867–1967.* Ravensburg, 1967.

Schwarz, M. *MdR. Biographisches Handbuch der Reichstage.* Hanover, 1965.

Simon, K. *Die württembergischen Demokraten. Ihre Stellung und Arbeit im Parteien- und Verfassungssystem in Württemberg und im Deutschen Reich 1890–1920.* Stuttgart, 1969.

Stegmann, D. *Die Erben Bismarcks: Parteien und Verbände in der Spätphase des Wilhelminischen Deutschlands; Sammlungspolitik, 1897–1918.* Cologne, 1970.

Stegmann, D. 'Wirtschaft und Politik nach Bismarcks Sturz. Zur Genesis der Miquelschen Sammlungspolitik 1890–1897', I. Geiss and B. J. Wendt (eds.), *Deutschland in der Weltpolitik des 19. und 20. Jahrhunderts. Fritz Fischer zum 65. Geburtstag.* Düsseldorf, 1973.

Stetter, F. J. 'Anfänge einer konservativen Partei in Württemberg', *Besondere Beilage des Staatsanzeigers für Württemberg,* Nr. 12, 31.12.1926.

Stürmer, M. (ed.) *Das kaiserliche Deutschland. Politik und Gesellschaft 1870–1918.* Düsseldorf, 1970.

Teichmann, U. *Die Politik der Agrarpreisstützung. Marktbeeinflussung als Teil des Agrarinterventionismus in Deutschland.* Cologne, 1955.

Tietz, G. *Hermann Tietz: Geschichte einer Familie und ihrer Warenhäuser.* Stuttgart, 1955.

Tirrell, S. R. *German Agrarian Politics after Bismarck's Fall.* N.Y., 1951.

Valentin, V. *Geschichte der deutschen Revolution von 1848–9.* 2 vols. Berlin, 1930–1.

Veblen, T. *Imperial Germany and the Industrial Revolution.* London, 1939.

Vogel, B., Nohlen, D., and Schultze, R.-O. *Wahlen in Deutschland.* Berlin, 1971.

Walker, M. *German Home Towns. Community, State and General Estate 1648–1871.* Ithaca, N.Y., 1971.

Wehler, H.-U. *Bismarck und der Imperialismus.* Cologne and Berlin, 1969.

Wehler, H.-U. *Krisenherde des Kaiserreichs 1871–1918. Studien zur deutschen Sozial- und Verfassungsgeschichte.* Göttingen, 1970.

Wehler, H.-U. *Das Deutsche Kaiserreich 1871–1918*. Göttingen, 1973.

Weinmann, A. *Die Reform der württembergischen Innenpolitik in den Jahren der Reichsgründung 1866–1870*. Göppingen, 1971.

Wernicke, J. *Kapitalismus und Mittelstandspolitik*. Jena, 1922.

Windell, G. C. *The Catholics and German Unity, 1866–71*. Minneapolis, 1954.

Winkler, H. A. 'Der rückversicherte Mittelstand. Die Interessen-verbände von Handwerk und Kleinhandel im deutschen Kaiserreich', W. Rüegg and O. Neuloh (eds.), *Zur soziologischen Theorie und Analyse des 19. Jahrhunderts*. Göttingen, 1971.

Witt, P.-C. *Die Finanzpolitik des deutschen Reiches von 1903–1913*. Lübeck and Hamburg, 1970.

Wolf, K. 'Ernst Lieber 1838–1902', *Nassauische Lebensbilder*, IV. Wiesbaden, 1950.

Zeender, J. K. *The German Center Party 1890–1906*. Philadelphia, 1976.

Zorn, W. 'Typen und Entwicklungskräfte deutschen Unternehmer-tums', K. E. Born (ed.), *Moderne deutsche Wirtschaftsgeschichte*. Cologne and Berlin, 1966.

Index